T0183426

Lecture Notes in Computer Science 12725

More information about this subseries at http://www.springer.com/series/7412

Edgar Roman-Rangel ·
Ángel Fernando Kuri-Morales ·
José Francisco Martínez-Trinidad ·
Jesús Ariel Carrasco-Ochoa ·
José Arturo Olvera-López (Eds.)

Pattern Recognition

13th Mexican Conference, MCPR 2021
Mexico City, Mexico, June 23–26, 2021
Proceedings

 Springer

Editors
Edgar Roman-Rangel ⓘD
Instituto Tecnológico Autónomo de México
Mexico City, Mexico

Ángel Fernando Kuri-Morales ⓘD
Instituto Tecnológico Autónomo de México
Mexico City, Mexico

José Francisco Martínez-Trinidad ⓘD
Instituto Nacional de Astrofísica, Óptica y
Electrónica
Puebla, Mexico

Jesús Ariel Carrasco-Ochoa ⓘD
Instituto Nacional de Astrofísica, Óptica y
Electrónica
Puebla, Mexico

José Arturo Olvera-López ⓘD
Autonomous University of Puebla
Puebla, Mexico

ISSN 0302-9743   ISSN 1611-3349   (electronic)
Lecture Notes in Computer Science
ISBN 978-3-030-77003-7   ISBN 978-3-030-77004-4   (eBook)
https://doi.org/10.1007/978-3-030-77004-4

LNCS Sublibrary: SL6 – Image Processing, Computer Vision, Pattern Recognition, and Graphics

This Springer imprint is published by the registered company Springer Nature Switzerland AG
The registered company address is: Gewerbestrasse 11, 6330 Cham, Switzerland

Preface

The Mexican Conference on Pattern Recognition 2021 (MCPR 2021) was the thirteenth event in the series organized by the Academic Division of Engineering of the Instituto Tecnológico Autónomo de México (ITAM) and the Computer Science Department of the National Institute for Astrophysics, Optics and Electronics (INAOE) of Mexico, under the auspices of the Mexican Association for Computer Vision, Neurocomputing and Robotics (MACVNR), which is a member society of the International Association for Pattern Recognition (IAPR). MCPR 2021 was due to be held in Mexico City, during June 23–26, 2021.[1]

This conference aims to provide a forum for the exchange of scientific results, practice, and new knowledge, promoting collaboration among research groups in Pattern Recognition and related areas in Mexico and around the world.

In this edition, as in previous years, MCPR 2021 attracted not only Mexican researchers but also worldwide participation. We received contributions from authors in 16 countries. In total 75 manuscripts were submitted, out of which 35 were accepted for publication in these proceedings and for presentation at the conference. Each of these submissions was strictly peer-reviewed by at least two members of the Program Committee, all of them experts in their respective fields of Pattern Recognition, which resulted in these excellent conference proceedings.

We were very honored to have as invited speakers such internationally recognized researchers as

- Prof. Lei Zhang, Cloud & Artificial Intelligence, Microsoft, USA.
- Prof. Alessandro Vinciarelli, School of Computing Science and the Institute of Neuroscience and Psychology, University of Glasgow, UK.
- Prof. Julian Fierrez, Escuela Politécnica Superior, Universidad Autónoma de Madrid, Spain.

We would like to thank all the people who devoted so much time and effort to the successful running of MCPR 2021. In particular, we extend our gratitude to all the authors who contributed to the conference. We give special thanks to the invited speakers, who shared their keynote addresses on various Pattern Recognition topics during the conference. We are also very grateful for the efforts and the quality of the reviews of all Program Committee members and additional reviewers. Their work allowed us to maintain the high quality of the contributions to conference and provided a conference program of high standard. Finally, but no less important, our thanks go to the Academic Division of Engineering of the Instituto Tecnológico Autónomo de México for providing key support to this event.

---

[1] The conference was held virtually due to the COVID-19 pandemic.

We are sure that MCPR 2021 provided a fruitful forum for Mexican Pattern Recognition researchers and the broader international Pattern Recognition community.

The next edition of MCPR will be held in Ciudad Juárez, Chihuahua, Mexico, in 2022.

June 2021

Edgar Roman-Rangel
Ángel Fernando Kuri-Morales
José Francisco Martínez-Trinidad
Jesús Ariel Carrasco-Ochoa
José Arturo Olvera-López

Organization

MCPR 2021 was sponsored by the Academic Division of Engineering of the Instituto Tecnológico Autónomo de México (ITAM) and the Computer Science Department of the National Institute of Astrophysics, Optics and Electronics (INAOE).

General Conference Co-chairs

Edgar Roman-Rangel	ITAM, Mexico
Ángel Fernando Kuri-Morales	ITAM, Mexico
José Francisco Martínez-Trinidad	INAOE, Mexico
Jesús Ariel Carrasco-Ochoa	INAOE, Mexico
José Arturo Olvera-López	BUAP, Mexico

Local Arrangement Committee

Alonso Mendiola Ricardo
Cervantes Cuahuey Brenda Alicia
Corvera Esmenjaud Susana
Salcedo González Ante
Vázquez Martínez Dulce María

Scientific Committee

Alexandre, L. A.	Universidade da Beira Interior, Portugal
Araujo, A.	Universidade Federal de Minas Gerais, Brazil
Benedi, J. M.	Universidad Politécnica de Valencia, Spain
Borges, D. L.	Universidade de Brasília, Brazil
Camargo, J.	Universidad Nacional de Colombia, Colombia
Castellanos, G.	Universidad Nacional de Colombia, Colombia
Das, A.	Indian Statistical Institute, Kolkata, India
Dos-Santos, J. A.	Universidade Federal de Minas Gerais, Brazil
Escalante-Balderas, H. J.	INAOE, Mexico
Esponda, F.	ITAM, Mexico
Facon, J.	Pontifícia Universidade Católica do Paraná, Brazil
Fierrez, J.	Universidad Autonoma de Madrid, Spain
Fumera, G.	University of Cagliari, Italy
Gatica-Perez, D.	Idiap Research Institute, Switzerland
Godoy, D.	UNICEN, Argentina
Goldfarb, L.	University of New Brunswick, Canada

Gomez-Gil, M. P.	INAOE, Mexico
Gómez-de-Silva-Garza, A.	ITAM, Mexico
Grau, A.	Universitat Politécnica de Catalunya, Spain
Gregorová, M.	HEG HES-SO, Switzerland
Gutierrez-Garcia, J. O.	ITAM, Mexico
Hernandez-Belmonte, U.	University of Guanajuato, Mexico
Heutte, L.	Université de Rouen, France
Hurtado-Ramos, J. B.	CICATA-IPN, Mexico
Jiang, X	University of Münster, Germany
Kampel, M.	Vienna Univerity of Technology, Austria
Kim, S. W.	Myongji University, South Korea
Kober, V.	CICESE, Mexico
Kostadinov, D.	University of Zurich, Switzerland
Krzyzak, A.	Concordia University, Canada
Lazo-Cortés, M. S.	INAOE, Mexico
Levano, M. A.	Universidad Católica de Temuco, Chile
Lizarraga-Morales, R.	University of Guanajuato, Mexico
Marchand-Maillet, S.	University of Geneva, Switzerland
Martínez-Carranza, J.	INAOE, Mexico
Mendoza, M.	Universidad Técnica Federico Santa María, Chile
Montes-Y-Gomez, M.	INAOE, Mexico
Montoliu, R.	Universidad Jaume I, Spain
Morales, M.	ITAM, Mexico
Morales, E.	INAOE, Mexico
Muszynski, M.	University of Geneva, Switzerland
Nappi, M.	Università degli Studi di Salerno, Italy
Oliveira, J. L.	Universidade de Aveiro, Portugal
Palagyi, K.	University of Szeged, Hungary
Pedrosa, G. V.	Universidade de Brasília, Brazil
Perez-Suay, A.	Universitat de València, Spain
Pina, P.	Instituto Superior Técnico, Portugal
Real, P.	University of Seville, Spain
Ruiz-Shulcloper, J.	UCI, Cuba
Salas, J.	CICATA-IPN, Mexico
San-Martin, C.	Universidad de la Frontera, Chile
Sanchez-Cortes, D.	Groupe Mutuel Holding SA, Switzerland
Sánchez-Salmerón, A. J.	Universitat Politècnica de València, Spain
Sansone, C.	Università di Napoli, Italy
Solorio, T.	University of Houston, USA
Sossa-Azuela, J. H.	CIC-IPN, Mexico
Sucar, L. E.	INAOE, Mexico
Tolosana, R.	Universidad Autónoma de Madrid, Spain
Valev, V.	Institute of Mathematics and Informatics, Bulgaria
Wang, C.	University of Geneva, Switzerland

Additional Referees

Alba-Cabrera, E.
Casavantes, M.
Chen, S.
Dubuis, A.
Ezra-Aragon, M.
García-Garví, A.
Jiménez-Guarneros, M.
Layana-Castro, P. E.
Lopez, J.
Luyet, G.
Medina-Pérez, M. A.
Navarro-Moya, F.
Ortega-Mendoza, R. M.
Pérez-Espinosa, H.

Sponsoring Institutions

Academic Division of Engineering of the Instituto Tecnológico Autónomo de México (ITAM)
National Institute of Astrophysics, Optics and Electronics of Mexico (INAOE)
Mexican Association for Computer Vision, Neurocomputing and Robotics (MACVNR)
National Council of Science and Technology of Mexico (CONACYT)

Contents

Image Processing and Analysis

Medical Applications of Pattern Recognition

Artificial Intelligence Techniques and Recognition

A Straightforward Framework for Video Retrieval Using CLIP

Jesús Andrés Portillo-Quintero[ID], José Carlos Ortiz-Bayliss[✉][ID], and Hugo Terashima-Marín[ID]

School of Engineering and Sciences, Tecnologico de Monterrey,
Av. Eugenio Garza Sada 2501, Monterrey, NL 64849, Mexico
a00226024@itesm.mx, {jcobayliss,terashima}@tec.mx

Abstract. Video Retrieval is a challenging task where the task aims at matching a text query to a video or vice versa. Most of the existing approaches for addressing such a problem rely on annotations made by the users. Although simple, this approach is not always feasible in practice. In this work, we explore the application of the language-image model, CLIP, to obtain video representations without the need for said annotations. This model was explicitly trained to learn a common space where images and text can be compared. Using various techniques described in this document, we extended its application to videos, obtaining state-of-the-art results on the MSR-VTT and MSVD benchmarks.

1 Introduction

Video is one of the most consumed forms of media available on the internet. The high consumption of this type of media requires obtaining suitable methods for finding videos that contain one or more features desired by the users. Most video browsers rely on annotations made by users to identify video contents. Although this solution is simple to implement, it comes at a high price. Relying on annotations to perform a query on videos requires an extensive description of the videos' innards and context. Unfortunately, this information may not be available. Thus, it is clear that a video retrieval system that can handle user's queries without the need for such annotations represents a relevant topic of study.

This document describes a video retrieval model, which, as its name implies, can retrieve the videos from a collection that are best described by a particular query (text). For example, "A woman is running" should return videos that contain women running, thus executing a text-to-video retrieval task (TVR). Given that the video retrieval architecture estimates the similarity between video and text, it can also perform the video-to-text retrieval (VTR) task. It consists of returning captions that best describe the query (video) from a set of description candidates. In either task, the system goal is that, given a query and a set of video-text pairs, it must return the ranking at which the corresponding opposite modality is positioned.

© Springer Nature Switzerland AG 2021
E. Roman-Rangel et al. (Eds.): MCPR 2021, LNCS 12725, pp. 3–12, 2021.
https://doi.org/10.1007/978-3-030-77004-4_1

The TVR and VTR tasks can be seen as methods by which video and text contents are funneled into a fixed-length representation using an embedding function. Since both projections fall in the same dimensional space, a similarity score can be applied, which can be used to rank elements from a set of prospects. Given that similarity metrics between text-video and video-text are equal, TVR and VTR are considered inverse operations. They only depend on the modality of the input prompt.

Some works extensively focus on the video representation by adding pre-trained models considered "experts". Each "expert" focuses on specific video contents such as sound, face detection, motion, among others. The information from all the experts is multiplexed by a complex gating mechanism [5,7]. Instead of starting from an elaborated video representation to train a common visual-text space, we propose to use a learned visual-text space to build a video representation. Similar to Mithun et al. [12], our approach consists of using pre-trained models that measure the similarity between image and text. Then, we extend this idea to handle videos. We experimented with several aggregation methods to comply with the extra temporal dimension.

In this work, we chose Contrastive Language-Image Pretraining (CLIP) as the base image-text model. CLIP is a state-of-the-art neural network, which is pre-trained for image-text pairs [14]. CLIP has proved that similarity learning can be used to train a visual encoder for downstream tasks such as classification, captioning, and clustering, to mention some. We harness the power of its visual representations to create a video representation that can be used directly with its original text encoder to bootstrap a neural network model for video retrieval. Since our work focuses on aggregation strategies of image features, our method is tested with Zero-Shots of the evaluation dataset. Hence, no parameter finetuning is exercised to improve retrieval results.

The remainder of this document is organized as follows. In Sect. 2 we provide the foundations of this investigation and an overview of the most relevant related works. Section 3 describes the experiments conducted, their main results, and their discussion. Finally, in Sect. 4, we present the conclusion and some ideas that may be worth exploring as part of the future work.

2   Background and Related Work

The work presented in this document is related to strategies used to construct a video encoder for video retrieval. It is straightforward to think that image features can serve as a proxy for video representations. Karpathy et al. [6] observed that a convolutional neural network (CNN) feature from a single frame could be discriminative enough for video classification, achieving just 1.3 fewer percentage points than the top accuracy model from the same work, which on its part included more visual and temporal information.

Mithun et al. [12] proved that it was possible to supersede the state-of-the-art video retrieval model by obtaining the average visual features obtained from an image-text model. This practice has been implemented on novel models, along with more elaborated video representations. For instance, the state-of-the-art in video retrieval has been pushed by models that implement a Mixture-of-Experts (MoE) paradigm [5,7,10,13]. The MoE approach proposes a complex video representation by multiplexing the outputs of several pre-trained models (known as "experts") that attend to particular aspects of video such as motion, face detection, character recognition, among others.

In this regard, we are aware that at most seven experts have been included in a video retrieval model [5]. Nonetheless, the current state-of-the-art implements a mixture of two experts, indicating that video-text representations may rescind the added complexity that multiple experts convey [13]. Patrick et al. propose that contrastive training used by most video retrieval systems encourages repulsive forces on independent, but similar, examples [13]. To alleviate this, they use a support set containing positive examples for each data point on a training batch, so the common video-text space must learn concept sharing. Nonetheless, contrastive training has been proved successful in image and video representation learning [2,9].

Contrastive training is a regime on which a model is inducted to pull similar data points together and push apart dissimilar ones on a latent space. The foundational mechanism of the Contrastive Language-Image Pretraining (CLIP) is the model used in this work. As the name states, the model is pre-trained on 400,000 image-text pairs collected from the Internet. As a siamese neural network, it is composed of an image (ViT-B/32) and text encoder (transformer) that funnel information into a common space where objects can be compared using cosine similarity [14].

3   Experiment and Results

This section provides a mathematical description of CLIP and how we can use it for VTR or TVR. Later, we describe the datasets and metrics considered for this work. Then, we detail the experiments and their main results, followed by a brief discussion of the most relevant findings.

3.1   CLIP as Video Representation

By using CLIP [14], we obtain the pre-trained functions $\omega(u) = \mathbf{w}$ and $\phi(t) = \mathbf{c_t}$, which encode image u and text t into $\mathbf{w}, \mathbf{c_t} \in \mathbb{R}^d$, where $d = 512$. Assume a video v is composed of s sampled frames such that $v = \{u_1, u_2, \ldots, u_s\}$. Consequently, we can calculate the embedding of each frame into a matrix $\mathbf{W} \in \mathbb{R}^{d \times s}$ so $\mathbf{W} = [\omega(u_1) = \mathbf{w_1}, \mathbf{w_2}, \ldots, \mathbf{w_s}]$. Therefore, the problem we try to solve is to find an aggregation function Λ that maps the input $\mathbf{W} \in \mathbb{R}^{d \times s}$ into a video representation $\mathbf{c_v} \in \mathbb{R}^d$. Then, with a video and text representations $\mathbf{c_v}$ and $\mathbf{c_t}$, we can compute a cosine similarity function (Eq. 1), which is useful for ranking the video-text pairs inside a dataset given a query of a specific modality.

$$sim(\mathbf{a}, \mathbf{b}) = \frac{\mathbf{a}^T \mathbf{b}}{\|\mathbf{a}\| \|\mathbf{b}\|} \tag{1}$$

3.2   Datasets

The proposed framework assumes a set $\mathcal{C}$ of videos and corresponding captions pairs in the form $\{\{(v_i, t_{ij})\}_{i=1}^{n}\}_{j=1}^{m(v_i)}$ where the number of captions per video may be non-uniform, hence m is a function of v. By design, some datasets are split into sections used for training and validation of results. We use the training splits to prove our hypothesis for the preliminary experiments, but final results are reported on tests split of their respective datasets.

The datasets involved in this work are listed below.

MSR-VTT is a dataset composed of 10,000 videos, each with a length that ranges from ten to 32 s and 200,000 captions. The training, validation and test splits are composed of 6,513, 497 and 2,990 videos, respectively, with 20 corresponding descriptions each [18]. The test set has been used in different ways in the literature. Then, we will refer to two common variations as Full [7] (containing all the 2,990 videos in the test set from MSR-VTT) and 1k-A [19] (containing only 1,000 videos from the 2,990 in the test set in MSR-VTT).

MSVD contains 1,970 videos, each with a length that ranges from one to 62 s. Train, validation and test splits contain 1,200, 100 and 670 videos, respectively [1]. Each video has approximately 40 associated sentences in English.

LSMDC is comprised 118,081 videos, each with a length that ranges from two to 30 s. The videos were extracted from 202 movies. The validation set contains 7,408 videos, and the test set 1,000 videos from movies independent from the training and validation splits [15].

All the frames were sampled from each video from the previously mentioned datasets to extract the frame features. Other datasets are related to this work but cannot be used include WIT (WebImageText) [14] and HT100M [11]. WIT is composed of 400,000 image-text pairs on which CLIP was trained on. Since WIT is an image-text dataset that cannot be used as a benchmark for video retrieval. HT100M is a dataset of 100 million video-text pairs, used only as a pre-training set for other Video Retrieval works [5,11,13,16].

3.3   Metrics

To conduct our experiments, we follow the testing methodologies used in previous works [5,7] and report standard retrieval metrics. For median rank (MdR), mean rank (MnR), and standard deviation of rank (StdR), the lower the value, the better the performance. In the case of recall at rank ($R@k$, where $k = \{1, 5, 10\}$), the higher the value, the better the performance. For datasets that involve multiple sentences per video —such as Full from MSR-VTT and MSVD test—, we follow the protocol used by Liu et al. [7] and use the minimum rank among all associated sentences to a given video query.

3.4   Exploratory Experiments

In the exploratory experiments, we empirically define two candidates for frame-level aggregation Λ functions. We conduct this set of preliminary experiments on a validation sample comprised of 1,000 video-text pairs from MSR-VTT. The first frame-level aggregation function is based on the idea that it is feasible to obtain reasonable video representations by only considering one frame sample [6]. Given the feature matrix $\mathbf{W} \in \mathbb{R}^{d \times s}$, we define $\Lambda_s(W) = W_{30} \in \mathbb{R}^d$ as a function that returns the features of the 30th frame. Since these videos contain approximately 30 frames per second, this is equivalent to sampling a frame from the first second of the video.

A second candidate for an aggregation function is proposed by Mithun et al. [12], who suggest that the average of frame-level features from videos can be used as an approximator for video representations. This method has extensively been used in other retrieval-related works [5,7,9,11,13]. Consequently, we define $\Lambda_{avg}(\mathbf{W}) = \bar{W} \in \mathbb{R}^d$, where $\bar{W}$ is the average value of matrix columns.

Given that videos present dynamic events in which several sequences of frames can represent completely different things, we used k-means as the method for aggregation [17]. With this implementation, the aggregation function follows the form $\Lambda_k(\mathbf{W}) = W \in \mathbb{R}^{d \times k}$, which returns k video embeddings. For evaluation purposes, we repeat the ranking procedure with the obtained independent video representations k times and register each query's minimum rank, then calculate the retrieval metrics.

Table 1. Text-to-video tetrieval results on the MSR-VTT validation set, using various aggregation functions.

Λ	R@1	R@5	R@10	MdR	MnR	StdR
Λ_s	24.9	46.1	56.9	7.0	64.61	149.21
Λ_{avg}	35.4	58.0	67.2	3.0	39.81	111.43
Λ_2	34.3	57.8	66.5	3.0	40.23	112.85
Λ_3	34.4	57.7	66.6	3.0	39.77	110.69
Λ_4	33.7	58.4	66.9	3.0	37.98	107.53
Λ_5	34.4	57.6	66.1	3.0	38.44	108.02
Λ_6	34.9	58.4	67.6	3.5	37.44	108.34
Λ_7	35.3	58.1	67.5	4.0	38.33	107.88
Λ_8	33.9	57.7	67.9	3.0	38.23	107.32
Λ_9	33.9	57.2	67.1	3.0	37.87	108.23
Λ_{10}	35.0	57.8	68.0	3.0	37.26	107.34

Based on the results depicted in Table 1, the average-based methods obtain the best results in terms of the metrics used. It is noticeable that, among k-means methods, there is no significant difference between the results. This may be because MSR videos do not exceed 32 s in length, which may not be enough to differentiate the centroids when creating the clusters. We appeal to Occam's Razor principle regarding the aggregation method and select Λ_{avg} for further experiments since it accomplishes a similar performance to k-means based aggregation methods, but with a lower calculation complexity.

3.5   Confirmatory Experiments

This section compares our video retrieval model against the state-of-the-art results for MSR-VTT, MSVD, and LSMDC datasets. In all the cases, we evaluate both the TVR and VTR tasks.

In MSR-VTT, we can supersede the R@1 score of the previous best model SSB [13] on the split 1k-A for the TVR task. However, we are positioned behind previous works on other recall metrics (Table 2). Besides, we consistently achieve state-of-the-art results on all the recall metrics in the Full split from MSR-VTT. In the MSVD dataset, we obtain state-of-the-art results on most of the retrieval metrics (Table 3). We suppose that models based on MoE, such as SSB [13] and CE [7], cannot use all of their implemented experts because the videos in MSVD lack audio information, so they have to rely exclusively on visual features. In LSMDC, we do not obtain state-of-the-art results, but we are positioned second-best (Table 4). Given that video descriptions in this dataset do not follow the form of a typical sentence, as they are designed to teach a model to recognize characters and interactions between movie scenes, we commend the robustness of CLIP's text encoder because it could adapt to a new sentence schema.

3.6   Discussion

Although we obtain outstanding results on different metrics and datasets, there are some things worth discussing. For example, our original supposition was that the ranking worsens as the video gets longer. To confirm or reject this idea, we conducted an experiment on set 1k-A from MSR-VTT (Fig. 1). Figure 1a depicts the video length in seconds (x-axis), the rank assigned to it (y-axis), the overall median is a red line, and the average rank is depicted as a blue line. As a video gets longer, we expected that it would be more difficult for the video representation to capture the temporal elements. Hence it would be ranked worse. However, it shows that ranking varies wildly from video length. Notice, there is a possible trend downwards. We claim that pattern results from a bigger sample size on shorter videos that allow for more outliers to appear (Fig. 1b). Also, in Fig. 1c we observe that, by grouping videos by length, there is no noticeable trend on rank (at least for videos present in the dataset).

We proceeded to look at the worst-ranked video-text pairs. We noticed that several sentences incorporated phrases like "a family is having a conversation" or "a man talking about a woman", hinting that sentences that were mainly describing audio content would be ranked worse. This conclusion is reinforced

Table 2. TVR and VTR results in the MSR-VTT dataset. M, H and W denote training on MSR-VTT, HT100M and WIT, respectively.

Method	Training	Test Set	TVR				VTR			
			R@1	R@5	R@10	MdR	R@1	R@5	R@10	MdR
JSFusion [19]	M	1k-A	10.2	31.2	43.2	13	-	-	-	-
HT100M [11]	H+M	1k-A	14.9	40.2	52.8	9	16.8	41.7	55.1	8
CE [7]	M	1k-A	20.9	48.8	62.4	6	20.6	50.3	64	5.3
AVLnet [16]	H+M	1k-A	27.1	55.6	66.6	4	28.5	54.6	65.2	4
MMT [5]	H+M	1k-A	26.6	57.1	**69.6**	4	27.0	57.5	69.7	3.7
SSB [13]	H+M	1k-A	30.1	**58.5**	69.3	3	**28.5**	**58.6**	**71.6**	**3**
CLIP	W	1k-A	**31.2**	53.7	64.2	4	27.2	51.7	62.6	5
VSE [12]	M	Full	5.0	16.4	24.6	47	7.7	20.3	31.2	28
VSE++ [12]	M	Full	5.7	17.1	24.8	65	10.2	25.4	35.1	25
Multi Cues [12]	M	Full	7.0	20.9	29.7	38	12.50	32.10	42.4	16
W2VV [3]	M	Full	6.1	18.7	27.5	45	11.8	28.9	39.1	21
Dual Enc. [4]	M	Full	7.7	22.0	31.8	32	13.0	30.8	43.3	15
E2E [9]	M	Full	9.9	24.0	32.4	29.5	-	-	-	-
CE [7]	M	Full	10.0	29.0	42.2	16	15.6	40.9	55.2	8.3
CLIP	W	Full	**21.4**	**41.1**	**50.4**	**10**	**40.3**	**69.7**	**79.2**	**2**

Table 3. TVR and VTR results in the MSVD dataset. D, H and W denote training on MSVD, HT100M and WIT, respectively.

Method	Training	TVR				VTR			
		R@1	R@5	R@10	MdR	R@1	R@5	R@10	MdR
VSE [12]	D	12.3	30.1	42.3	14	34.7	59.9	70.0	3
VSE++ [12]	D	15.4	39.6	53.0	9	-	-	-	-
Multi Cues [12]	D	20.3	47.8	61.1	6	-	-	-	-
CE [7]	D	19.8	49.0	63.8	6	-	-	-	-
Support-set Bottleneck [13]	H+D	28.4	60.0	72.9	4	-	-	-	-
CLIP	W	**37**	**64.1**	**73.8**	**3**	**59.9**	**85.2**	**90.7**	**1**

Table 4. TVR and VTR results in the LSMDC dataset. L, H and W denote training on LSMDC, HT100M and WIT, respectively.

Method	Training	TVR				VTR			
		R@1	R@5	R@10	MdR	R@1	R@5	R@10	MdR
JSFusion [19]	L	9.1	21.2	34.1	36	**12.3**	**28.6**	**38.9**	**20**
CE [7]	L	11.2	26.9	34.8	25.3	-	-	-	-
MMT [5]	H+L	**12.9**	**29.9**	**40.1**	**19.3**	-	-	-	-
CLIP	W	11.3	22.7	29.2	56.5	6.8	16.4	22.1	73

by the fact that our model scored the best on MSVD, a dataset that by design does not contain any audio track, and text descriptions are based on what can be visualized.

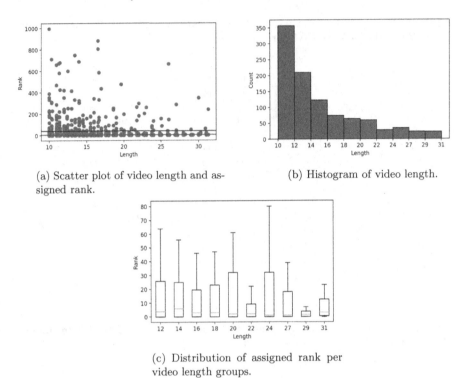

(a) Scatter plot of video length and assigned rank.

(b) Histogram of video length.

(c) Distribution of assigned rank per video length groups.

Fig. 1. Analysis on relation of video length and assigned rank on TVR task using the 1k-A test splits. (Color figure online)

4   Conclusion and Future Work

This work presents the first implementation of CLIP to obtain video features. Our method works by leveraging its learned common image-text space without the need for parameter finetuning (Zero-Shot). We apply an aggregation function to frame-level features, common in other video retrieval works. Our work focuses only on visual and text modalities, as it supersedes methods that implement a complex mixture of pre-trained models obtaining state-of-the-art results on the MSVD and MSR-VTT datasets[1].

One potential application of this CLIP-derived implementation is to retrieve specific moments inside videos. Also, it is yet unseen how will our video representation behave if tested as a video classifier. This methodology might be helpful to create a video representation that is based on CLIP for longer durations. For example, other works have used frame features to construct a graph that can change through time [8]. Such a representation could keep the strong text align-

---

[1] The code is publicly available at: https://github.com/Deferf/CLIP_Video_Represen tation.

ment suitable for video retrieval. Also, our work can be used as an expert on a future MoE video retrieval system.

Acknowledgments. This research was partially supported by ITESM Research Group with Strategic Focus on Intelligent Systems.

References

1. Chen, D., Dolan, W.B.: Collecting highly parallel data for paraphrase evaluation. In: Proceedings of the 49th Annual Meeting of the Association for Computational Linguistics: Human Language Technologies, pp. 190–200 (2011)
2. Chen, T., Kornblith, S., Norouzi, M., Hinton, G.: A simple framework for contrastive learning of visual representations. In: International Conference on Machine Learning, pp. 1597–1607. PMLR (2020)
3. Dong, J., Li, X., Snoek, C.G.M.: Predicting visual features from text for image and video caption retrieval. IEEE Trans. Multimed. **20**(12), 3377–3388 (2018)
4. Dong, J., et al.: Dual encoding for zero-example video retrieval. In: Proceedings of the IEEE/CVF Conference on Computer Vision and Pattern Recognition, pp. 9346–9355 (2019)
5. Gabeur, V., Sun, C., Alahari, K., Schmid, C.: Multi-modal transformer for video retrieval. In: Vedaldi, A., Bischof, H., Brox, T., Frahm, J.-M. (eds.) ECCV 2020. LNCS, vol. 12349, pp. 214–229. Springer, Cham (2020). https://doi.org/10.1007/978-3-030-58548-8_13
6. Karpathy, A., Toderici, G., Shetty, S., Leung, T., Sukthankar, R., Fei-Fei, L.: Large-scale video classification with convolutional neural networks. In: Proceedings of the IEEE conference on Computer Vision and Pattern Recognition, pp. 1725–1732 (2014)
7. Liu, Y., Albanie, S., Nagrani, A., Zisserman, A.: Use what you have: video retrieval using representations from collaborative experts. In: BMVC (2019)
8. Mao, F., Wu, X., Xue, H., Zhang, R.: Hierarchical video frame sequence representation with deep convolutional graph network. In: Proceedings of the European Conference on Computer Vision (ECCV) Workshops (2018)
9. Miech, A., Alayrac, J.B., Smaira, L., Laptev, I., Sivic, J., Zisserman, A.: End-to-end learning of visual representations from uncurated instructional videos. In: Proceedings of the IEEE/CVF Conference on Computer Vision and Pattern Recognition, pp. 9879–9889 (2020)
10. Miech, A., Laptev, I., Sivic, J.: Learning a text-video embedding from incomplete and heterogeneous data (2020)
11. Miech, A., Zhukov, D., Alayrac, J.B., Tapaswi, M., Laptev, I., Sivic, J.: Howto100m: Learning a text-video embedding by watching hundred million narrated video clips. In: Proceedings of the IEEE/CVF International Conference on Computer Vision, pp. 2630–2640 (2019)
12. Mithun, N.C., Li, J., Metze, F., Roy-Chowdhury, A.K.: Learning joint embedding with multimodal cues for cross-modal video-text retrieval. In: Proceedings of the 2018 ACM on International Conference on Multimedia Retrieval, pp. 19–27 (2018)
13. Patrick, M., et al.: Support-set bottlenecks for video-text representation learning. In: International Conference on Learning Representations (2021)
14. Radford, A., et al.: Learning transferable visual models from natural language supervision (2021)

15. Rohrbach, A., Rohrbach, M., Tandon, N., Schiele, B.: A dataset for movie description. In: Proceedings of the IEEE Conference on Computer Vision and Pattern Recognition, pp. 3202–3212 (2015)
16. Rouditchenko, A., et al.: AVLnet: learning audio-visual language representations from instructional videos (2020)
17. Sun, C., Myers, A., Vondrick, C., Murphy, K., Schmid, C.: Videobert: a joint model for video and language representation learning. In: Proceedings of the IEEE/CVF International Conference on Computer Vision, pp. 7464–7473 (2019)
18. Xu, J., Mei, T., Yao, T., Rui, Y.: MSR-VTT: a large video description dataset for bridging video and language. In: Proceedings of the IEEE Conference on Computer Vision and Pattern Recognition, pp. 5288–5296 (2016)
19. Yu, Y., Kim, J., Kim, G.: A joint sequence fusion model for video question answering and retrieval. In: Proceedings of the European Conference on Computer Vision (ECCV), pp. 471–487 (2018)

Inferential Rules for Identifying Answers in TOEFL Texts

Meliza Contreras González(✉) , Mireya Tovar Vidal ,
and G. De Ita

Benemerita Universidad Autónoma de Puebla,
Facultad de Ciencias de la Computación, Puebla, Mexico
{mtovar,deita}@cs.buap.mx

Abstract. Knowledge modeling is required to analyze the properties and relationships in a specific domain. Several mechanisms are used to represent knowledge; one of them is the logical rule that is an intuitive way to represent schemes through a structure that facilitates matching a premise with a corresponding conclusion.

In the case of the reading comprehension section in the TOEFL accreditation exams, it is necessary to analyze which pattern is linked to the question and related to the answer, so that from this scheme and the complementary information provided by the documents, a correct solution can be found. One advantage of using inferential rules is that it yields a deterministic result instead of making probabilistic management. In this paper, we propose inferential rules to model patterns to answer questions about TOEFL academic texts.

Keywords: Inference pattern · Rules · Semantic relationships

1 Introduction

Readers of texts in languages other than their native one have two challenges: translating text to their native language and mapping the structure from the passage sentences they know of the foreign language [7]. In the Test of English as a Foreign Language (TOEFL), in particular, the reading comprehension section, to answer the questions, the reader builds a model of knowledge representation, which requires applying inferential processes to understand the meaning of the text [7].

Efforts have been made to improve understanding through tips, strategies, rules identification, and practices. However, in most of the cases, it does not consider the context that is a fundamental element in the brain's mental representation to generate inference patterns and to build a network of related concepts from sentences. This work is intended to show the inference patterns with rules modeling and the semantic relations present in the TOEFL academic texts to facilitate the selection of the correct answers.

The paper's content is divided as follows: Sect. 2 shows preliminary concepts about semantic relationships and modeling rules. In Sect. 3 the state of the art of

© Springer Nature Switzerland AG 2021
E. Roman-Rangel et al. (Eds.): MCPR 2021, LNCS 12725, pp. 13–22, 2021.
https://doi.org/10.1007/978-3-030-77004-4_2

research about inference and patterns are presented, while in Sect. 4, a methodology for pattern extraction is defined. In Sect. 5, the inferential patterns are mentioned and an example is shown. Finally, the conclusions and future work are presented in Sect. 6.

2   Preliminary Concept

2.1   Semantic Relationships

Semantics is the study of the meaning of words, sentences, and expressions of a language. All the words that maintain a relationship of meaning between them are part of the same semantic field. Semantic relationships include relations between clauses or between words [1].

A word is a hyponym of another if its meaning is included in it. For example, a lion is a hyponym of an animal an animal is a hyperonym of a lion.

Synonymy is a semantic phenomenon that occurrs when the same concept or idea can be expressed with two or more different words [1].

Antonymy is a semantic phenomenon that occurs when two words have an opposite meaning, e.g., bad and good [1].

Other relationships called semantic roles focus on explaining both the syntactic structure and the meaning of words.

2.2   Modeling Rules

An expert system can be defined as an intelligent program that uses knowledge and inference procedures to solve complex problems. The problems that are solved can be classified according to their nature, in deterministic or stochastic [2].

The rules in an intelligent system are considered as a deterministic representation of a knowledge. In Fig. 1, the general scheme of rule representation is shown; the rules possess an antecedent (premise) and a consequent (conclusion) [2]. In this case, each rule has a group condition CG_i within the conditional block connected between *or* operators. The result is given, or it is said that it is accepted or rejected.

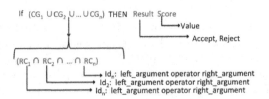

Fig. 1. Example of rules specification [2]

Within the CG_i, we have a set of applied rules. If any of the rules are invalid, then automatically that group is already invalid because *and* operator is used, then as the conditional has the *or* operator, it is required that at least some of these CG_i will be valid, the result can be given. The rule's conditions RC_i are defined with a *left* argument, an *operator*, and an *right* argument [2], in Fig. 1 appears. In our case, a rule-based approach is used because the correct answer is required in a deterministic way.

3   Related Work

Cognitive models study how human beings learn, think, and remember. For example, Kinstch and Van Dijk model [5] has interrelated elements that fuse cognitive psychology and predicate logic for support in the process of reading comprehension, which is interesting from a nonmonotonic reasoning point-of-view.

Other models are mentioned in [4], Miller and Johnson-Laird, where they show their interest in the relationship between perception and language. In their model, events are associated with lexical labels, and perception is seen as an activity of conceptualization referring to schemes, the determination of a pattern from a document's structure is not considered but rather a global representation of the information which could be too dense to query.

Vallejos [10] presents another tool called soploon, based on artificial intelligence mechanisms to provide a virtual assistant to determine errors in the object-oriented paradigm.

In the case of Garcia-Gorrostieta [6], they introduce a logic system that support computer engineering students. Their system allows, in the first instance, to determine the type of arguments, the validation of arguments from lexicons and classifications, and identify the type of arguments to evaluate in order to recognize if the arguments are correct or not.

4   Methodology

A corpus of 300 TOEFL academic texts available in [3] was thoroughly reviewed. These texts have a three-element structure: first, a passage is described, generally of less than one page, where, according to the text type, descriptions with academic content are mentioned: narrative, expositive or argumentative. The second element corresponds to questions battery related to passage text type. It is worth mentioning that it was possible to observe and analyze each passage type from the review. The third element corresponds to the answer options for each question. They have the characteristic that there are always four possible answers, and only one is the correct one.

Once the passages were reviewed, each text's structure was discovered; the direct relationship between the passage text and answer-question block was analyzed. Thus, a set of patterns was found that allows, in the first instance, to characterize the type of text.

On the other hand, from the answer-question block, it is possible to review what is being evaluated in the passage according to certain semantic properties that the passage possesses. Some classes of passages, are:

- Expositive texts: certain properties focus on the description of a particular topic, the distinct components or properties that it possesses (meronyms), paths that can be similar or different from others, categorization relationships such as hyperonyms and hyponyms.
- Narrative texts: they focus on describing historical events considering factual data such as dates, places, and events.
- Argumentative texts: are the most complex and least frequent passages. Their characteristics include hypotheses on any particular topic, opinions about the hypotheses, and in many cases, it is required to analyze through a summary of the total passage in order to recognize the main idea of the passage.

After reviewing the Corpus properties, it was necessary to establish a specific method in order to describe patterns in the passage. From the texts' reviews, there are two methods for processing the texts. The bottom-up and the top-down approaches. In the first instance it is necessary to determine the type of text to analyze.

In the case of argumentative texts, it was observed that the reader could confuse, if the text was either expositive or narrative, considering that an opinion mentions some property, for example, definitions or events. For this reason, the pattern extraction procedure should be universal and applicable to any class of passage.

Therefore with the bottom-up approach, the steps are: analyze the answer-question block, extract the semantic content. The answer options had the consistency that each of the distractors corresponded to the same semantic field.

Once the semantic field of the answers was verified, we proceeded to analyze the question. Precise characteristics were found according to the type of text; another important element, the context, was identified in this researching. After analyzing all the questions with their possible answer options, a mental model can be generated to process the text of the passage without being distracted from the rest of the elements.

However, it was necessary to formally identify the question-answer blocks according to the type of text, which was modeled employing cognitive blocks. In order to characterize an specific type of text, it is necessary to avoid ambiguity. If a reader doubts about the class of the passage, then it is neccesary to validate the cognitive blocks' in order to recognize the class of the passage. Based on these elements, the following section shows the rules used to determine the patterns according to each type of text and the Algorithm 1 used in the process. In our case, we have adapted this rule by considering the cognitive blocks that characterize the question-answer block of each type of text.

5   Inference Route from Cognitive Patterns

In Fig. 2, we show an example of a TOEFL passage. The passage is the class of expositive text, the topic is about the nature of viruses.

The passage is from the expository text class; the topic deals with viruses' behavior and properties. Thus, to find the correct answers, it is required to transform the text's sentences into predicates that correspond to known patterns earlier classified from the TOEFL passages review (step 1 in Algorithm 1). According to rule-based systems, each type of question and cognitive block's patterns propose a scheme of rules.

From that patterns raised we have the rule specification: IF (condition group) THEN action, where the group of conditions allows to determine the type of text to infer the correct answer from the evaluation of each response according to the patterns generated considering the context.

Topic: Virus

The term 'virus is derived from the Latin word for poison. or slime. It was originally applied to the noxious stench emanating from swamps that was thought to cause a variety of diseases in the centuries before microbes were discovered and specifically linked to illness. But it was not until almost the end of the nineteenth century that a true virus was proven to be the cause of a disease.

The nature of viruses made them impossible to detect for many years even after bacteria had been discovered and studied. Not only are viruses too small to be seen with a light microscope, they also cannot be detected through their biological activity, except as it occurs in conjunction with other organisms. In fact, viruses show no traces of biological activity by themselves. Unlike bacteria, they are not living agents in the strictest sense Viruses are very simple pieces of organic material composed only of nucleic acid, either DNA or RNA, enclosed in a coat of protein made up of simple structural units.(Some viruses also contain carbohydrates and lipids.) They are parasites, requiring human, animal, or plant cells to live. The virus replicates by attaching to a cell and injecting its nucleic acid.' once inside the cell, the DNA or RNA that contains the virus' genetic information takes over the cell's biological machinery, and the cell begins to manufacture viral proteins rather than its own.

1. Which of the following is the best title for the passage.

(A) New Developments in Viral Research   (B) Exploring the Causes of Disease (C) DNA: Nature's Building Block   (D) Understanding Viruses

2. Before microbes were discovered It was believed that some diseases were caused by

(A) germ-carrying insects   (B) certain strains of bacteria (C) foul odors released from swamps (D) slimy creatures living near swamps

3. The word "proven" in line 4 is closest meaning to which of the following.

(A) Shown   (B) Feared   (C) Imagined   (D) Considered

4. The word nature" in line 6 is closest in meaning to which of the following?

(A) Self-sufficiency (B) Shapes   (C) Characteristics (D) Speed

5. All of the following may be components of a virus EXCEPT

(A) RNA (B) plant cells (C) carbohydrates (D) a coat of protein

6. The author implies that bacteria were investigated earlier than viruses because

(A) bacteria are easier to detect   (B) bacteria are harder to eradicate (C) viruses are extremely poisonous (D) viruses are found only in hot climates

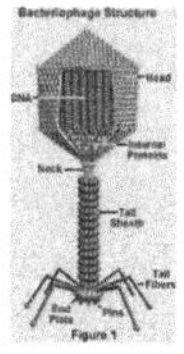

Fig. 2. Example of Expositive Text with answer-question block [3]

Figure 3a shows an adaptation of the group condition ($CB_{texttype}$) in order to apply the next step of the methodology, which is the determination of the class of the passage (step 2 in Algorithm 1).

For this, in the premise, the validation of each one of the cognitive blocks $CB_{texttype}$ employs an exclusive *or* operator as a connector operator, considering that each passage is the only one from one type. Also, for each case in the condition, there is one consequence action in the inference pattern.

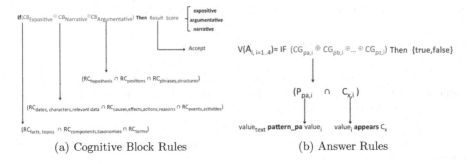

(a) Cognitive Block Rules   (b) Answer Rules

Fig. 3. Rules

Each of the cognitive blocks has own rule conditions $RC_{pattern}$ according to the definition (steps 3 to 10 in Algorithm 1). For expositive texts, rule conditions have patterns as facts and topics; components, taxonomies and terms. There must be at least one occurrence for each of the block elements that correspond to the expository text.

The narrative texts have three rule conditions that are required to be true; the first one corresponds to the presence of dates, characters, or relevant data; it requires evidence of the causes, effects, actions or reasons, and also of the events and activities that characterize this type of text.

Argumentative texts require a hypothesis, the positions, and phrases or structures to identify them.

Once the cognitive blocks have been validated and the type of the founded text has been returned, the next step is to find the correct answer based on the question's context. For this, a conditional block will be related to a particular answer over the four possible answers. In Fig. 3b the answer rules are shown (step 12 in Algorithm 1).

There are no partially correct results given the deterministic rule in Fig. 4. The premise has a group condition $CG_{pattern,answer}$ according to a pattern that coincides with the answer option. For that reason, the notation is considered as the pattern from letters a to z, considering that there can be several patterns, and the variable i is used as a second subscript that corresponds to the four possible answers.

Each type of answer associated one inference pattern. $CG_{pattern,i}$, $i = 1, 2, 3, 4$ contains the following rule: it must exist at the same time. The first step is to determine if the value of the answer corresponds to one of the possible inference patterns.

The second step consists in determining if the answer's value corresponds to one of the patterns (condition $P_{pattern,i}$) concerning to the passage text (step 16 to 19 in Algorithm 1), and also, it must be fulfilled that the answer or the distractor is related to the context (condition $C_{x,i}$). This rule was established in this way because it may be the case that the distractor corresponds to the semantic field, but there is no evidence of such content in the text, which is related to the context of the question; therefore, if it does not exist in the context, it can be discarded and in this case, the result would be false (step 20 in Algorithm 1). In Fig. 4, an inference pattern is shown.

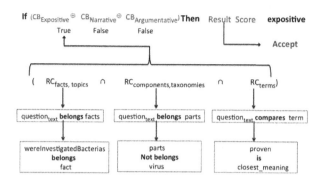

Fig. 4. Text category verification

On the other hand, according to the pattern, at the time of verification on the premise, only one of the patterns will be valid, therefore, only one of the patterns corresponds to the question context. Consequently, only one pattern will correspond to the semantic field value, and it coincides with the definition inside the passage.

It is worth mentioning that a particular distractor can take correspondence with a pattern, but it could not appear in the context. If all the group conditions are false for having the exclusive or operator, the deterministic answer would be false. Next, we will see a practical example of how these rules would be used.

An example of an explanatory text is shown with the relationship of viruses as the main topic. Here we can observe in the first instance; the questions contain the elements according to the cognitive block considering the topic, components, and comparisons.

In the case of synonyms, we can characterize the text as expositive when we fulfill these elements. For example, the first element, as a rule, bacteria were investigated, corresponds to what would be a fact because it gives a description that was made. Thus, this element corresponds to rules condition of topic and facts, then a question that corresponds to the components is found, in this case: which components do not belong to the viruses, see Fig. 5.

However, it is possible that a negative operator (except) appears in the text. Hence, this condition also present the rule as true. Finally, we find one of the questions that compare terms with the proved verb, considering its closest meaning that implies the comparison according to the synonymy with other terms. Thus, the three cognitive blocks of expository texts are satisfied.

Consequently, in narrative and argumentative texts, these relations do not correspond since the cognitive blocks of the other blocks are not found. Therefore it is false, so the rule shows the expositive text, and hence, it is accepted.

Figure 6 shows a deterministic way to identify the answer from the question. A typical class of this text is for example: All the following may be components of a virus EXCEPT?. The phrase except is a negative premise, hence there is an operator not within the conditional that contains the expositive patterns found according to the block question answer that was made in the Corpus analysis.

As patterns in expositive texts are presented, the holonyms, meronyms, hyponyms, synonyms, antonyms. Figure 6 illustrates the three examples, the incorrect answer is generated with these rules, as shown in this figure.

The analysis start with one incorrect answer, in this case $A_1 = RNA$ (see Fig. 6a). The conditional rule is applied in this case: we verify if the left argument virus corresponds with the holonym operator with respect to the right argument.

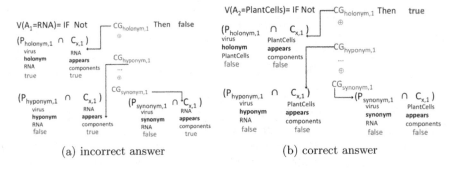

(a) incorrect answer   (b) correct answer

Fig. 5. Examples of answer rules

In this case, it is true since there is evidence within the passage described as a component. We have the validation that RNA appears as the right argument. The result is true since there is evidence within the passage that it is described as a component.

On the other hand, we have the validation that in the context, RNA appears as part of the elements of the passage, hence it is also true in the question of the other patterns in the hyponyms, and it is false because the relation of the virus with RNA is only a holonymy and not a hyponymy. The result is false in the question of the RNA context appears; therefore, it is true.

Finally, in the synonymy question, it gives us in the context that if RNA appears, that is true, but the property that virus is synonymous with RNA is not fulfilled; therefore, they are false, and the only true one is the holonymy relation.

However, the negation is required in the premise; that is, the holonymy property must not exist; consequently, the premise must be false, see Fig. 6b.

The process for the answers three and four; carbohydrates and a protein coat, respectively, is similar to the answer one because, in the passage, these three elements are described as components of the viruses.

Concerning to the answer two, which are plant cells, it makes the same type of premise that negates the condition. In this case, no property is being validated

---

Algorithm 1 algorithm for inferring correct answers in TOEFL texts

---

Input: TOEFL Passage
Output: answers

1: Generate the knowledge base of the passage by transforming the text to predicates $left\_argument$ KBproperty $right\_argument$.
2: Process the questions to $left\_argument\ Q_z Property\ right\_argument$ to obtain the cognitive block.
3: Apply the rule to determine the type of text on the obtained $Q_z Property$
4: switch $(Q_z Properties)$:
5: case $(RC_{facts,topics} \cap RC_{components,taxonomies} \cap RC_{terms})$:
6: return Expositive
7: case: $(RC_{dates,characters,relevantdata}$ $\cap$ $RC_{causes,effects,actions,reasons}$ $\cap$ $RC_{events,activities})$:
8: return Narrative
9: case: $(RC_{hypothesis} \cap RC_{positions} \cap RC_{phrases,structures})$:
10: return Argumentative
11: **for** each question Q_z, $z = 1 \ldots n$ **do**
12:    **for** each answer, A_i of Q_z **do**
13:       Apply the rule according to the pattern and context.
14:       ban=false
15:       switch(A_i):
16:       case $(p_{a,i}(A_i))$: ban=true
17:       case $(p_{b,i}(A_i))$:ban=true
18:       . . .
19:       case $(p_{z,i}(A_i))$:ban=true
20:       **if** $(ban$ and $C_{x,i})$ **then**
21:          return "A_i is the answer to question Q_z."
22:       **end if**
23:    **end for**
24: **end for**

---

according to the passage's text that indicates that viruses are a holonomy of plant cells; hence it is false.

Also, it can be said that plant cells do not appear in the components of the passage. Therefore, the result is false in the same way in the relation of hyponymy and synonymy, no pattern can be said to be true, and it does not appear in the context; consequently, the three elements that form the premise are false, and by the rule of exclusive gold it will be false since the values are equal.

Therefore, this premise's negation is true, which implies that the correct answer to the statement that it is not a component is precisely the answer two. With this method, it is possible to determine the correct answer based on the patterns corresponding to each type of text.

6 Conclusions and Future Work

The identification rules to support the deduction of a correct answer is an intuitive method that relies on logical formalism. In our case, we have founded the traditional rule scheme to our needs from the Corpus Analysis of the type of texts found in the TOEFL test. In the case of down-top analysis, the questions are first processed, then the type of the text is verified according to the cognitive blocks, and finally, the patterns are extracted.

According to the type of text, we determine which pattern is correct and the correct answer considering both the verified patterns and the context regarding the passage's information.

As a future work, an interface can be developed to these rules and passages text from a lexicon with a knowledge base and the inference engine in order to provide the correct answer to the user.

References

1. Campo y Garrido, N.: Relaciones semánticas entre las palabras: hiponimia, sinonimia, polisemia, homonimia y antonimia. Los cambios de sentido. Contribuciones a las Ciencias Sociales **1**(1), 1–10 (2010)
2. Castillo, E., Gutiérrez, J.M., Hadi, A.S.: Expert Systems and Probabilistic Network Models. Springer-Verlag, United States (1997)
3. Chuvanan University, pp. 60–73. http://www.cvauni.edu.vn/. Last Accessed 4 Sep 2018
4. Dizier, S., Viegas, E.: Computational Lexical Semantics. Cambridge University Press, England (1995)
5. Kintsch, W., Dijk, T.: Toward a model of text comprehension and production. Psychol. Rev. **85**(1), 363–394 (1978)
6. García, J., López, A., González, S.: Argumentative relation identification in academic texts. J. Intell. Fuzzy Syst. **39**(1), 1–11 (2020)
7. MacMillan, F.: Lexical patterns in the reading comprehension section of the TOEFL test. Revista do GEL **1**(3), 143–172 (2006)
8. Amostoy, M.: La investigación sobre el desarrollo y la enseñanza de las habilidades de pensamiento. Revista Electronica de Investigación Educativa **4**(1), 1–10 (2002)
9. Miller, J.R., Kintsch, W.: Readability and recall of short prose passages: a theoretical analysis. J. Exp. Psychol. Hum. Learn. Mem. **6**(4), 335–354 (1980)
10. Vallejos, S., Berdun, L.S., Armentano, M.G., Soria, A., Teyseyre, A.R.: Soploon: a virtual assistant to help teachers to detect object oriented errors in students' source codes. Comput. Appl. Eng. Educ. **26**, 1–14 (2018)

Automatic Detection of Injection Attacks by Machine Learning in NoSQL Databases

Heber I. Mejia-Cabrera[1](✉) , Daniel Paico-Chileno[1](✉) ,
Jhon H. Valdera-Contreras[2](✉) , Victor A. Tuesta-Monteza[1](✉) ,
and Manuel G. Forero[2](✉)

[1] LABSIS, Grupo TIAP,
Universidad Señor de Sipán, Pimentel, Peru
{hmejia,pchilenodaniel,vtuesta}@crece.uss.edu.pe
[2] Semillero Lún, Facultad de Ingeniería, Grupo D+Tec, Universidad de Ibagué, Ibagué,
Colombia
vcontrerasjhon@crece.uss.edu.pe, manuel.forero@unibague.edu.co

Abstract. NoSQL databases were created for the purpose of manipulating large
amounts of data in real time. However, at the beginning, security was not important
for their developers. The popularity of SQL generated the false belief that NoSQL
databases were immune to injection attacks. As a consequence, NoSQL databases
were not protected and are vulnerable to injection attacks. In addition, databases
with NoSQL queries are not available for experimentation. Therefore, this paper
presents a new method for the construction of a NoSQL query database, based
on JSON structure. Six classification algorithms were evaluated to identify the
injection attacks: SVM, Decision Tree, Random Forest, K-NN, Neural Network
and Multilayer Perceptron, obtaining an accuracy with the last two algorithms of
97.6%.

Keywords: Classification · Machine learning · Injection attack · NoSQL · Data
set construction · JSON · Data security

1 Introduction

In recent years NoSQL data managers have been the best solution for the availability of
real-time information [1]. Technologies such as Big Data and the Internet of Things are
revolutionizing society. Therefore, companies such as Facebook, Google and Amazon,
among others, have had the need to create their own NoSQL databases to better satisfy
their customers and serve very large databases. Depending on the type of data to be
stored, NoSQL databases can be classified into different categories such as documents,
key-value, columns, graphs and memory [2].

© Springer Nature Switzerland AG 2021
E. Roman-Rangel et al. (Eds.): MCPR 2021, LNCS 12725, pp. 23–32, 2021.
https://doi.org/10.1007/978-3-030-77004-4_3

The popularity of SQL resulted in the false belief that NoSQL databases would not be affected by injection attacks. Meanwhile, companies such as The Open Application Security Project (OWASP) continue to rank injection attacks among the most dangerous risks in web applications. Thus, the Parse Server platform and the Fornite authentication API suffered injection attacks from a misconfigured domain using regular expressions (RegEx) [3]. Therefore, security in NoSQL is a critical aspect, but unfortunately at the beginning it was not the main concern of its designers. As a consequence, NoSQL has performance problems in existing defensive solutions to injection attacks. Islam, et all. point out that the development of large applications has increased the popularity of NoSQL databases. However, given their vulnerability to injection attacks, tools have been developed for their detection using supervised learning models and synthetic minority oversampling techniques (SMOTE) for the selection of features for training and evaluation, obtaining an accuracy of 93.5% using a Neural Network [4].

Eassa et al. claim that NoSQL data managers are the best solution for many companies due to the constant data growth and the availability of information in real time. However, their security system is unknown. Thus, web applications connected to these databases suffer constant injection attacks by cybercriminals, who exploit the security by finding holes for unauthorized access and information theft. However, very few works have been published on methods for detecting attacks on NoSQL databases [5]. Among the few works, an architecture called DNIARS, based on the RESTFUL web service, can be mentioned, which employs a detection function to compare database queries with non-malicious query patterns stored in another database called NoSQL Engines, obtaining a 21% error rate, in the analysis of 168 415 requests. One of the major difficulties in developing methods to identify injection attacks in NoSQL databases is that there are no free databases available that can be used for research. In contrast, there are multiple protection works developed for SQL databases [6, 7, 14–16]. Given the need to improve the security of NoSQL databases, this paper presents a procedure for the construction of a NoSQL query database and a comparative study of six classifiers for detecting injection attacks.

2   Material

Since there are no NoSQL databases available on the network, which are previously labeled with benign and malicious queries, it was necessary for the development of this work, to build a database composed of 509 records of NoSQL queries. Figure 1 shows the flowchart of the process followed for database development and query simulation, following the JSON document structure.

Table 1 presents the source of the queries, their context, label and NoSQL query string.

The biggest security breach threat occurs at login, where it is very common to find default credentials and even databases with disabled authentication, so most attacks occur in these cases. Examples of attacks are given by combining comparison operators such as "$gt" (greater than) and "$ne" (not equal to). Thus, if the operator "$gt" is used to evaluate a value that is not in the database and evaluating this result with the operator "$ne"; the final result will be positive and in this way the protection is broken obtaining

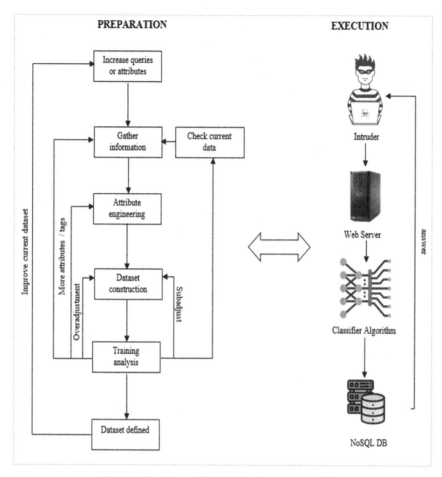

Fig. 1. Flowchart of NoSQL database construction.

Table 1. Characterization of benign and malicious queries in NoSQL databases.

N°	Query NoSQL	Label	Context	Source
1	db.usuarios.find({usuario:valor_1, contrasenia:valor_2})	Benign	Sessions	[8]
2	db.usuarios.find({usuario:{$gt:'"'}, contraseña: {$gt:'"'}})	Malicious	Sessions	[8]
3	db.logins.find({username:valor_1, password: valor_2	Benign	Sessions	[9]
4	db.logins.find({username: {$ne:1}, password: {$ne: 1})	Malicious	Sessions	[9]

the records of the collection. Similarly, clauses such as "$where", "$regex" and addition operators such as "$or" and "$and", which are a type of variables that alter the data sent in Javascript to the server through the HTTP GET method, can be used for the same purpose.

Attribute definition was performed using REGEXPER to extract regular expressions and define a pattern based on the JSON document structure as shown in Fig. 2.

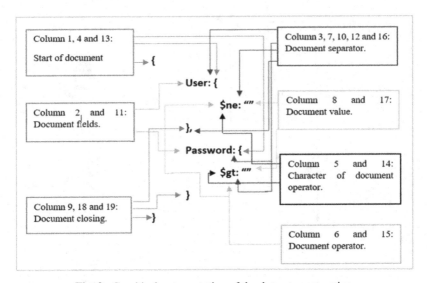

Fig. 2. Graphical representation of the dataset construction.

According to Fig. 2, in the JSON structure, each character or string is an attribute of the dataset. Among the most known attributes are start, end, operator, field and value.

Once the JSON structure was acquired, it was labeled as a benign or malicious query, then decomposed and separated into attributes of the dataset as seen in Table 2.

To verify whether the number of entries and attributes in the database was sufficient, a loss assessment was made by performing a logistic regression. If the training and validation losses were significantly separated, attributes and examples were increased. 450 malicious and 59 benign queries were defined in the database, which can be freely accessed [10] (Table 3).

The Regexper tool [11] was used to decompose a query into its basic parts. The machine learning techniques were developed in Java language, employing the Weka 3.8 library [12], running on an Intel Core i5-7200U CPU @ 2.50 GHz 2.70 GHz, 8 GB RAM, AMD Radeon 530 2 GB graphics card, operating on a Microsoft Windows 10 environment.

Table 2. Dataset construction - attributes.

Feature	Value	Description
Column 1	[0–255]	123: Determines the ASCII code of start character of the JSON structure
Column 2	[0–11]	Determines the possible value of the field within a query of the JSON structure
Column 3	[0–255]	58: Determines the ASCII code of the separator character in the JSON structure
Column 4	[0–255]	123: Determines the ASCII code of start character of the JSON structure
Column 5	[0–255]	36: Determines the ASCII code for the dollar character that is part of the JSON structure operator
Column 6	[0–6]	Determines the possible value of the operator within the query in a JSON structure
Column 7	[0–255]	58: Determines the ASCII code of the separator character in the JSON structure
Column 8	[0–4]	Represents a value that can be entered within a query of the JSON structure
Column 9	[0–255]	125: Determines the ASCII code of the closing character of the JSON structure
Column 10	[0–255]	44: Determines the ASCII code of the separator character in the JSON structure
Column 11	[0–11]	Determines the possible value of the field within a query of the JSON structure
Column 12	[0–255]	58: Determines the ASCII code of the separator character in the JSON structure
Column 13	[0–255]	123: Determines the ASCII code of start character of the JSON structure
Column 14	[0–255]	36: Determines the ASCII code for the dollar character that is part of the JSON structure operator
Column 15	[0–6]	Determines the possible value of the operator within the query in a JSON structure
Column 16	[0–255]	58: Determines the ASCII code of the separator character in the JSON structure
Column 17	[0–4]	Represents a value that can be entered within a query of the JSON structure
Column 18	[0–255]	125: Determines the ASCII code of the closing character of the JSON structure
Column 19	[0–255]	125: Determines the ASCII code of the closing character of the JSON structure

Table 3. Dataset tags.

Source	Label	Description
Query	Benign	Determines the query according to the corresponding attributes
	Malicious	

Table 4. Classification algorithms with better performance in detecting injection attacks on SQL databases.

N°	Classifier	Accuracy	Source
1	Neural netwoks	95.30%	[13]
2	Random forest	93.60%	[13]
3	Support vector machine	95.40%	[13]
4	K-NN	92.00%	[5]
5	Decision trees	93.40%	[5]
6	Multilayer perceptron	95.30%	[13]

3   Method

Once the database was built, six of the classifiers with the best performance in identifying SQL injection attacks, shown in Table 5, were evaluated, adjusting the parameters to obtain the highest accuracy in the NoSQL dataset.

Table 5. Best accuracy results obtained with the classifiers evaluated.

Classifier	Parameters	
	Name	Value
Support vector machine	Function kernel	Radial base
	Function kernel	Polynomial
	Function kernel	Sigmoidal
Decision tree	No parameters	Null
Random forest	Out-of-sample cases %	10
	Number of iterations	150–200
	Number of Trees	160–200
Neural network	Learning rate	0.03–0.05
	Epochs	2000–2500
	Number of hidden layers	3–4
Multilayer perceptron	Learning rate	0.03–0.05
	Epochs	2000–2500
	Number of hidden layers	3–4
	Nodes for each hidden layer	10, 5, 6 10, 6, 6, 10
K-nearest neighbours	Number of nearest neighbours	5–7

Eighty percent of the samples were used for training and 20% for evaluation, using the attributes shown in Table 2, as descriptors. Table 4 shows the parameters used and the range of values selected to tune them.

4 Results

Table 6 presents the tuning parameters that yielded the highest accuracy with the classifiers evaluated and Table 8 the following performance measures: accuracy, precision, recall, F-Score and AUC for each classifier. Figure 3 shows the precision, recall and F-score obtained with the same methods. Table 7 shows the confusion matrix for each algorithm, where B represents benign query and M represents malicious query.

Table 6. Parameters used for classifiers.

Classifier	Parameter name	Value
Decision tree	No parameters	Null
Random forest	Out-of-sample cases %	10
	Number of iterations	200
	Number of trees	200
Multi-layer perceptron	Learning rate	0.05
	Epochs maximum	2000
	Number of hidden layers	4
Neural network	Learning rate	0.05
	Epochs maximum	2000
	Number of hidden layers	4
	Nodes for each concealed	10, 6, 6, 10
Support vector machine	Type of SVM	C-SVC, C = 1
	Kernel function	Radial base function: $e\left(-\frac{\|x_1 - x_2\|^2}{2\sigma^2}\right)$
	Class weights	{1,1}
K-nearest neighbours	Number of nearest neighbours	5

Table 7. Confusion matrix of the algorithms.

		Classification										
		Decision tree		Multilayer perceptron		K-NN		Neural network		Random forest		SVM	
		B	M	B	M	B	M	B	M	B	M	B	M
Real	Benign	261	44	297	8	295	10	297	8	294	11	278	27
	Malicious	10	194	4	200	53	151	4	200	42	162	50	154

Table 8. Performance measures obtained with the descriptors evaluated.

Classifier algorithm	Accuracy	Precision	Recall	F-Score	AUC
Support vector machine	84.9%	84.8%	91.1%	87.6%	83.3%
K-nearest neighbours	87.6%	84.8%	96.7%	90.4%	96.6%
Neural network	97.6%	98.7%	97.4%	98.0%	98.9%
Multilayer perceptron	97.6%	98.7%	97.4%	98.0%	98.9%
Decision tree	89.4%	96.3%	85.6%	90.6%	94.6%
Random forest	89.6%	87.5%	96.4%	91.7%	97.4%

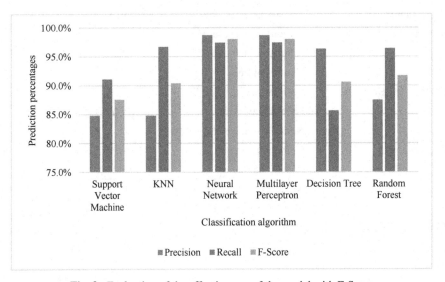

Fig. 3. Evaluation of the effectiveness of the model with F-Score

As shown in Table 8, the best results were obtained with the Neural Network and the Multilayer Perceptron, whose architectures are shown in Figs. 4 and 5, obtaining an accuracy of 97.6%, precision 98.7%, recall 97.4%, F-Score 98.0% and AUC of 98.9%, above the performance obtained by Islam et al. [4].

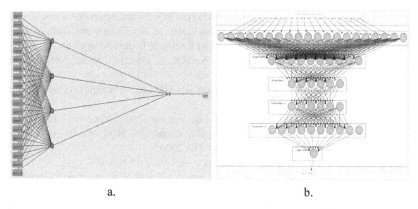

a.   b.

Fig. 4. Neural network architectures. a. Architecture of the multilayer perceptron that achieved the best performance. b. Architecture of the neural network that achieved the best performance.

5 Conclusions

Security against NoSQL injection attacks does not receive the necessary attention, due among other reasons to the difficulty of accessing a NoSQL query database. Therefore, in this research, a procedure for the construction of a dataset with 509 NoSQL queries was presented, finding a pattern in its structure consisting of 19 attributes, as well as benign and malicious labeling. Six of the classification algorithms that presented better results in the identification of injection attacks in SQL databases were evaluated, finding that neural networks and the multilayer perceptron allow obtaining the highest accuracy, identifying 97.6% of the attacks performed. One of the major difficulties in developing methods to detect injection attacks on NoSQL databases is the unavailability of example datasets. To contribute to this type of research, the database is now available through internet.

References

1. Eassa, A., El-Bakry, H., Al-Tarawneh, O., Salama, A.: NoSQL racket: a testing tool for detecting NoSQL injection attacks in web applications. Int. J. Adv. Comput. Sci. Appl. **8**, 614–622 (2017). ResearchGate, Fuzhou, China
2. Ma, H., Wu, T., Chen, M., Yan, R., Pan, J.: A parse tree-based NoSQL injection attacks detection mechanism. J. Inf. Hiding Multimed. Signal Process. **8**, 916–928 (2017). ResearchGate, Fuzhou, China
3. APISecurity.   https://apisecurity.io/issue-15-fortnite-hack-tls-mitm-attacks-sql-injections-for-nosql/. Accessed 24 Jan 2019
4. Islam, R., Islam, S., Ahmed, Z., lqbal, A., Shahriyar, R.: Automatic detection of NoSQL injection using supervised learning. In: 43rd Annual Computer Software and Applications Conference (COMPSAC), pp. 760 – 769. IEEE, Milwaukee, USA (2019)
5. Eassa, A., Elhoseny, M., El-Bakry, H., et al.: NoSQL injection attack detection in web applications using RESTful service. Programm. Comput. Softw. **44**, 435–444 (2018). Springer, Cairo, Egypt

6. Hasan, M., Balbahaith, Z., Tarique, M.: Detection of SQL injection attacks: a machine learning approach. In: International Conference on Electrical and Computing Technologies and Applications (ICECTA), pp. 1–6. IEEE, Ras Al Khaimah, United Arab Emirates (2019)
7. Ron, A., Bronshtein, E., Shulman-Peleg, A.: No SQL, no injection? Exam. NoSQL Secur. J. 1, 1–4 (2015). ResearchGate
8. Websecurify.   https://blog.websecurify.com/2014/08/hacking-nodejs-and-mongodb.html. Accessed 14 Aug 2020
9. InfoQ. https://www.infoq.com/articles/nosql-injections-analysis/. Accessed 18 June 2017
10. Researchgate. https://www.researchgate.net/publication/350671150_NoSQL_dataset
11. Regexper. https://regexper.com/. Accessed 08 Oct 2020
12. WEKA. https://www.cs.waikato.ac.nz/ml/weka/. Accessed 25 Nov 2020
13. Zhang, K.: A machine learning based approach to identify SQL injection vulnerabilities. In: 34th IEEE/ACM International Conference on Automated Software Engineering (ASE), pp. 1286–1288. IEEE, San Diego, CA, USA (2019)
14. Ross, K., Moh, M., & Moh, T.: Multi-Source Data Analysis and Evaluation of Machine Learning Techniques for SQL Injection Detection. In: Proceedings of the ACMSE 2018 Conference (ACMSE '18), pp. 1–8. ACM, New York, NY, USA (2018)
15. Singh, G., Kant, D., Gangwar, U., Singh, U., Pratap, A.: SQL Injection detection and correction using machine learning techniques. In: Satapathy, S., Govardhan, A., Raju, K., Mandal, J. (eds.) Emerging ICT for Bridging the Future - Proceedings of the 49th Annual Convention of the Computer Society of India (CSI). Advances in Intelligent Systems and Computing, vol. 337, pp. 435–442. Springer, Cham (2015). https://doi.org/10.1007/978-3-319-13728-5_49
16. Tripathy, D., Gohil, R., Halabi, T.: Detecting SQL injection attacks in cloud SaaS using machine learning. In: 2020 IEEE 6th International Conference on Big Data Security on Cloud (BigDataSecurity), IEEE International Conference on High Performance and Smart Computing, (HPSC) & IEEE Intl Conference on Intelligent Data and Security (IDS), pp. 145–150. IEEE, Baltimore, MD, EE. UU (2020)

Automatic Recognition of Learning-Centered Emotions

Yesenia N. González-Meneses[1]([✉]) [iD], Josefina Guerrero-García[1] [iD],
Carlos Alberto Reyes-García[2] [iD], and Ramón Zatarain-Cabada[3] [iD]

[1] Facultad de Ciencias de la Computación, BUAP, Av. San Claudio y 14 Sur, Col. San Manuel
Edificio CCO3, Ciudad Universitaria, Puebla, Mexico
[2] Ciencias Computacionales, INAOE, Luis Enrique Erro 1, Tonantzintla, Puebla, Mexico
`kargaxxi@inaoep.mx`
[3] TecNM, Campus Culiacán, Culiacán, Sinaloa, Mexico
`ramon.zc@culiacan.tecnm.mx`

Abstract. In this article, we present the research project in which we make a proposal for the recognition of emotions focused on learning, by identifying units of action on the faces of students. The learning-centered emotions that are recognized are *bored* and *interested*. This work begins with the capture of images of faces of college students performing a learning activity in real-time and ends with the recognition of emotions. A video of the learning process is recorded, frames are obtained, and then used to identify reference points of each student's face, which is triangulated to obtain geometric characteristics. The latter are used by a fuzzy inference algorithm that assigns a membership degree to 16 action units related to the emotions of *bored* and *interested*. Pattern recognition algorithms such as support vector machine, k-nearest neighbors, assemble of trees and neural networks are trained with the percentage of the membership of each action unit. After testing training models under different configurations, better results are observed with a neural network with an accuracy of 83%.

Keywords: Learning-centered emotions · Action units · Automatic recognition

1 Introduction

Learning-centered emotion (LCE) recognition is a task immersed in educational software development as part of student modeling. The purpose of identifying students' emotions in real time while interacting with software in a learning process is that they can receive feedback according to level obtained but also considering their emotional state, since this is decisive in the acquisition of knowledge. This way, the data set collected in the student modeling module in educational software, such as intelligent tutoring systems, are taken into consideration so that it automatically makes decisions about new teaching strategies according to the information contained in that module, such as the cognitive level of the student, their level of learning, but most importantly, their emotional state, since it has an important influence on the learning process. Nowadays, this issue takes on relevance due to the increase in the use of information technologies in the educational

© Springer Nature Switzerland AG 2021
E. Roman-Rangel et al. (Eds.): MCPR 2021, LNCS 12725, pp. 33–43, 2021.
https://doi.org/10.1007/978-3-030-77004-4_4

area, since we currently have millions of children and young people studying through all kinds of online courses.

At the beginning of this work, one of the main areas of opportunity was the lack of databases with information obtained from students carrying out a learning activity in real time, a really important factor to be able to start a process of identifying LCE. Since it is not the same to have facial expressions obtained from people watching a movie, tv commercials, or videos to facial expressions of people immersed in a learning process, with the former we can obtain expressions of primary emotions such as happiness, sadness, or anger; but it is very difficult to capture expressions of secondary emotions such as those focused on learning (e.g., interest, boredom, or frustration). The first part of this work began with the search of databases of expressions and physiological signals of LCE. After conducting an analysis of the state of the art on databases with emotional information obtained from educational contexts, we identified the lack of this type of information available publicly. It forced us to start from the capture of the data necessary for the identification of LCE. We took on the task of acquiring different devices to capture behavioral data and physiological data from students performing a learning activity. This involved from the implementation of a heart rate sensor to obtain heart beats, the use of thermal cameras to measure temperature levels of the face and the use of video cameras to record the expression of the student's face. To start the data capture, it was necessary to formalize a protocol, which included the specifications of the devices to be used, the educational software, the activities to be carried out as part of the experiment and the writing of an informed consent in which each participant was informed about the data to be captured, the use that would be given to it, and the authorization of their participation and use of data on a voluntary basis.

Another area of opportunity is itself the identification of LCE based on data from different signals such as video, heart rate and facial temperature. In this work we begin with the analysis of the student's face, taking the frames of the recorded videos. In a future stage of the project, the other signals will be added to achieve better recognition by integrating different types of data. In each frame every facial expression is broken down into individual components of muscle movement, called Action Units (AUs) according to the Facial Action Coding System (FACS) of [1]. For the identification of AUs, the reference points are first located on the face of each student with which the face is triangulated to obtain geometric characteristics. These are used by a fuzzy inference algorithm that assigns a degree of membership for 16 AUs related to the emotions of bored and interested. With the degree of membership of the action units for each emotion, machine learning algorithms such as k-nearest neighbors (KNN), assemble of trees, support vector machine (SVM) and neural networks (NN) are trained.

In the next section we summarize the state of the art on the development of databases with information from students in a learning process and of works that identify LCE, presenting a summary of their scope. In Sect. 3 we explain how the data capture was organized and carried out, as well as the creation of the database. In Sect. 4 we describe the strategies and configurations to test different machine learning algorithms and the results obtained with each classification model. In Sect. 5 we analyze the results and finally we present our conclusions and future work.

2   Stated of the Art

In the first part of this section, we present a summary of the databases that are available on the web, some provided by universities and others directly by work groups that are dedicated to automatic recognition of emotions. In the second part we present an analysis of the most recent works around automatic recognition of LCE.

2.1   Databases of Physiological and Behavioral Signals of LCE

The databases of emotional expressions can be formed by a set of images, videos, voice recordings, readings of the heart rate, facial temperature, galvanic level, and other physiological data obtained through different devices. Its content is related to the context in which they were achieved and the way in which emotions were generated. Thus, we can find databases with information captured in particular contexts and databases created from acted-out or spontaneous emotions captured in real time. These two aspects are decisive in the training, testing and validation of algorithms for the development of automatic systems for identifying emotions in a particular context such as the LCE. Most of the databases are based on the theory of emotions [2], which assumes the existence of six basic emotions on a discrete scale (happiness, sadness, disgust, surprise, fear, and anger) and an approximate set of 30 secondary emotions, but in large numbers their content corresponds only to basic emotions, leaving out the secondary emotions, the classification in which the LCE is found (interest, boredom, frustration, confusion, excitement, and surprise). Regarding how to generate emotions, the ideal method is to capture them spontaneously, since its naturalness differs from those acted-out in intensity, configuration, and duration. Our interest lies in hybrid databases that contain both imaging and physiological data. The DEAP database [3], contains physiological recordings (of EEG) and facial video of an experiment where 32 volunteers watched a sub-set of 40 music videos, this is the only one of this type publicly available.

Table 1 summarizes the characteristics of the three most popular facial expression databases available publicly. These correspond to facial expressions of basic emotions, that have been captured while testers perform diverse activities.

Table 2 shows the database details of spontaneous facial expressions. These correspond to emotions focused on the learning process that have been captured while students carry out an activity within a natural environment. Some of them contain physiological data, but unfortunately are not available publicly, nor do they provide information about the characteristics of data; much less, these don't detail the procedures that were made.

2.2   Automatic Recognition of Learning-Centered Emotions

Even though we began researching the state of the art regarding automatic recognition of emotions, it was necessary to narrow it down and focus on works that dealt, specifically, with learning-centered emotions. Most of the studies found aim to identify basic emotions in diverse contexts (approx. 80%), while only few of them target emotions within an educational setting (approx. 20%). From the latter, we encounter works e.g., [15] that make use of convolutional neuronal nets in order to recognize LCE. They run tests using three databases: RaFD, posed facial expression database containing images

Table 1. Databases facial expressions of basic emotions

Database	Facial expression	# of subjects	Number of images/videos	Type
Extended Cohn-Kanade Dataset (CK+) [4]	Neutral, sad, surprise, happy	123	593 image sequence (327) sequence having discrete emotion labels)	Posed & spontaneous smiles
Induced Natural Emotion Database (Belfast) [5]	Relaxed, sad, amusement, surprised, fearful, anger, disgusted	37 Male 45 Female	492	Induced
Affectiva [6]	7 basic emotions, 20 expressions and 13 emojis	–	7,860,463	Spontaneous

Table 2. Databases of facial expressions that correspond to learning-centered emotions

Database	Facial expression	Number of subjects	Number of images/videos	Type/Software Tool
Own database [7]	Frustrated, confused, sad, joyful, anguished, and fearful	39 students	30 to 60 min for student	Spontaneous/Intelligent Tutor System
Own database [8]	Interested, bored, frustrated, confused, surprised, pleasured, curios, happy and neutral	22 college students	Images	Spontaneous /Learning administrator system
Own database [9, 10] y [11]	Interested, bored, frustrated, and excited	8 students	Video and EGG (discrete emotion labels)	Spontaneous/Intelligent Tutor System
Own database [12, 13] y [14]	Pleasure, frustrated, confused, interested, and bored	137 students	Video and the BROMP observation method	Spontaneous/Educational game Physics Playground

of 8 basic emotions, and two spontaneous databases created by themselves especially with content of LCE of eight students. Emotions recognized are the following: *engaged, excited, bored,* and *relaxed.* The work concludes that, within literature, there is no work that applies the deep learning approaches to recognize of emotions in educational environments. The precision achieved when using the RaFD database is close to 95%, while databases left reach 88% and 74% respectively.

In [16], they propose a computer-assisted method aimed to instructors of certain schools, where students with mental disorders or emotional problems are taught with a system that works with usable technologies and intelligent recognition of emotions. The emotion recognition module begins with the capture of the brain headband signal. After extracting characteristics, these are processed with two classifiers: support vector machine and k-close neighbors with a cross-validation of 10 iterations. The emotions they recognize are happiness, calm, sadness, and fear. They conclude that the EEG from brain headbands is increasingly used for emotion recognition due to its low cost and easy access. The contribution of their proposal is focused on the recognition of emotions and the responses to the emotions of the students to improve their learning capacities. This work identifies basic emotions and although it analyzes the behavior of students in a teaching process, it does not focus on recognizing emotions focused on learning. Identified emotions are happiness, calm, sadness, and fear. The study concludes that EEG from brain headbands is increasingly used for emotion recognition due to its low cost and easy access. The contribution of the proposal is focused on the recognition of emotions and its students' responses so that learning capacities can be improved. This research identifies basic emotions and, although it analyzes the behavior of students in teaching processes, it does not deepen in recognizing learning-centered emotions.

In [11], a binary local pattern for the recognition of LCE is implemented. The purpose of this work is to build a database of spontaneous facial expressions corresponding to affective states in education so that it can be used in different intelligent tutorial systems, as seen in other literature like [10, 17] and [18]. The data capture technologies used are video and EEG headsets (Emotiv-EPOC). The learning-centered emotions perceived are frustration, boredom, engagement, and enthusiasm. To build their database, they take photographs of the students' facial expressions and, considering the affective state detected with the EEG signals, they proceed to label images. When using an SVM, they obtained an accuracy of 80% with a standard deviation of 2%.

In [19], authors try to improve the detection of sensor-free affection through "deep learning" specifically with Recurrent Neural Networks (RNNs). Human coders observed the students as they made use of the online learning platform and tagged the students' affect at 20-s intervals. The labeled emotions were bored, frustrated, confused, focused, and impossible to code. Their data was obtained from 646 students from 6 different schools. They obtain statistical characteristics, by time interval. They use the tags and features in three deep learning models: traditional recurrent neural network (RNN), closed recurrent unit neural network (GRU), and long-short term memory network (LSTM). The best results are obtained for an area under the curve, AUC = 0.78% with RNN.

In articles by [12] and [13] computer-vision, learning analysis and computational learning were used to detect students' affect in a real environment (a school's computer lab) with at least thirty students. The students moved, gestured, and talked to each other, which made the task difficult. Despite these challenges, they were able to detect boredom, confusion, delight, frustration, and interest. They use the RELIEF-F statistical characteristic selection algorithm, on a total of 78 facial characteristics and 3 characteristics of gross body movements. They use 14 different classifiers, including Bayesian classifiers, logistic regression, classification by clustering (with k-means), C4.5 trees, etc., using standard implementations of the WEKA (Waikato Environment for Knowledge Analysis) computational learning tool. They present the best recognition rate by classifier: boredom 64% (k-means), confusion 74% (Bayes net), pleasure 83% (Naïve Bayes), interest 64% (Bayes net) and frustration 62% (Bayes net). They clearly identify that the distribution of affective states depends on the interface used. Another similar investigation of them is the present in [20].

3 Data Capture for the Automatic Identification of Learning-Centered Emotions

For this stage, a computer laboratory of the Polytechnic University of Puebla (UPPue) was equipped. We installed the different devices, a web cam, a thermal camera, and the heart rate sensor. College engineering students were recorded using a MOOC (Massive Open Online Courses) about basic algebra. The data capture process per student lasted 40 min, which included the explanation of the experiment in which they would participate, the signature of the informed consent document, the introduction to the topic, the development, and a final evaluation. With the captured data, a database was created consisting of 393,928 data files (4,803 per experiment, included 1 file of the pulse sensor, 4,801 of thermal camera and 1 of the webcam). For this work we are using the video files (*wmv*) of 82 students. The creation of the database is part of stage two in the methodology proposed for the recognition of LCE presented in [21] which also includes the following steps described in this work for the training of algorithms, classification of the emotions and validation of the results.

3.1 Video Preprocessing

Human manual tagging was done first. For this, two people involved in the project were trained. In order to capacitate them, the FACS Manual [2] was used both theoretically and practically, performing some exercises simultaneously with the two human taggers. Through observation from second zero to the last one, the videos to be tagged were scrolled through. Videos that did not contain the complete recording of the experiment or in which students wore glasses were removed.

To carry out manual labeling, the most representative AUs of the interested and bored emotions were identified to be considered in their identification. The selection of AUs associated with each emotion was determined taking as reference those used by different authors to identify basic emotions. Most authors use only some of the first 27 AUs. For example, in The Emotional Intelligence Academy (https://www.eiagroup.com) and in [22], they use 17 AUs to recognize basic emotions. In the iMotions company they use 14 [23]. In accordance with the consensus of human taggers and taking the aforementioned works as reference, for this research we selected 16 AUs associated with the interested and bored emotions. The presence of these AUs in the facial expression are the base for their labeling.

After tagging the videos, the following strategies are executed: noise elimination, treatment of isolated or missing data, elimination of inconsistencies and duplicates. (In this case, the contrast of the image was improved, using histogram equalization.) Subsequently, the detection and automatic segmentation of the face is carried out, eliminating the background, and identifying reference points of eyes, eyebrows, mouth, nose, and contour of the face with an AAM (Active Appearance Models) algorithm, which retrieves 68 pairs of points, which describe the shape of the face. In Fig. 1, we can appreciate the facial landmarks for a frame of the video.

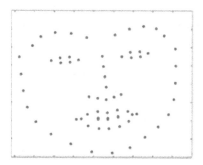

Fig. 1. Facial landmarks obtained from a frame of the video.

The last step is the alignment of facial landmarks; A method is used to align the reference points through a heuristic model based on affine transformations. The applied transformations are rotation, normalization, correction, and translation to align the neutral state (first frame of the video) with the facial expression (input image).

3.2 Feature Extraction

In this step, the magnitude and orientation of the reference points of the neutral frame (first) and of the final frame are calculated. A triangular shape of the facial reference points is obtained, the vector of triangle areas (ta) is generated, the changes in size of the facial areas of the current frame according to the neutral frame are calculated. A feature vector of dimension 243 is generated with the magnitude, orientation, and areas of the triangles. To include all the characteristics in a simpler manner, the facial reference points of 10 selected areas of the face are grouped under two different schemes: average and maximum. The eye and mouth areas are added, creating the feature vectors "car_avg" and "car_max". This reduces the dimensionality of the feature vector from 243 to two vectors with 22 features each.

After this process, the vector of AUs characteristics is obtained. The vectors "car_avg" and "car_max" are used to train a Fuzzy inference model for the recognition of AUs [24]. The Fuzzy model outputs a vector of AUs characteristics with a membership value for each AU, this is the input to train the algorithms.

4   Automatic Recognition of Learning-Centered Emotions with Machine Learning Algorithms

After analyzing the state of the art in terms of automatic emotion recognition, we tested most of the machine learning algorithms under different configuration models and identified those that delivered the best results when processing our data. The selected algorithms were SVM, KNN, assemble of trees and NN. These were trained under various classification schemes, changing the percentages of training data (60%, 70% and 80%) and test (40%, 30% and 20%), the number of folds for cross validation (3, 5, and 10), using for all of them 16 characteristics obtained from the membership values of the AUs that were previously selected. For each type of algorithm, the Bayesian optimization process was executed.

In all runs, the algorithm was executed with an expected improvement per second plus acquisition function. The function evaluates the expected amount of improvement in the objective function, ignoring the values that cause an increase in the objective and establishes a second in the time weighting for the acquisition function. The optimization algorithm was run in 100 iterations and without training time limit. The execution of the neural network in the validation was evaluated with the increase in the cross-entropy error.

The proposed classification schemes were trained, experiments with SVM, KNN, assemblies and NN were executed using all versions that Matlab® has implemented for each algorithm. Subsequently, the Bayesian optimization process was executed for each algorithm. The results of all the training tests carried out were analyzed and 9 of the best 57 were selected, those that gave the best results for accuracy. For our data, the classification scheme with the best behavior is that of NN. With the classification models of these algorithms, the validation was performed on the data reserved for tests.

5   Results Analysis

For the validation of the results, evaluation metrics are used such as accuracy, precision, rate of true positives, rate of false positives and the data from the confusion matrix. The analysis is made considering the models with the best results. Table 3 shows the results of each one of the executed tests with the selected classification models; accuracy and precision per class are shown. The group of metrics with the best evaluation for the selected classification models are those of NN. This classification model achieves an accuracy of 83%, and the best accuracy percentage for the bored and interested emotions. Regarding the next best result for accuracy, there is the assemble of trees with 79%. The KNN model follows, with an accuracy of 76.4% and a precision for the "*interested*" class of 84%, same as the NN. Very closely there is the SVM model, with an accuracy of 76.24%, but with lower precision scores for both emotions.

Table 3. Results of the evaluated classification models

#	Algorithm	*Accuracy*	*Precision* bored	*Precision* interested
1	SVM	76.24%	26%	82.24%
2	KNN	76.40%	32%	**84%**
4	Assemble of trees	79%	36%	83%
3	Neural network	**83%**	**66%**	**84%**

6 Conclusions

The classification models with the best results were neuronal network, assemble of trees, KNN and SVM, trained with a group of data of 60%, and tested with 40% and a crossed evaluation of 5 folds. The configuration for the NN was made with 70% of data for training, 15% for validation and 15% for testing. The obtained results allow us to conclude that with a general accuracy = 83%, the predictions of the NN were correct. The precision = 66%, for the "bored" class, indicates predictions are often correct. Precision = 84% for the "interested" class indicates that, when predicted, it is often correct, not only for NN, but also the KNN algorithm.

The evaluation metrics for the best four classification models indicate a good recognition of the "interested" emotion, reaching an 84% of precision, far above the most similar work done in the past [12] y [13] that reached a precision of 64%. For the "bored" emotion, the 66% precision achieved is also above the 64% obtained by the works mentioned. The lowest precision recorded for the "bored" emotion is attributed to the fact that we have a lower number of frames from different persons for this emotion, due to the complexity of obtaining frames for this expression in real time and distinguish it from, for example, a frustrated emotion and despite applying data balancing techniques, the fact that there are more faces for the "interested" emotion than for the "bored" emotion is still reflected. Having this in mind, future works would have to include the capture of more data for the "bored" emotion. Another work that has been proposed is executing algorithms of deep learning with the objective of obtaining better percentages of recognition when processing images. There is also, as a pending task, integrating heart rate and temperature data to create more complex characteristic vectors that give us the possibility of improving recognition percentages and proposing new strategies for automatic recognition of learning-centered emotions.

References

1. Hjortsj, C.-H., Ekman, P., Friesen, W.V., Hager, J.C., Facs, F., Facs, F.M.: Sistema de Codificación Facial, pp. 1–8 (2019)
2. Paul, E., Rosenberg, E.L.: What the Face Reveals: Basic and Applied Studies of Spontaneous Expression Using the Facial Action Coding System (FACS), Second. Oxford Scholarship Online, San Francisco (2012)
3. Soleymani, M., Member, S., Lee, J.: DEAP: a database for emotion analysis using physiological signals. IEEE Trans. Affect. Comput. **3**(1), 18–31 (2012)

4. Lucey, P., Cohn, J.F., Kanade, T., Saragih, J., Ambadar, Z.: The extended Cohn-Kanade dataset (CK+): a complete facial expression dataset for action unit and emotion-specified expression. In: 2010 IEEE Computer Society Conference on Computer Vision and Pattern Recognition Workshops (CVPRW), no. July, pp. 94–101 (2010)

5. Sneddon, I., Mcrorie, M., Mckeown, G., Hanratty, J.: Belfast induced natural emotion database. IEE Trans. Affect. Comput. **3**(1), 32–41 (2012)

6. El Kaliouby, R., Picard, R.W.: Affective database. MIT Media Laboratory. https://www.aff ectiva.com. Accessed 08 Apr 2019

7. Nye, B., et al.: Analyzing learner affect in a scenario-based intelligent tutoring system. In: André, E., Baker, R., Hu, X., Rodrigo, M., du Boulay, B. (eds.) AIED 2017. LNCS (LNAI), vol. 10331, pp. 544–547. Springer, Cham (2017). https://doi.org/10.1007/978-3-319-61425-0_60

8. Xiao, X., Pham, P., Wang, J.: Dynamics of affective states during MOOC learning. In: André, E., Baker, R., Hu, X., Rodrigo, M., du Boulay, B. (eds.) AIED 2017. LNCS (LNAI), vol. 10331, pp. 586–589. Springer, Cham (2017). https://doi.org/10.1007/978-3-319-61425-0_70

9. Zataraín, R., Barrón, M.L., Glez, F., Reyes-García, C.A.: An affective and web 3.0 based learning environment for a programming language. Telemat. Inform. (2017)

10. Barrón-Estrada, M.L., Zatarain-Cabada, R., Aispuro-Medina, B.G., Valencia-Rodríguez, E.M., Lara-Barrera, A.C.: Building a corpus of facial expressions for learning-centered emotions. Res. Comput. Sci. **129**, 45–52 (2016)

11. Zatarain-Cabada, R., Barrón-Estrada, M., González-Hernández, F., Oramas-Bustillos, R., Alor-Hernández, G., Reyes-García, C.: Building a corpus and a local binary pattern recognizer for learning-centered emotions. In: Pichardo-Lagunas, O., Miranda-Jiménez, S. (eds.) MICAI 2016. LNCS (LNAI), vol. 10062, pp. 524–535. Springer, Cham (2016). https://doi.org/10.1007/978-3-319-62428-0_43

12. Bosch, N., et al.: Detecting student emotions in computer-enabled classrooms. In: International Joint Conference on Artificial Intelligence, IJCAI, vol. 2016-Janua, pp. 4125–4129 (2016)

13. Bosch, N., D'mello, S.K., Ocumpaugh, J., Baker, R.S., Shute, V.: Using video to automatically detect learner affect in computer-enabled classrooms. In: ACM Transactions on Interactive Intelligent Systems, vol. 6, no. 2, pp. 1–26 (2016)

14. Bosch, N., et al.: Automatic detection of learning-centered affective states in the wild. In: Proceedings of the 20th International Conference on Intelligent User Interfaces, IUI 2015, pp. 379–388 (2015)

15. González-Hernández, F., Zatarain-Cabada, R., Barrón-Estrada, M.L., Rodríguez-Rangel, H.: Recognition of learning-centered emotions using a convolutional neural network. J. Intell. Fuzzy Syst. **34**(5), 3325–3336 (2017)

16. Mehmood, R., Lee, H.: Towards building a computer aided education system for special students using wearable sensor technologies. Sensors **17**(317), 1–22 (2017)

17. Zatarain-Cabada, R., Barron-Estrada, M.L., González-Hernández, F., Rodríguez-Rangel, H.: Building a face expression recognizer and a face expression database for an intelligent tutoring system. In: Proceedings of the IEEE 17th International Conference on Advanced Learning Technologies, ICALT 2017, no. 2161–377X/17, pp. 391–393 (2017)

18. Barrón-Estrada, M.L., Zatarain-Cabada, R., Oramas-Bustillos, R., González- Hernández, F.: Sentiment analysis in an affective intelligent tutoring system. In: IEEE 17th International Conference on Advanced Learning Technologies (2017)

19. Botelho, A.F., Baker, R.S., Heffernan, N.T.: Improving sensor-free affect detection using deep learning. In: André, E., Baker, R., Hu, X., Rodrigo, M., du Boulay, B. (eds.) AIED 2017. LNCS (LNAI), vol. 10331, pp. 40–51. Springer, Cham (2017). https://doi.org/10.1007/978-3-319-61425-0_4. ISBN 978-3-319-61424-3

20. Monkaresi, H., Bosch, N., Calvo, R., D'Mello, S.: Automated detection of engagement using video-based estimation of facial expressions and heart rate. IEEE Trans. Affect. Comput. **8**(1), 15–28 (2017)
21. González-Meneses, Y.N., Guerrero-García, J., Reyes-García, C.A., Olmos-Pineda, I., González-Calleros, J.M.: Methodology for automatic identification of emotions in learning environments. Res. Comput. Sci. **5**(148), 89–96 (2019)
22. Wegrzyn, M., Vogt, M., Kireclioglu, B., Schneider, J., Kissler, J.: Mapping the emotional face. How individual face parts contribute to successful emotion recognition. PLoS One **12**(5), 1–15 (2017)
23. Farnsworth, B.: Facial Action Coding System (FACS) – A Visual Guidebook. Boston, USA (2019)
24. Morales-Vargas, E., Reyes-García, C.A., Peregrina-Barreto, H.: On the use of action units and fuzzy explanatory models for facial expression recognition. PLoS One **14**(10), 1–13 (2019)

Pattern Recognition Techniques

Unsupervised Feature Selection Methodology for Analysis of Bacterial Taxonomy Profiles

Saúl Solorio-Fernández[✉]🆔, J. A. Carrasco-Ochoa,
and José Fco. Martínez-Trinidad

Computer Sciences Department,
Instituto Nacional de Astrofísica, Óptica y Electrónica,
Luis Enrique Erro # 1, Santa María Tonantzintla, 72840 Puebla, Mexico
{sausolofer,ariel,fmartine}@inaoep.mx

Abstract. Unsupervised Feature Selection is an area of research that currently has received much attention in the scientific community due to its wide application in practical problems where unlabeled data arise. One of these problems is profiling the structure of bacterial communities in the oceans, where it is required to identify and select relevant features from unlabeled marine sediment samples. This paper introduces a methodology to identify and select a set of relevant features in this field. To select a subset of relevant features, we rely on a synergy between ranking-based unsupervised feature selection methods, an introduced internal validation index, and a clustering algorithm. According to the results obtained in our analyses, the proposed methodology can select those features that best discover cluster structures in this kind of data.

Keywords: Unsupervised feature selection · Feature ranking-based methods · Feature subset selection methodology · Bacterial community structure profiles

1 Introduction

When analyzing the structure of ocean bacterial community profiles, it is known that deep-water marine sediments exhibit an outstanding level of bacterial diversity whose study is of great interest to the scientific community in this field [1,2]. The collected sediment samples (objects) are essentially unsupervised, i.e., the objects do not have an a priori classification, and the labeling process is commonly done in the data exploratory analysis stage based on the features that describe the objects in the sample. For the labeling process, it is important to determine those features that could define "natural" and "interesting" cluster structures in the collected data [3]. In this task, unsupervised feature selection methods [3,4] can greatly support the researcher since their main objective is to try to identify good features that best define cluster structures without needing the class labels. Specifically, ranking-based unsupervised feature selection

© Springer Nature Switzerland AG 2021
E. Roman-Rangel et al. (Eds.): MCPR 2021, LNCS 12725, pp. 47–56, 2021.
https://doi.org/10.1007/978-3-030-77004-4_5

methods (RUFSM) have become very popular in recent years due to their efficiency, scalability, and simplicity [4]. Unsupervised ranking-based feature selection methods use distinct criteria to evaluate each feature's importance, obtaining an ordered list (ranking) where features are arranged according to their relevance. However, although these methods are commonly used in practice, one drawback is that they do not provide a subset of features as output; therefore, the user must manually establish a threshold to choose the final number of features to select. This decision is difficult since researchers profiling the structure of bacterial communities in the oceans usually do not have additional information or criteria to help guide them in selecting the best feature subset. Moreover, in this scenario, researchers do not have any information to decide which particular feature selection method might be the most appropriate for their problem.

This paper presents a feature selection methodology to select a subset of features from the results of a pool of ranking-based unsupervised feature selection methods. The idea is to create a positive synergy between the ranking-based methods, a defined internal validation index, and a specific clustering algorithm to identify and select a good subset of features that best discover cluster structures in the data. The methodology introduced in this paper was applied in a real-world dataset used to analyze bacterial taxonomy profiles, getting good results regarding the quality of the selected features.

The rest of this paper is organized as follows. In Sect. 2, we provide a brief review of the raking-based unsupervised feature selection methods used in our study. In Sect. 3, we describe the proposed methodology. The analysis of bacterial taxonomy profiles is presented and discussed in Sect. 4. Finally, Sect. 5 concludes this paper and enunciates further research on this topic.

2   Raking-Based Unsupervised Feature Selection Methods

In the literature, the ranking-based unsupervised feature selection methods can be classified as Statistical, Similarity/Spectral, Information Theory, and Sparse Learning-based methods [4]. Some of the most representative and relevant methods on the categories mentioned above, used in this paper's proposed methodology, are briefly described below.

Variance: Variance [3] is one of the most simple ranking-based methods for evaluating a single feature's importance in an unsupervised context. The idea is that higher variance features are more relevant for building good cluster structures. This statistical-based method weights and ranks features according to their variance in the dataset.

SUD: Sequential backward selection method for Unsupervised Data [5] weights features using a distance-based similarity entropy measure. The idea is to calculate the entropy that is generated after removing one feature at a time from the whole set of features. Features are ordered from the most relevant (which produces the highest entropy after removing it) to the least relevant feature (lowest entropy).

LS: Laplacian Score [6] is a similarity/spectral feature selection method that measures a feature's relevancy using the Laplacian matrix derived from the similarities among objects. The idea is to weigh each feature measuring how this feature preserves the pre-defined graph structure represented by the Laplacian matrix [7]. This method gets a feature ranking according to the Laplacian score associated with each feature.

SVD-Entropy: SVD-Entropy (ranking-based version) [8] selects those features that best represent the data, measuring the data matrix's entropy through its singular values. Each feature's Contribution to the Entropy (CE) is evaluated through a leave-one-out comparison, and the features are sorted according to their respective CE values.

SPEC: SPECtrum decomposition [9] is another similarity/spectral feature selection method that evaluates the importance of the features using the concept of *consistency*[1] regarding the structure of the graph induced from the objects' similarities. Feature evaluation is performed by measuring each feature's consistency against the nontrivial eigenvectors of the Laplacian matrix through some *score functions*. The final result is an ordered list whose elements are set from the most to the least consistent (relevant) feature.

USFSM: Unsupervised Spectral Feature Selection Method for mixed data [10] is a feature selection method based on Spectral Feature Selection [11]. USFSM ranks features according to their consistency in the dataset by analyzing the spectrum distribution changes (spectral gaps) of the Normalized Laplacian matrix when each feature is excluded from the whole set of features separately. Features are sorted in descending order according to their respective spectral gaps score values.

UDFS: Unsupervised Discriminative Feature Selection method [12] weights features simultaneously using the discriminative information in the scatter matrices and feature correlations. UDFS addresses the feature selection problem by considering the trace criterion [13] into a constrained regression problem optimized through an efficient optimization algorithm. Features are ranked according to their score values in descending order.

NDFS: Nonnegative Discriminative Feature Selection method [14] performs feature selection exploiting the discriminative information and feature correlations in a unified framework. First, NDFS uses spectral analysis [15] to learn pseudo-class labels (defined as non-negative real values). Then, a regression model with $l_{2,1}$ norm regularization [16] is optimized through a special solver, also proposed in this work. Features are ranked from the most relevant (those most related to the pseudo-class labels) to the least relevant ones.

It is important to highlight that the particular set of methods described above were selected because they are based on different metrics and frameworks and because they are widely used in practice by researchers.

---

[1] A feature is consistent if it takes similar values for the objects that are close to each other and dissimilar values for far apart objects.

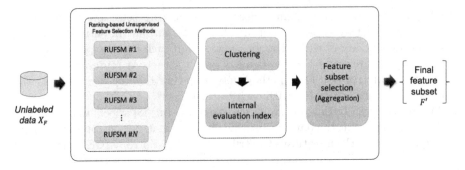

Fig. 1. General diagram of the proposed Unsupervised Feature Selection methodology.

3   Proposed Methodology

One of the major problems of applying feature selection is choosing an appropriate method for a particular dataset. Each feature selection method has its strengths and weaknesses, and its performance generally depends on multiple factors such as dataset type, number of features, number of objects, etc. Thus, some knowledge is generally required to select a suitable method for each particular case [17,18]. On the other hand, since the task associated with this problem is of unsupervised nature, it is also necessary to define a clustering algorithm and a criterion for evaluating its results. In Fig. 1, we show the general diagram of the proposed unsupervised feature selection methodology, and in the following paragraphs, the details about the steps followed into each stage are provided.

1. Let $X_F = \{x_1, x_2, \ldots, x_m\}$ be a collection of m unlabeled objects described by a set of n features $F = \{f_1, f_2, \ldots, f_n\}$, and let $R = \{r_1, r_2, \ldots, r_N\}$ be a pool of N Ranking-based Unsupervised Feature Selection Methods. We first apply each ranker r_i, $i = 1 \ldots N$ to the original dataset X_F. As a result, we will obtain a list $L = \{l_1, l_2, \ldots, l_N\}$, containing the feature rankings produced by each ranker r_i.
2. For each $l_i \in L$ obtain the corresponding *average ranking quality value* v_i and the *best cut point* p_i. The v_i value indicates how good is the feature ranking l_i; meanwhile, p_i is an index that indicates the best cut-off point in this feature ranking. To complete this stage, the next steps are followed:

   - Using a defined clustering algorithm, perform clustering over $X_{l_i^1}$, which is the dataset described just by the first feature in l_i. Afterwards, cluster $X_{l_i^2}$ which is the dataset described by the first two features in l_i, and so on, until evaluating $X_{l_i^{n'}}$, which is the dataset described by the first n' features in the ranking, being $n' \leq n$. The corresponding clustering results will be $C = \{c_{l_i^1}, c_{l_i^2}, \ldots, c_{l_i^{n'}}\}$.
   - For each element $c \in C$, evaluate its clustering quality using a defined internal evaluation index [19]. The respective clustering quality evaluations will be $Q = \{q_{l_i^1}, q_{l_i^2}, \ldots, q_{l_i^{n'}}\}$.

– Compute the v_i value, which is obtained by averaging the clustering quality evaluations in Q. Likewise, p_i will be the index associated with the best value[2] in Q.

3. The last step is the *ranking aggregation* procedure, which consists of selecting from L the final feature subset $F' \subseteq F$ using a suitable aggregation function. To complete this step, the following operations are performed:

– Select the best N' ($N' \leq N$) feature rankings from L, i.e., those with best *average ranking quality values*, as well as their corresponding *best cut points*.
– From the best feature rankings selected (previous step), obtain their corresponding *best-cut-off point feature subsets* and assign them to L', i.e.,

$$L' = \{l_1^{p_1}, l_2^{p_2}, \ldots, l_{N'}^{p_{N'}}\}$$

– Get the final feature subset F', which is obtained from the union of the elements in L'. Therefore the aggregation function is defined as:

$$F' = \bigcup_{i \in L'} F_{l_i^{p_i}} \tag{1}$$

where $F_{l_i^{p_i}}$ is the set of features obtained from *best-cut-off point feature subset* $l_i^{p_i}$.

Note that the proposed methodology can be applied over any set of ranking-based unsupervised feature selection methods, clustering algorithm, and clustering quality evaluation measure, making it applicable to a wide variety of problems in the unsupervised context.

4   Analysis of Bacterial Taxonomy Profiles

In order to illustrate the use of the proposed unsupervised feature selection methodology, we apply it over the swGoM sediments dataset [1]. This is a real-world ocean bacterial community structure profiles dataset composed of 87 abiotic numerical features with no missing values and 61 objects extracted from the Southwestern Gulf of Mexico. The features are categorized into five groups: Total Metals, Adsorbed Metals, Organic Matter, Total Hydrocarbons, and Aliphatic Hydrocarbons. For this dataset, as a pre-processing step, because some features have ranges of values with different scales (which could affect the outcome of feature selection methods, clustering algorithms, and internal evaluation measures), the features were standardized. That is, each dimension was normalized to obtain a mean 0 and standard deviation of 1.

For grouping the samples, we use the well-known k-means clustering algorithm [20], and for evaluating its clustering results, the Calinski-Harabasz (CH)

---

[2] Maximum or minimum, depending on the internal evaluation index used.

index [21] was employed. We chose the CH index because it shares the same basis with the k-means algorithm and because they often produce good results when running together [19]. However, due to most of the internal evaluation indices (including the CH index) have a bias[3] regarding the cardinality of the feature subsets evaluated [3,22], in our methodology, to evaluate more fairly the quality of the clusters, we propose to use a partially modified version of the CH index proposed in [23], which we called as Normalized Calinski-Harabasz (NCH) index, and it is defined as:

$$NCH\left(T\right) = \frac{tr\left(S_b^{(X_T)}\right)}{tr\left(S_w^{(X_T)}\right)} \times \frac{m-k}{k-1} \times |T| \tag{2}$$

where X_T is the dataset described by the candidate feature subset $T \subseteq F$, $S_w^{(X_T)}$ and $S_b^{(X_T)}$ are the corresponding within-class scatter and between-class scatter matrices [3], respectively, $tr(\cdot)$ represents the trace of these scattering matrices, m is the number of objects, and k is the number of clusters. This modification tries to counteract the bias and causes the Calinski-Harabasz index to assess the candidate feature subsets more fairly. Therefore, the best feature subset will be the one with the largest value for the index defined in Eq. 2.

On the other hand, following the idea to consider only those features at the beginning of the ranking (the most relevant), the number of features to evaluate in the feature ranking (denoted as the parameter n' in our methodology) was set equal to $n' = 50\%$ of the dataset's total number of features. Meanwhile, based on our experiments' best quality results, the number of best feature rankings to select (denoted as the parameter N' in our methodology) was chosen as $N' = 3$. For the k-means clustering algorithm, the number of clusters was also set to $k = 3$ since according to [1], there are three distinct groups in the data.

The implementations of the ranking-based unsupervised feature selection methods used in our experiment were taken from their respective authors with the parameters recommended by themselves. Meanwhile, for the k-means clustering algorithm, we used the implementation included in the Weka machine learning software [24] using the default parameter values and fixing $k = 3$ as mentioned earlier. All experiments were run in Matlab R2018a with Java 8.02, using a computer with an Intel Core i7-5820K 3.3 GHz processor with 32 GB DDR4 RAM, running 64-bit Microsoft Windows 10 operating system.

4.1 Results and Discussion

In Fig. 2, we can see the ranking evaluation results over the SwGoM dataset. Figure 2a, show the clustering quality results (NCH values) of the different subsets of features evaluated according to the ranking produced by each ranking-based method. Furthermore, as a reference, in this figure, we also included the

---

[3] The value computed by these indices increases or decreases monotonically regarding the number of features.

clustering quality obtained considering the whole set of features (original). Figure 2b, on the other hand, shows the average ranking quality values and the corresponding best cut points (numbers in parenthesis) of these feature rankings. As we can see in Fig. 2b, the best results (best average ranking) were obtained by SVD-Entropy, SUD, and Laplacian Score with best cutoff points in 11, 2, and 14, respectively. This can be corroborated in Fig. 2a, where it is possible to see that the ranking produced by these methods is clearly better than the rest of the methods. Furthermore, the quality obtained with these ranking methods is better than considering the original set of features.

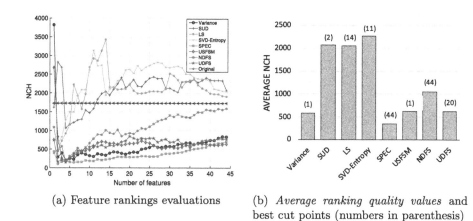

(a) Feature rankings evaluations

(b) *Average ranking quality values* and best cut points (numbers in parenthesis)

Fig. 2. Feature rankings evaluations and *average ranking quality values* on the feature ranking produced by the ranking-based methods on the SwGoM dataset.

Consequently, the feature rankings (first 20 features) produced by the ranking-based methods and the final feature subset F' selected are shown on Table 1. From this Table, it is possible to observe that, according to our methodology, the feature subset $F' = \{7, 14, 19, 6, 15, 13, 5, 17, 9, 11, 4, 23, 22, 21\}$, belonging to the Aliphatic Hydrocarbons features group [1], is the most important to define clusters structures in the data. This can be verified in Fig. 3, where a well-formed cluster clearly separated from the rest can be observed using the features 7, 14, and 19 (Fig. 3b); meanwhile, selecting the first features of the ranking obtained from SPEC (which is the worst method according to the *average ranking quality values*) these structures are not distinguished clearly, since the values of some these features follow a uniform distribution (see Fig. 3a). Moreover, the NCH index value reached with F' is 3, 432, which is better than any of the individual rankings (not considering the trivial solution). This means that our methodology can effectively identify and select relevant features in the Southwestern Gulf of Mexico's bacterial community structure profiles dataset.

Table 1. Feature rankings produced by the ranking-based methods (first 20 features) and final feature subset F' selected on SwGoM dataset.

Ranking position	Feature ranking								F'
	Variance	SUD	LS	SVD-Entropy	SPEC	USFSM	NDFS	UDFS	
1	30	5	13	7	87	49	54	9	{7
2	9	6	21	14	86	47	21	56	14
3	4	7	19	9	85	48	38	55	19
4	52	54	7	15	84	54	1	38	6
5	17	4	14	6	83	38	7	54	15
6	28	9	15	19	82	60	12	5	13
7	19	11	6	13	81	52	53	11	5
8	18	12	23	17	80	43	47	32	17
9	1	35	5	5	79	50	22	10	9
10	70	13	9	11	78	64	23	35	11
11	32	19	11	4	77	53	19	8	4
12	7	21	17	21	76	35	6	47	23
13	64	14	4	22	75	51	48	15	22
14	36	53	22	38	74	26	13	1	21}
15	11	20	53	23	73	45	82	12	
16	42	22	25	53	72	83	49	25	
17	49	15	39	52	71	78	14	18	
18	61	38	16	25	70	62	71	22	
19	80	8	12	54	69	28	69	46	
20	35	50	24	44	68	42	26	16	

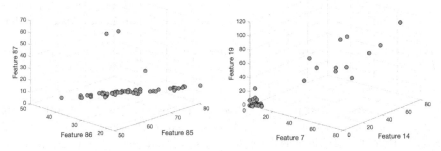

(a) First three features from SPEC ranking   (b) Features f_7, f_{14}, and f_{19} from F'

Fig. 3. SwGoM dataset in different feature dimensional spaces according to (a) the first three ranked features of SPEC and (b) three features selected from the feature subset F'.

5   Conclusions and Future Work

In this paper, we introduced a methodology to solve the feature subset selection problem by using unsupervised feature ranking-based methods. Our methodology combines the advantages of using a pool of unsupervised ranking-based methods with a normalized internal validation index and a clustering algorithm.

It results in a positive synergy between the involved elements that allows selecting a subset of features that discover good cluster structures in the data.

To show our methodology's effectiveness, we tested it on a real-world unlabeled bacterial community structure profiles dataset of Mexico's Southwestern Gulf. The results have shown that our methodology is useful for identifying and selecting relevant features that allow defining good cluster structures in the data, showing the advantages of applying ranking-based feature selection methods on unsupervised data.

Finally, an interesting future research direction is to perform a study combining unsupervised ranking-based methods and feature subset selectors, aiming to allow our methodology to improve its performance in terms of clustering quality. Furthermore, since our methodology is independent of the type of input data, we will also consider its application on other datasets as future work.

Acknowledgements. The first author gratefully acknowledges the Instituto Nacional de Astrofósica, Óptica y Electrínica (INAOE) for the collaboration grant awarded for developing this research. We also thank E. Ernestina Godoy-Lozano and collaborators to provide the data for the analysis presented in this paper.

References

1. Godoy-Lozano, E.E., et al.: Bacterial diversity and the geochemical landscape in the southwestern Gulf of Mexico. Front. Microbiol. **9**, 2528 (2018)
2. Wang, Y., et al.: Comparison of the levels of bacterial diversity in freshwater, intertidal wetland, and marine sediments by using millions of illumina tags. Appl. Environ. Microbiol. **78**(23), 8264–8271 (12 2012)
3. Dy, J.G., Brodley, C.E.: Feature selection for unsupervised learning. J. Mach. Learn. Res. **5**, 845–889 (2004)
4. Solorio-Fernández, S., Carrasco-Ochoa, J.A., Martínez-Trinidad, J.F.: A review of unsupervised feature selection methods. Artif. Intell. Rev. **53**(2), 907–948 (2020)
5. Dash, M., Liu, H., Yao, J.: Dimensionality reduction of unsupervised data. In: Proceedings Ninth IEEE International Conference on Tools with Artificial Intelligence, pp. 532–539. IEEE Computer Society (1997)
6. He, X., Cai, D., Niyogi, P.: Laplacian score for feature selection. In: Advances in Neural Information Processing Systems 18, vol. 186, pp. 507–514 (2005)
7. Chung, F.R.K.: Spectral Graph Theory. Reprinted edn, vol. 92. American Mathematical Soc. (1997)
8. Varshavsky, R., Gottlieb, A., Linial, M., Horn, D.: Novel unsupervised feature filtering of biological data. Bioinformatics **22**(14), e507–e513 (2006)
9. Zhao, Z., Liu, H.: Spectral feature selection for supervised and unsupervised learning. In: Proceedings of the 24th International Conference on Machine Learning, pp. 1151–1157. ACM (2007)
10. Solorio-Fernández, S., Martínez-Trinidad, J.F., Carrasco-Ochoa, J.A.: A new unsupervised spectral feature selection method for mixed data: a filter approach. Pattern Recogn. **72**, 314–326 (2017)
11. Zhao, Z.A., Liu, H.: Spectral Feature Selection for Data Mining. CRC Press (2011)
12. Yang, Y., Shen, H.T., Ma, Z., Huang, Z., Zhou, X.: L2,1-Norm regularized discriminative feature selection for unsupervised learning. In: IJCAI International Joint Conference on Artificial Intelligence, pp. 1589–1594 (2011)

13. Fukunaga, K.: Introduction to Statistical Pattern Recognition, vol. 22. Academic Press (1990)

14. Li, Z., Yang, Y., Liu, J., Zhou, X., Lu, H.: Unsupervised feature selection using nonnegative spectral analysis. Proc. Natl. Conf. Artif. Intell. **2**, 1026–1032 (2012)

15. Ng, A.Y., Jordan, M.I., Weiss, Y.: On spectral clustering: analysis and an algorithm. In: Advances in Neural Information Processing Systems, pp. 849–856 (2002)

16. Argyriou, A., Evgeniou, T., Pontil, M.: Convex multi-task feature learning. Mach. Learn. **73**(3), 243–272 (2008)

17. Seijo-Pardo, B., Porto-Díaz, I., Bolón-Canedo, V., Alonso-Betanzos, A.: Ensemble feature selection: homogeneous and heterogeneous approaches. Knowl.-Based Syst. **118**, 124–139 (2017)

18. Bolón-Canedo, V., Alonso-Betanzos, A.: Ensembles for feature selection: a review and future trends. Inf. Fusion **52**, 1–12 (2019)

19. Liu, Y., Li, Z., Xiong, H., Gao, X., Wu, J.: Understanding of internal clustering validation measures. In: 2010 IEEE 10th International Conference on Data Mining (ICDM), pp. 911–916. IEEE (2010)

20. MacQueen, J.B.: Some methods for classification and analysis of multivariate observations. In: Proceedings of 5-th Berkeley Symposium on Mathematical Statistics and Probability, vol. 1, pp. 281–297 (1967)

21. Calinski, T., Harabasz, J.: A dendrite method for cluster analysis. Commun. Stat. - Theory Methods **3**(1), 1–27 (1974)

22. Morita, M., Sabourin, R., Bortolozzi, F., Suen, C.Y.: Unsupervised feature selection using multi-objective genetic algorithms for handwritten word recognition. In: Seventh International Conference on Document Analysis and Recognition, 2003. Proceedings, pp. 666–670. IEEE (2003)

23. Solorio-Fernández, S., Carrasco-Ochoa, J., Martínez-Trinidad, J.: A new hybrid filter–wrapper feature selection method for clustering based on ranking. Neurocomputing **214** (2016)

24. Hall, M., Frank, E., Holmes, G., Pfahringer, B., Reutemann, P., Witten, I.H.: The WEKA data mining software: an update. SIGKDD Explor. Newsl. **11**(1), 10–18 (2009)

A Comparative Study of Two Algorithms for Computing the Shortest Reducts: MiLIT and MinReduct

Vladímir Rodríguez-Diez[1,2]([✉]), José Fco. Martínez-Trinidad[3],
J. A. Carrasco-Ochoa[3], Manuel S. Lazo-Cortés[4], and J. Arturo Olvera-López[1]

[1] Benemérita Universidad Autónoma de Puebla,
Faculty of Computer Science, Language & Knowledge Engineering Lab,
Ciudad Universitaria, Puebla, Puebla, Mexico
[2] Universidad de Camagüey, Circunvalación Nte. km $5\frac{1}{2}$, Camagüey, Cuba
vladimir.rodriguez@reduc.edu.cu
[3] Instituto Nacional de Astrofísica, Óptica y Electrónica,
Coordinación de Ciencias Computacionales, Luis Enrique Erro # 1,
Tonantzintla, Puebla, Mexico
[4] TecNM|Instituto Tecnológico de Tlalnepantla, Av. Instituto Tecnológico s/n,
Tlalnepantla de Baz, State of Mexico, Mexico

Abstract. Rough set reducts are irreducible attribute subsets preserving discernibility information of a decision system. Computing all reducts has exponential complexity regarding the number of attributes in the decision system. Given the high computational cost of this task, computing only the reducts of minimum length (the shortest reducts) becomes relevant for a wide range of applications. Two recent algorithms have been reported, almost simultaneously, for computing these irreducible attribute subsets with minimum length: MiLIT and MinReduct. MiLIT was designed at the top of the Testor Theory while MinReduct comes from the Rough Set Theory. Thus, in this paper, we present a comparative study of these algorithms in terms of asymptotic complexity and runtime performance.

Keywords: Typical testor · Minimum-length · Shortest reduct

1 Introduction

Rough Set Theory (RST) [11] Reducts are minimal attribute subsets preserving the discernibility capacity of the whole set of attributes [12]. Reducts have been found useful for feature selection [9] and classification [10] among others. The main drawback of reducts is that computing the complete set of reducts for a decision system is an NP-hard problem [18]. However, most of the times, only a subset of reducts is necessary for real applications [4]. The set of all reducts with the minimum length (the shortest reducts) is particularly relevant for such

© Springer Nature Switzerland AG 2021
E. Roman-Rangel et al. (Eds.): MCPR 2021, LNCS 12725, pp. 57–67, 2021.
https://doi.org/10.1007/978-3-030-77004-4_6

applications, since it is a representative sample of all reducts [19]. Recently, the algorithm MinReduct, for computing all the shortest reducts, was reported [15].

Testor Theory [2] separately developed the concept of Typical Testor. Typical Testor and Reduct concepts are so close [3] that algorithms designed for computing typical testors can be used for computing reducts and vice versa [6]. Typical testors have been used for feature selection [16] and some other real-world applications [20]. Since computing all typical testors is also NP-hard, a significant runtime reduction can be obtained from computing only the set of all the minimum-length typical testors. For this purpose, the **Mi**nimum **L**ength **I**rreducible **T**estors (MiLIT) algorithm was recently proposed [13]. The authors reported indeed two variants of MiLIT: the first one using an in-place search based on **N**ext **C**ombination (next attribute subset) calculation (NC) and the other one using a search with **P**runing based on **F**eature and **R**ow **C**ontribution (PFRC).

The almost simultaneous publication of these algorithms that solve an equivalent problem deserves a comparative study. Thus, in this work, we present such a study with the aim of providing application suggestions and some foundations for the development of future algorithms. To this end, we will first provide a common theoretical framework for describing the algorithms under study. Then, a description in terms of asymptotic complexity will be presented. Finally, an experimental assessment of the three algorithms will be carried out over synthetic and real-world decision systems.

The rest of this paper is structured in the following way. In Sect. 2, some basic concepts from RST and the pruning properties used by the algorithms under study are presented. In Sect. 3, we describe the algorithms with an special emphasis in their asymptotic time complexity. Then, in Sect. 4, we present our experimental assessment and the discussion of the results. Finally, our conclusions appear in Sect. 5.

2   Theoretical Background

In this section, we introduce the main concepts of Rough Set Theory, as well as the definitions and propositions supporting the pruning strategies used in MiLIT and MinReduct. Notice that although MiLIT algorithms are designed in the top of Testor Theory, we will use concepts from Rough Set Theory for describing these algorithms.

In RST, a decision system (DS) is a table with rows representing objects while columns represent attributes. We denote by U a finite non-empty set of objects $U = \{x_1, x_2, ..., x_n\}$ and A is a finite non-empty set of attributes. For every attribute in A there is a mapping: $a : U \to V_a$. The set V_a is called the *value set* of a. Attributes in A are further divided into condition attributes C and decision attributes D such that $A = C \cup D$.

Decision attributes D induce a partition of the universe U into decision classes. Usually, we are interested in those classes induced by an attribute subset B that correspond to the decision classes. To this end, the *B-positive region of*

D, denoted as $POS_B(D)$, is defined as the set of all objects in U such that if two of them have the same value for every attribute in B, they belong to the same decision class.

A subset $B \subseteq C$ is a decision *reduct* of DS relative to D if:

1. $POS_B(D) = POS_C(D)$.
2. B is a minimal subset (regarding inclusion) fulfilling condition 1.

Decision reducts have the same capability as the complete set of condition attributes for discerning between objects from different classes (Condition 1), and every attribute in a reduct (typical testor) is indispensable for holding Condition 1 (Condition 2). A super-reduct (testor) is a set B that fulfills Condition 1, regardless of Condition 2. Decision reducts are called just reducts, for simplicity.

The *Binary Discernibility Matrix* is a binary table representing the discernibility information of objects belonging to different classes. The element $m(i, j, c)$ regarding two objects x_i and x_j and a single condition attribute $c \in C$ is defined as:

$$m(i, j, c) = \begin{cases} 1 \text{ if } c(x_i) \neq c(x_j) \\ 0 \text{ otherwise} \end{cases}$$

The *Simplified Binary Discernibility Matrix* is a reduced version of the binary discernibility matrix after applying absorption laws. In Testor Theory [5] this concept is called *Basic Matrix*, and we will adopt this term for the rest of this document, because it is simple and explicit. From the basic matrix of a decision system all reducts can be computed [21].

2.1   Pruning Properties Used by the Algorithms Under Study

The reader can find the proof and a more detailed explanation of the following propositions in [13, 15].

Definition 1. *B is a super-reduct iff in the sub-matrix of the basic matrix formed by the columns corresponding to the attributes in B, there is no zero row (a row with only zeros).*

The attribute contribution, presented in Definition 2, is used by MinReduct and PFRC-MiLIT.

Definition 2. *Given $B \subseteq C$ and $x_i \in C$ such that $x_i \notin B$. x_i contributes to B iff the sub-matrix of the basic matrix formed with only those attributes in B has more zero rows than that matrix formed with attributes in $B \cup \{x_i\}$.*

The pruning based on Definition 2 is supported by Proposition 1.

Proposition 1. *Given $B \subseteq C$ and $x_i \in C$ such that $x_i \notin B$. If x_i does not contribute to B, then $B \cup \{x_i\}$ cannot be a subset of any reduct.*

The algorithms under study search for super-reducts (testors) instead of reducts (typical testors) supported by the following proposition, which was first introduced in [22]. This simplification reduces the cost of candidate subsets evaluations.

Proposition 2. *Let $B \subseteq C$, if B is one of the shortest super-reducts of a basic matrix, then it is also one of the shortest reducts.*

MiLIT and MinReduct, as in many other algorithms for reduct (and typical testor) computation [7,14,17] arrange the basic matrix to reduce the search space. The arrangement consist in moving one of the rows with the fewest number of 1's in the basic matrix to the top, and all columns in which this row has 1, are moved to the left. This arrangement reduces the attribute subsets evaluated by these algorithms which follow a traversing order that resembles the lexicographical order. The search can be stopped after all the attribute subsets that include an attribute of the columns having a 1 in the first row of the basic matrix are evaluated. For the rest of the attribute subsets in the search space (in the lexicographical order), the first row is always a zero row.

For PFRC-MiLIT the following proposition was presented:

Proposition 3. *Given $B \subseteq C$ and $x_i \in C$ such that $x_i \notin B$. If there exist a zero row in the sub-matrix of the basic matrix formed by the attributes in $B \cup \{x_i\}$, that is also a zero row in the sub-matrix formed by the remaining attributes on the right side of x_i. Then $B \cup \{x_i\}$ cannot be a subset of any reduct.*

Proposition 4 is used by MinReduct in order to avoid the unnecessary evaluation of super-sets of a reduct. If a given attribute subset does not hold this proposition, Condition 2 of the reduct definition cannot be met because it has excluding (redundant) attributes. The verification of Proposition 4 is called exclusion evaluation.

Proposition 4. *Given $B \subseteq C$, if B is a subset of a reduct, $\forall x_i \in B$ exists at least one row in the sub-matrix formed by the attributes in B that has a 1 in the column corresponding to x_i and 0 in all other columns.*

3   MiLIT and MinReduct Algorithms

We present here a brief description of the three algorithms under study. In the subsequent explanation, the asymptotic time complexity of each algorithm is detailed. For this purpose, the number of rows in the basic matrix is denoted by m, the number of columns is denoted by n, the number of 0's in the first row of the arranged basic matrix is denoted by n_0 and the length of the shortest reducts is denoted by k.

3.1   NC-MiLIT

The key pruning goal of any algorithm designed for computing the shortest reducts consist in evaluating only attribute subsets with a length not higher than that of the shortest reducts (k). Unfortunately, the length of the shortest reducts cannot be known a priori. In fact, the idea of estimating by an approximate algorithm this length and then use it as a parameter for the exact algorithm computing all the shortest reducts was reported in [8].

Both versions of the MiLIT (NC and PFRC) ensure the evaluation of only attribute subsets with a length not higher than k by their traversing order.

For each candidate subset evaluated by NC-MiLIT the super-reduct property is verified by means of Definition 1. This verification has a time cost of $\Theta(m \times k)$. The number of evaluations can be precisely determined for this algorithm. To the number of subsets that can be generated with length lower than or equal to k with the n attributes (Eq. 1) we must subtract the avoided evaluations of those attribute subsets that do not include an attribute of the columns having a 1 in the first row (Eq. 2).

$$C(n, k) = \sum_{i=1}^{k} \binom{n}{i} \tag{1}$$

$$C(n_0, k) = \sum_{i=1}^{\min(n_0, k)} \binom{n_0}{i} \tag{2}$$

Thus, the time complexity of the NC-MiLIT algorithm can be expressed by Eq. 3

$$T_{NC} = \Theta\left((m \times k)\left(\sum_{i=1}^{k}\binom{n}{i} - \sum_{i=1}^{\min(n_0, k)}\binom{n_0}{i}\right)\right) \tag{3}$$

3.2   PFRC-MiLIT

The PFRC-MiLIT algorithm includes the verification of contribution (Proposition 1) and the zero row remanence (Proposition 3) for each evaluated candidate. The idea is to avoid subsets that are super-sets of any candidate with a non contributing attribute or with remanent zero rows, since they cannot form reducts. Both properties can be verified in time $\Theta(m \times k)$ which makes no difference with NC-MiLIT in terms of asymptotic complexity. However, this evaluation process requires more computation time, but a great number of candidates can be avoided in this way. In practical terms, this pruning is achieved by means of a queue data-structure in which those subsets that will not lead to a reduct are not enqueued.

For PFRC-MiLIT, the time complexity computed by Eq. 3 is the upper bound. This can be expressed as it is shown in Eq. 4. The actual number of candidates evaluated depends on the distribution of the data in the basic matrix.

The authors of MiLIT claim that in sparse matrices these avoided subsets are very common, which seems obvious after Proposition 3.

$$T_{PFRC} = O\left((m \times k)\left(\sum_{i=1}^{k}\binom{n}{i} - \sum_{i=1}^{\min(n_0,k)}\binom{n_0}{i}\right)\right) \tag{4}$$

3.3   MinReduct

MinReduct traverses the search space of attribute subsets using a depth-first search. When a new attribute is added to the current attribute subset candidate, it is verified for contribution as in Definition 2. This verification can be computed in a time $\Theta(m)$ by means of a binary cumulative mask. If the new attribute contributes, the current candidate is evaluated for the super-reduct condition, otherwise the new attribute is discarded and several subsets are pruned. Evaluating the super-reduct condition as in Definition 1 requires also a time $\Theta(m)$ by means of the same binary cumulative mask. This cumulative computation can be achieved because of the traversing order followed by this algorithm. The disadvantage of this traversing order is that some subsets with a length higher than that of the shortest reducts may be evaluated.

The main pruning property of MinReduct consists in avoiding the evaluation of candidates with length higher than the shortest reduct found so far. Since the length of the shortest reducts is unknown at the beginning of the algorithm, the asymptotic upper bound of the number of candidates evaluated by MinReduct (ss) can be expressed by Eq. 5.

$$ss = O\left(\sum_{i=1}^{k}\binom{n}{i} - \sum_{i=1}^{\min(n_0,k)}\binom{n_0}{i} + f(n)\right) \tag{5}$$

In Eq. 5, $f(n)$ represents the number of subsets with length higher than k that are evaluated before the first of the shortest reducts is found. There are many algorithms for estimating k in a time proportional to n [8]. However, estimating k a priori makes no significant improvement to MinReduct because the algorithm itself will find a good estimate in a relatively short runtime. Therefore, we can substitute Eq. 5 by Eq. 6, which is the same upper bound of evaluated candidates than PFRC-MiLIT.

$$ss = O\left(\sum_{i=1}^{k}\binom{n}{i} - \sum_{i=1}^{\min(n_0,k)}\binom{n_0}{i}\right) \tag{6}$$

In MinReduct, the time complexity for the evaluation of subsets that do not include the last column of the arranged basic matrix (c_{max}) is $\Theta(m)$. The worst case time complexity for those subsets including c_{max} is $\Theta(nm)$, because the exclusion evaluation may be required. The number of such subsets ($ss_{c_{max}}$) has an asymptotic upper bound as shown in Eq. 7.

$$ss_{c_{max}} = O\left(\frac{1}{n-1}\sum_{i=1}^{k}\binom{n}{i} - \frac{1}{n_0-1}\sum_{i=1}^{\min(n_0,k)}\binom{n_0}{i}\right)$$

$$ss_{c_{max}} = O\left(\frac{1}{n}\sum_{i=1}^{k}\binom{n}{i} - \frac{1}{n_0}\sum_{i=1}^{\min(n_0,k)}\binom{n_0}{i}\right) \tag{7}$$

Thus, we can compute the upper bound of the asymptotic time complexity (T_{MR}) for MinReduct by the following expression:

$$T_{MR} = O\left(m * ss + mn * ss_{c_{max}}\right) \tag{8}$$

$$T_{MR} = O\left(m\left[\sum_{i=1}^{k}\binom{n}{i} - \sum_{i=1}^{\min(n_0,k)}\binom{n_0}{i}\right] + mn\left[\frac{1}{n}\sum_{i=1}^{k}\binom{n}{i} - \frac{1}{n_0}\sum_{i=1}^{\min(n_0,k)}\binom{n_0}{i}\right]\right)$$

$$T_{MR} = O\left(m\left[2\sum_{i=1}^{k}\binom{n}{i} - \left(1 + \frac{n}{n_0}\right)\sum_{i=1}^{\min(n_0,k)}\binom{n_0}{i}\right]\right) \tag{9}$$

4 Experimental Comparison

In this section, an experimental comparison of MiLIT and MinReduct is presented. For this experiment, 500 randomly generated basic matrices with 2000 rows and 30 columns are used. These dimensions were selected as in [14], to keep the runtime for the algorithms within reasonable boundaries. These basic matrices have densities of 1's uniformly distributed in the range (0.20-0.80). In addition, the algorithms were tested over 13 decision systems taken from the UCI machine learning repository [1] and 15 high dimension synthetic basic matrices. All experiments were run on a PC with a Core i3-7100 Intel processor at 3.90 GHz, with 8 GB in RAM, running GNU/Linux. We thankfully acknowledge the authors of MiLIT [13] for sharing the source code of their Java implementations of the MiLIT algorithm.

Figure 1 shows the average runtime for MiLIT (NC and PFRC) and MinReduct as a function of the density of 1's over the 500 synthetic basic matrices. The 500 matrices were divided into 15 bins by discretizing the range of densities, for clarity purposes. As it can be seen in Fig. 1, MinReduct was the fastest in general.

Figure 2 shows the runtime of MiLIT (NC and PFRC) and MinReduct for 13 matrices with 1200 rows and density 0.33 with a number of columns ranging from 30 to 54. These matrices were included in order to explore the performance of the algorithms when the number of attributes increases. For these matrices MinReduct was also the fastest algorithm without any apparent relation to the number of attributes of the basic matrix.

Table 1 shows the runtime of MiLIT (NC and PFRC) and MinReduct (MR), in milliseconds, for 13 decision systems taken from the UCI machine learning

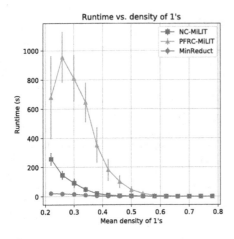

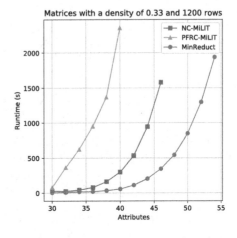

Fig. 1. Average runtime vs. density of 1's for MinReduct and MiLIT.

Fig. 2. Runtime for matrices with 1200 rows and density 0.33.

repository and two high dimension synthetic basic matrices. This is a more heterogeneous experiment in terms of density and dimensions than our two previous experiments. The first columns in Table 1 shows the name of the dataset, the number of attributes (Atts), the number of rows in the basic matrix (Rows), the density of the basic matrix (Dens), the number of shortest reducts (Nsol) and the length of the shortest reducts (Len). Decision systems in Table 1 are sorted in ascending order regarding the density of their basic matrix. Although MinReduct was the fastest in most cases, for the first three matrices, PFRC-MiLIT showed a significant runtime reduction regarding MinReduct and NC-MiLIT. This result corresponds to the benefits expected from the application of Proposition 3 for sparse matrices.

4.1 Discussion

As a result of these experiments carried out over 528 matrices, NC-MiLIT was the fastest algorithm in 11 matrices with no significant runtime reduction in any case. On the contrary, PFRC-MiLIT was the fastest algorithm in only three matrices, but it showed a significant runtime reduction in those matrices.

PFRC-MiLIT incorporates pruning strategies over the feature power set to make fewer evaluations than NC-MiLIT. Although using a breadth-first search for finding all the shortest reducts guarantees that no subset with length higher than k is evaluated, it is less efficient in terms of time and space, than the traditional depth-first search used in most algorithms for reduct computation. Thus, from our experiments we conclude that the evaluation of Proposition 3 for sparse matrices is the main contribution of PFRC-MiLIT. In [13] an upper threshold density of 0.3 was estimated for the application of PFRC-MiLIT. After our experiments, we recommend to reduce this value to 0.15.

Table 1. Runtime (in seconds) over synthetic and real-world data.

Name	Atts	Rows	Dens	Nsol	Len	MR	NC	PFRC
Keyword-activity	37	26	0.04	1	25	396	1111342	**6**
Soybean	35	28	0.11	29	11	283	23021	**8**
QSAR-biodeg	42	40	0.12	2	13	264	254220	**132**
Anneal	38	62	0.21	15	7	**18**	135	50
Dermatology	35	1103	0.34	137	6	**96**	125	695
Student-mat	32	6253	0.43	21	6	174	**159**	27387
Lung-cancer	57	237	0.47	112	4	**25**	56	81
Arrhythmia	279	52951	0.54	5	1	**5**	192	186
Optdigits (train)	64	29758	0.59	185	4	**278**	1989	12986
Landsat (test)	36	7980	0.74	6	14	**1.6E6**	>12.6E6	>12.6E6
1500 × 150	150	1500	0.75	228778	4	**2286**	21998	37855
250 × 600	600	250	0.84	170	2	269	**104**	127
SPECT Heart	22	2284	0.90	17	3	**<1**	2	1
Ozone	72	5751	0.93	239	2	**7**	87	141
Sonar	60	426	0.95	2612	4	**191**	1607	4843

5 Conclusions

In this paper we present a comparative study of MiLIT and MinReduct: two recent algorithms for computing all the shortest reducts (minimum length irreducible testors). Although MiLIT comes from the Testor Theory and MinReduct comes from the Rough Set Theory, both algorithms are intended to solve an equivalent algorithmic task. A description of the algorithms in terms of asymptotic complexity was presented. Finally, an experimental comparison over synthetic basic matrices and real-world decision systems taken from the UCI machine learning repository was carried out.

From our experiments, we have concluded that PFRC-MiLIT is the fastest algorithm for sparse basic matrices with densities under 0.15. The main advantage of PFRC-MiLIT relays on the evaluation of the zero row remanence on these sparse matrices. We have also found that the breadth-first search used in MiLIT is less efficient than the traditional depth-first search used in MinReduct, for candidate evaluation. Thus, MinReduct was faster than MiLIT for basic matrices with densities above 0.15 in most cases.

An interesting study for future work would be assessing the performance of verifying the zero row remanence using a depth-first search, for sparse basic matrices. A deeper study involving basic matrices with densities under 0.15 is needed for providing a stronger conclusion on sparse basic matrices.

References

1. Bache, K., Lichman, M.: UCI machine learning repository (2013)

2. Cheguis, I.A., Yablonskii, S.V.: About testors for electrical outlines. Uspieji Matematicheskij Nauk (In Russian) **4**(66), 182–184 (1955)
3. Chikalov, I., et al.: Three Approaches to Data Analysis. Springer, Heidelberg (2013). https://doi.org/10.1007/978-3-642-28667-4
4. Jiang, Yu., Yu, Y.: Minimal attribute reduction with rough set based on compactness discernibility information tree. Soft. Comput. **20**(6), 2233–2243 (2015). https://doi.org/10.1007/s00500-015-1638-0
5. Lazo-Cortés, M., Ruiz-Shulcloper, J., Alba-Cabrera, E.: An overview of the evolution of the concept of testor. Pattern Recogn. **34**(4), 753–762 (2001)
6. Lazo-Cortés, M., Martínez-Trinidad, J., Carrasco-Ochoa, J., Sánchez-Díaz, G.: On the relation between rough set reducts and typical testors. Inf. Sci. **294**, 152–163 (2015)
7. Lias-Rodríguez, A., Sánchez-Díaz, G.: An algorithm for computing typical testors based on elimination of gaps and reduction of columns. Int. J. Pattern Recognit Artif Intell. **27**(08), 1350022 (2013)
8. Lin, T.Y., Yin, P.: Heuristically fast finding of the shortest reducts. In: Tsumoto, S., Słowiński, R., Komorowski, J., Grzymała-Busse, J.W. (eds.) RSCTC 2004. LNCS (LNAI), vol. 3066, pp. 465–470. Springer, Heidelberg (2004). https://doi.org/10.1007/978-3-540-25929-9_55
9. Nguyen, S.H., Szczuka, M.: Feature selection in decision systems with constraints. In: Flores, V., et al. (eds.) IJCRS 2016. LNCS (LNAI), vol. 9920, pp. 537–547. Springer, Cham (2016). https://doi.org/10.1007/978-3-319-47160-0_49
10. Own, H.S., Yahyaoui, H.: Rough set based classification of real world Web services. Inf. Syst. Front. **17**(6), 1301–1311 (2014). https://doi.org/10.1007/s10796-014-9496-3
11. Pawlak, Z.: Rough sets. Int. J. Comput. Inform. Sci. **11**(5), 1–51 (1982)
12. Pawlak, Z.: Rough Sets: Theoretical Aspects of Reasoning About Data, vol. 9. Springer, Heidelberg (1991). https://doi.org/10.1007/978-94-011-3534-4
13. Piza-Dávila, I., Sánchez-Díaz, G., Lazo-Cortés, M.S., Villalón-Turrubiates, I.: An algorithm for computing minimum-length irreducible testors. IEEE Access **8**, 56312–56320 (2020)
14. Rodríguez-Diez, V., Martínez-Trinidad, J., Carrasco-Ochoa, J., Lazo-Cortés, M.: A new algorithm for reduct computation based on gap elimination and attribute contribution. Inf. Sci. **435**, 111–123 (2018)
15. Rodríguez-Diez, V., Martínez-Trinidad, J.F., Carrasco-Ochoa, J.A., Lazo-Cortés, M.S., Olvera-López, J.A.: MinReduct: a new algorithm for computing the shortest reducts. Pattern Recogn. Lett. **138**, 177–184 (2020)
16. Ruiz-Shulcloper, J.: Pattern recognition with mixed and incomplete data. Pattern Recognit Image Anal. **18**(4), 563–576 (2008)
17. Sanchez-Díaz, G., Lazo-Cortés, M.: CT-EXT: an algorithm for computing typical testor set. In: Rueda, L., Mery, D., Kittler, J. (eds.) CIARP 2007. LNCS, vol. 4756, pp. 506–514. Springer, Heidelberg (2007). https://doi.org/10.1007/978-3-540-76725-1_53
18. Skowron, A., Rauszer, C.: The discernibility matrices and functions in information systems. In: Słowiński, R. (ed.) Intelligent Decision Support, vol. 11, pp. 331–362. Springer, Heidelberg (1992). https://doi.org/10.1007/978-94-015-7975-9_21
19. Susmaga, R.: Computation of shortest reducts. Found. Comput. Decis. Sci. **23**(2), 119–137 (1998)
20. Torres, M.D., Torres, A., Cuellar, F., Torres, M.D.L.L., Ponce De León, E., Pinales, F.: Evolutionary computation in the identification of risk factors. Case of TRALI. Expert Syst. Appl. **41**(3), 831–840 (2014)

21. Yao, Y., Zhao, Y.: Discernibility matrix simplification for constructing attribute reducts. Inf. Sci. **179**(7), 867–882 (2009)
22. Zhou, J., Miao, D., Feng, Q., Sun, L.: Research on complete algorithms for minimal attribute reduction. In: Wen, P., Li, Y., Polkowski, L., Yao, Y., Tsumoto, S., Wang, G. (eds.) RSKT 2009. LNCS (LNAI), vol. 5589, pp. 152–159. Springer, Heidelberg (2009). https://doi.org/10.1007/978-3-642-02962-2_19

Extremal Topologies
for the Merrifield-Simmons Index
on Dynamic Trees

P. Bello$^{(\boxtimes)}$ ⓘ, M. Rodríguez, and G. De Ita ⓘ

Benemérita Universidad Autónoma de Puebla, Facultad de Ciencias de la
Computación, Av. San Claudio y 14 sur, Puebla 72000, Mexico
{pbello,deita}@cs.buap.mx

Abstract. In this article, we study the recognition of extremal topologies for the Merrifield-Simmons index in the space of tree graphs. We
analyze how to obtain the maximum and the minimum number of independent set on these topologies when a new vertex v is joined to a tree
T_n via a new edge $\{v_p, v\}$, with $v_p \in V(T_n)$ and $v \notin V(T_n)$.

We show that $i(T_n \cup \{\{v_p, v\}\})$ is minimum when v is a new leaf node,
and its father v_p was also a leaf node in T_n. In addition, the father v_h of
v_p has a maximal degree in T_n, and as a last criterion, v_p has a maximal eccentricity into the nodes in T_n with maximal degree. On the other
hand, we show that $i(T \cup \{\{v_p, v\}\})$ is maximum when v is linked to a
vertex v_p with maximal degree in T_n, and v_p has a greater number of
neighbors with minimal degree in T_n.

Keywords: Counting independent sets · Merrifield-Simmons index ·
Extremal topologies · Dynamic trees

1 Introduction

Merrifield and Simmons showed the correlation between the number of independent sets of G, denoted $i(G)$, and the boiling points of the molecular graph
represented by G [11]. This is one of the main reasons why the number of independent sets of a graph G, in the area of mathematical chemistry, is called the
Merrifield-Simmons index (M-S) of G. However, in the area of graph theory, $i(G)$
is called the Fibonacci number of G.

The Merrifield-Simmons index is a significant topological index of the structural chemistry of the molecular graph G [2,5]. A topological index is a map
from the set of chemical compounds represented by molecular graphs to the
set of real numbers. Many topological indices are closely correlated with some
physico-chemical characteristics of the underlying compounds. The Merrield-
Simmons index is one of the topological indices whose mathematical properties

In memory of Miguel Rodríguez.

© Springer Nature Switzerland AG 2021
E. Roman-Rangel et al. (Eds.): MCPR 2021, LNCS 12725, pp. 68–77, 2021.
https://doi.org/10.1007/978-3-030-77004-4_7

were studied in some detail in [7]. The M-S index and the Hosoya index are some of the most popular topological indices in chemistry.

The recognition of extremal topologies on graphs has been a significant study on the pattern structural recognition area [5]. Especially, in graph theory, several works deal with the characterization of extremal graphs with respect to Hosoya and Merrifield-Simmons indices for different topology graphs, such as trees, unicyclic graphs, and certain structures containing pentagonal and hexagonal cycles [1,2,4–6,9].

Given a tree T_n with n nodes, it is known that the topology with a minimum number of independent sets corresponds to the path $i(P_n) = F_{n+2}$. Meanwhile, the topology with the maximum value for the number of independent sets correspond to the start: $i(S_n) = 2^{n-1} + 1$ [3]. In [10], the largest number of maximal independent sets that any tree T_n of order n can have is determined. This work also shows a linear time algorithm for the computation of the number of maximal independent sets for any input tree.

Two of the works related to our analysis to determine extremal values for the M-S index on trees are the works of Li et al. [7] and Lv et al. [8]. In [7], the maximum value for $i(T(n, k))$, which corresponds to the tree of n vertices and diameter k, is determined. Meanwhile, in [8] Lv et al. shows how to determine the topology for the tree of n vertices with maximum degree k and which, at the same time, corresponds to the maximum value for the M-S index. In comparison to their methods of fixing the tree parameters, in our analysis we consider any input tree T_n of order n. As a matter of fact, the initial topology of T_n will change, since a new leaf node v will be inserted to T_n. Therefore, a dynamic topology for the input tree should be considered. In our analysis, we determine the topology that must have $(T_n \cup \{\{v_p, v\}\})$ with $v_p \in V(T_n), v \notin V(T_n)$ that corresponds with the extremal values (maximum and minimum) of the M-S index on any tree $(T_n \cup \{\{v_p, v\}\})$.

The basic strategy for determining the number of independent sets is based on the model counting of a monotone conjunctive normal form (CNF). A model counting algorithm converts the input CNF formula into a graph, and the counting of independent sets is applied on a graph.

In the following section, we introduce some needed notation for this paper. In section three, we show the analysis for obtaining extremal values for the Marrifield-Simmons index on dynamic trees. In section four, some instances illustrating the obtained results are shown. Last section presents the conclusions.

2   Preliminaries

Let $G = (V, E)$ be an undirected graph with a set of vertices V and a set of edges E. It is assumed that G is a simple graph, that is, it does not have loops nor parallel edges. Sometimes, we denote an edge $\{u, v\} \in E$ in abbreviated form as uv. The *neighborhood* of $x \in V$ is the set $N(x) = \{y \in V : xy \in E\}$, and its *closed neighborhood* is $N(x) \cup \{x\}$, which is denoted by $N[x]$. The degree of a vertex x in the graph G, denoted by $\delta_G(x)$, is $|N(x)|$. The degree of the graph G is $\Delta(G) = \max\{\delta_G(x) : x \in V\}$.

A path between two vertices v and w, denoted as P_{vw}, or simply as P_n, is a sequence of edges: $v_0v_1, v_1v_2, \ldots, v_{n-1}v_n$ such that $v = v_0$, $v_n = w$, and $v_kv_{k+1} \in E$, for $0 \le k < n$; the length of the path is n. A simple path is a path where $v_0, v_1, \ldots, v_{n-1}, v_n$ are all distinct. A simple cycle is a non-empty path, where the first and last vertices are identical. For $u, v \in V(G)$, $d(u, v)$ denotes the distance between u and v in G, which is the length of the shortest path between u and v.

An acyclic graph is a graph that does not contain cycles. The connected acyclic graphs are called *trees*, and a connected graph is a graph where for any pair of vertices there is a path connecting them. It is not difficult to infer that in a tree there is a unique path connecting any two pair of its vertices. We denote by P_n, T_n, S_n and K_n to the path, tree, the start graph and the complete graph, respectively, all of them containing n vertices.

We say that $G' = (V', E')$ is a subgraph of $G = (V, E)$ if $V' \subset V$ and $E' \subset E$. If $V' = V$, then G' is called a spanning subgraph of G. If G' contains all the edges of G that join two vertices in V', then G' is said to be induced by V'.

We denote $d(T)$ as the diameter of the tree T, which is defined as $d(T) = max\{d(u, v) : u, v \in V(T)\}$. Let $T(v)$ be a tree T with root vertex v. The vertices in a tree with degree equal to one are called leaves or pendant nodes, while the non roots nodes of degree greater than one are called internal nodes of the tree. In this work, we consider a graph $G = (V, E)$ by the set of edges forming E.

A subset $S \subseteq V$ is called independent, when every $u, v \in S$ implies that $uv \notin E$. $I(G)$ denotes the set of all independent sets of G. Let $v \in V(G)$, we denote as $I_v(G) = \{S \in I(G) : v \in S\}$ and $I_{-v}(G) = \{S \in I(G) : v \notin S\}$. The corresponding counting problem on independent sets, denoted by $i(G)$, consists of counting the number of independent sets of a graph G. Computing $i(G)$ is a $\sharp$P-complete problem for graphs G, where $\Delta(G) \ge 3$. The computation of $i(G)$ remains $\sharp$P-complete even if it is restricted to 3-regular graphs [12].

Some reduction rules have been useful to count combinatorial objects on graphs. Particularly, the following rules are commonly used:

1. Vertex reduction rule: let $v \in V(G)$,

$$i(G) = i(G - v) + i(G - (N[v]))$$

2. Edge division rule: let $e = \{x, y\} \in E(G)$,

$$i(G) = i(G - e) - i(G - (N[x] \cup N[y]))$$

3   Counting Independent Sets

The following Lemmas and the Corollary will be useful for our analysis. They show that given an initial graph $G = (V, E)$, if new edges are added to $E(G)$, then $i(G)$ decreases. Meanwhile, if new vertices are added to $V(G)$, then $i(G)$ increases, even if the new vertices are connected to all original $v \in V(G)$.

Lemma 1. *Let $G = (V, E)$ be an undirected graph, let $x, y \in V(G)$, and $e = \{x, y\} \notin E(G)$, then $i(G) > i(G \cup e)$.*

Proof. Let $S_e = \{S \in I(G) : x, y \in S\}$ be the independent sets in G containing the two vertices $x, y \in V$. $|S_e| > 0$ since at least the set $\{x, y\} \in S_e$ because $e \notin E(G)$. As, $i(G \cup e) = i(G) - |S_e|$ then $i(G) > i(G \cup e)$.

Lemma 2. *Let $G = (V, E)$ be an undirected graph, and let $x \notin V$. Let $G_1 = G \cup \{\{x, v\} : \forall v \in V\}$, then $i(G_1) = i(G) + 1$.*

Proof. $I(G_1) = I(G) \cup \{\{x\}\}$, since there are no more independent sets including x and any other vertex from V. Then, $i(G_1) = i(G) + 1$.

Corollary 1. *Let $G = (V, E)$ be an undirected graph, and let x, v be two vertices, such that $x \notin V$, $v \in V$. Let $G_1 = G \cup \{\{x, v\}\}$, then $i(G_1) > i(G)$.*

Proof. According to the previous lemma, $i(G_1) = i(G) + 1$ when there are no more edges between x and any other vertex $v \in V$. If any edge $\{v, x\}$ is omitted in $E(G_1)$, then G_1 is even greater than $i(G) + 1$. In any case, $i(G_1) > i(G)$.

In this section we study the recognition of extremal topologies for the Merriffeld-Simmons index on the space of tree structures.

3.1   Computing Independent Sets on Trees

Let $T = (V, E)$ be a rooted tree at a vertex $v_r \in V$. We traverse T in postorder.

Let $\mathcal{F}_i = \{T_i\}, i = 1, \ldots, n$ where $\mathcal{F}_i$ is a family of induced subgraphs, it is $T_i = (V_i, E_i), V_i \subset V, E_i \subset E$, and each V_i is built as $V_i = \{v_1, \ldots v_i\}$ of V. We associate to each vertex $v_i \in V$ a pair (α_i, β_i) with $\alpha_i = |I_{-v_i}(T_i)|$, which means that α_i is the number of subsets in $I(T_i)$ where v_i does not appear. Meanwhile, $\beta_i = |I_{v_i}(T_i)|$ conveys the number of subsets in $I(T_i)$, where v_i appears. Therefore, $i(T_i) = \alpha_i + \beta_i$.

The first pair (α_1, β_1) is $(1, 1)$ since the induced subgraph $T_1 = \{v_1\}, I(T_1) = \{\emptyset, \{v_1\}\}$ given that v_1 is a pendant vertex of T_n. The new pair $(\alpha_{i+1}, \beta_{i+1})$ is built from the previous one by a Fibonacci sequence, as it can be seen in Eq. (1).

$$(\alpha_{i+1}, \beta_{i+1}) = (\alpha_i + \beta_i, \alpha_i) \tag{1}$$

When a node $v_i \in V(T_n)$ has more than one child, then the Hadamard product among the $(\alpha_{i_j}, \beta_{i_j}), j = 1, \ldots, k$ is formed in order to obtain (α_i, β_i). The following algorithm shows how to compute $i(T)$ for a tree T.

The computation of $i(T)$ is done while T is traversing in post-order by the Algorithm 1. Algorithm 1 returns the number of independent sets of a rooted tree T in time of order $O(n + m)$, which is the necessary time for traversing T in post-order.

Algorithm 1. Linear_Tree(T)

Require: A tree T
Ensure: i(T)
   Traversing T in post-order, and when a node $v \in T$ is left, assign:
   if v is a leaf node in T **then**
      $(\alpha_v, \beta_v) = (1, 1)$
   else if v is the root node of T **then**
      return $\alpha_v + \beta_v$
   else if $u_1, u_2, ..., u_k$ are the child nodes of v, as we have already visited all child nodes,
   then each pair $(\alpha_{u_j}, \beta_{u_j})$ $j = 1, ..., k$ has been determined based on recurrence (1)
   then
      Let $\alpha_v = \prod_{j=1}^{k} \alpha_{v_j}$ and $\beta_v = \prod_{j=1}^{k} \beta_{v_j}$.
   end if

3.2   The Case for Adding a Pendant Vertex

Let $T_n \in \mathcal{T}(n)$ be a tree and let $v \notin V(T_n)$ be a new vertex. We consider the problem of finding where to connect v to T_n, preserving the structure of the tree, and with the aim of obtaining extremal values for the Merrifield-Simmons index on $i(T_n \cup \{\{v_p, v\}\})$, with $v_p \in V(T_n)$.

In this work is necessary to define the concept of *eccentricity* for a node of a tree. Let $v \in V(T_n)$, the eccentricity of v is $max_{w \in V(T_n)}\{|P_{vw}| : P_{vw}$ is the path joining w with $v\}$. The path P_{vw} is unique in topology trees.

We consider $v \notin V(T_n)$ as a new pendant node linked to T_n using the node $v_p \in V(T_n)$ as the father node of v, forming the new tree $T' = (T_n \cup \{\{v_p, v\}\})$. Let us denote $(T_n \cup \{\{v_p, v\}\})$ as $(T_n \cup_{v_p} v)$. We analyze the number of independent sets of $(T_n \cup_{v_p} v)$ by using the vertex reduction rule applied on the vertex v.

$$i(T_n \cup_{v_p} v) = i(T_n) + i(T_n - \{v, v_p\}). \tag{2}$$

From Eq. (2), we see that $i(T_n)$ is an invariant since its value is independent from the place of v_p in T_n. Then, the extremal values for Eq. (2) are based only on the term $i(T_n - \{v, v_p\})$ which becomes the first objective function to optimize.

Since the node v to be added to T_n will be a leaf of T', then the father v_p of v is its unique neighbor, this is $N(v) = \{v_p\}$. let us consider the computation of the minimum value for $i(T_n - \{v, v_p\})$. Notice that $i(T_n, \{v_p\}) = i(T_n - \{v, v_p\})$ since $v \notin V(T_n)$. In order to minimize $i(T_n, \{v_p\})$ we have that $(T_n, \{v_p\})$ would be kept as an unique connected component, and it is achieved when v_p is a leaf node of T_n.

Let $w \in V(T_n)$ the father node of v_p. We apply the vertex reduction rule on w for computing $i(T_n - \{v_p\}) = i(T_n - \{v, v_p\})$.

$$i(T_n - \{v_p\}) = i(T_n - \{w, v_p\}) + i(T_n - N[w]). \tag{3}$$

The function $i(T_n - N[w])$ will get a minimum value when $|N[w]|$ has a maximum value, therefore w must have a maximum degree in T_n, and w must

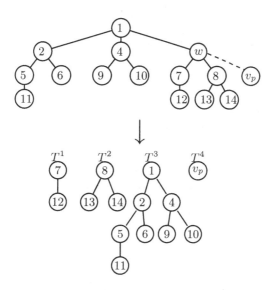

Fig. 1. Decomposing the tree considering w as the root node

have at least one pendant vertex as a child node. The optimization of the function $i(T_n - \{w, v_p\})$ expresses the original problem in a recursive form, and for this second calling, consider the case of deleting two nodes from the original tree T_n instead of only one node.

Let us consider that T_n is arranged with w as the root node, which is denoted as T^w. If $k = \delta(w)$ is the degree of w, then there are k subtrees $T^1, \ldots, T^k$ from T^w whose father is w. One of those subtrees is formed by the leaf node v_p. Let us assume $T^k = \{v_p\}$. An example of this decomposition is given in Fig. 1.

Hence, the function $i(T_n - \{w, v_p\})$ can be written as:

$$i(T_n - \{w, v_p\}) = (\prod_{j=1}^{k-1} i(T^j)). \tag{4}$$

The value $(\prod_{j=1}^{k-1} i(T^j))$ obtains a minimal value when the components $i(T^j)$ have a maximal number of asymmetric values, that is, when w has a maximal eccentricity with respect to other internal nodes with the same degree in T_n, and $(\prod_{j=1}^{k-1} i(T^j))$ will become minimal.

The order for holding the conditions for v_p is relevant in order to be part of the minimum of $i(T_n \cup_{v_p} v)$. The main criterion is that v_p must be a leaf node of T_n. Among the possible leave nodes, the father w of v_p must have a maximal degree in T_n. Finally, if both criteria are hold by different nodes, then v_p must have a maximal eccentricity with respect to other similar internal nodes of T_n. An example of a tree where the first two criteria are hold for minimazing $i(T_n \cup_{v_p} v)$ is illustrated in Fig. 2.

When a unique $w \in T_n$ holds the above conditions (v_p is a leaf node whose father w in T_n is the internal node with maximum degree in T_n, and v_p has a maximal eccentricity in T_n) with respect to any other internal node in T_n, then the node v_p where v was linked, in order to minimize $i(T_n \cup_{v_p} v)$, has been found in linear time. This is of $O(|T_n|)$.

Nonetheless, it could be that T_n has several nodes $W = \{w_1, \ldots, w_r\}$ that hold the above conditions. Thus, we enumerate $i(T_n - \{\{w_i, v_p\}\})$ on a leaf node v_p of each $w_i \in W$. As the counting of $i(T_n - \{\{w_i, v_p\}\})$ is done in $O(n)$ time, then the computation of $i(T_n - \{\{w_i, v_p\}\})$ on each $w_i \in W$ is done in $O(r \cdot n)$ time. Also, we can see that r is less than the total number of nodes in T_n; therefore $(r < n)$. Hence, the total complexity time to find the location v_p that minimizes $i(T_n \cup_{v_p} v)$ hold a complexity time of order $O(n^2)$.

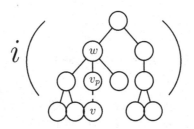

Fig. 2. Building the minimum M-S index on a tree

We analyze now the case for maximizing $i(T_n \cup_{v_p} v)$. Here, we apply once more time the vertex division rule on v. The Eq. (5) is the result of applying such rule.

$$i(T_n \cup_{v_p} v) = i(T_n) + i(T_n - \{v, v_p\}). \tag{5}$$

We can identify that the term $i(T_n)$ in Eq. (5) is an invariant, then it can be considered as a constant value. Therefore, the objective function to maximize is $i(T_n - \{v, v_p\})$.

Since the node v to be inserted to T_n will be a new leaf that is not part of T_n, then $i(T_n - \{v_p\}) = i(T_n - \{v, v_p\})$. In addition, the father v_p of v is unique: $N(v) = \{v_p\}$. Hence, $i(T_n - \{v_p\})$ has a maximum value when a maximum number of subtrees are generated when v_p is removed from T_n. This depends on the degree of disconnection resulting on $(T_n - \{v_p\})$. Thus, the main condition in order to maximize the number of subtrees in $(T_n - \{v_p\})$, is that v_p must have a maximal degree in T_n.

Now, let us suppose that w is an adjacent node to v_p in T_n. We compute $i(T_n - \{v_p\})$ using the vertex division rule on w, and we get:

$$i(T_n - \{v_p\}) = i(T_n - \{w, v_p\}) + i(T_n - N[w]). \tag{6}$$

Both terms in Eq. (6) are the multi-objective functions that have to be optimized. The function $i(T_n - N[w])$ will achieve a maximum value when $|N[w]|$ is the minimum possible. Therefore, w must have a minimal degree in T_n. For example, w must be a leaf node of T_n. As second condition for v_p is that it must be adjacent to a leaf node. Notice that it is possible to have different nodes in T_n holding both conditions.

The optimization of the function $i(T_n - \{w, v_p\})$ expresses the original problem in a recursive form, and in the second calling, there are two nodes to be deleted from the original tree T_n instead of only one node. Also, notice that the conditions for the maximum of $i(T_n \cup_{v_p} v)$ establish dual conditions for the minimum of $i(T_n \cup_{v_p} v)$.

With the aim of maximizing $i(T_n \cup_{v_p} v)$, the node v_p which is the father of v, must be an internal node with a maximal degree that has leaf nodes as adjacent nodes. An example of a tree where these criteria are hold for maximizing $i(T_n \cup_{v_p} v)$ is illustrated in Fig. 3.

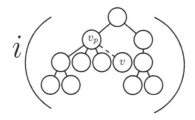

Fig. 3. Building the Maximum M-S Index on a Tree

We deal with the case where T_n has a set of nodes $W = \{v_1, \ldots, v_r\}$ holding similar conditions. Each $v_i \in W$ has a maximal degree in T_n and it is adjacent to leaf nodes of T_n. The other case is that T_n has only nodes holding to be maximal and without leaf nodes in T_n. In those cases, it is necessary to calculate $i(T_n \cup_{v_i} v)$ on each $v_i \in W$.

Since the computation of $i(T_n \cup_{v_i} v)$ is done in $O(n)$ time, then to get the minimum of those values, it requires a complexity time of order $O(r \cdot n)$. On the other hand, r is less than the number of nodes in T_n: $(r < n)$. Thus, the total complexity time to find the position v_p that maximizes $i(T_n \cup_{v_p} v)$ has a complexity time upper bounded by $O(n^2)$.

4   Examples

Some examples of the application of our proposals to determine the node v_p that optimizes the values of $i(T_n \cup \{\{v_p, v\}\})$ are presented in this subsection. Let us consider as first instance the tree T_n in Fig. 4. We search the node v_p such that $i(T_n \cup_{v_p} v)$ gets extremal values when the new leaf node v is linked to T_n through the node $v_p \in V(T_n)$.

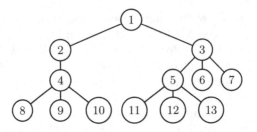

Fig. 4. Looking for $v_p \in V(T_n)$ where $i(T_n \cup \{\{v_p, v\}\})$ achieves extremal values

With the aim to minimize $i(T_n \cup_{v_p} v)$, the leaf nodes of T_n are examined. We look for the leaf node with a parent of maximum degree in T_n. The leaf nodes whose father are the nodes: v_3, v_4 and v_5 hold a previous condition. The eccentricity for the nodes v_4 and v_5 is maximal. Hence, we compute the values $i(T_n \cup \{\{v_9, v\}\})$ and $i(T_n \cup \{\{v_{11}, v\}\})$, choosing the minimum between both as the minimum for $i(T_n \cup_{v_p} v)$. In this case, $i(T_n \cup \{\{v_9, v\}\})$ achieves a minimum value of $i(T_n \cup_{v_p} v)$ for any position of $v_p \in V(T_n)$

On the other hand, we explore the position of v_p such that $(T_n \cup_{v_p} v)$ achieves an extremal maximum topology for the M-S index. We have that the nodes: v_3, v_4 and v_5 have a maximum degree in T_n. But the nodes v_4 and v_5 have a maximum number of leaf nodes (nodes of minimal degree), then $i(T_n \cup \{\{v_4, v\}\})$, and $i(T_n \cup \{\{v_5, v\}\})$ have to be computed in order to recognize which one achieves a maximum value. In this case, the maximum for $i(T_n \cup_{v_p} v)$ is achieved with $v_p = v_4$. Example 2: Let us regard the tree in Fig. 5. In this tree, the nodes: v_1, v_3, v_5 and v_9 have maximal degree in T_n, and all of them have at least one leaf child node. Thus, all of those nodes hold the first two criteria for inserting v and getting a minimum for $i(T_n \cup_{v_p} v)$. However, node v_9 has a greater eccentricity than the remaining nodes; therefore, the position of v_p that minimizes the function $i(T_n \cup \{\{v_p, v\}\})$ is with $v_p = v_{15}$ or $v_p = v_{16}$.

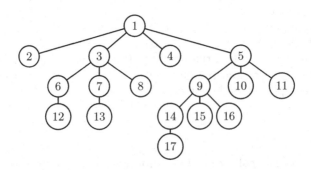

Fig. 5. Looking for $v_p \in V(T_n)$ where $i(T_n \cup \{\{v_p, v\}\})$ achieves extremal values

For the same tree, the position where $i(T_n \cup_{v_p} v)$ is maximized, is in the parent node of v_{15} and v_{16}. Thus, $v_p = v_9$. Therefore, $i(T_n \cup \{\{v_9, v\}\})$ maximizes the Merrifield-Simmons index when T_n is extended by a new leaf node v.

Notice that in this case, the value $i(T_n \cup \{\{v_p, v\}\})$ is similar for the positions $v_p = v_{14}$, $v_p = v_{15}$ and $v_p = v_{16}$.

5   Conclusions

The recognition of extremal topologies on trees is relevant in the optimization of topological invariants of chemical compounds modeled by arborescent molecular graphs [7,8,10]. We have considered here, the case of how to extend a given tree T_n through a new node v, keeping the structure of tree, and achieving extremal values for the M-S index for the new tree.

Given a tree T_n of order n, a node $v \notin V(T_n)$, and $v_p \in V(T_n)$, the M-S index of $(T \cup \{\{v_p, v\}\})$ will be minimum when v_p is a leaf node in T_n. In addition, the father v_h of v_p has a maximal degree in T_n, and as a last criterion, v_p has a maximal eccentricity into the nodes of T_n with maximal degree.

On the other hand, the M-S index of $(T \cup \{\{v_p, v\}\})$ achieves a maximum value when v is linked to a node v_p with maximal degree in T_n, and v_p has a greater number of neighbors with a minimal degree in T_n.

References

1. Pedersen, A.S., Vestergaard, P.D.: The number of independent sets in unicyclic graphs. Discret. Appl. Math. **152**(1–3), 246–256 (2005)
2. Deng, H.: The smallest Merrifield-Simmons index of $(n, n+1)$-graphs. Math. Comput. Model. **49**(s1–2), 320–326 (2009)
3. Prodinger, H., Tichy, R.F.: Fibonacci numbers of graphs. Fibonacci Q. **20**(1), 16–21 (1982)
4. Deng, H.: Catacondensed benzenoids and phenylenes with the extremal third-order Randić index. MATCH Commun. Math. Comput. Chem. **64**(2), 471–496 (2010)
5. Wagner, S., Gutman, I.: Maxima and minima of the Hosoya index and the Merrifield-Simmons index. Acta Appl. Math. **112**, 323–346 (2010). https://doi. org/10.1007/s10440-010-9575-5
6. Shiu, W.C.: Extremal Hosoya index and Merrifield-Simmons index of hexagonal spiders. Discret. Appl. Math. **156**(15), 2978–2985 (2008)
7. Li, X., Zhao, H., Gutman, I.: On the Merrifield-Simmons index of trees. MATCH Commun. Math. Comput. Chem. **54**, 389–402 (2005)
8. Lv, X., Yu, A.: The Merrifield-Simmons and Hosoya indices of trees with a given maximum degree. MATCH Commun. Math. Comput. Chem. **56**, 605–616 (2006)
9. Cao, Y., Zhang, F.: Extremal polygonal chains on k-matchings. MATCH Commun. Math. Comput. Chem. **60**, 217–235 (2008)
10. Herbert, S.W.: The number of maximal independent sets in a tree. Siam J. Alg. Disc. Meth. **7**(1), 125–130 (1986)
11. Merrifield, R.E., Simmons, H.E.: Topological Methods in Chemistry. Wiley, New York (1989)
12. Greenhill, C.: The complexity of counting colourings and independent sets in sparse graphs and hypergraphs. Comput. Complex. **9**(1), 52–72 (2000). https://doi.org/10.1007/PL00001601

Experimental Comparison of Oversampling Methods for Mixed Datasets

Fredy Rodríguez-Torres[(✉)] [iD], J. A. Carrasco-Ochoa[iD],
and José Fco. Martínez-Trinidad[iD]

Instituto Nacional de Astrofísica Óptica y Electrónica, 08544 San Andres Cholula,
Puebla, Mexico
{frodriguez,ariel,fmartine}@inaoep.mx

Abstract. In supervised classification, the class imbalance problem
causes a bias that results in poor classification for the minority class.
To face this problem, particularly in supervised classification with mixed
data, some oversampling methods for mixed data have been reported in
the literature. However, there is no experimental study comparing and
evaluating these methods in a common setting. Therefore, in this paper,
we present an experimental comparison of state-of-the-art oversampling
methods designed specifically for mixed datasets. Our study reports the
best oversampling methods for mixed data in terms of oversampling quality, taking into account the imbalance ratio, and runtime.

Keywords: Class imbalance · Oversampling methods · Mixed data

1 Introduction

The class imbalance problem occurs when, in a dataset, one of two classes has
fewer objects (minority class) compared with the other class (majority class).
This causes a classification bias towards the majority class resulting in poor classification performance for the minority class, which usually is the most important
class in a supervised classification task.

In the literature, we can find many oversampling methods for solving the
class imbalance problem [4–9,11,12,14–16,18,20,21,25,27] which were designed
to work with numerical data. However, in practice we can find class imbalance
problems where objects are described by numerical and non-numerical features
[13,17,22,24]. This kind of problems have been little studied in the literature,
therefore in this paper we will compare state-of-the-art oversampling methods
for mixed datasets, on different public standard mixed datasets under the same
framework.

The following sections of this work are organized as follows: In Sect. 2, the
oversampling methods for mixed data used in our experiments are described.
Section 3 details the experimental setup. In Sect. 4, we present our results of
the comparison performed. And finally, in Sect. 5, our conclusions and future
research directions are provided.

© Springer Nature Switzerland AG 2021
E. Roman-Rangel et al. (Eds.): MCPR 2021, LNCS 12725, pp. 78–88, 2021.
https://doi.org/10.1007/978-3-030-77004-4_8

2   Oversampling Methods for Mixed Data

In this section, we describe the oversampling methods for mixed datasets reported in the literature.

All of them are based on SMOTE [5,9], this is an oversampling method designed for datasets with only numerical features. The main idea of SMOTE is generating synthetic objects in a random way between objects of the minority class and their k-nearest neighbors. For generating a synthetic object, SMOTE computes the feature differences between an object of the minority class and one of its k-nearest neighbors, randomly selected. After this computation, each one of these feature differences is multiplied by a random number in [0.0-1.0], and these multiplied differences are added to each corresponding feature of the object of the minority class under consideration, obtaining the feature values for the new synthetic object.

SMOTE-NC [5]: This method was published jointly with SMOTE [5] as a version able to work with mixed datasets. One of the differences between SMOTE and SMOTE-NC is that SMOTE-NC uses a modified Euclidean distance for computing the k-nearest neighbors when not all features are numerical. Another difference is that, for non-numerical features, SMOTE-NC selects the most frequent value among the k-nearest neighbors of the object of the minority class under consideration as the value for the corresponding feature in the new synthetic object.

SMOTE-HVDM [2,9,21,23,27]: This method generates synthetic objects in the same way as SMOTE-NC, but instead of using the modified Euclidean distance proposed in SMOTE-NC, SMOTE-HVDM uses HVDM [28] for computing the distances between the objects of the minority class and finding the k-nearest neighbors.

LNE-SMOTE [19]: This method generates values for the numeric features by randomly generating values between the value of the object under consideration and one of its k-nearest neighbors (randomly selected), but it skews the generation of the value according to the safe-level value between the object under consideration and its selected neighbor as in Safe-Levels-SMOTE [14]. And, for non-numerical features, the value for the feature in the new synthetic object is selected as the most frequent value.

MNDO-NC [10]: In the first stage, this method computes the correlation between the minority class's numerical features identifying three types of correlations: low, medium, and high. Then, for generating synthetic objects for numerical features, MNDO-NC uses the mean value into the minority class as the value for the features with low correlation with other features. And, for features with medium correlation with others, it uses random values generated through a univariate distribution as the value for these features. Finally, for features with a high correlation with other features, MNDO-NC generates random values based on a multivariate distribution and it uses them as values for the corresponding features. In a second stage, MNDO-NC computes the k-nearest neighbors of the generated synthetic objects into the minority class (using only the numerical features of the first stage), and, for each non-numerical feature of each generated synthetic object, MNDO-NC uses the most frequent value among its k-nearest neighbors as the value for the non-numerical feature in the synthetic object.

SMOTER [26]: This method generates synthetic objects for numerical features in the same way as in SMOTE [5]. For non-numerical features, it randomly selects one of the two values among the object under consideration and one of its k-nearest neighbors (randomly selected).

SMOGN [3]: This method is based on SMOTER [26], but, if the distance between an object of the minority class and one of its k-nearest neighbors (randomly selected) is less than half of the median of the distances between the object under consideration and its k-nearest neighbors, then SMOGN works as SMOTER, otherwise, it adds Gaussian Noise on each numerical feature of the object under consideration and these feature values are used as the values for a new synthetic object.

As it can be seen, only a few oversampling methods have been designed for mixed datasets compared with the many others designed for numerical datasets. Furthermore, to the best of our knowledge, no experimental comparison between these methods has been reported; hence this is addressed in this paper.

3   Experimental Setup

For the evaluation of the oversampling methods for mixed data, we use all imbalanced mixed datasets from the KEEL repository [1] shown in Table 1. These mixed datasets have a 5-fold cross-validation partition available at the KEEL

Table 1. Mixed datasets used for our experiments

Dataset	# Features		# Objects	IR
	Numerical	Non-numerical		
abalone9-18	7	1	731	16.40
lymphography-normal-fibrosis	3	15	148	23.67
kddcup-guess_passwd_vs_satan	26	15	1642	29.98
abalone-3_vs_11	7	1	502	32.47
abalone-17_vs_7-8-9-10	7	1	2338	39.31
abalone-21_vs_8	7	1	581	40.50
kddcup-land_vs_portsweep	26	15	1061	49.52
abalone-19_vs_10-11-12-13	7	1	1622	49.69
abalone-20_vs_8-9-10	7	1	1916	72.69
kddcup-buffer_overflow_vs_back	26	15	2233	73.43
kddcup-land_vs_satan	26	15	1610	75.67
kddcup-rootkit-imap_vs_back	26	15	2225	100.14
abalone19	7	1	4174	129.44

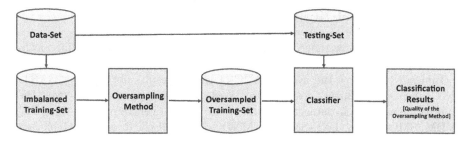

Fig. 1. Scheme used for evaluating the oversampling quality of an oversampling method.

repository. Table 1 shows, left to right, the dataset name, the number of features of each type (numerical and non-numerical), the number of objects, and the Imbalance Ratio (IR), respectively; datasets appear in ascending order according their IR.

In our experiments, the oversampling quality produced by an oversampling method will be assessed through a supervised classifier. For this, the classifier will be feed with the output of an oversampling method, that is, the oversampled training set, which jointly with a testing set will produce a classification result by using an evaluation measure for the experiments we used AUC (Area Under Curve). If we now provide the same testing set and the original training dataset (without oversampling) to the same classifier, we will get another classification result. Since the only thing that changed was the training set, then the difference in the classification results can be attributed to the oversampling method used. In this way, if under this scheme the training dataset is changed using each one of the oversampled training data produced by the different oversampling methods, this will allow us to compare the oversampling methods through the quality of classification obtained. A scheme of this process is shown in Fig. 1. Additionally, we measure the runtime (in seconds), that each oversampling method spent for oversampling the minority class on each mixed dataset. For our experiments, we used MATLAB R2020a in a computer with an AMD FX-8320 3.50 GHz processor with 16 GB DDR4 RAM, running 64-bit Windows 10.

Since all of the oversampling methods used in our experiments generate random numbers for building synthetic objects, they were applied 10 times, and the average classification result is reported. In this experiment, we used $k = 5$ for computing the k-nearest neighbors for all the oversampling methods, which is the value most commonly used in the literature. Later, we compare the results obtained when using $k = 3$ and $k = 7$.

For our experiments, we used the supervised classifiers CART, KNN ($K = 5$), and Naive Bayes, three of the classifiers most commonly used for evaluating oversampling methods. The classification results were assessed through AUC, the most common evaluation measure for class imbalance problems.

4   Experimental Results

In this section, we show the experimental comparison of the oversampling methods for mixed data of the state-of-the-art as described in Sect. 2.

Tables 2 to 4 show the average AUC of the 10 results obtained by CART, KNN, and Naive Bayes, respectively. Each classifier was applied over the minority class of each dataset of Table 1 (see rows) oversampled by SMOTE-HVDM, SMOTE-NC, LNE-SMOTE, MNDO-NC, SMOTER, and SMOGN (see columns). These tables are divided into two parts, the first part with the datasets with an $IR < 50$ and the second part with the datasets with an $IR > 50$. The highest average result of each classifier in each group of datasets is highlighted in bold.

Table 2. Average AUC results of CART for the datasets of Table 1.

Dataset	Method					
	SMOTE-HVDM	SMOTE-NC	LNE-SMOTE	MNDO-NC	SMOTER	SMOGN
abalone9-18	0.739	0.749	0.725	0.733	0.724	0.728
lymphography-normal-fibrosis	0.933	0.849	0.938	0.750	0.943	0.869
kddcup-guess_passwd_vs_satan	0.989	0.989	0.997	0.989	0.989	0.989
abalone-3_vs_11	1.000	1.000	1.000	1.000	1.000	0.993
abalone-17_vs_7-8-9-10	0.732	0.687	0.736	0.678	0.701	0.617
abalone-21_vs_8	0.843	0.830	0.796	0.853	0.827	0.775
kddcup-land_vs_portsweep	1.000	1.000	0.979	1.000	1.000	1.000
abalone-19_vs_10-11-12-13	0.564	0.544	0.556	0.534	0.557	0.535
Average AUC for datasets with $IR < 50$	**0.850**	0.831	0.841	0.817	0.843	0.813
abalone-20_vs_8-9-10	0.723	0.690	0.632	0.745	0.725	0.636
kddcup-buffer_overflow_vs_back	1.000	1.000	1.000	1.000	1.000	1.000
kddcup-land_vs_satan	1.000	1.000	0.999	1.000	1.000	1.000
kddcup-rootkit-imap_vs_back	1.000	1.000	0.973	1.000	1.000	1.000
abalone19	0.540	0.541	0.501	0.529	0.553	0.506
Average AUC for datasets with $IR > 50$	0.852	0.846	0.821	**0.855**	**0.855**	0.828

Table 2 shows that applying SMOTE-HVDM allows the CART classifier to obtain a higher average AUC than those obtained when other oversampling methods are applied on mixed datasets with $IR < 50$. However, for those datasets with $IR > 50$, when applying MNDO-NC and SMOTER the CART classifier obtains a sightly higher average AUC than when SMOTE-HVDM is applied.

Table 3. Average AUC results of KNN for the datasets of Table 1.

Dataset	Method					
	SMOTE-HVDM	SMOTE-NC	LNE-SMOTE	MNDO-NC	SMOTER	SMOGN
abalone9-18	0.797	0.797	0.744	0.587	0.799	0.586
lymphography-normal-fibrosis	0.712	0.789	0.734	0.796	0.711	0.740
kddcup-guess_passwd_vs_satan	1.000	0.999	0.988	1.000	1.000	0.930
abalone-3_vs_11	1.000	1.000	0.994	1.000	1.000	0.952
abalone-17_vs_7-8-9-10	0.819	0.794	0.794	0.556	0.811	0.536
abalone-21_vs_8	0.813	0.855	0.764	0.806	0.810	0.594
kddcup-land_vs_portsweep	0.979	0.979	0.996	0.972	0.979	0.935
abalone-19_vs_10-11-12-13	0.629	0.611	0.618	0.531	0.634	0.500
Average AUC for datasets with $IR < 50$	**0.844**	0.829	0.829	0.781	0.843	0.722
abalone-20_vs_8-9-10	0.778	0.830	0.772	0.583	0.789	0.502
kddcup-buffer_overflow_vs_back	0.983	0.983	0.983	0.960	0.983	0.908
kddcup-land_vs_satan	0.999	0.999	0.999	0.980	0.999	0.945
kddcup-rootkit-imap_vs_back	0.998	0.987	0.999	0.860	1.000	0.807
abalone19	0.689	0.725	0.587	0.500	0.706	0.500
Average AUC for datasets with $IR > 50$	0.890	0.868	0.868	0.776	**0.895**	0.732

On the other hand, in Table 3, we can see that when SMOTE-HVDM is applied, it allows the KNN classifier to obtain the highest average AUC on mixed datasets with $IR < 50$. While, when SMOTER is applied, it allows the KNN classifier to obtain the highest average AUC on those datasets with $IR > 50$.

Furthermore, Table 4 shows that for the Naive Bayes classifier, as in previous Tables, when SMOTE-HVDM is applied on datasets with $IR < 50$ it allows to get the highest average result. However, for this classifier, on datasets with $IR > 50$ applying MNDO-NC allows to obtain the highest average result.

From the three previous tables, we can observe that, among all the revised oversampling methods, SMOTE-HVDM, SMOTER, and MNDO-NC are the ones that got the best results in terms of the supervised classification results that can be obtained when they are used for balancing a training set. Particularly, SMOTE-HVDM and SMOTER show being the oversampling methods that allow the classifiers to obtain the best AUC in mixed datasets with $IR < 50$, while MNDO-NC and SMOTER allow to obtain the best AUC in mixed datasets with $IR > 50$.

Additionally, we show the results obtained by using values for $k = 3$ and $k = 7$ on each evaluated oversampling method. All methods were applied in the same conditions as in the previous experiments but changing only the value of k. In Table 5, we show the average AUC result for the datasets of Table 1,

Table 4. Average AUC results of Naive Bayes for the datasets of Table 1.

Dataset	Method					
	SMOTE-HVDM	SMOTE-NC	LNE-SMOTE	MNDO-NC	SMOTER	SMOGN
abalone9-18	0.719	0.728	0.681	0.718	0.717	0.538
lymphography-normal-fibrosis	0.910	0.747	0.839	0.650	0.870	0.903
kddcup-guess_passwd_vs_satan	0.973	0.982	0.939	0.983	0.972	0.993
abalone-3_vs_11	0.993	0.967	1.000	1.000	1.000	0.991
abalone-17_vs_7-8-9-10	0.697	0.681	0.678	0.673	0.696	0.560
abalone-21_vs_8	0.795	0.789	0.784	0.784	0.796	0.744
kddcup-land_vs_portsweep	0.969	0.969	0.980	0.969	0.969	0.989
abalone-19_vs_10-11-12-13	0.650	0.651	0.522	0.578	0.645	0.493
Average AUC for datasets with $IR < 50$	**0.838**	0.814	0.803	0.795	0.833	0.776
abalone-20_vs_8-9-10	0.701	0.698	0.687	0.734	0.701	0.551
kddcup-buffer_overflow_vs_back	0.983	0.983	0.966	0.983	0.983	0.983
kddcup-land_vs_satan	0.949	0.949	0.973	0.949	0.949	0.969
kddcup-rootkit-imap_vs_back	0.977	0.961	0.971	0.980	0.977	0.915
abalone19	0.675	0.687	0.650	0.723	0.675	0.500
Average AUC for datasets with $IR > 50$	0.857	0.856	0.849	**0.874**	0.857	0.782

according to the IR (< 50 or > 50), obtained by CART, KNN, and Naive Bayes classifiers when they are trained with the oversampled training sets produced by SMOTE-HVDM, SMOTE-NC, LNE-SMOTE, MNDO-NC, SMOTER, and SMOGN using $k = 3$ and $k = 7$.

Table 5 shows that the revised oversampling methods have a similar oversampling quality result for the different used k-values. Most of the average AUC results, obtained when $k = 5$, are close to the results obtained when $k = 3$, or $k = 7$. Moreover, the conclusions observed regarding the best methods for different levels of the IR are preserved when using different values for k showing SMOTE-HVDM, MNDO-NC, and SMOTER as the best options. Therefore, from the results shown in Tables 2, 3, 4, and 5 we can see that SMOTE-HVDM and SMOTER are the oversampling methods that allow the classifiers to obtain the best AUC in mixed datasets with $IR < 50$. In contrast, MNDO-NC and SMOTER get the best AUC in mixed datasets with $IR > 50$.

Finally, for comparing the runtime of the evaluated oversampling methods, we measured their runtime for oversampling each dataset of Table 1. Table 6 shows the runtime, in seconds, for fully balancing every mixed datasets of Table 1 with the oversampling methods SMOTE-HVDM, SMOTE-NC, LNE-SMOTE, MNDO-NC, SMOTER, and SMOGN (see columns). The last row shows the sum

Table 5. Average AUC results of CART, KNN, and Naive Bayes classifiers for the datasets of Table 1 when using $k = 3$ and $k = 7$; according the IR level (< 50 or > 50)

IR	Classifier	k value	Method					
			SMOTE-HVDM	SMOTE-NC	LNE-SMOTE	MNDO-NC	SMOTER	SMOGN
<50	CART	3	0.835	0.827	0.808	0.815	**0.836**	0.805
		7	0.847	0.832	0.806	0.816	**0.850**	0.809
	KNN	3	0.838	**0.842**	0.837	0.820	0.839	0.717
		7	**0.849**	0.837	0.827	0.830	0.848	0.715
	Naive Bayes	3	0.813	0.808	0.815	0.795	**0.822**	0.770
		7	0.829	0.801	0.812	0.795	**0.831**	0.776
>50	CART	3	0.843	0.837	0.831	**0.855**	0.845	0.829
		7	**0.859**	0.846	0.837	0.858	0.852	0.826
	KNN	3	0.885	**0.889**	0.875	**0.889**	0.886	0.721
		7	**0.898**	0.889	0.873	0.897	**0.898**	0.735
	Naive Bayes	3	0.857	0.858	0.848	**0.874**	0.857	0.782
		7	0.852	0.854	0.823	**0.874**	0.854	0.780

Table 6. Runtime in seconds spent by SMOTE-HVDM, SMOTE-NC, SMOTE-LNE, MNDO-NC, SMOTER and SMOGN for fully balancing the datasets of Table 1.

Dataset	Time of:					
	SMOTE-HVDM	SMOTE-NC	LNE-SMOTE	MNDO-NC	SMOTER	SMOGN
abalone9-18	0.3	0.3	25.9	0.7	0.1	0.1
lymphography-normal-fibrosis	5.4	10.2	3783.0	9.3	8.7	9.3
kddcup-guess_passwd_vs_satan	0.6	0.2	95.1	0.7	0.2	0.2
abalone-3_vs_11	0.2	0.1	55.7	0.4	0.1	0.1
abalone-17_vs_7-8-9-10	1.9	2.8	1025.0	2.8	2.5	3.0
abalone-21_vs_8	0.3	0.1	74.2	0.5	0.1	0.1
kddcup-land_vs_portsweep	7.7	17.5	5803.9	11.0	16.9	17.5
abalone-19_vs_10-11-12-13	1.0	0.7	564.3	1.5	0.9	1.1
abalone-20_vs_8-9-10	1.1	1.7	804.4	1.7	1.4	1.8
kddcup-buffer_overflow_vs_back	3.8	8.2	3272.1	4.1	9.2	9.6
kddcup-land_vs_satan	9.0	9.6	4191.8	10.1	9.4	9.9
kddcup-rootkit-imap_vs_back	3.7	4.7	1894.3	6.8	3.8	4.3
abalone19	7.6	17.9	6024.9	11.9	16.4	17.2
sum	**42.6**	74.0	27614.6	61.5	69.7	74.2

of the runtimes on every datasets for each oversampling method. The lower sum is highlighted in bold.

In Table 6, we can see that the runtime of SMOTE-HVDM is shorter than the runtimes of the other evaluated oversampling methods for mixed data. However, the runtimes of SMOTE-NC, MNDO-NC, SMOTER and SMOGN are also short and close to those of SMOTE-HVDM. Also, it can be noticed that LNE-SMOTE is the oversampling method that takes longer to oversample each dataset. This is due to the generation process of synthetic objects in LNE-SMOTE since this method takes into account the objects of the minority class together with the objects of the majority class for computing the k-nearest neighbors; unlike all other methods that only use the minority class objects.

5 Conclusions

This paper shows an experimental comparison among state-of-the-art oversampling methods specifically designed to work on mixed data. We assessed the oversampling methods in terms of the oversampling quality regarding the imbalance ratio (IR), and the runtime spent by each oversampling method.

From our experimental results, we can conclude that, SMOTE-HVDM, MNDO-NC, and SMOTER are the oversampling methods for mixed data that allow getting balanced datasets which, when fed to a classifier, improve its classification results compared with the results that can be obtained by using the other evaluated oversampling methods. We can conclude from our experiments that SMOTE-HVDM and SMOTER got the best results in mixed datasets with $IR < 50$. While MNDO-NC, and SMOTER got the best results in mixed datasets with $IR > 50$. On the other hand, the results show that all revised oversampling methods have good oversampling quality results independently of the value of k used for computing the k-nearest neighbors. In terms of runtime, SMOTE-HVDM, MNDO-NC, and SMOTER were the fastest oversampling methods, with similar runtimes, while LNE-SMOTE was the slowest method since it computes the k-nearest neighbors for the minority class in the whole dataset.

In future researches, we will make experimental comparisons of oversampling methods that work with mixed data over large imbalanced datasets.

Acknowledgments. The corresponding author thanks the National Council of Science and Technology of Mexico for partly support this work through a scholarship grant.

References

1. Alcalá-Fdez, J., et al.: Keel data-mining software tool: data set repository, integration of algorithms and experimental analysis framework. J. Multiple-Valued Logic Soft Comput. **17** (2011)
2. Borowska, K., Stepaniuk, J.: Imbalanced data classification: a novel re-sampling approach combining versatile improved SMOTE and rough sets. In: Saeed, K., Homenda, W. (eds.) CISIM 2016. LNCS, vol. 9842, pp. 31–42. Springer, Cham (2016). https://doi.org/10.1007/978-3-319-45378-1_4
3. Branco, P., Torgo, L., Ribeiro, R.P.: SMOGN: a pre-processing approach for imbalanced regression. In: First International Workshop on Learning with Imbalanced Domains: Theory and Applications, pp. 36–50. PMLR (2017)
4. Bunkhumpornpat, C., Sinapiromsaran, K., Lursinsap, C.: Safe-level-SMOTE: safe-level-synthetic minority over-Sampling TEchnique for handling the class imbalanced problem. In: Theeramunkong, T., Kijsirikul, B., Cercone, N., Ho, T.-B. (eds.) PAKDD 2009. LNCS (LNAI), vol. 5476, pp. 475–482. Springer, Heidelberg (2009). https://doi.org/10.1007/978-3-642-01307-2_43
5. Chawla, N.V., Bowyer, K.W., Hall, L.O., Kegelmeyer, W.P.: SMOTE: synthetic minority over-sampling technique. J. Artif. Intell. Res. **16**, 321–357 (2002)
6. Chen, B., Xia, S., Chen, Z., Wang, B., Wang, G.: RSMOTE: a self-adaptive robust smote for imbalanced problems with label noise. Inf. Sci. **553**, 397–428 (2020)

7. Dong, H., He, D., Wang, F.: SMOTE-XGBoost using tree Parzen estimator optimization for copper flotation method classification. Powder Technol. **375**, 174–181 (2020)
8. Douzas, G., Bacao, F.: Geometric SMOTE a geometrically enhanced drop-in replacement for smote. Inf. Sci. **501**, 118–135 (2019)
9. Fernández, A., Garcia, S., Herrera, F., Chawla, N.V.: SMOTE for learning from imbalanced data: progress and challenges, marking the 15-year anniversary. J. Artif. Intell. Res. **61**, 863–905 (2018)
10. Fujita, H., Selamat, A.: Multivariate normal distribution based over-sampling for numerical and categorical features. In: Advancing Technology Industrialization Through Intelligent Software Methodologies, Tools and Techniques: Proceedings of the 18th International Conference on New Trends in Intelligent Software Methodologies, Tools and Techniques (SoMeT_19), vol. 318, p. 107. IOS Press (2019)
11. Guan, H., Zhang, Y., Xian, M., Cheng, H., Tang, X.: SMOTE-WENN: solving class imbalance and small sample problems by oversampling and distance scaling. Appl. Intell. **51**, 1–16 (2020)
12. Guo, S., Chen, R., Li, H., Zhang, T., Liu, Y.: Identify severity bug report with distribution imbalance by CR-SMOTE and ELM. Int. J. Softw. Eng. Knowl. Eng. **29**(02), 139–175 (2019)
13. Hämäläinen, W., Nykänen, M.: Efficient discovery of statistically significant association rules. In: 2008 Eighth IEEE International Conference on Data Mining, pp. 203–212. IEEE (2008)
14. Han, H., Wang, W.-Y., Mao, B.-H.: Borderline-SMOTE: a new over-sampling method in imbalanced data sets learning. In: Huang, D.-S., Zhang, X.-P., Huang, G.-B. (eds.) ICIC 2005. LNCS, vol. 3644, pp. 878–887. Springer, Heidelberg (2005). https://doi.org/10.1007/11538059_91
15. Kovács, G.: An empirical comparison and evaluation of minority oversampling techniques on a large number of imbalanced datasets. Appl. Soft Comput. **83**, 105662 (2019)
16. Kovács, G.: Smote-variants: a python implementation of 85 minority oversampling techniques. Neurocomputing **366**, 352–354 (2019)
17. Kurgan, L.A., Cios, K.J., Tadeusiewicz, R., Ogiela, M., Goodenday, L.S.: Knowledge discovery approach to automated cardiac SPECT diagnosis. Artif. Intell. Med. **23**(2), 149–169 (2001)
18. Liang, X., Jiang, A., Li, T., Xue, Y., Wang, G.: LR-SMOTE-an improved unbalanced data set oversampling based on k-means and SVM. Knowl.-Based Syst. **196**, 105845 (2020)
19. Maciejewski, T., Stefanowski, J.: Local neighbourhood extension of smote for mining imbalanced data. In: 2011 IEEE Symposium on Computational Intelligence and Data Mining (CIDM), pp. 104–111. IEEE (2011)
20. Maldonado, S., López, J., Vairetti, C.: An alternative smote oversampling strategy for high-dimensional datasets. Appl. Soft Comput. **76**, 380–389 (2019)
21. Rodriguez-Torres, F., Carrasco-Ochoa, J.A., Martínez-Trinidad, J.F.: Deterministic oversampling methods based on smote. J. Intell. Fuzzy Syst. **36**(5), 4945–4955 (2019)
22. Rögnvaldsson, T., You, L., Garwicz, D.: State of the art prediction of HIV-1 protease cleavage sites. Bioinformatics **31**(8), 1204–1210 (2015)
23. Sáez, J.A., Luengo, J., Stefanowski, J., Herrera, F.: SMOTE-IPF: addressing the noisy and borderline examples problem in imbalanced classification by a resampling method with filtering. Inf. Sci. **291**, 184–203 (2015)

24. Sidana, S., Laclau, C., Amini, M.R.: Learning to recommend diverse items over implicit feedback on PANDOR. In: Proceedings of the 12th ACM Conference on Recommender Systems, pp. 427–431 (2018)
25. Sun, J., Li, H., Fujita, H., Fu, B., Ai, W.: Class-imbalanced dynamic financial distress prediction based on Adaboost-SVM ensemble combined with smote and time weighting. Inf. Fus. **54**, 128–144 (2020)
26. Torgo, L., Ribeiro, R.P., Pfahringer, B., Branco, P.: SMOTE for regression. In: Correia, L., Reis, L.P., Cascalho, J. (eds.) EPIA 2013. LNCS (LNAI), vol. 8154, pp. 378–389. Springer, Heidelberg (2013). https://doi.org/10.1007/978-3-642-40669-0_33
27. Torres, F.R., Carrasco-Ochoa, J.A., Martínez-Trinidad, J.F.: SMOTE-D a deterministic version of SMOTE. In: Martínez-Trinidad, J.F., Carrasco-Ochoa, J.A., Ayala-Ramírez, V., Olvera-López, J.A., Jiang, X. (eds.) MCPR 2016. LNCS, vol. 9703, pp. 177–188. Springer, Cham (2016). https://doi.org/10.1007/978-3-319-39393-3_18
28. Wilson, D.R., Martinez, T.R.: Improved heterogeneous distance functions. J. Artif. Intell. Res. **6**, 1–34 (1997)

Shortening the Candidate List for Similarity Searching Using Inverted Index

Karina Figueroa[1]([⊠])[iD], Antonio Camarena-Ibarrola[1][iD], and Nora Reyes[2][iD]

[1] Universidad Michoacana de San Nicolás de Hidalgo, Morelia, Michoacán, Mexico
{karina.figueroa,camarena}@umich.mx
[2] Departamento de Informática, Universidad Nacional de San Luis, San Luis,
Argentina
nreyes@unsl.edu.ar

Abstract. Similarity searching consists of retrieving elements from a database that are closest to a given query. One strategy selects some elements as references and uses them to organize the whole database. With these reference points, it is possible to obtain a candidate list that contains the answer to the query and the rest of the database can be discarded for a while. In this article, a new strategy for reducing the candidate list is proposed. According to the experiments presented, it is possible to reduce the size of the list by up to 35%.

1 Introduction

Proximity or similarity searching is a significant task on several important fields, such as pattern recognition, retrieval of multimedia information, computational biology, etc. In the problems associated with these fields, there are normally huge databases involved and a similarity measure that evaluates how similar the elements are between them. Usually, the similarity is modeled and defined by experts in each application with a distance function. The distance function is habitually expensive to compute in terms of I/O operations and time complexity. When a query is given, the goal is to answer it with the minimum number of distance evaluations [13].

In order to reduce the searching costs, an index is built during the preprocessing time. When a query is given (query time) the index is used to find the most promissory set of elements (i.e. the candidate list) avoiding sequential search through the whole database. Basically, there are two main similarity queries: *Range queries* and *K-Nearest Neighbor queries*.

A *Range query* $R(q,r)$ retrieves the objects enclosed in the "ball" centered on a given query object q with radius r; formally, $R(q,r) = \{u \in \mathbb{X}, d(u,q) \leq r\}$.

A *K-Nearest Neighbor* query $NN_K(q)$ retrieves the K elements of $\mathbb{U}$ that are closest to q, that is, $NN_K(q)$ is a set such that for all $x \in NN_K(q)$ and for all $y \in (\mathbb{U} \setminus NN_K(q))$, $d(q,x) \leq d(q,y)$, and $|NN_K(q)| = K$.

In this work, we present an improvement of [8] where a *candidate list* was obtained from a metric inverted index. Our proposal consists of considering a

© Springer Nature Switzerland AG 2021
E. Roman-Rangel et al. (Eds.): MCPR 2021, LNCS 12725, pp. 89–97, 2021.
https://doi.org/10.1007/978-3-030-77004-4_9

small set well selected from the inverted list. This work is organized as follows: In Sect. 2 the previous work is explained in detail. Our proposal is described in Sect. 3 and the experiments which support our improvement are shown in Sect. 4. Finally, some conclusions and future work are discussed in Sect. 5.

2   Previous Work

Similarity searching problem has been extensively studied. There are three main families of algorithms: Pivot-based algorithm [4,10] (it works in low dimensional spaces); Partition-based algorithm (it works in high dimension with a huge preprocessing time) [3,11]; and the Permutation-based algorithm [1,2,5].

The context of this work is related to three references mainly: the permutation-based algorithm [2], the inverted index file [1], and a recent inverted index [8].

2.1   Permutation-Based Algorithm

In [2] the *Permutation-Based Algorithm (PBA)* was introduced and the idea was extended in [5]. Essentially, the goal is to keep an index to depict how the database is seen according to the perspective of some chosen points called permutants or reference points. The purpose of this index is to avoid distance evaluations at solving similarity searching queries.

During the preprocessing time, a subset of the database is choosen $\mathbb{P} \subseteq \mathbb{U}$, $\mathbb{P} = \{p_1, \ldots, p_k\}$, this is the set of permutants, where $|\mathbb{P}| = k$. Each object in the database $u \in \mathbb{U}$ computes its distance to all the permutants, $\forall p \in \mathbb{P}, d(u, p)$; that is, $D_u = (d(p_1, u), \ldots, d(p_k, u))$, where $D_u^1 = d(p_1, u)$. Then, it sorts them in increasing order, where ties are broken in any consistent order. The *permutation* of u, Π_u is defined as the position of each $p \in \mathbb{P}$ after D_u was sorted, the authors used $\Pi_u^{-1}(p_i)$ to identify the position of element p_i in permutation Π_u.

In order to fix ideas, lets introduce an example, let be $k = 6$, and $\mathbb{P} = \{p_1, \ldots, p_6\}$. Then, for an element u, let $D_u = (4, 2, 2, 6, 1, 4)$ the distances between u and each $p \in \mathbb{P}$; that is, $d(p_1, u) = 4, d(p_2, u) = 2$ and so on. $\Pi_u = (5, 2, 3, 1, 6, 4)$, then $\Pi_u^{-1}(p_1) = 4, \Pi_u^{-1}(p_2) = 2$, and so on; that is, $\Pi_u^{-1} = (4, 2, 3, 6, 1, 5)$. All the permutations are the index; hence, the index can be kept with $n \times k$ integers.

The hypothesis is that two identical elements must have the same permutation, while two close or similar objects should have similar permutations. Therefore, when similar objects to a given query q are searched the key is to find similar permutations. There are several approaches to measure how similar two permutations are [12], but the authors in [2] recommend using the Spearman Footrule metric.

$$F(u, q)_k = F(\Pi_u, \Pi_q) = \sum_{i=1}^{k=|\mathbb{P}|} |\Pi_u^{-1}(p_i) - \Pi_q^{-1}(p_i)| \tag{1}$$

For example, let be $\Pi_q = (1, 3, 5, 2, 6, 4)$, according to Eq. 1 and using the Π_u previously computed considering $\mathbb{P} = \{p_1, \ldots, p_6\}$, $|\mathbb{P}| = k = 6$ then:

$$F(u, q)_k = |4 - 1| + |2 - 4| + |3 - 2| + |6 - 6| + |1 - 3| + |5 - 5| = 8 \quad (2)$$

In finding the most similar permutations, $O(n)$ Spearman Footrule distances have to be computed. However, $F(u, q)$ is not expensive to compute since it is linear in k. When Π_u is computed for all u, the list can be sorted in increasing order by the similarity given by the Spearman Footrule metric (Eq. 1). The authors showed that the most promissory elements to the query are very likely to be in the first positions of this order. Notice that this is where an additional index is important.

Metric Inverted File. In [1] the authors proposed using an inverted file to find the most similar permutations to the query's permutation. During the pre-processing time, as in the previous section, they compute the permutation for each element in the database. Then, they introduce a parameter $m_i \leq k$ and all the permutations are trimmed, taking only the first m_i elements.

In the inverted file, each permutant $p \in \mathbb{P}$ keeps a list of pairs (u, ψ), where u is an element, and ψ is the position of p in the permutation Π_u. Of course, $\psi \leq m_i$.

For example, let be $m_i = 4$ and consider our $\Pi_u = (5, 2, 3, 1, 6, 4)$. The list for permutant p_5 will have the pair $(u, 1)$, the list for permutant p_2 will have the pair $(u, 2)$, and so on. The index in this proposal is this inverted file, which needs to keep $2 \times n \times m_i$ integers. Let $\mathbb{I}_{p_j}$ the inverted index list for permutant p_j.

$$\mathbb{I}_{p_j} = \{(u, \psi) \mid \Pi_u^{-1}(p_j) = \psi \leq m_i\} \quad (3)$$

During the querying time, a new parameter m_s was introduced, where $m_s \leq m_i \leq k$. The authors, in [1], proposed to carry out the union of all the inverted index lists for the first m_s elements of Π_q^{-1}, so the m_s closest permutants will be considered.

$$\mathbb{C} = \bigcup_{i=1}^{m_s} \mathbb{I}_p, \quad p \in \Pi_q(i), \quad (4)$$

In our running example (i.e. $\Pi_q = (1, 3, 5, 2, 6, 4)$), let be $m_s = 3$. Hence, the lists of permutants p_1, p_3, and p_5 will be processed, it means, just the first 3 permutants will be considered. In order to compute the similarity between the permutations of u and q (see the example in Eq. 2), from the lists of p_1, p_3, p_5. In this case we are able to compute $|4 - 1|, |3 - 2|, |1 - 3|$, but when some value is missing, the authors proposed using $m_i + 1$. Basically, they compute $F'(u, q)$ for each element in the database, see Eq. 5.

$$F'(u, q) = \begin{cases} |\Pi_u^{-1}(p_i) - \Pi_q^{-1}(p_i)| & \text{if } \Pi_q^{-1}(p_i) \leq m_s \text{ and } \Pi_u^{-1}(p_i) \leq m_i \\ m_i + 1 & \text{otherwise.} \end{cases} \quad (5)$$

It can be noticed that for any permutant p_i, if $\Pi_q^{-1}(p_i) \leq m_s$ then p_i is at the first m_s permutants in the permutation of q (Π_q); and if $\Pi_u^{-1}(p_i) \leq m_i$ then there is a pair $(u, \psi = \Pi_u^{-1}(p_i))$ in the list of p_i in the inverted file.

The authors in [8] proposed using a short inverted list, using just the object without the position; that is, $u \in \mathbb{U}$ which $\Pi_u^{-1}(p_j) \leq m_i$. The new inverted list proposed was:

$$\mathbb{I}'_{p_j} = \{(u) \mid \Pi_u^{-1}(p_j) \leq m_i\} \tag{6}$$

They also keep the permutations trimmed; that is, the size of the permutation is m_i and the complete permutation for the query.

$$F^*(u, q)_{m_i} = F^*(\Pi_u, \Pi_q) = \sum_{i=1}^{m_i} |i - \Pi_q^{-1}(\Pi_u(i))| \tag{7}$$

However, in all these strategies the size of the candidate list is almost the same as that of the whole database. In [6], the authors used a prefix tree to keep similar permutations on the same disk page. In that paper, the authors searched the common prefix (there are not enough details about how it was computed). There are also other data structures for the permutation-based algorithm [9].

3   Proposal

Our proposal is to use the Inverted List as in Eq. (6), compute the similarity between Candidate List as Eq. (7), with a different value of m_s for each query, it will be called m_{s_r}. Each query is different and the number of closest permutants considered should depend on the query's radius. The new Candidate List $\mathbb{C}'$ will be

$$\mathbb{C}' = \bigcup_{i=1}^{m_{s_r}} \mathbb{I}_p, \quad p \in \Pi_q(i), \tag{8}$$

The new parameter would be a function of the search radius r, and α will be a percentage of r. That is, some permutations should start with the same permutant as the query. However, other nearby elements might begin with another permutant (perhaps the one in 2nd position of the query permutation). Let D_u^* the sorted D_u, where $D_{u_1}^*$ is the distance to the closest permutant. Formally, it will be as follows:

$$m_{s_r} = j, \text{ where } j = \max_{j=1}^{m_s} \text{ such that } D_{u_j}^* \leq D_{u_1}^* + \alpha r \tag{9}$$

4   Experimental Results

In order to evaluate the performance of our proposal, some experiments were run in synthetic and real-world datasets. The synthetic databases allow us to learn how dimension affects our method. While the real ones show their behavior in practical situations. The performance of our proposed technique is measured in terms of distance computations.

In the following table there is a summary of the acronyms used:

Acronym	Description
PP	Permutation-based technique [2]
Pi	Inverted index [1]
Pm	The new proposal
Ps	This is as Pi, using m_s instead m_i
α	Fraction of radius query

4.1   Synthetic Databases

This dataset is composed by vectors uniformly distributed in the unitary cube, with 100,000 vectors in $\mathbb{R}^d$ with $d \in \{32, 64\}$, using Euclidean distance to measure how far they are to each other.

First, the results in dimension 32 and 64 are shown in Fig. 1, in this case, $\alpha = 0$. In this plot the performances of PP, Pi, Ps and Pm are shown. The best performance is that of Pm. Notice that it is possible to get the nearest neighbor using less distances with a short candidate list, about 39% less, for $\alpha = 0$. Precision was 98%, 99.5% and 99.84% for $\alpha = (0, 0.05, 0.1)$ respectively, the results are shown in Fig. 2.

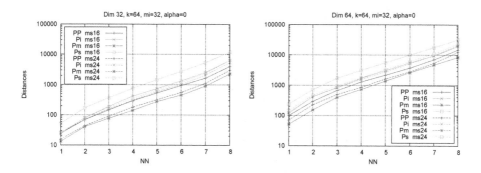

Fig. 1. Synthetic database, dimension 32 and 64.

In Fig. 2 at the left side, the vertical axis shows the size of candidate list, m_{s_r} was (1,2,3) in dimension 32 and (1,3,7) in dimension 64.

In Fig. 2 at the right side, the vertical axis is the size of each inverted list, the horizontal axis has no label because each size do not correspond to a specific permutant. These sizes were sorted in increasing order. The idea was just to show an ordered plot.

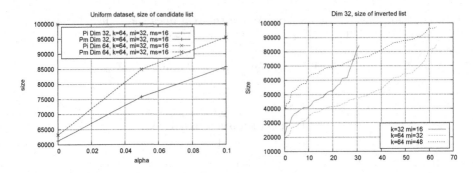

Fig. 2. Size of the candidate list in synthetic datasets.

4.2   NASA Images

This dataset consists of 20-dimensional vectors which were generated from images downloaded from NASA (available at http://www.dimacs.rutgers.edu/ Challenges/Sixth/software.html), where duplicate vectors were eliminated. We used the Euclidean distance to compare the feature vectors of this collection of images. The size of this dataset is 40,150 feature vectors, the size indexed was 39,650, the rest were used as queries (500).

Our proposal outperforms the others as can be seen in Fig. 3. The candidate list was reduced. It is important to mention that in these experiments, the precision was 100% and it was used just 1 permutant, that is $m_{s_r} = 1$.

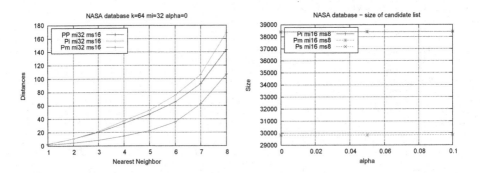

Fig. 3. NASA Dataset, left side the distances need to retrieve nearest neighbor. On the right side, the size of the candidate list is shown.

In Fig. 5 (right side) the size of the inverted list is shown for each one. Notice that in this case, in general, each list has almost half of elements.

4.3   Colors

The 2nd real-world database used consists of 112,682 color histogram in 112-dimensional feature vectors. This dataset is available from SISAP project's metric space benchmark set [7]. The size of this database is 112,850 vectors. The size of the query set is 500, each not being part of the indexed elements.

For this database, the performance is shown in Fig. 4. Notice that the best performance is for Pm (left side) and the candidate list was shorted (right side). In this case, with since $\alpha = 0$ the 100% of precision was obtained, m_{s_r} was (1, 3, 4) for $\alpha = (0, 0.05, 0.1)$ respectively.

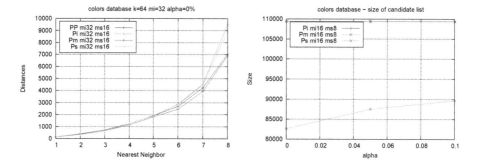

Fig. 4. Color dataset. Left side the distances needed to retrieve the nearest neighbor. On the right side, the size of the candidate list is shown. (Color figure online)

In Fig. 5 (left side), the size of each inverted list is shown. Observe that each inverted list is large.

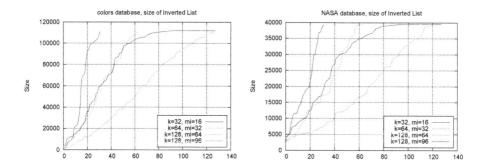

Fig. 5. Distribution of the permutants in real-world databases.

5 Discussion and Future Work

In this paper, a new strategy to reduce the size of the candidate list was introduced. We observed a high concentration of elements in almost every inverted list. When the union of several inverted lists is carried out, almost the whole database is considered.

The proposed strategy allows using one or just a few inverted lists, even if there were a uniform distribution between permutants. For example, if $n = 100,000$ and there were 64 permutants, each list would have almost 1,500 elements (considering that the lists are disjoint), but when using $m_i = 32$, we get at least $50,000$ elements in the candidate list.

An interesting experiment, for the final version, will be to use a strategy to select good permutants and compare them with the experimental results shown here.

The candidate list can be shorted if a similar rule for the 2nd or 3rd permutant could be considered as described in Eq. 9.

References

1. Amato, G., Savino, P.: Approximate similarity search in metric spaces using inverted files. In: Lempel, R., Perego, R., Silvestri, F. (eds.) 3rd International ICST Conference on Scalable Information Systems, INFOSCALE 2008, Vico Equense, Italy, 4–6 June 2008, p. 28. ICST/ACM (2008). https://doi.org/10.4108/ICST. INFOSCALE2008.3486
2. Chávez, E., Figueroa, K., Navarro, G.: Proximity searching in high dimensional spaces with a proximity preserving order. In: Gelbukh, A., de Albornoz, Á., Terashima-Marín, H. (eds.) MICAI 2005. LNCS (LNAI), vol. 3789, pp. 405–414. Springer, Heidelberg (2005). https://doi.org/10.1007/11579427_41
3. Chávez, E., Navarro, G.: A compact space decomposition for effective metric indexing. Pattern Recogn. Lett. **26**(9), 1363–1376 (2005)
4. Chávez, E., Navarro, G., Baeza-Yates, R., Marroquín, J.: Proximity searching in metric spaces. ACM Comput. Surv. **33**(3), 273–321 (2001)
5. Chávez, E., Figueroa, K., Navarro, G.: Effective proximity retrieval by ordering permutations. IEEE Trans. Pattern Anal. Mach. Intell. (TPAMI) **30**, 1647–1658 (2008). http://doi.ieeecomputersociety.org/10.1109/TPAMI.2007.70815
6. Esuli, A.: PP-Index: using permutation prefixes for efficient and scalable approximate similarity search. In: LSDR-IR Workshop (2019)
7. Figueroa, K., Navarro, G., Chávez, E.: Metric spaces library (2007). http://www. sisap.org/Metric_Space_Library.html
8. Figueroa, K., Reyes, N., Camarena-Ibarrola, A.: Candidate list obtained from metric inverted index for similarity searching. In: Martínez-Villaseñor, L., Herrera-Alcántara, O., Ponce, H., Castro-Espinoza, F.A. (eds.) MICAI 2020. LNCS (LNAI), vol. 12469, pp. 29–38. Springer, Cham (2020). https://doi.org/10.1007/978-3-030-60887-3_3
9. Mohamed, H., Marchand-Maillet, S.: Quantized ranking for permutation-based indexing. Inf. Syst. **52**, 163–175 (2015). https://doi.org/10.1016/j.is.2015.01.009
10. Patella, M., Ciaccia, P.: Approximate similarity search: a multi-faceted problem. J. Discrete Algorithms **7**(1), 36–48 (2009)
11. Samet, H.: Foundations of Multidimensional and Metric Data Structures. The Morgan Kaufman Series in Computer Graphics and Geometic Modeling, 1st edn. Morgan Kaufmann Publishers, University of Maryland at College Park (2006)

12. Skala, M.: Counting distance permutations. J. Discrete Algorithms **7**(1), 49–61 (2009). https://doi.org/10.1016/j.jda.2008.09.011
13. Zezula, P., Amato, G., Dohnal, V., Batko, M.: Similarity Search - The Metric Space Approach. Advances in Database Systems. Springer, Boston (2006). https://doi.org/10.1007/0-387-29151-2

Neural Networks and Deep Learning

Neuroevolution for Sentiment Analysis in Tweets Written in Mexican Spanish

José-Clemente Hernández-Hernández[(✉)], Efrén Mezura-Montes,
Guillermo-de-Jesús Hoyos-Rivera, and Omar Rodríguez-López

Artificial Intelligence Research Institute, University of Veracruz,
Sebastián Camacho 5, 91000 Xalapa-Enruíquez, Veracruz, Mexico
{emezura,ghoyos}@uv.mx

Abstract. In this article we propose a special kind of Neuroevolution, called NeuroEvolution of Augmenting Topologies (NEAT), which is based on a genetic algorithm, that is then used to generate an artificial neural network to analyze tweets written in Mexican Spanish, and then labeling them as positive, negative and neutral. Classification performance of neural networks generated through neuroevolution is compared to other Machine Learning approaches, such as Support Vector Machines, Naïve-Bayes, and a handcrafted neural network. This is made through a 10-fold cross validation. As it will be explained in this paper, statistical results suggest that the Neuroevolution neural network generated is simpler than the generated by hand, and gets a competitive performance with respect to the other compared methods.

Keywords: Neuroevolution · Sentiment analysis · Evolutionary computing · Neural networks

1 Introduction

Sentiment Analysis (SA), called Opinion Mining, is the field of study that analyzes the opinions that are related on a topic or an object in a web page or social network [6], such as Twitter, ending up in the text automatic labeling in different polarity sentiments. e.g., positive, negative or neutral.

It is common to see that an opinion includes many features such as the aspect of an entity to which the opinion refers and the time in which the opinion is expressed, all of them used to extract the main sentiment of such opinion. In this paper a symbolic technique is used to construct a vector representation of opinions to later labeling them with different polarity sentiments (see Sect. 3).

Several approaches in SA for sentiment classification include Machine Learning (ML) algorithms based on supervised learning [17]. Moreover, in recent years, Deep Learning (DL) techniques haven been used as well to tackle such problem, obtaining promising results [1,20]. On the other hand, few research works in SA report the usage of Evolutionary Computing (EC) and such scarce work is more evident regarding Neuroevolution (NE) [15]. Therefore, in this work we propose

© Springer Nature Switzerland AG 2021
E. Roman-Rangel et al. (Eds.): MCPR 2021, LNCS 12725, pp. 101–110, 2021.
https://doi.org/10.1007/978-3-030-77004-4_10

to adopt the so-called NeuroEvolution of Augmenting Topologies (NEAT) [16], for evolving a neural network so as to above mentioned task to label opinions.

This paper includes Support Vector Machines and also the Naïve-Bayes classifier, both of them traditional ML techniques, as source comparison against the NEAT evolved neural network. We also include a handcrafted neural network in the performance assessment to be able compare the complexity of the evolved neural network structure. In this particular work, the classification task will consider tweets in Mexican Spanish labeled with three different tags: *positive*, *negative* or *neutral* sentiments.

The rest of the paper is organized as follows: Sect. 2 presents the related research works on tweets classification. Section 3, describes the proposed vector representation and the neuroevolution-based approach to classify tweets written in Mexican Spanish. Section 4, details the experimental design, the obtained results and their corresponding discussion. Finally, Sect. 5 summarizes the conclusions and future work.

2 Related Works

Traditionally two main approaches have been reported in the literature for text classification in SA: (1) research works that use polarity lexicons and (2) ML algorithms to approximate classification [1] with an important use of DL and neural networks [19].

For the classification through the use of lexicons, the label of a text can be obtained from the polarity of the words inside the document [7]. However, this approach depends on the classification quality of the used dictionary. In [2] it is depicted the construction of SentiWordNet 3.0, which is an improved version of SentiWordNet 1.0 [3]. This dictionary has words whose polarity was calculated through sets of synonyms. On the other hand in [12] a lexicon for Spanish words was developed by labeling the words by a group of experts. Here, the words were divided into different sets of emotions. In [14], a dictionary of terms in Spanish was created, assigning to each of them a polarity value in the range $[-1, 1]$ in $\mathbb{R}$. The closer the value of a word is to -1, the more negative it will be, and the closer the value is to 1, the more positive the word will be.

With respect to the ML algorithms, it has been reported the implementation of Support Vector Machines (SVM), Naïve-Bayes (NB) and Maximum Entropy (ME) [8,9,11,13,17]. Thanks to the develop of DL, new proposals have also been proposed, many using Recurrent Neural Networks (RNN), CNN and Long Short-Term Memory (LSTM) [1,18–20]. Those SA dedicated approaches have also been applied to the sentiment analysis of tweets in different languages [4], tweets related to products and services [10] and for other types of data, such as movie reviews and questions [5].

Finally, the NE has been used for classification in other languages such as Polish, in this case with *feed-forward* neural networks, deep belief neural networks, NB and SVM, where the accuracy performance was compared with NeuroEvolution of Augmenting Topologies [15]. As far as the authors know, the use of NE for SA over tweets is particularly recent and research works are reported in other languages different to Spanish. Motivated by the above described, this research work introduces the NE to the analysis of tweets written in Mexican Spanish.

3 Proposed Approach

The tweets used in this work were collected and manually labelled in three different polarity sentiments, *positive, negative* and *neutral*. These tweets are part of the mexican political context and correspond to *trendin topics* occurred during the selected dates for the data collection, some of them were provided by the CEOA[1]. The tweets were preprocessed and later used to train the compared algorithms. Table 1 shows their corresponding distribution.

Table 1. Number of tweets per polarity.

Positive	Negative	Neutral
3160	4579	4754

With the aim of evaluate the performance of the algorithms by using the classes indicated in Table 1, the experiments are divided in two phases: the former considers only positive and negative sentences, while the latter uses the three categories. The details of both experiments are presented in Sect. 4.

3.1 Data Preprocessing

Stopwords, hashtags, mentions, punctuation marks, numbers and URLs, were removed in the preprocessing step, and the tweets were transformed into lower-case, and then tokenized. We also added manually labeled *emojis* and *emoticons* with positive, neutral and negative (1, 0 and −1, respectively). Furthermore, each word within the tweets that does not appear in the lexicon created in [14] was added its respective polarity value, calculated by Eq. (1):

$$P = \frac{TP - TN}{T} \tag{1}$$

where TP and TN are, respectively, the number of positive and negative tweets where the token appears, and T is the sum of TP and TN. Emojis, emoticons, and the new words were added, whit their respective polarity value, to the lexicon created in [14]. Later, once the lexicon was extended, all of its elements were separated, with their respective value, into 20 different sets that divide the interval $[-1, 1]$ equitably. Each of these subintervals, called *polarity levels*, is a coordinate of the vector that represents a tweet.

---

[1] Centro de Estudios de Opinión y Análisis de la Universidad Veracruzana.

						Polarity level															
	1	2	3	4	5	6	7	8	9	10	11	12	13	14	15	16	17	18	19	20	s
$t_1 =$	0	0	0	0	0	0	0	-0.3	-0.2	0	0.04	0	0.28	0.33	0	0.51	0	0	0	1	POS
$t_2 =$	-1	0	0	-0.7	0	-0.5	0	-0.3	-0.2	0	0	0	0	0	0	0	0	0	0	0	NEG

Fig. 1. Continuous vector representation of two tweets, it can be seen that one of the tweets has more negative sentiment than other.

Then, in order to create the vector of a certain message, the elements included in the extended lexicon were assigned, according to their polarity value, to one of the vector's polarity levels. The final value corresponding to each level will be the average of all the element polarity values assigned to it (see Fig. 1).

This representation aims at extending the lexicon used to one which contains the terms placed in the tweets used for training and, in addition, to capture the usage that is given to those words within the context where the tweets were extracted from. In this way, we can label the tweets using the associated vector: the more values are in the levels 1 to 10, the more negative the tweet will be, and, correspondingly, the more values are in levels 11 to 20, the more positive the tweet will be. Figure 2 shows a negative and positive tweet, respectively.

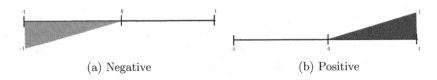

(a) Negative   (b) Positive

Fig. 2. Graphic representation of negative tweets (a) and positive tweets (b).

3.2   Parameter Settings for NEAT

NeuroEvolution of Augmenting Topologies (NEAT), is a genetic algorithm that searches for structures, activations functions and weights of an Artificial Neural Network (ANN) [16]. NEAT replaces the Stochastic Gradient Descent over the weights and the engineering design by hand of an ANN structure. In this case, NEAT is used to generate an ANN for classifying the pre-processed tweets.

NEAT introduces three important elements: (1) for the individual and genome representation, NEAT uses historical markings, that allows identifying shared historical connections in the crossover operator applied to individuals; (2) NEAT also uses speciation to separate the evolved ANNs, based on the so-called innovation, into different species; and finally (3) based on the fitness function used, the evolved ANNs can increase (if necessary) or decrease their complexity. The representation of a potential solution involves information about a node (neuron) and its type: (1) input, also called sensor, (2) hidden or (3) output node. Such representation also specifies the activation functions, connections,

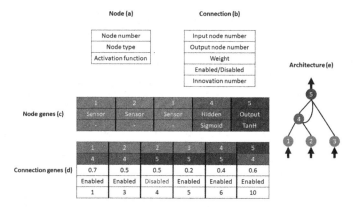

Fig. 3. Individual genotype representation; being (a) and (b) the models of node and connection, (c) and (d) the node and connection genes and (e) the network phenotype.

and their corresponding weight values, as well as the node state, enabled or disabled, and the innovation number. This is graphically shown in Fig. 3.

An ANN can be differentiated by its topology. Each connection within a network contains a number allowing to identify it, called innovation number. When an ANN is changed by the mutation operator with respect to its structure, e.g., when a node or a connection is added, a global number is incremented by 1, assigning it as the innovation number to such created connection between nodes.

The mutation operator can update the structure of the network and its weights, as well as the activation function of a node. On the other hand, the crossover operator involves the innovation number of each connection gene from any two selected individuals. If two given networks are to be reproduced, the innovation number allows identifying the similarity of both networks. The resulting offspring contains the connections where the innovation number matches between the two parent networks. The connections only appearing in one of the parent networks are called *disjoint*, and those beyond the range of the shorter network are called *excess*. Per example, if crossing the next two networks A & B: $A = [1, 2, 4, 5, 6]$ and $B = [1, 2, 3, 4, 6, 7, 8]$, we can detect that the *disjoint* connections are 5 (for parent network A) and 3 (for parent network B), and the *excess* ones are 7 and 8 (for parent network B). The resulting offspring contains the union of both initial connections as shown below:

$$O = [1, 2, 3, 4, 5, 6, 7, 8]$$

In the case of the speciation among ANNs, Eq. 2 shows the coefficients and elements to differentiate two networks:

$$\delta = \frac{c_1 E}{N} + \frac{c_2 D}{N} + c_3 * \bar{W} \tag{2}$$

where E and D are the number of exceeded and disjoint connections, respectively, W is the average weight of matching genes, c_1, c_2, c_3 reflect the importance of the three factors mentioned, respectively, and the factor N is the number of genes in the larger of both networks. A network from the species X will be part of the species Y when similarity, δ, against another network, taken randomly from the species Y, is less than the compatibility threshold, δ_t (user-defined parameter). The network from species X is evaluated against networks from the existing species. If only species X exists and the similarity with respect to any selected network to be compared is higher, a new species is created considering the network which is being evaluated as its first member.

Here we use NEAT with a population of 20 individuals, 100 generations, one elite individual and 30% of crossover rate. The networks are fully connected with only the sigmoid activation function for both experiments (see Sect. 4). There are 20 neurons in the input layer, 0 in the hidden layer, where the algorithm can add new neurons when necessary, and, depending on the number of categories, 2 or 3 in the output layer.

For both experiments the factors coefficients are $c_1 = 1$, $c_2 = 1$ and $c_3 = 0.5$ with $\delta_t = 3$, and the probability of adding a connection or a node is 20%. The mutation and replacement values, for the first experiment, are 20% and 10% respectively, while for the second experiment is 5% for both values.

4   Experiments and Results

The experiments were performed using Python 3.6 and a computer with AMD Ryzen 5 3500 with 4 cores to 2.10 GHz, 12 GB RAM and Windows 10 of 64 bits. For comparison purposes we used the following algorithms: (1) NB[2], (2) SVM[3], both with the default parameters of the Scikitlearn library, and (3) a handcrafted neural network with 20 neurons in the input layer, 19 nodes in the hidden layer and 2 or 3 in the output one, depending the number of categories considered (called ANN-FF). The neural network obtained by NEAT is called from now on as ANN-NEAT, and NEAT was executed using its Python library[4].

A 10-fold cross-validation was performed to compare the results obtained by the SVM, NB, ANN-FF and ANN-NEAT algorithms. The first experiment, called P, consisted of classifying tweets as positive or negative (two classes), while the second, called S, added the neutral category. To validate the results, the 95%-confidence non-parametric *Wilcoxon rank-sum* test was applied to the samples of results.

Table 2 shows the results obtained in experiment P (two classes). As it can be seen, ANN-NEAT obtains statistically similar results to the compared methods, even against the manually-generated neural network ANN-FF.

Table 3, on the order hand, shows the results of the second experiment (S). In this case ANN-NEAT outperforms NB, while the comparison against SVM

---

[2] https://scikit-learn.org/stable/modules/naive_bayes.html#gaussian-naive-bayes.

[3] https://scikit-learn.org/stable/modules/svm.html#svm-mathematical-formulation.

[4] https://neat-python.readthedocs.io/en/latest/neat_overview.html.

Table 2. First experiment (P) accuracy results per classifier; "≈" means that the statistical test doesn't find significative differences between the method in the corresponding column and ANN-NEAT.

Split	NB	SVM	ANN-FF	ANN-NEAT
1	0.9625	0.9587	0.9625	**0.9677**
2	0.9522	0.9612	0.9612	**0.9651**
3	0.9638	0.9638	0.9651	**0.9690**
4	0.9561	**0.9599**	**0.9599**	0.9561
5	0.9599	**0.9677**	0.9638	**0.9677**
6	0.9651	**0.9703**	0.9677	0.9638
7	0.9664	0.9638	0.9664	**0.9677**
8	**0.9638**	0.9612	0.9612	0.9574
9	0.9587	0.9548	**0.9612**	**0.9612**
10	0.9612	0.9599	0.9625	**0.9638**
Avg.	0.9610	0.9621	0.9632	**0.9639**
Std. Dev.	0.0044	0.0045	0.0025	0.0045
Stat. test	≈	≈	≈	–

and ANN-FF indicated that no significant differences were found with respect to ANN-NEAT.

Table 3. Second experiment (S) accuracy results per classifier; where "≈" means that the statistical test doesn't find significative differences between the method in the corresponding column and ANN-NEAT. On the other hand, "−" indicates that ANN-NEAT statistically overcomes the method in the corresponding column.

Split	NB	SVM	ANN-FF	ANN-NEAT
1	0.7994	0.8288	0.8312	**0.8352**
2	0.8032	0.8176	0.8256	**0.8296**
3	0.7998	0.8295	0.8311	**0.8399**
4	0.8191	**0.8399**	0.8383	0.8383
5	0.8006	**0.8295**	0.8279	0.8263
6	0.8070	0.8199	0.8207	**0.8247**
7	0.8118	0.8335	**0.8385**	0.8295
8	0.7934	0.8167	0.8215	**0.8223**
9	0.8143	0.8287	**0.8367**	0.8343
10	0.8311	0.8423	**0.8487**	0.8471
Avg.	0.8075	0.8286	0.8315	**0.8327**
Std. Dev.	0.0118	0.0087	0.0084	0.0077
Stat. test	–	≈	≈	–

Even though the differences in the obtained results by ANN-NEAT with respect to the compared methods were not statistically significant in most cases, Fig. 4 includes the classification rates obtained in a boxplot graph. It is interesting to note that in both, first experiment (P) and more clearly in the second experiment (S), the ANN-NEAT performance tends to be better. In fact, in the experiment (S) ANN-NEAT provided the best and more consistent results.

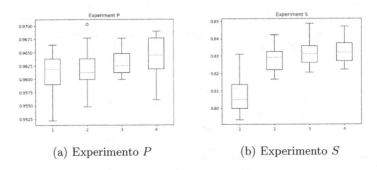

(a) Experimento P (b) Experimento S

Fig. 4. Boxplot diagram per classifier. 1) NB, 2) SVM, 3) ANN-FF, 4) ANN-NEAT.

Furthermore, the structures of the neural networks obtained by NEAT were analyzed with respect to the handcrafted neural network. The results show a significant decrease in the neurons of the hidden layer (maximum 3 and 4 in the hidden layer for the P and S experiment, respectively, with respect to 19 neurons). Therefore, the number of connections was significantly reduced (see Table 4). It was interesting to observe that in a *split* of the P experiment (the 6th to be precise), ANN-NEAT removed a neuron from the input layer, so it can be considered as an attribute selection process added to neuroevolution, similar to the process carried out by FeatureSelection-NEAT (FS-NEAT). It should be noted that the initial neural network in NEAT had 40 and 60 connections, respectively, which indicates NEAT's ability to reduce the complexity of the model by optimizing the classification rate.

Table 4. Number of neurons in the input and hidden layer, and connections in the neural networks generated by NEAT.

Split	Experiment P			Experiment S		
	Input	Hidden	Connections	Input	Hidden	Connections
1	20	0	37	20	0	56
2	20	0	37	20	0	54
3	20	2	38	20	0	56
4	20	1	39	20	0	56
5	20	0	35	20	4	64
6	19	0	32	20	1	57
7	20	3	42	20	0	55
8	20	0	37	20	0	54
9	20	2	41	20	0	55
10	20	1	40	20	0	59

5   Conclusions and Future Work

In this work neuroevolution was applied to the analysis of feelings in tweets written in Mexican Spanish. Two experiments were performed, one with two classes (positive and negative tweets) and another with three classes (the neutral class was added) using the neural network generated by NEAT against a manually-generated neural network and also against two classifiers (NB and SVM). The results, validated by the 95%-confidence Wilcoxon rank-sum test, indicated that the neural network generated by NEAT obtained similar results to those of the compared methods, being even better than NB in the case of three classes, and that their design (number of neurons in the hidden layer and in one case in the input layer) was significantly simplified with respect to the handcrafted neural network.

It is important to mention that, given the computational cost of neuroevolution, the search capacity of NEAT was limited by using only the activation function *Sigmoid* and default connections. However, even with those limitations, NEAT managed to find a simplified model that obtained even better results than other methods, including the manually generated neural network, which is more complex. It is true that the process of generating the model is computationally intensive, but the resulting model performs very efficiently.

Part of the future work is to revisit the representation of the tweets and look for other options that lead to a better ranking. Finally, other Neuroevolution techniques such as HyperNEAT, for Deep Learning, will be tested.

Acknowledgments. The authors are grateful for the support of the Centro de Estudios de Opinión y Análisis of the Universidad Veracruzana in the process of collecting tweets. The first author and the fourth author are grateful for the support of the National Council of Science and Technology (CONACyT), through a scholarship to carry out graduate studies at Universidad Veracruzana.

References

1. Ain, Q.T., et al.: Sentiment analysis using deep learning techniques: a review. Int. J. Adv. Comput. Sci. Appl. **8**(6), 424–433 (2017). https://doi.org/10.14569/IJACSA.2017.080657
2. Baccianella, S., Esuli, A., Sebastiani, F.: SENTIWORDNET 3.0: an enhanced lexical resource for sentiment analysis and opinion mining. In: Proceedings of the 7th International Conference on Language Resources and Evaluation, LREC 2010, pp. 2200–2204 (2010)
3. Esuli, A., Sebastiani, F., Moruzzi, V.G.: SENTIWORDNET: a publicly available lexical resource for opinion mining. In: Language, pp. 417–422 (2006)
4. González, J.A., Hurtado, L.F., Pla, F.: ELiRF-UPV at TASS 2018: sentiment analysis in twitter based on deep learning. In: CEUR Workshop Proceedings, pp. 37–44 (2018)
5. Kim, Y.: Convolutional neural networks for sentence classification. In: Proceedings of the 2014 Conference on Empirical Methods in Natural Language Processing, EMNLP 2014, pp. 1746–1751 (2014). https://doi.org/10.3115/v1/d14-1181

6. Liu, B.: Sentiment analysis and opinion mining (2012). https://doi.org/10.2200/S00416ED1V01Y201204HLT016
7. Mozetič, I., Grčar, M., Smailović, J.: Multilingual twitter sentiment classification: the role of human annotators. PLoS ONE **11**(5), e0155036 (2016). https://doi.org/10.1371/journal.pone.0155036
8. Neethu, M.S., Rajasree, R.: Sentiment analysis in twitter using machine learning techniques. In: 2013 4th International Conference on Computing, Communications and Networking Technologies, ICCCNT 2013, pp. 1–5 (2013). https://doi.org/10.1109/ICCCNT.2013.6726818
9. Pang, B., Lee, L., Vaithyanathan, S.: Thumbs up? Sentiment classification using machine learning techniques. In: Proceedings of the Conference on Empirical Methods in Natural Language Processing (EMNLP), pp. 79–86, July 2002. https://doi.org/10.3115/1118693.1118704
10. Paredes-Valverde, M.A., Colomo-Palacios, R., Salas-Zárate, M.D.P., Valencia-García, R.: Sentiment analysis in Spanish for improvement of products and services: a deep learning approach. Sci. Program. **2017** (2017). https://doi.org/10.1155/2017/1329281
11. Pla, F., Hurtado, L.F.: ELiRF-UPV en TASS 2013: Análisis de sentimientos en twitter. In: CEUR Workshop Proceedings (2013)
12. Rangel, I.D., Sidorov, G., Guerra, S.S.: Creación y evaluación de un diccionario marcado con emociones y ponderado para el español. Onomazein **29**(1), 31–46 (2014). https://doi.org/10.7764/onomazein.29.5
13. Read, J.: Using emoticons to reduce dependency in machine learning techniques for sentiment classification. In: Proceedings of the Conference on 43rd Annual Meeting of the Association for Computational Linguistics, ACL 2005, pp. 43–48, June 2005. https://doi.org/10.3115/1628960.1628969
14. Rodríguez López, O., de Jesús Hoyos Rivera, G.: A simple but powerful word polarity classification model. In: Martínez-Villaseñor, L., Batyrshin, I., Marín-Hernández, A. (eds.) MICAI 2019. LNCS (LNAI), vol. 11835, pp. 51–62. Springer, Cham (2019). https://doi.org/10.1007/978-3-030-33749-0_5
15. Sobkowicz, A.: Automatic sentiment analysis in Polish language. In: Ryżko, D., Gawrysiak, P., Kryszkiewicz, M., Rybiński, H. (eds.) Machine Intelligence and Big Data in Industry. SBD, vol. 19, pp. 3–10. Springer, Cham (2016). https://doi.org/10.1007/978-3-319-30315-4_1
16. Stanley, K.O., Miikkulainen, R.: Evolving neural networks through augmenting topologies evolutionary computation. Evol. Comput. **10**(2), 99–127 (2002). https://doi.org/10.1162/106365602320169811
17. Sun, S., Luo, C., Chen, J.: A review of natural language processing techniques for opinion mining systems. Inf. Fusion **36**, 10–25 (2017). https://doi.org/10.1016/j.inffus.2016.10.004
18. Young, T., Hazarika, D., Poria, S., Cambria, E.: Recent trends in deep learning based natural language processing. IEEE Comput. Intell. Mag. **13**(3), 55–75 (2018). https://doi.org/10.1109/MCI.2018.2840738
19. Yue, L., Chen, W., Li, X., Zuo, W., Yin, M.: A survey of sentiment analysis in social media. Knowl. Inf. Syst. **60**(2), 617–663 (2018). https://doi.org/10.1007/s10115-018-1236-4
20. Zhang, L., Wang, S., Liu, B.: Deep learning for sentiment analysis: a survey. Wiley Interdisc. Rev. Data Min. Knowl. Disc. **8**(4), 1–25 (2018). https://doi.org/10.1002/widm.1253

Neovascularization Detection on Optic Disc Region Using Deep Learning

Cesar Carrillo-Gomez[1] ⓘ, Mariko Nakano[1](✉) ⓘ, Ana Gonzalez-H.Leon[2] ⓘ,
Juan Carlos Romo-Aguas[2] ⓘ, Hugo Quiroz-Mercado[2] ⓘ,
and Osvaldo Lopez-Garcia[1] ⓘ

[1] Instituto Politecnico Nacional, Coyoacan, Mexico City, Mexico
mnakano@ipn.mx
[2] Hospital Dr. Luis Sánchez-Bulnes, Asociación Para Evitar La Ceguera, Mexico City, Mexico

Abstract. Diabetic Retinopathy (DR) is one of the biggest eye diseases affecting the worldwide population. The DR presents several damages in the retina depending on its grade of advance, although the damages are asymptomatic in almost all cases. The presence of neovascularization (NV) is considered as the worse stage in the DR, and the patients of this stage require urgent treatment to avoid partial or total blindness. Timely detection of the new vessels in the retina can lead to an adequate treatment to avoid vision loss. In this work, we present automatic detection of neovascularization in the optic disc region (NVD) using a deep learning algorithm. We evaluate several deep neural networks (DNNs) to classify between health optic disc region and NVD. The better DNNs are DenseNet-161 and Efficientnet-B7, which show 93.3% and 92.0% accuracy and 89.5% and 84.2% in sensitivity, respectively. In the computational complexity, DenseNet-161 has a lower number of trainable parameters than that of Efficientnet-B7. To train the DNNs appropriately, we construct a labeled dataset from one of the largest public datasets, bounding NV regions in the retinal images.

Keywords: Diabetic Retinopathy · Neovascularization · Deep learning · Deep neural networks · Automatic diagnostic

1 Introduction

Diabetic Retinopathy (DR) is a complication derived from diabetes, due to high blood sugar levels the retina is damaged, and it can cause blindness if proper treatment is not applied. In Mexico, this disease is one of the most frequent causes of blindness due to the high number of patients with diabetes. According to the "Asociación Mexicana de Retina", it is estimated that around two and a half million patients in Mexico suffer from some level of DR, and out of these around 300,000 suffer from the most advanced stage of DR, which tends to cause total blindness [1]. According to the International Council of Ophthalmology, DR can be divided into 5 stages [2], as shown in Table 1.

One of the principal symptoms of proliferative DR is the presence of neovascularization which is the sprouting of new vessels from pre-existent vessels. The presence of

© Springer Nature Switzerland AG 2021
E. Roman-Rangel et al. (Eds.): MCPR 2021, LNCS 12725, pp. 111–120, 2021.
https://doi.org/10.1007/978-3-030-77004-4_11

Neovascularization (NV) can cause vitreous hemorrhage or can pull the retina causing traction retinal detachment [3]. When traction retinal detachment involves the macula, which is responsible for reading and driving vision, severe visual loss occurs. So, the patients with NV detected require urgent treatment to avoid partial and total blindness.

Table 1. International classification of diabetic retinopathy and diabetic macular edema [2]

Diabetic retinopathy grade	Visible elements in the eye
Proliferative DR	Severe nonproliferative DR and 1 or more of the following: - Neovascularization - Vitreous/preretinal hemorrhage
Severe nonproliferative DR	Moderate nonproliferative DR with any of the following: - Intraretinal hemorrhages ($\geq$20 in each quadrant) - Definite venous beading (in 2 quadrants) - Intraretinal microvascular abnormalities (in 1 quadrant)
Moderate nonproliferative DR	Microaneurysms and other signs (dot and blot hemorrhages, hard exudates, cotton wool spots)
Mild nonproliferative DR	Microaneurysms only
No apparent DR	No abnormalities

The NV can be found in the whole retinal region, but one of the most frequent places to find them is around the optic disc, denominated as NV in the optic disc (NVD), while NV in other regions of the retina is called NVE (neovascularization elsewhere). For people without training, it is hard to identify the presence of NV in regions such as the optic disc where many healthy vessels are present. The creation of a system capable of detecting accurately the presence of NV can significantly reduce human errors as well as the number of resources used for this task. The patients detected the NV can receive timely treatments to avoid their vision loss.

Recently machine learning approaches, especially deep learning-based approaches, are introduced for automatic diagnostic of several diseases in medicine [4, 5]. The use of deep learning allows us efficient image classifications and object segmentation and detection, without the need for extended feature engineering. In ophthalmology, some automatic systems have been proposed [6–13], such as automatic quality assessment of retinal images [6], the automatic detection of lesions caused by the DR [7, 8], the detection of vessels in the eye fundus image [9], and other eye diseases [10]. In the literature, relatively few NV detection systems based on machine learning have been proposed [11–13]. Yu et al. proposed the NVD detection algorithm using a support vector machine (SVM) together with Gabor-based vessel segmentation and feature extractions from segmented vessels [11]. The line operators are used in [12] to segment the different types of vessels, in which fine vessels are considered as candidates of new vessels and some features are extracted from them. Finally, the SVM is used to discriminate new vessels from normal vessels. In [13], several vascular patterns are extracted and classified into normal and abnormal vessels using a classifier based on m-Mediods. All these methods firstly extract features from segmented vessels and then some classifiers are applied to classify the regions into NV or not NV using extracted features. Generally, the extracted features vary depending on the quality of the retinal image and the presence of other lesions, then classification accuracies also vary depending on these factors. As shown in [11] there is still a lack of data for test purposes, and the available data presents an imbalance which makes it hard to compare between the proposed methods.

In this paper, we present a deep learning based NVD detection system, in which we firstly evaluate several configurations of the deep neural networks (DNNs), considering that the variation of optic disc (OD) region is large among individuals and fundus cameras used to take images, and the OD regions with and without NV are highly similar, especially initial stage of the presence of NV. To train the DNNs adequately, we constructed our database from a public database [14], bounding NVs in the OD regions. The experimental results show good performance at classifying healthy without NV and non-healthy optic discs with NV, especially, we attained an accuracy of 93.3% using DenseNet-161.

The rest of this paper is organized as follows. In Sect. 2, we describe the constructed database, which is split into the training set and validation set for the DNNs and test set for evaluation of DNNs. The DNNs used for evaluations are described in Sect. 3 and in Sect. 4 we provide the experimental results, finally in Sect. 5, some conclusions obtained in this work together with discussions are provided.

2 Database Generation and Analysis

2.1 Database

On one hand, we have several improvements in the deep learning community where more effective networks and new architectures are being implemented, while on the other hand we still lack information to process for important tasks such as detection of Neovascularization. There are a few databases available publicly to work with [11] where images are classified into different categories according to the International Classification of Diabetic Retinopathy and Diabetic Macular Edema scheme [2].

For this scope, a database from the Kaggle competition was used. This database contains the largest number of retinal images within available public databases. The training set of this database is labeled as 5 different DR grades mentioned in Table 1, however, images do not contain any annotation about the lesions of DR, such as microaneurysm, exudates, and new vessels. So, we must create our database with NV annotation using bounding boxes. Considering that new vessels are one of the principal symptoms in the proliferative DR, the ophthalmologists create a ground truth annotation from 709 images of this category. This database presents an inconvenience due to the imbalanced problem, in which a few images with new vessels are found in optic disc regions.

From a total of 709 images classified in the proliferative DR stage in [14], a total of 470 annotations of neovascularization were found in 358 images, because some images contain more than two annotations of NV. This number of images with NV can be considered still very few to train efficiently DNNs and this number must be increased to improve deep learning-based NV detection system.

In 358 images with annotations of new vessels, we analyzed each annotated bounding box. The annotated images keep the same resolution; however, these have considerable variations in illumination, contrast, and blurriness. Figure 1 shows some examples of the retinal images with NV annotations together with optic disc annotation. As shown by Fig. 1, illumination and contrast are varied among images.

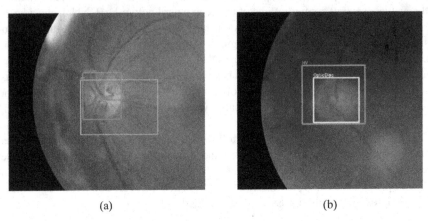

(a)   (b)

Fig. 1. Examples of annotation of neovascularization together with optic disc annotation

2.2 Preprocessing of Datasets

Due to the nature of new vessels, which proliferate randomly in any direction, the size of the bounding box that encloses new vessels varies considerably. The size of the biggest bounding box is larger than the optic disc, while some bounding boxes have a very tiny size. This variation of sizes of bounding boxes makes it difficult to use directly as training data. Therefore, filtering by the size of bounding boxes (area of the bounding box) was carried out using the number of pixels inside of the box. Figure 2 shows a histogram of the number of pixels within the bounding box using all bounding boxes of new vessels. From Fig. 2, we can observe that there are a few bounding boxes with a large number of pixels ($>1 \times 10^6$), however, these cases may cause the degradation of the classification performance.

Figure 3 shows the distribution of the sizes of bounding boxes after the filtering operation. The thresholds for lower and upper limits were chosen manually where the lower limit is equal to 4×10^4 and the upper limit is equal to 5×10^5. This filtering operation eliminates outliers: huge bounding boxes and very tiny bounding boxes, however at the same time the total number of annotations containing new vessels is reduced to 304.

Now, one last step was performed to create a database for NVD, in which final bounding boxes must contain optic discs with new vessels. For the extraction of such images, we looked for cases where an intersection between the bounding box of the optic disc and that of the new vessels was found. As shown in Fig. 4. where the red box represents the bounding box of the optic disc, the green box represents the presence of

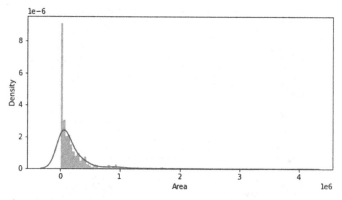

Fig. 2. Distribution of the area of the bounding boxes containing new vessels.

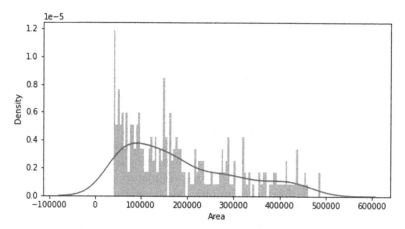

Fig. 3. Distribution of size of bounding boxes with new vessels

new vessels near the optic disc. From these two regions, a new region marked as the blue box containing both regions can be created. A total of 187 images with new vessels and optic discs were obtained.

We select 187 bounding boxes of the optic disc without the presence of new vessels, which will belong to the healthy optic disc class. To select them more properly, we first calculate the mean values of width and height of the optic disc with new vessels, which are previously annotated by experts. These mean values are multiplied randomly by values within [0.5, 1.5] and applied for the selection of 187 healthy optic disc bounding boxes. In this manner, we can create healthy optic disc bounding boxes of similar size to the NVD bounding boxes, finally, we get a balanced dataset composed of 187 NVD regions and 187 healthy optic disc regions.

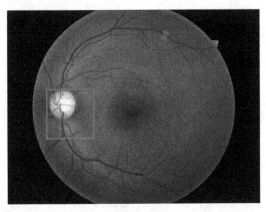

Fig. 4. Example of the intersection of two regions (Color figure online)

3 Deep Learning Approach

As mentioned before, after filtering the data the database size was reduced and the size and pixel values of interested regions vary among each other. Therefore, to use a deep learning approach, certain operations must be performed. First, data normalization must be done by changing the pixel values of the images to have a 0.5 mean and standard deviation of 0.5. With the data normalization, we can prevent the values from increasing rapidly, this was done in the three-color channels: Red, Green, and Blue.

To increase the training performance, a data augmentation technique was used. Random flipping in vertical and horizontal directions was applied, as well as random rotation from 0 to 180°. Due to the differences in color and illumination found between images, a color jitter was also applied where brightness, contrast, and saturation were changed randomly for each image in each epoch. The last method used as data augmentation was a resizing in the smallest side of the image, this was done to effectively use the pre-trained filters of the network. These data augmentation techniques were applied only for the training set using a seed to keep reproductivity between each network. Due to the lack of data for training, a new set of images were dynamically created by applying the data augmentation process each epoch on the training set, the number of new images is set to be the same size as the training set. Freezing layers didn't show a significant improvement, therefore the whole networks were trained.

State of the art networks have shown good performance in multiclass classification problems such as ImageNet challenge, therefore these networks tend to be useful for simple tasks such as binary classification, although retinal images are very different from natural images. In this scope, different off-the-shelf networks have been used for the classification of optic discs with new vessels (NVD regions) and healthy optic discs without the presence of new vessels. Old architectures such as VGG16 [15] tend to have a lack of performance against newer architectures with fewer parameters like Resnet [16] and DenseNet-161 [17]. In the past years, some new networks such as Effiicentnet-B7 [18] have shown an amazing performance although the number of parameters increases.

Table 2. Comparison in the number of parameters of the networks used.

Network	Number of parameters	Input size
VGG16	~134 M	224 × 224
Resnet18	~11 M	224 × 224
DenseNet161	~26 M	224 × 224
Efficientnet-B7	~64 M	600 × 600

As shown in Table 2 the number of parameters is very different among each network, which is directly related to the processing time it takes to be trained and the required memory size for storage of parameters. Finally, for the training of the networks the data was divided into 70% for training, 15% for validation, and the rest 15% for the final test, keeping all sets balanced. The workstation used for training had a CPU with an Intel(R) Xenon (R) at 2.30 GHz, 12 GB in RAM, and a Tesla P8 GPU.

4   Experimental Results

To train the networks a manual search of the optimal value for the learning rate was done, being it around 0.00001 for all networks. Based on the results of the validation set, the best model after training for 100 epochs was chosen for each architecture and applied to the test set. To show the performance among the different architectures, four metrics, which are accuracy, precision, specificity, and sensitivity value, were calculated. These metrics are expressed by (1)–(4).

$$accuracy = \frac{True\ Positive + True\ Negative}{Total\ data} \tag{1}$$

$$precision = \frac{True\ Positive}{True\ Positive + False\ Positive} \tag{2}$$

$$specificity = \frac{True\ Negative}{True\ Negative + False\ Positive} \tag{3}$$

$$sensitivity = \frac{True\ Positive}{True\ Positive + False\ Negative} \tag{4}$$

In Table 3, a summary shows the performance of each network to classify the optic disc region into two classes: NVD and healthy optic disc using the test set, which is not used during the training process. The NVD contains new vessels, and the healthy optic disc does not contain any new vessels. Considering that the medical purpose, it is worse to classify an NVD as a healthy one when it has the presence of neovascularization. Therefore, the sensitivity value is very important.

According to the global performance shown in Table 3, DenseNet-161 and Efficientnet-B7 show a good performance over the other two networks. Although

Table 3. Performance of the classification using test set.

Network	Accuracy	Precision	Sensitivity	Specificity
VGG16	78.7%	73.9%	89.5%	67.6%
Resnet	84.0%	80.9%	89.5%	78.4%
DenseNet-161	**93.3%**	97.1%	**89.5%**	97.3%
Efficientnet-B7	92.0%	**100%**	84.2%	**100%**

Efficientnet-B7 shows higher performance in precision and specificity than DenseNet-161, the latter shows better accuracy and sensitivity. Considering the value of sensitivity is important in medicine because the lower value of this metric means that patients with NV are not detected and as a consequence of this, they cannot receive timely treatment to avoid partial and total blindness. As part of the visualization of the results, the Receiver Operation Characteristic (ROC) curves for each model are shown in Fig. 5.

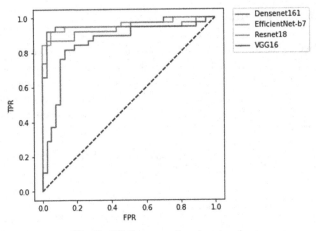

Fig. 5. ROC curves of each network

As seen in Fig. 5 the overall performance of the networks is good, being EfficientNet just a little below Densenet-161, although in terms of computational complexity, given by Table 2, DenseNet has a number of trainable parameters less than half the size of EfficientNet, which provides an important advantage in practice.

Finally, in Fig. 6 we provide some examples of optic disc images. Figure 6(a) shows an example that DNN is correctly detected as NVD, Fig. 6(b) is an example that the DNN classified correctly as a healthy optic disc, while Fig. 6(c) is an image that DNN classified erroneously NVD as a healthy optic disc. As shown by Fig. 6(c), it is very difficult to observe very thin new vessels in the region.

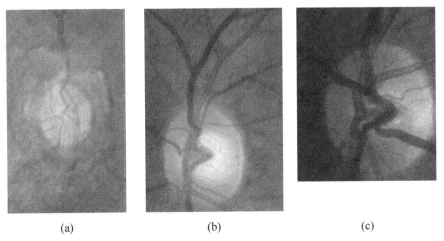

(a)   (b)   (c)

Fig. 6. (a) NVD classified as NVD, (b) healthy optic disc classified correctly, (c) NVD classified as a healthy optic disc.

5   Conclusions

This paper proposes to find the presence of neovascularization in the optic disc region (NVD). We demonstrate that it is possible to achieve such a task using deep learning with state-of-the-art networks, such as VGG16, Resnet, DenseNet, and EfficientNet. We evaluated these DNNs using several metrics, such as accuracy, precision, sensitivity, and specificity. From the evaluation results, we consider that DenseNet-161 shows a better performance, obtaining 93.3% in accuracy and 89.5% in sensitivity. In NVD detection, the false-negative error, in which NVD is diagnosed as a healthy optic disc, is critical, because the patients with new vessels miss a timely treatment to avoid partial and total blindness. Considering above mentioned issue, the DenseNet-161 is a better option in an automatic NVD detection system, because it provides a higher value in sensitivity than the EfficientNet. From computational complexity points of view, DenseNet-161 has fewer trainable parameters than that of the EfficientNet, which means that the trained DenseNet-161 can operate under smaller storage requirements than EfficientNet, and also DenseNet-161 is faster than the EfficientNet. It is important to mention that a further increase in the database size must be done to obtain a more reliable performance evaluation. The construction of a reliable automatic NVD detection system is our future work, which can be incorporated into an automatic DR grading system.

References

1. Asociación Mexicana de Retina: Retinopatía diabetíca. https://amretina.org/info01.html. Accessed 18 Feb 2021
2. ICO Guidelines for Diabetic Eye Care. https://www.icoph.org. Accessed 18 Feb 2021
3. Campochiaro, P.: Ocular neovascularization. J. Mol. Med. (Berlin, Germany) **91**(3), 311–21 (2013)

4. Litjens, G., et al.: A survey on deep learning in medical image. Med. Image Anal. **42**(12), 60–88 (2017)
5. Tajbakhsh, N., et al.: Convolutional neural networks for medical image analysis: full training or fine tuning. IEEE Trans. Med. Imaging **35**(5), 1299–1312 (2016)
6. Calderon, G., et al.: A teleophthalmology support system based on the visibility of retinal elements using the CNNs. Sensors **20**, 2838 (2020)
7. Gulshan, V., et al.: Development and validation of a deep learning algorithm for detection of diabetic retinopathy in retinal fundus photographs. JAMA J. Am. Med. Assoc. **316**(22), 2402–2410 (2016)
8. Oh, K., Kong, H., Leem, D., Lee, H., Seo, H., Yoon, S.: Early detection of diabetic retinopathy based on deep learning and ultra-wide-field fundus images. Sci. Rep. **11**(1), 1–9 (2021)
9. Vega, R., et al.: Retinal vessel extraction using Lattice Neural Networks with dendritic processing. Comput. Biol. Med. **58**, 20–30 (2015)
10. Choi, R., et al.: Variability in plus disease identified using a deep learning-based retinopathy of prematurity severity scale. Ophthalmol. Retina **4**(10), 1016–1021 (2020)
11. Yu, S., Xiao, D., Kanagasingan, Y.: Machine learning based automatic neovascularization detection on optic disc region. IEEE J. Biomed. Health Inform. **22**(3), 886–894 (2018)
12. Welikala, R., et al.: Automated detection of proliferative diabetic retinopathy using a modified line operator and dual classification. Comput. Method Prog. Biomed. **114**, 247–261 (2014)
13. Akram, M., Khalid, S., Tariq, A., Javed, M.: Detection of neovascularization in retinal images using multivariate m-Medios based classifier. Comput. Med. Imaging Graph. **37**, 346–357 (2013)
14. Diabetic Retinopathy Detection-identify signs of diabetic retinopathy in eye images. https://www.kaggle.com/c/diabetic-retinopathy-detection/data. Accessed 18 Feb 2021
15. Simmonyan, K., Zisserman, A.: Very deep convolutional networks for large-scale image recognition. In: 3rd International Conference on Learning Representations, ICLR 2015, San Diego, USA (2015)
16. He, K., Zhang, X., Ren, S., Sun, J.: Deep residual learning for image recognition. In: IEEE Computer Vision and Pattern Recognition, Las Vegas, USA, pp. 770–778 (2016)
17. Huang, G., Liu, Z., Van Der Maaten, L., Weinberger, K.: Densely connected convolutional networks. In: IEEE Computer Vision and Pattern Recognition, pp. 2261–2269 (2017)
18. Ran, M., Le, Q.V.: EfficientNet: rethinking model scaling for convolutional neural networks. In: Conference on Machine Learning, pp. 10692–10700 (2019)

Metric Localisation for the NAO Robot

Oswualdo Alquisiris-Quecha[1][✉] [iD] and Jose Martinez-Carranza[1,2] [iD]

[1] Computer Science Department, Instituto Nacional de Astrofísica, Óptica y Electrónica, INAOE, Puebla, Mexico
{oswualdoaq,carranza}@inaoep.mx
[2] Computer Science Department, University of Bristol, Bristol, UK

Abstract. We present a metric localisation approach for the NAO robot based on the methodology of depth estimation using optical flow in a frame-to-frame basis. We propose to convert optical flow into a 2-channel image from which images patches of 60×60 are extracted. Each patch is passed as input to a Convolutional Neural Network (CNN) with a regressor in the last layer, thus a depth value is estimated for such patch. A depth image is formed by putting together all the depth estimates obtained for each patch. The depth image is coupled with the RGB image and then passed to the well known ORB-SLAM system in its RGB-D version, this is, a visual simultaneous localisation and mapping approach that uses RGB and depth images to build a 3D map of the scene and use it to localise the camera. When using the depth images, the estimates are recovered with metric. Hence, the NAO's position can be estimated in metres. Our approach aims at exploiting the walking motion of the robot, which produces image displacements in consecutive frames, and by taking advantage from the fact that the NAO's walking motion could be programmed to be performed at constant speed. We mount a depth camera on the NAO's head to produce a training dataset that associates patch RGB images with depth values. Then, a CNN can be trained to learn the patterns in between optical flow vectors and the scene depth. For evaluation, we use one of the in-built NAO's camera. Our experiments show that this approach is feasible and could be exploited in applications where the NAO requires a localisation systems without depending on additional sensors or external localisation systems.

Keywords: Depth estimation · Deep learning · CNN · SLAM · Optical flow · NAO robot

1 Introduction

The importance of a robot being able to localise itself in an environment lies in the ability to interact with the environment without any physical damage while sensing any objects in it and their characteristics. It is clear that locating and navigating is trivial for a person, but for a robot, this task becomes complex. One of the main challenges within the field of robotics is autonomous single-camera navigation, in which camera images are processed frame-by-frame. However, the NAO robot is an example of a robotic platform that generates an oscillatory movement when walking. Hence, it is not possible to obtain clear and noise-free images to be analysed correctly in subsequent

© Springer Nature Switzerland AG 2021
E. Roman-Rangel et al. (Eds.): MCPR 2021, LNCS 12725, pp. 121–130, 2021.
https://doi.org/10.1007/978-3-030-77004-4_12

processes, so this remains a challenge under the erratic movements typical of moving robots.

In order to address this problem, various techniques have been proposed, always trying to compensate for the movement of the robot by implementing stabilisation systems on RGB images. However, using this type of images, it is possible to obtain blurred reference points (a common problem in RGB images) when the robot moves and consequently the loss of precision. Therefore, the use of optical flow techniques is considered, which can represent a relative estimate of depth according to the behaviour of their flow vectors. Altogether with Deep Learning techniques, optical flow can be exploited to estimate the depth of objects in a scene without requiring the additional sensors. The argument is to take advantage of the optical flow vectors generated by the natural erratic movement that humanoid robots produce when moving around their environment.

For this reason, a monocular vision-based method is proposed for the NAO robot's metric navigation, without the need for additional hardware. Under this approach, a first previous work has been carried out, shown in [1], where the input images fed to the system are images processed in a 3D colour space assigned according to the value of the optical flow. This image is passed to a CNN encoder-decoder to generate an estimated depth image. Unfortunately, this first approach turned out to be very slow, taking more than 1 s to generate a depth image.

In contrast, in this current work, optical flow is used directly as input to a CNN architecture in the form of small patches, and the output of the network is a single depth estimate. We use the DenseNet-169 architecture as the basis to obtain a convolutional regressor from it. This architecture is implemented in such a way that it is possible to adjust the density level of the depth estimates. That is, depending on the task to be performed as well as the hardware with which the robot is equipped, the precision of the estimate can be adjusted.

2   Related Work

There are several works that address the problem of autonomous navigation using monocular images. However, many of them choose to use more sensors to the devices as in [5, 17], which leads to the fact of significantly reducing the autonomy time of the robot, whereby adding additional weight it causes greater instability when performing movements of the robot in its environment. As well as using SLAM techniques as in [10, 15, 16] and Deep Learning for the estimation problem as in [3, 6, 7] or by merging both as presented by [12, 18], where many of the architectures used require great computing power. However, robotic systems have limited computing power on board.

Within the literature, there are few works where optical flow techniques are used for the problem of depth estimation in a single image as in [4, 13], where most of them use optical flow as a complementary technique to enhance the main method. However, the use of optical flow has become attractive to be used for mobile robots, for instance, in [9] the authors propose a CNN network to estimate the distance of an object in a 3D scene by using visual characteristics from optical flow. The input to the CNN is the estimation of the optical flow. The ultrasonic sensors is used as ground truth. The application to the system is that of monocular robotic navigation through obstacle avoidance. Various works have used optical flow in drones as in [11], where the optical flow is used to perform fast but safe landing manoeuvres or as presented in [14] in which the estimation of the depth by merging optical flow and camera pose values.

3 Methodology

The proposed method is presented in Fig. 1. The general idea is to use state of the art convolutional neural network that best suits the established needs, that is, a network that enables depth estimation given a single image, generated from the optical flow vectors, as input to the system, as well as a depth estimator using a convolutional regressor.

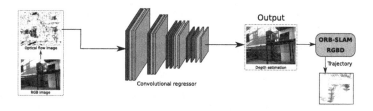

Fig. 1. General methodology

The modification of a CNN network is analysed to obtain a convolutional regressor, where the input for the network is a 2-channel image composed of the *du* and *dv* components of the resulting optical flow vectors when applying the Farneback method [2], and with this, perform the depth estimation of areas of interest, where together with the ORB-SLAM system a map is generated, and the position of the robot is obtained.

This begins with the acquisition of images directly from the camera of the NAO robot. The images are processed to obtain their corresponding optical flow image. The latter are processed to generate patches, which become inputs of the convolutional regressor to estimate the depth for each patch. Finally, all the depth are put together to form a depth image. The original RGB image and the generated depth image are passed to the ORB-SLAM in its RGB-D version to estimate the map and the position of the robot during its movement.

For this implementation, the dataset presented in Sect. 4 is used as training data for the Densenet-169 network. This network has various advantages compared to other state-of-the-art networks. For instance, the Densenet-169 network mitigates the problem of gradient fading, strengthens the spread and reuse of features and requires fewer parameters. Originally, this architecture was designed to be used in images consisting of three channels (usually RGB images) as input data to the system and is used in classification tasks since it is designed to classify 1000 different classes.

However, to our purposes, the network has been modified to operate with our dataset and for the task of estimating the metric depth of the environment. This modification consists of the following: the input image has now 2-channel, that is, the *du* and *dv* components obtained from the optical flow vectors; furthermore, the last layer is a fully-connected layer with a single output. In this sense, the network has become a convolutional regressor-type architecture where the fully connected layer operates as a linear regressor of the system.

4 Description of the Dataset

Our dataset was generated with the help of an Asus Xtion sensor, placed the head of the NAO robot. In order to characterise the images with the erratic movement of the robot, as it moves, the NAO robot is positioned at a distance of 3.5 m facing towards the wall up. The robot will be made to walk towards the wall getting closer up to 40 cm w.r.t wall. The walking will generate a radial expansive optical flow from which the dataset will be created.

For each 640×480 pixel image, the complete set of optical flow images and their corresponding depth images are taken. For each image in the dataset, 80 patches of 60×60 pixels is extracted. The Ground Truth depth for each patch is calculating by averaging the depth values of the patch in its corresponding sub-image of the depth image. This dataset is intended to be used in regression tasks using convolutional networks, known as convolutional regression. The dataset is made up of 504,080 images, of which they are divided into three categories: Training, Validation and Testing with 322,613, 100,817 and 80,650 data respectively. Each group consists of the optical flow du and dv components which are represented by a 2-channel image. Likewise, their corresponding scalar representing the average depth value is also stored (See Fig. 2).

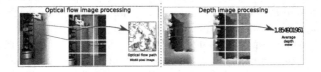

Fig. 2. Generation of the dataset

5 Training

For the training process, we use the dataset described in Sect. 2. Within the optimizer configuration used, the ADAM optimizer is selected with learning rate values of 0.001 and betas $\beta_1 = 0.9$, $\beta_2 = 0.999$ (default betas of the optimizer itself), the training process is carried out using a batch size 256 size for 100 times. The general architecture is presented in Fig. 3, in which the flow of the data related to the training process and depth estimation of the proposed method is depicted.

For the loss function, Mean Square Error Loss (MSELoss) is used, which implements a criterion that measures the mean square error (L2 squared norm) between each element in input x and the objective y. This loss function is denoted as $loss(x, y) =$

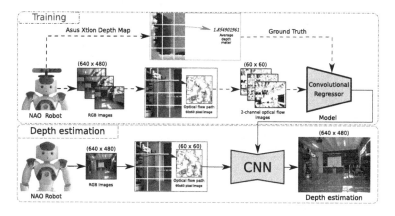

Fig. 3. General description of training and depth estimation

$(x - y)^2$. Where x is the current value and y is the value predicted by the architecture. The convolutional regressor training process with the configuration and parameters mentioned above took 7 d, 13 h, 31 min, 41 s to complete, obtaining a model with the trained weights. The training was carried out using a computer with an Intel® CoreTM i5-7300HQ CPU @ 2.50 GHz × 4, 8 GB of DDR4 RAM, with Nvidia GeForce GTX 1050 GPU with 640 Cuda Cores, the computer operates on the Ubuntu 18.04.2 LTS operating system in the 64 bit version.

6 ORB-SLAM RGBD

ORB-SLAM is a popular real-time SLAM implementation enabled to use a monocular, stereo or RGB-D camera to obtain input images on a frame-to-frame basis. The system calculates the trajectory of the camera while building sparse 3D reconstruction of the environment, is capable of detecting loops and relocating the camera in real time [8]. In the particular case of the RGB-D camera, both the map and camera estimates are recovered in the world's scale. Therefore, the ORB-SLAM RGBD system is a metric SLAM method.

Because the NAO robot does not have a depth sensor, it is necessary to provide an alternative to the RGB-D camera in order to recover the metric trajectory of the robot. By using architecture proposed in Sect. 3, we manage to generate an estimated depth image that can be coupled with the current RGB image obtained with the NAO's camera. Thus, enabling us to use RGB-D ORB-SLAM. Figure 4 shows a general overview of the system, where you can see the flow of data through the modules involved and their interconnections through the common data transmission and reception channel of the ROS system.

7 Experiments and Results

Various experiments were carried out for validation. It should be noted that the depth image is generated by the proposed CNN architecture and not from an external depth

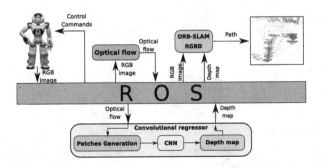

Fig. 4. General diagram of the interconnection of modules

sensor, so this technique continues to be a depth estimation technique using a monocular approach. It is necessary to clarify that for the experiments carried out; no previous image was built. Likewise, no assumption was made about the scene and the environment.

To validate the depth estimate of the proposed method, an analysis of the error obtained between the depth value predicted by the architecture and the actual depth value (obtained from the RGB-D sensor) is performed. This process is repeated for the number of patches to be processed. We calculate the RMSE value of average error, the mean, median, among others. These values can be seen in Table 1.

Table 1. Quantitative evaluation of the convolutional regressor

RMSE	Average	Median	Standard deviation	Minimum	Maximum	Number of images	Number of patches
1.257497 m	0.995430 m	0.812298 m	0.768388 m	0.000030 m	4.266205 m	300	24,000

Our proposed method is also assessed using the mean of the Absolute Trajectory Error (ATE). This measures the difference between the points of the trajectory estimated by ORB-SLAM and the true trajectory obtained with a motion capture system, the Vicon system. Since the Vicon system and ORB-SLAM have different reference systems, it is not possible to calculate the error directly. Therefore, a realignment of the translation and rotation values obtained from both systems is first performed using the Iterative Closest Point (ICP) algorithm. Note that we do not perform any scale adjustment. After aligning both trajectories, the ATE error calculation is applied.

As a first experiment, the NAO walks along a 6-meter square path. During the entire trajectory, the robot maintains its sight forward, having a wall insight at a minimum distance of 1.5 m and maximum of 3 m, the route is made without generating rotational turns with the robot, see Fig. 5.

In Table 2, the results of experiment 1 are concentrated through six runs using the NAO robot, in each one the ATE analysis is applied. It can be seen that the average error generated from the path by the NAO robot is approximately 60 cm (cm) and a maximum error of 1.11 m (m).

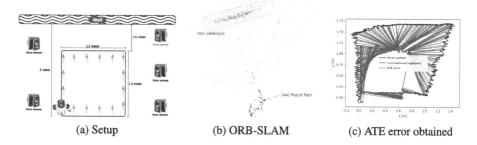

(a) Setup   (b) ORB-SLAM   (c) ATE error obtained

Fig. 5. Setup and result of experiment 1

Table 2. Results obtained from experiment 1

Experiment 1	ATE	Relative error	Mean	Median	Standard deviation	Min	Max
Test 1	0.472090 m	7.8681%	0.414832 m	0.323480 m	0.225351 m	0.100502 m	1.028387 m
Test 2	0.442785 m	7.3796%	0.442785 m	0.390867 m	0.200976 m	0.019855 m	0.770647 m
Test 3	0.791380 m	13.1896%	0.778789 m	0.829457 m	0.140609 m	0.437600 m	1.054863 m
Test 4	0.693241 m	11.5539%	0.631699 m	0.547518 m	0.285549 m	0.244373 m	1.426973 m
Test 5	0.558198 m	9.3031%	0.492768 m	0.426733 m	0.262229 m	0.052486 m	1.045850 m
Test 6	0.677523 m	11.2920%	0.617406 m	0.551779 m	0.279011 m	0.178363 m	1.310711 m
Averages	**0.605869 m**	**10.0976%**	**0.563046 m**	**0.511639 m**	**0.232287 m**	**0.172196 m**	**1.106238 m**

The second experiment is carried out according to Fig. 6, where displacements without rotational turns are analysed in order to observe the precision of the trajectory generated by proposed method. In this experiment, it is possible to obtain the robot's displacement path as well as the detection of the wall surface. This clarifies the fact that it is possible to generate the tracking of a trajectory using the convolutional regressor as a generator of depth images of the environment in conjunction with the ORB-SLAM system.

The ATE error analysis is presented in the Table 3, where there is an average error of approximately 47 cm along the path. According to the results, a minimum error of 12 cm and a maximum of 1.10 m is obtained.

Table 3. Results obtained from experiment 2

Experiment 2	ATE	Relative error	Mean	Median	Standard deviation	Min	Max
Test 1	0.320059 m	8.2064%	0.296167 m	0.298163 m	0.121337 m	0.043369 m	0.622565 m
Test 2	0.698582 m	17.9123%	0.636239 m	0.608065 m	0.288475 m	0.160160 m	1.481530 m
Test 3	0.359224 m	9.2107%	0.323904 m	0.287433 m	0.155330 m	0.132085 m	0.963596 m
Test 4	0.293510 m	7.5258%	0.231726 m	0.197894 m	0.180142 m	0.061379 m	1.321294 m
Test 5	0.600417 m	15.3951%	0.563856 m	0.534911 m	0.206316 m	0.245262 m	1.053263 m
Test 6	0.552650 m	14.1705%	0.477011 m	0.396976 m	0.279075 m	0.127640 m	1.192376 m
Averages	**0.470740 m**	**12.0702%**	**0.421483 m**	**0.387240 m**	**0.205112 m**	**0.128315 m**	**1.105771 m**

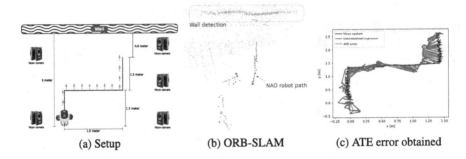

| (a) Setup | (b) ORB-SLAM | (c) ATE error obtained |

Fig. 6. Setup and result of experiment 2

As a last experiment, the robot moves in a straight line a distance of three meters towards a wall, stopping at a safe distance of 0.5 m. A sidewall is located at a distance of one meter along the trajectory (See Fig. 7). In this experiment, the path generated by proposed system can be observed, where the detection of the two walls is observed during the path of the robot.

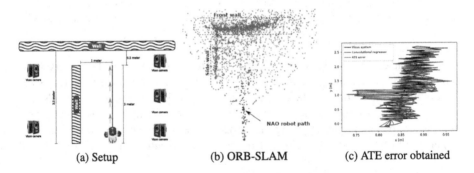

| (a) Setup | (b) ORB-SLAM | (c) ATE error obtained |

Fig. 7. Setup and result of experiment 3

The result of the ATE error is concentrated in Table 4. The average error value obtained of 24 cm is considered to be the result of the NAO robot pitching when walking, considering the measurement obtained by the Vicon system.

As a comparison between the experiments carried out, the averages of each experiment are concentrated to validate the operation of the Convolutionary Regression concentrates in Table 5.

We should highlight that this work does not focus on the precision of navigation, as this largely depends on the application to which the robot will be used. In contrast, this work focuses on validating that the method is functional to estimate the depth image and the position of the robot in its environment during navigation, using only optical flow images to perform this task.

Table 4. Results obtained from experiment 3

Experiment 3	ATE	Relative error	Mean	Median	Standard deviation	Min	Max
Test 1	0.067472 m	2.2490%	0.055529 m	0.049922 m	0.038328 m	0.010024 m	0.144965 m
Test 2	0.428005 m	14.2666%	0.288156 m	0.233465 m	0.316471 m	0.038139 m	1.607486 m
Test 3	0.132282 m	4.4093%	0.118231 m	0.109934 m	0.059329 m	0.015495 m	0.271140 m
Test 4	0.156278 m	5.2090%	0.141891 m	0.145754 m	0.065498 m	0.026210 m	0.340418 m
Test 5	0.488837 m	16.2943%	0.434939 m	0.451333 m	0.223135 m	0.019258 m	0.969946 m
Test 6	0.217138 m	7.2376%	0.185494 m	0.157850 m	0.112875 m	0.038103 m	0.462322 m
Averages	**0.248335 m**	**8.2776%**	**0.204040 m**	**0.191376 m**	**0.135939 m**	**0.024538 m**	**0.632712 m**

Table 5. General comparison of the various experiments

Experiments	ATE	Relative error	Mean	Median	Standard deviation	Min	Max
Experiment 1	0.605869 m	10.0976%	0.563046 m	0.511639 m	0.232287 m	0.172196 m	1.106238 m
Experiment 2	0.470740 m	12.0702%	0.421483 m	0.387240 m	0.205112 m	0.128315 m	1.105771 m
Experiment 3	0.248335 m	8.2776%	0.204040 m	0.191376 m	0.135939 m	0.024538 m	0.632712 m

8 Conclusions and Future Work

In this work, an architecture for depth estimation is proposed and implemented using optical flow vectors using the DenseNet-169 architecture as the basis. The architecture is implemented in such a way that it is possible to adjust the density level of the depth estimates. That is, depending on the task to be carried out as well as the hardware with which the robot is equipped, the architecture can work correctly.

It is important to mention that the depth values obtained from the proposed method in conjunction with the ORB-SLAM system generate metric maps of the environment expressed in meters. Therefore, given the nature of the implementation, a metric depth estimator is obtained under a monocular approach, without requiring external sensors to which the robot is equipped.

In the experiments, it was observed that to obtain better results; it is necessary to perform a navigation with trajectories with a small amount of rotations on the yaw axis of the robot. This is due to the fact that this generates sudden movements, together with the heading motion in the robot when moving, resulting in tracking errors.

According to the experiments carried out, it is concluded that the erratic movement induced in the NAO's head while walking can be exploited by observing the optical flow and that it is possible to exploit it to learn the metric depth of the environment with respect to the robot. Our results indicate that our approach is feasible, and we are confident that it could be used on other erratic motion robotic platforms for estimating the metric depth of the environment.

As future work, we propose to explore new CNN network architectures in order to reduce processing time and obtain better results in the resulting depth images, as well as to explore new data augmentation policies. Since images are used, the intention is to adjust the source code to be used directly in graphics cards to speed up the processing of both the optical flow analysis and the generation of patches of the input image. Therefore, alternatives could be explored using CUDA to parallelism certain processes.

References

1. Alquisiris-Quecha, O., Martinez-Carranza, J.: Depth estimation using optical flow and CNN for the NAO robot. Res. Comput. Sci. **148**(11), 49–58 (2019)
2. Farnebäck, G.: Two-frame motion estimation based on polynomial expansion. In: Bigun, J., Gustavsson, T. (eds.) SCIA 2003. LNCS, vol. 2749, pp. 363–370. Springer, Heidelberg (2003). https://doi.org/10.1007/3-540-45103-X_50
3. Gil, C.R., Calvo, H., Sossa, H.: Learning an efficient gait cycle of a biped robot based on reinforcement learning and artificial neural networks. Appl. Sci. **9**(3), 502 (2019)
4. Ho, H.W., de Croon, G.C.H.E., Chu, Q.: Distance and velocity estimation using optical flow from a monocular camera. Int. J. Micro Air Veh. **9**(3), 198–208 (2017)
5. Hornung, A., Wurm, K.M., Bennewitz, M.: Humanoid robot localization in complex indoor environments. In: IROS, pp. 1690–1695 (2010)
6. Li, R., Wang, S., Long, Z., Gu, D.: UnDeepVO: monocular visual odometry through unsupervised deep learning. In: 2018 IEEE International Conference on Robotics and Automation (ICRA), pp. 7286–7291. IEEE (2018)
7. Lobos-Tsunekawa, K., Leiva, F., Ruiz-del Solar, J.: Visual navigation for biped humanoid robots using deep reinforcement learning. IEEE Robot. Autom. Lett. **3**(4), 3247–3254 (2018)
8. Mur-Artal, R., Tardós, J.D.: ORB-SLAM2: an open-source SLAM system for monocular, stereo, and RGB-D cameras. IEEE Trans. Robot. **33**(5), 1255–1262 (2017)
9. Ponce, H., Brieva, J., Moya-Albor, E.: Distance estimation using a bio-inspired optical flow strategy applied to neuro-robotics. In: 2018 International Joint Conference on Neural Networks (IJCNN), pp. 1–7. IEEE (2018)
10. Rioux, A., Suleiman, W.: Autonomous slam based humanoid navigation in a cluttered environment while transporting a heavy load. Robot. Auton. Syst. **99**, 50–62 (2018)
11. Scheper, K.Y.W., de Croon, G.C.H.E.: Evolution of robust high speed optical-flow-based landing for autonomous MAVs. Robot. Auton. Syst. **124**, 103380 (2020)
12. Tiwari, L., Ji, P., Tran, Q.-H., Zhuang, B., Anand, S., Chandraker, M.: Pseudo RGB-D for self-improving monocular slam and depth prediction. arXiv preprint, page arXiv:2004.10681 (2020)
13. Wang, C., Ji, T., Nguyen, T.-M., Xie, L.: Correlation flow: robust optical flow using kernel cross-correlators. arXiv preprint arXiv:1802.07078 (2018)
14. Wang, K., Shen, S.: Flow-motion and depth network for monocular stereo and beyond. IEEE Robot. Autom. Lett. **5**(2), 3307–3314 (2020)
15. Wen, S., Othman, K.M., Rad, A.B., Zhang, Y., Zhao, Y.: Indoor SLAM using laser and camera with closed-loop controller for NAO humanoid robot. In: Abstract and Applied Analysis, vol. 2014. Hindawi (2014)
16. Wen, S., Zhang, Z., Ma, C., Wang, Y., Wang, H.: An extended Kalman filter-simultaneous localization and mapping method with Harris-scale-invariant feature transform feature recognition and laser mapping for humanoid robot navigation in unknown environment. Int. J. Adv. Robot. Syst. **14**(6), 1729881417744747 (2017)
17. Xu, X., Hong, B., Guan, Y.: Humanoid robot localization based on hybrid map. In: 2017 International Conference on Security, Pattern Analysis, and Cybernetics (SPAC), pp. 509–514. IEEE (2017)
18. Zhou, H., Ummenhofer, B., Brox, T.: DeepTAM: deep tracking and mapping. In: Ferrari, V., Hebert, M., Sminchisescu, C., Weiss, Y. (eds.) ECCV 2018. LNCS, vol. 11220, pp. 851–868. Springer, Cham (2018). https://doi.org/10.1007/978-3-030-01270-0_50

Multi-source Transfer Learning for Deep Reinforcement Learning

Jesús García-Ramírez[✉] [iD], Eduardo Morales[iD], and Hugo Jair Escalante[iD]

Instituto Nacional de Astrofísica Óptica y Electrónica (INAOE),
Sta. Maria Tonantzintla, 72840 Puebla, Mexico
{gr_jesus,emorales,hugojair}@inaoep.mx

Abstract. Deep reinforcement learning has obtained impressive performance in challenging tasks in recent years. Nevertheless, it has important limitations such as long training times and the number instances that are needed to achieve acceptable performance. Transfer learning offers an alternative to alleviate these limitations. In this paper, we propose a novel method for transferring knowledge from more than one source tasks. First, we select the best source tasks using a regressor that predicts the performance of a pre-trained model in the target task. Then, we apply a selection of relevant convolutional kernels for the target task in order to find a target model with similar number of parameters compared to the source ones. According to the results, our approach outperforms the accumulated reward obtained when learning from scratch in 20.62% using lower parameters (about 56% of the total, depending on the specific game).

Keywords: Transfer learning · Deep reinforcement learning · Multi source transfer

1 Introduction

Deep Reinforcement Learning (DRL) is the combination of Reinforcement Learning (RL) and Deep Learning (DL). DRL takes advantage of both approaches, from RL learning by interacting with the environment and from DL the ability to take raw data as input. Despite its effectiveness, DRL has two main limitations namely, the large number of instances that are need to achieve acceptable performance and demanding computational resources. Transfer Learning (TL) offers an alternative to reduce the training times in DRL while maintaining and even improving the performance of training a model from scratch.

DRL is commonly used when the state space is large and classical RL approaches are not applicable, an example of these tasks is the Atari video games scenario. The first algorithm that showed impressive results in the Atari domain was the so called Deep Q-Network (DQN) [9] that outperformed human-level performance in 30/47 games using frames as input for a Convolutional Neural Network (CNN).

© Springer Nature Switzerland AG 2021
E. Roman-Rangel et al. (Eds.): MCPR 2021, LNCS 12725, pp. 131–140, 2021.
https://doi.org/10.1007/978-3-030-77004-4_13

Some relevant works of TL in DRL have been proposed so far. Some of them use expert instances (e.g., [6,7,16,20]), however, gathering expert derived data could be difficult. In this work, we train an agent for the problem at hand with pre-trained models instead of using expert instances. Other approaches use imitation learning with a distillation strategy to obtain a reduced model for the task at hand (e.g., [13]), a problem with these methods is that finding the reduced model is very expensive and time consuming process by itself. Instead in this work we propose an approach in which pre-trained models are transferred to a new task. Pan et al. [10], propose a multi-source TL for DRL, where they train three models to learn a new task, one model finds a hidden representation, another learns the features and the last one is used to train the agent.

In this work, we propose a novel TL method that takes advantage from the knowledge of different source tasks. The proposed method selects two source tasks using a regression model that predicts the performance of a pre-trained model in the target task. Then, a selection of relevant convolutional kernels is applied to each source task. We add a convolutional layer to learn a new representation that combines the information from the selected kernels while the transferred kernels are frozen to accelerate the training process. We report an experimental evaluation of the proposed method in the challenging domain of Atari video games. According to the results, the proposed approach obtains negative transfer in few games that are difficult to transfer. Also, the jumpstart and final performance shows that there exists an improvement from the beginning until the end of the training process. Finally, it is also observed that better learning curves are obtained with the proposed approach compared with training the same task from scratch. The code and additional material of this work are publicity available: https://github.com/gr-jesus/Multi_Source_DRL.

2   Related Work

Several related works of TL in DRL have been proposed. AlphaGo [16] could be seen as a transfer of human experts games to train a certain task. In Atari games similar approaches were proposed, some of them pre-train the models with human expert instances [20] or initialize the experience replay (stack of instances used to train the agent) with expert episodes [6,7]. Nevertheless, collecting expert episodes can be difficult and the games scores are bias to the experts' performance.

Other approaches are based on a distillation strategy (a.k.a policy distillation) [13], where experience replay, produced by a teacher model, is used to train a new model for the same task but with considerable fewer parameters. Parisotto et al. [12], propose an approach where the output of the hidden layers from the teacher model are imitated through a loss function. Kickstarting DRL [14] uses the teacher-student schema but the student access to different teachers and the trajectories are used to learn a new model as close as possible to the teachers. This approaches tries to learn a teacher's policy via an imitation approach, that can run in hardware with limited resources. However, they learn a model for the same task, while we try to learn a new task using different source models.

Some initial efforts for transferring knowledge to a new task have been proposed. Cruz et al. [5] present initial experiments using a traditional fine-tuning approach and transferring the convolutional layers to learn a new task. Mittel et al. [8] use a generative adversarial neural network to find a useful representation for different games. These works present initial efforts for transfer knowledge to a new task, but their experiments are applied to few tasks and they use only one source model. In contrast in this work we show how to effectively use information from more than one model.

The most similar work to ours is that proposed by Pan et al. [10], they use a two-step transfer approach. First, a hidden representation for the available source tasks is learned using a CNN. Then, the agent for the target task imitates the features and the policy of the source task network using a loss function. This approach is difficult to apply because three or more models are trained to learn a new task: the source task models, the feature regression network, and the target task. We propose to learn a new task using a one-step TL, here we apply a fine-tuning approach and only the new model is trained.

3   Background

In this section we briefly present background information on Deep Reinforcement Learning and Transfer Learning.

3.1   Deep Reinforcement Learning

An RL problem can be modeled as a Markov Decision Process (MDP), that is a 5-tuple (S, A, P, R, γ): a state space S, an action space A, a probability state transition function $P(s'|s, a)$, a reward function R, and a discount factor γ [17].

In RL an agent interacts with a representation of the environment and the goal is to maximize the expected accumulated reward. Nevertheless, with large state spaces (e.g., Atari games [1]), it is difficult to find a suitable policy. To deal with this problem, a supervised learner is used to approximate the policy (the Q-value or both).

To test the proposed method we use DQN [9], this is the first work that obtains human performance in 29/49 Atari games using the same neural network architecture and the same hyperparameters for all their experiments using only frames of the video games as input. Two of the most important contributions of DQN are: the experience replay, an stack of instances that are used to train the CNN and the target network, a copy of the online network (this network update their weights as the instances are selected) used to select the actions during the training, their weights are updated after a number of steps.

3.2   Transfer Learning

Transfer learning offers an alternative to reduce the training time and the instances that are needed to achieve good performance in the target tasks. TL can be used when the instances in the target are few or to accelerate the training process.

According to Qiang Yang et al. [19], TL uses a source task with sufficient label examples to obtain a conditional distribution $P(Y_s|X_s)$, using a marginal distribution $P(X_s)$, where $X_s = \{x_1, x_2, \ldots, x_n\}$ are the instances and $Y_s = y_1, \ldots, y_k$ are the labels of the source task. The target task has few examples, insufficient to approximate the conditional distribution $P(X_t|Y_t)$. TL can approximate the conditional probability distribution of the target task using $P(X_s)$, $P(X_s|Y_s)$, and $P(X_t)$ [11]. One potential problem of TL is negative transfer, that appears when training with information from a source task has worse results than training the agent from scratch.

4   Multi-source Transfer Learning

In this section, we introduce the proposed method for transferring from two source tasks in DRL. We propose a method to solve two important questions of TL [19]: how to select among a set of source tasks and what information to transfer to the target task. In the following subsections we present the different stages of the proposed method.

4.1   Source Task Selection

In order to select the source tasks for transferring to a new target task we learn a regression model for predicting the expected performance of a pre-trained model in the target task. The goal of this model is to approximate the expected performance of source tasks into the final problem and use this approximation to select the tasks that seem more promising. For learning the regressor, we use information derived from the response of source models when images from the target tasks are feed. Specifically, we observe that pre-trained models that produce uniform feature maps with those inputs obtain lower performance than those that produce outputs with more diverse (informative) values. To estimate the diversity of values in the pre-trained models we calculate the entropy of feature maps [15]. If the convolutional layers of the pre-trained models (sources) produce uniform outputs with a sample of target inputs, their entropy values will be lower than those outputs with diverse values. We also consider the similarities between the action spaces of the source and target tasks, for this we codify both, source and target, action spaces in one-hot encoding and combined them with the entropies of the feature maps.

We train a regression model with information about the entropies of the feature maps and the similarities between action spaces. To obtain the entropies of the source tasks, a sample of the target task is evaluated in the pre-trained models, then we discretize the feature maps and find the entropy value of each one. Finally, the mean of every entropy value in the sample is used as the value of the convolutional kernels. A one-hot encoding of the action spaces is used with the entropies as input feature are the inputs of the regression model, where the performance of the pre-trained model in the new task is used as the output of the regressor. We train the regressor using 12 Atari games as described in Sect. 5.

We select Random Forest (RF) [2] as the algorithm to build the regressor because of their performance in regression tasks. Some important hyperparameters were modified in order to find the best ones, to evaluate this we use the mean squared error and the precision of the ranking of source tasks at the first, second and third position. The precision consider source task that obtain positive transfer at each position according to Eq. 1.

$$presicion\ at\ k = \frac{true\ positives\ at\ k}{k} \tag{1}$$

4.2   Relevant Convolutional Kernels Selection

Once the regression model is trained to predict the performance of a pre-trained model, we select the two best source tasks according to the regressor. Transfering the entire model produces a more complex model than the source ones. We hypothesize that it is not necessary to transfer the whole model of the source tasks and that we can construct a combined model from two source models of similar size as the original model.

Taking into account the entropies produced by the pre-trained model, we only transfer those ones with the highest entropy values. In order to obtain a model with a shared representation but with a similar architecture to the source tasks, we consider to transfer half of the convolutional kernels in each convoutional layer. For example, if we use in the source tasks the architecture proposed by Mnhi et al. [9], where the convolutional layers consist of three convolutional layers with {32, 64, 64} kernels, for each pre-trained model we only transfer {16, 32, 32} kernels.

4.3   Transfer Learning Stage

In this section we describe the TL process in the proposed method. The proposed architecture can be seen in Fig. 1, the first part of the architecture consists of the convolutional kernels selected from each source task (those kernels with the highest entropy value). In the proposed approach, the weights of those kernels are frozen simplifying the learning process. Then, both representations are joined and a convolutional layer is added in order to learn a new representation combining the information from both models. Finally, we use a fully connected layer and the output layer with actions available for each agent.

The architecture shown in Fig. 1 is used to train the new agent, the target model has a considerably lower number of parameters (parameters $\in$ [2,302,675-2,308,450] depending the number of actions), 56.92% with respect to the source models (parameters $\in$ [4,044,963-4,052,658] depending the number of actions). The two source tasks with the highest predicted performance by the regressor are selected for transferring to the new task. Also, we tune the hyperparameters

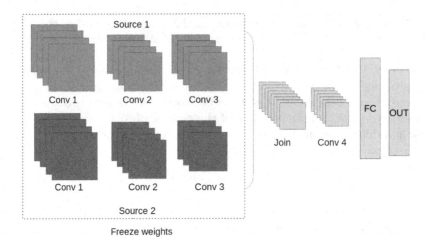

Fig. 1. Used architecture for the proposed method. The two source tasks transfer half of the pre-trained models, in order to use the learned representation we freeze the weights of the transferred convolutional layers. We also add a convolutional layer to learn a shared representation.

of DQN algorithm to reduce the instability of the learning curves, specifically we reduce the value of the learning rate and increase the batch size. In the training of the new task we fine-tune only the new layers added to the model.

5   Experimental Results

In this section we show the experiments of the proposed method. The aim of the experiment is to show that transferring from multiple source tasks is an effective methodology that compares favorably with a model trained from scratch. To validate our experiments we use the DQN algorithm with Atari games. First, we describe the building of the regression model. Then, we describe the training of different games and the obtained results.

To obtain the training set for training the regressor, we use examples of transferring and fine-tuning the convolutional layers to a new target task. We selected twelve Atari games, shown in the first part of Table 1 and we exhaustively transfer between all these games to find the performance of the pre-trained models in a target task. For these experiments we used dopamine-rl library [4] and the same hyperparameters proposed for the DQN algorithm.

We build the regression model using SciKitLearn library [3], where we changed some of the hyperparameters to improve performance. In particular, using 47 trees and mean squared error as quality measure, we obtained the lowest error and the best precision in the first, second and third position according to the ranking of the selected source tasks (the rest of hyperparameters have the default values proposed by SciKitLearn).

For the TL stage we used the architecture of Fig. 1, the source tasks are selected by the ranking obtained by the regression model. We selected half of the convolutional kernels with the highest entropy values for each source task, these weights are frozen in order to optimize less parameters.

In order to reduce the instability of the learning curves, we increased the batch size from 32 to 64 and we reduced the learning rate from 0.00025 to 0.000025 (see Fig. 2). The rest of hyperparameters are the same proposed in dopamine-rl. We run three independent experiments for each game because of the instability of the DQN algorithm.

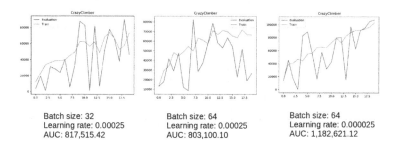

Batch size: 32
Learning rate: 0.00025
AUC: 817,515.42

Batch size: 64
Learning rate: 0.00025
AUC: 803,100.10

Batch size: 64
Learning rate: 0.000025
AUC: 1,182,621.12

Fig. 2. Hyperparameter tuning for DQN algorithm, we increase the batch size and reduce the learning rate in order to reduce the instability of the learning curves.

To validate our experiments we use the metrics proposed by Taylor [18]: jumpstart, the initial gain in performance at the first iteration; maximum reward during the training; final performance after training; transfer ratio, a comparison between the learning curves from scratch and the learning curves with transfer learning. For the first three metrics values higher than one means positive transfer and for the transfer ratio values higher than zero means better behaviour of the learning curves when training with transfer.

We use eighteen more games that are not used during the training of the regression, these games can be seen in the second part of Table 1. We select the two pre-trained models with the highest predicted performance, these source tasks can be seen in the second and third columns of Table 1. We report the mean and the geometric mean to reduce the influence of some outliers.

The evaluation results from the selected games are shown in Table 1. Taking into account the maximum obtained reward during training, in 20/30 games there is a positive transfer, in 4/30 there is a neutral transfer (the mean of the game is higher than the lower score obtained during training without transfer), and in 6/30 games there is a negative transfer.

According to the mean of all the games with the used metrics we can conclude: (i) the jumpstart for the games is better than training from scratch, $mean=12.4583$, however some source task lose this gain because of the instability of the learning curves (e.g., Kung-Fu Master); (ii) the final performance obtained an improvement of 18.08% with respect to training from scratch; (iii)

Table 1. Results of the proposed method. We use the metrics proposed by Taylor et al. [18]: jumpstart (JS), Final Performance (FP)

Objetivo	Fuente 1	Fuente 2	JS	FP	TR	MAX
Crazy Climber	Time Pilot	Tennis	0.8338	0.8932	0.1173	1.0088
Star Gunner	Robotank	Freeway	0.6668	1.9575	0.2962	1.8991
Boxing	Freeway	Tennis	2.0434	1.0522	0.0817	1.0286
Freeway	Robotank	Pong	0.0426	1.4605	0.3854	1.4602
Pong	Video Pinball	Kangaroo	7.1500	1.0124	0.1570	1.0037
Robotank	Tennis	Jamesbond	0.9002	1.0847	0.1078	1.0090
Up & Down	Time Pilot	Tennis	0.3402	0.7841	0.1683	1.0242
Atlantis	Star Gunner	Robotank	0.5174	6.7524	12.6039	5.4547
Breakout	Freeway	Robotank	0.7885	0.5136	−0.0939	0.8960
Space Invaders	Jamesbond	Assault	0.6806	0.7111	−0.0797	0.7681
Video Pinball	Pong	Robotank	0.3596	0.6313	0.3905	1.3653
Gopher	Tennis	Time Pilot	2.2107	1.0250	0.3121	1.1148
Assault	Kung-Fu Master	Ice Hockey	0.8008	0.6643	−0.1422	0.6398
Beam Rider	Jamesbond	Demon Attack	0.7771	0.8536	−0.0730	0.8546
Fishing Derby	Time Pilot	Ice Hockey	0.9667	1.1303	−0.1121	0.9194
Hero	Pong	Asterix	1.4214	1.1813	0.1686	1.1848
Kangaroo	Tennis	Ice Hockey	0.8082	1.4319	0.3102	1.2543
Name This Game	Tennis	Ice Hockey	1.2221	0.8893	0.3339	1.1060
Road Runner	Freeway	Kangaroo	6.9509	0.6475	0.1049	1.0011
Tutankham	Ice Hockey	Jamesbond	0.4853	1.0931	0.2051	1.2418
Asterix	Time Pilot	Kung-Fu Master	0.9504	0.6286	−0.3223	0.6842
Demon Attack	Jamesbond	Freeway	0.4516	0.7017	−0.0124	0.9485
Ice Hockey	Freeway	Tennis	0.7323	1.6125	0.1762	0.9735
Krull	Star Gunner	Tennis	1.4189	1.1382	0.2268	1.0392
Tennis	Beam Rider	Kangaroo	2.2500	0.9174	−0.5259	1.0400
Enduro	Tennis	Freeway	0.0000	1.1100	0.1853	1.0969
Jamesbond	Ice Hockey	Tennis	1.5169	1.1261	0.5857	1.1688
Kung-Fu Master	Asterix	Tennis	332.2752	0.8196	0.0371	0.8296
Time Pilot	Kangaroo	Pong	1.5970	1.1553	0.6064	1.1797
Qbert	Freeway	Robotank	2.4931	0.4464	−0.1123	0.9038
Mean			12.4583	1.1808	0.5362	1.2062
Geometric Mean			0.5909	0.9996	−	1.0930

the learning curves obtained better performance than training without transfer, this is because of the hyperparameters tuning process of the DQN algorithm; finally, taking into account the maximum score obtained by the agents, there is an improvement of 20.62% with respect to training from scratch. Considering the best out of three experiments per game, a mean gain of 5.8 h is obtained with the proposed method.

6   Conclusions and Future Work

In this work we presented a TL formulation for DRL using multiple source tasks, our approach selects from a set of available source tasks two useful pre-trained models for the target task. We fine-tune the added layers and the transferred ones are frozen in order to reduce the training time. Nevertheless, the main limitation of our method is that some experiments transferring the convolutional layers are needed to train the regression model.

The general performance of the evaluation metrics shows that transfer from two source task is better than training from scratch. Jumpstart and final performance show an improvement from the beginning until the end of the training process, the transfer ratio shows better performance of the learning curves compared with the training without transfer. Finally, there exists an improvement of the maximum score of 20.62% with respect to training from scratch. Also, the number of parameters of the target task is considerably lower than source ones (between [56.92%–56.96%], depending the target game), consequently the model could be used in hardware with limited resources.

In future work we will like to apply the proposed approach to other domains such as classification tasks. We will also try to improve the performance of the games that obtain negative transfer using a different hyperparameter setting.

Aknowledgements. The authors thankfully acknowledge computer resources, technical advice and support provided by Laboratorio Nacional de Supercómputo del Sureste de México (LNS), a member of CONACYT national laboratories with projects No. 201901047C and 202002030c. We also want to acknowledge the Laboratorio Nacional de Supercómputo del Bajio with project No. 2020.1. Jesús García-Ramírez acknowledges CONACYT for the scholarship that supports his PhD studies associated to CVU number 701191.

References

1. Bellemare, M.G., Naddaf, Y., Veness, J., Bowling, M.: The arcade learning environment: an evaluation platform for general agents. JAIR **47**, 253–279 (2013)
2. Breiman, L.: Random forests. Mach. Learn. **45**(1), 5–32 (2001)
3. Buitinck, L., et al.: API design for machine learning software: experiences from the scikit-learn project. In: ECML PKDD Workshop: Languages for Data Mining and Machine Learning, pp. 108–122 (2013)
4. Castro, P.S., Moitra, S., Gelada, C., Kumar, S., Bellemare, M.G.: Dopamine: a research framework for deep reinforcement learning (2018). http://arxiv.org/abs/1812.06110
5. de la Cruz, G., Du, Y., Irwin, J., Taylor, M.: Initial progress in transfer for deep reinforcement learning algorithms, July 2016
6. Cruz, Jr., G.V., Du, Y., Taylor, M.E.: Jointly pre-training with supervised, autoencoder, and value losses for deep reinforcement learning. arXiv preprint arXiv:1904.02206 (2019)
7. Hester, T., et al.: Deep Q-learning from demonstrations. In: Proceedings of the AAAI Conference on Artificial Intelligence, vol. 32 (2018)

8. Mittel, A., Munukutla, S., Yadav, H.: Visual transfer between Atari games using competitive reinforcement learning. arXiv preprint arXiv:1809.00397 (2018)
9. Mnih, V., et al.: Human-level control through deep reinforcement learning. Nature **518**(7540), 529 (2015)
10. Pan, J., Wang, X., Cheng, Y., Yu, Q.: Multisource transfer double DQN based on actor learning. IEEE Trans. Neural Netw. Learn. Syst. **29**(6), 2227–2238 (2018)
11. Pan, S.J., Yang, Q.: A survey on transfer learning. IEEE Trans. Knowl. Data Eng. **22**(10), 1345–1359 (2009)
12. Parisotto, E., Ba, J.L., Salakhutdinov, R.: Actor-mimic: deep multitask and transfer reinforcement learning. arXiv preprint arXiv:1511.06342 (2016)
13. Rusu, A.A., et al.: Policy distillation. arXiv preprint arXiv:1511.06295 (2015)
14. Schmitt, S., et al.: Kickstarting deep reinforcement learning. arXiv preprint arXiv:1803.03835 (2018)
15. Shannon, C.E.: A mathematical theory of communication. Bell Syst. Tech. J. **27**(3), 379–423 (1948)
16. Silver, D., et al.: Mastering the game of go with deep neural networks and tree search. Nature **529**(7587), 484 (2016)
17. Sutton, R.S., Barto, A.G., et al.: Introduction to Reinforcement Learning. MIT Press, Cambridge (2018)
18. Taylor, M.E., Stone, P.: Transfer learning for reinforcement learning domains: a survey. JMLR **10**(Jul), 1633–1685 (2009)
19. Yang, Q., Zhang, Y., Dai, W., Pan, S.J.: Transfer Learning. Cambridge University Press, Cambridge (2020)
20. Zhang, X., Ma, H.: Pretraining deep actor-critic reinforcement learning algorithms with expert demonstrations (2018)

Efficient Training of Deep Learning Models Through Improved Adaptive Sampling

Jorge Ivan Avalos-López[1]([✉]), Alfonso Rojas-Domínguez[1] [ID],
Manuel Ornelas-Rodríguez[1] [ID], Martín Carpio[1] [ID], and S. Ivvan Valdez[2] [ID]

[1] Tecnológico Nacional de México/Instituto Tecnológico de León, 37290 León, México
avaloslj2014@licifug.ugto.mx
[2] Centro de Investigación en Ciencias de Información Geoespacial A.C.,
76703 Querétaro, México

Abstract. Training of Deep Neural Networks (DNNs) is very computationally demanding and resources are typically spent on training-instances that do not provide the most benefit to a network's learning; instead, the most relevant instances should be prioritized during training. Herein we present an improved version of the Adaptive Sampling (AS) method (Gopal, 2016) extended for the training of DNNs. As our main contribution we formulate a probability distribution for data instances that minimizes the variance of the gradient-norms w.r.t. the network's loss function. Said distribution is combined with the optimal distribution for the data classes previously derived by Gopal and the improved AS is used to replace uniform sampling with the objective of accelerating the training of DNNs. Our proposal is comparatively evaluated against uniform sampling and against Online Batch Selection (Loshchilov & Hutter, 2015). Results from training a Convolutional Neural Network on the MNIST dataset with the Adadelta and Adam optimizers over different training batch-sizes show the effectiveness and superiority of our proposal.

Keywords: Deep learning · Convolutional Neural Networks · Gradient Descent · Importance Sampling

1 Introduction

During the past decade, the increase in available data and computational power (development of graphics cards with higher computing capacity) as well as important theoretical developments, propelled the advent of Deep Learning (DL) techniques and their further dominance in several pattern recognition applications such as computer vision, pattern classification, natural language processing, forecasting and so on [1].

The bottleneck of DL models is their training; due to the very large amounts of data to be processed and the millions of trainable parameters, the training process is usually very computationally expensive [2], although relatively simple. The standard method for training many deep neural networks (DNNs), in particular for classification tasks,

---

A. Rojas-Domínguez and S. Ivvan Valdez—CONACYT Research Fellow.

E. Roman-Rangel et al. (Eds.): MCPR 2021, LNCS 12725, pp. 141–152, 2021.
https://doi.org/10.1007/978-3-030-77004-4_14

is stochastic gradient descent (SGD) and its variations. A network is presented with a set of examples, an error function is computed and the gradient of this error function is back-propagated through the network in order to determine the necessary adjustments to its parameters. In practice, instead of adjusting the network one data instance at a time, the training dataset is divided into so-called mini-batches of fixed size and the network is trained on one mini-batch (i.e. on a few data instances) at a time.

The conventional way of forming the mini-batches is through uniform sampling of the data instances, but recently there have been efforts to develop strategies to accelerate the training of DNNs through more efficient sampling schemes. In 2016, Loshchilov & Hutter [4] and Alain et al. [7] explored adaptive and intelligent selection mechanisms that focus computing resources on the *most informative* examples; this is called *Importance Sampling* (IS). In 2017 Katharopoulos & Fleuret [3] proposed a *biased importance sampling*, based on a biased gradient estimate designed to reduce the variance over the stochastic gradients.

Such novel sampling strategies are built around the idea that not all samples are equally important in the training process and the most relevant instances should be prioritized to accelerate learning. Said strategies employ either the loss-values or the gradient-norms as measures of the importance, but none has used both measures jointly. Sampling based on the gradient-norms tends to show better performance, but the advantage over using loss-values is not too large [3]. Meanwhile, using the gradient-norm is more computationally expensive than using the loss-value. Developing a method that combines the two measures is an interesting idea, which we explore in this work.

Following the same guiding principle as previous works we propose a new IS scheme that accelerates the training of Convolutional Neuronal Networks (CNNs) by focusing the computation on the samples that minimize the variance of the gradients w.r.t. the loss function. As such, this work is an extension of Gopal's work [5] for the training of DNNs; specifically we propose a novel probability distribution to perform IS. Our proposal is validated using a CNN trained on the MNIST classification task and we demonstrate that our strategy speeds up the training procedure compared to the standard sampling scheme (uniform sampling) as well as compared to the proposal of Loshchilov & Hutter [4], a method considered in the state of the art.

2   Related Work

Several strategies to improve the convergence of SGD have been described in the literature. Most of these are focused on improving the way in which data instances are selected to form the training mini-batches. We refer to said strategies as *Selective Sampling* strategies. The key idea behind these methods is to design a non-uniform distribution to replace the uniform distribution that is usually employed to sample training instances.

In the literature, we have identified two approaches to the problem of Selective Sampling. The first approach constructs a probability distribution according to the gradient norm of each training instance; this is done with the objective of reducing the variance between the gradients of the sampled instances. Under this approach, Katharopoulos & Fleuret [3] proposed to accelerate the training of a DNN using a probability distribution based on the gradient-norm of each instance; they ranked the instances w.r.t. their loss-value and then sampled these based on that ranking. They also derived an upper bound on the gradient-norm, and used it to estimate the most convenient moments to switch between uniform sampling and IS along the training process. Similarly, Alain et al. [7] employed the gradient-norm to define each instance's importance. Zhao & Zhang [8] and Needell et al. [9] showed that the optimal sampling distribution is proportional to the per-instance gradient-norm and established a clear connection with the variance of the gradient estimates of SGD. Gopal [5] defined a distribution of classes that is directly proportional to the norm of the gradients, in order to sample from those classes with instances that lead to the maximum reduction in the variance of the gradients.

The second approach to Selective Sampling consists of constructing a probability distribution based on the loss value of each individual training instance. The loss function is a measure of how well a model can solve particular instances. If the loss of an instance is high then it should be sampled more frequently so that the model can have more opportunities to learn to solve it. The idea is to preferably supply the DNN with instances that are harder to classify or forecast, since this should make the learning process more efficient. Following this approach, Loshchilov & Hutter [4] employed the loss to define each instance's importance, ranked the instances w.r.t. their latest known loss value and built a probability distribution that decays exponentially as a function of that ranking. Likewise, Schaul [10] and Katharopoulos & Fleuret [11] use the loss to create their sampling distributions. They keep a history of losses for previously seen instances and for new training iterations they sample instances proportionally to that loss.

Besides Selective Sampling strategies there have also been other proposals to optimize the training of DNNs. Fan et al. [6] used reinforcement learning to train a neural network that selects instances in order to optimize the convergence of a second neural network. Joseph et al. [13] designed a mini-batch selection strategy based on the maximization of a submodular function that captures relevant information from the data used to speed up the training. Zhao & Zhang [14] divided the data set into clusters with low variance, and then strategically sampled mini-batches from those clusters. Finally, Wu et al. [15] designed a distribution that maximizes the diversity of the losses in a training batch.

Our proposed IS is an extrapolation and modification of the Adaptive Sampling (AS) algorithm of Gopal [5] to DL models, with the addition of a redefined probability distribution that combines the gradient and the loss of individual instances and of the mini-batches. This addition is possible due to important contributions by Katharopoulos & Fleuret [3, 11]. The details of our proposal are provided in the following section.

3   Adaptive Sampling for Deep Learning

Let $D = \{(x_1, y_1), (x_2, y_1), \ldots, (x_N, y_N)\}$, $x_i \in \mathbb{R}^n$, $y_i \in \mathbb{R}^m$, $\forall i = 1, \ldots, N$ be the training set, where X represents a set of data instances and Y their set of labels, $\varphi(x_i; \theta) : \mathbb{R}^n \to \mathbb{R}^m$ be a Deep Learning model for classification of m classes, parameterized by vector θ, and $L(\varphi(x_i; \theta), y_i) : \mathbb{R}^m \to \mathbb{R}^+$ be the loss function to be minimized during training. Training with SGD means finding the optimum vector θ^*, usually by solving:

$$\theta^* = \underset{\theta}{\operatorname{argmin}}\, E_{x_i \sim \mathcal{U}}\big[L(\varphi(x_i; \theta), y_i)\big] = \underset{\theta}{\operatorname{argmin}}\, \frac{1}{N} \sum_{i=1}^{N} L(\varphi(x_i; \theta), y_i), \qquad (1)$$

where $\mathcal{U}$ represents the uniform distribution. Guillaume et al. [16] showed that SGD is a powerful tool to optimize the sampling distribution of Monte Carlo (MC) estimators, motivating the idea of employing a sampling distribution which is not constant through time. IS can be seen as a method to estimate (1), surrogating a uniform distribution with a non-uniform one. Thus we have a MC estimator of the form [16]:

$$\theta^* = \operatorname*{argmin}_{\theta} E_{x_i \sim \mathcal{V}}\big[\zeta(x_i)L(\varphi(x_i;\theta), y_i)\big] = \operatorname*{argmin}_{\theta} \frac{1}{N}\sum_{i=1}^{N}\frac{1}{\mathcal{V}(x_i)}L(\varphi(x_i;\theta), y_i), \quad (2)$$

where $\zeta(x_i) = \frac{\mathcal{U}(x_i)}{\mathcal{V}(x_i)}$ is called the importance weight and $\mathcal{V}$ the *importance distribution* [16].

Following the work of Gopal [5], we associate *side information* to each x_i. This side information can represent a class label, a measure that is inherent to each instance, or it can be any tag associated with x_i that enables us to create a partition C of dataset D: $C = \{c_1, c_2, \ldots, c_k\}, c_j = \left\{x_1^j, x_2^j, \ldots, x_{m_j}^j\right\} \forall j = 1, 2, \ldots, k$. That is, the N instances are split into k mutually exclusive bins, which are not necessarily balanced.

Let us now define a probability distribution over the bins: $P = \{p_1, p_2, \ldots, p_k\}, p_j = P(C = c_j)$; and a probability distribution over the elements of each bin: $Q^j = \left\{q_1^j, q_2^j, \ldots, q_{|I_j|}^j\right\}, q_i^j = P\left(c_j = x_{i\in I_j}^j\right)$, where $I = \{I_1, I_2, \ldots, I_k\}$ are index sets of the partition C. In our notation a superindex is used to indicate the j-th bin and a subindex indicates the i-th element of the corresponding j-th bin.

Assuming that P and Q^j are independent, the probability of picking the i-th training instance is given by:

$$P(X = x_i) = p_j q_i^j. \quad (3)$$

Using this result, and defining $\mathcal{V}(x_i)$ as $p_j q_i^j$, we can rewrite (2) as:

$$\theta^* = \operatorname*{argmin}_{\theta} \frac{1}{N}\sum_{c_j \in C}\sum_{i \in c_j}\frac{1}{p_j q_i^j}L\left(\varphi\left(x_i^j;\theta\right), y_i^j\right). \quad (4)$$

This problem is solved by gradient descent, so we require the gradient d^t at training iteration t:

$$d^t = \frac{1}{N}\frac{1}{p_j q_i^j}\nabla_\theta L\left(\varphi\left(x_i^j;\theta^{t-1}\right), y_i^j\right). \quad (5)$$

As our main contribution, we propose to employ non-uniform distributions for both P and Q^j, defined to reduce the total variance of the gradients and improve the estimate of the descent direction.

Formally, we define two minimization problems, (6) and (11) respectively: the first one is the minimization of the gradient variance w.r.t P, assuming a fixed Q^j; the second problem is the counterpart of the first one, i.e. the minimization of the gradient variance w.r.t Q^j assuming a fixed P. The first problem is:

$$\min_{P} V[d^t] = \min_{p_1, \ldots, p_k}\left(\mathbb{E}\big[d^{tT}d^t\big] - \mathbb{E}[d^t]^{T}\mathbb{E}[d^t]\right). \quad (6)$$

The solution to (6) is due to Gopal [5] and gives the optimal distribution P at the t-th iteration:

$$p_j \propto \frac{1}{N} \sqrt{\sum_{i \in c_j} \frac{1}{q_i} \left\| \nabla_\theta L\left(\varphi\left(x_i^j; \theta^{t-1}\right), y_i^j\right) \right\|^2}. \tag{7}$$

Using Gopal's idea of reformulating the uniform distribution as the product of one distribution for the bins times a second distribution for the instances, i.e. $1/N = (|c_j|/N)(1/|c_j|)$, from (4) we have:

$$\frac{1}{N} \sum_{c_j \in C} \sum_{i \in c_j} \frac{1}{p_j q_i} L\left(\varphi\left(x_i^j; \theta\right), y_i^j\right) = \sum_{c_j \in C} \frac{1}{p_j} \frac{|c_j|}{N} \frac{1}{|c_j|} \sum_{i \in c_j} \frac{1}{q_i} L\left(\varphi\left(x_i^j; \theta\right), y_i^j\right). \tag{8}$$

So, we have the following optimization problem defined only for the instances of a particular bin:

$$\theta_j^* = \underset{\theta}{argmin} \; \frac{1}{|c_j|} \sum_{i \in c_j} \frac{1}{q_i} L\left(\varphi\left(x_i^j; \theta\right), y_i^j\right), \forall j = 1, \ldots, k. \tag{9}$$

For which the gradient d_j^t at training iteration t is:

$$d_j^t = \frac{1}{q_i^j} \frac{1}{|c_j|} \nabla_\theta L\left(\varphi\left(x_i^j; \theta^{t-1}\right), x_i^j\right). \tag{10}$$

Then, akin to (6) we pose the minimization of the gradient variance, but this time w.r.t. Q^j:

$$\min_{Q^j} V\left[d_j^t\right] = \min_{q_1, \ldots, q_{|I_j|}} \left(\mathbb{E}\left[d_j^{t\mathrm{T}} d_j^t\right] - \mathbb{E}\left[d_j^t\right]^{\mathrm{T}} \mathbb{E}\left[d_j^t\right]\right), \forall j = 1, \ldots, k, \tag{11}$$

where we can find the following expectations:

$$\mathbb{E}\left[d_j^{t\mathrm{T}} d_j^t\right] = \sum_{i \in c_j} q_i^j \frac{1}{\left(q_i^j\right)^2} \frac{1}{\left(|c_j|\right)^2} \left\| \nabla_\theta L\left(\varphi\left(x_i^j; \theta^{t-1}\right), x_i^j\right) \right\|^2, \tag{12}$$

$$\mathbb{E}\left[d_j^t\right] = \sum_{i \in c_j} q_i^j \frac{1}{|c_j|} \frac{1}{q_i^j} \nabla_\theta L\left(\varphi\left(x_i^j; \theta^{t-1}\right), x_i^j\right) = \frac{1}{|c_j|} \sum_{i \in c_j} \nabla_\theta L\left(\varphi\left(x_i^j; \theta^{t-1}\right), x_i^j\right). \tag{13}$$

Notice that $\mathbb{E}\left[d_j^t\right]$ is independent of q_i^j and we can ignore it. We are left with $\mathbb{E}\left[d_j^{t\mathrm{T}} d_j^t\right]$ and proceed to minimize the variance following Gopal's solution (details are found in [5]). Finally, the optimal distribution Q^j at the t-th iteration is given by:

$$q_i^j \propto \frac{1}{|c_j|} \left\| \nabla_\theta L\left(\varphi\left(x_i^j; \theta^{t-1}\right), y_i^j\right) \right\|. \tag{14}$$

Intuitively, (3) can be understood as two consecutive selection procedures: first, according to (7) we pick bins which have a larger gradient contribution relative to other bins; then according to (14) we sample the instances with the larger gradient contribution within that bin. The motivation behind this proposal is that these two selection procedures result in more efficient sampling of training data instances than uniform sampling, which should be translated into a reduction of the time required to train a DNN.

3.1 Computational Cost

There are three major problems in computing the probability distributions (7) and (14).

1. For (7), it is impractical to reset the optimal sampling distribution after each iteration. The solution proposed by Gopal [5] is to update p_j every β iterations, which means to re-sample a few training instances from each bin (the appropriate amount of instances depends on the mini-batch size). The downside of this approach is that there is a new hyper-parameter β to be tuned.
2. For (14), computing the gradient norm for an individual instance requires computing a square root for each instance (notice that this is not required in (7)). Katharopoulos & Fleuret [11] show that sampling using the loss exhibits similar variance reducing properties to sampling according to the gradient norm. Using that result, we replace (14) with:

$$q_i^j \propto L\left(\varphi\left(x_i^j; \theta\right), y_i^j\right).$$ (15)

3. The last difficulty is found in computing the gradient norm. Deep Learning models are characterized by having hundreds of thousands or millions of parameters (e.g. *RestNet-50* has 23 million trainable parameters [19]), so that computing the full gradient becomes prohibitive. In order to overcome this obstacle, Katharopoulos & Fleuret [3] derived an upper-bound of the gradient norm:

$$\hat{G}_i \equiv \left\|\nabla_{\theta_t^l} L\left(\varphi\left(x_i^j; \theta^{t-1}\right), y_i^j\right)\right\|^2 \geq \left\|\nabla_\theta L\left(\varphi\left(x_i^j; \theta^{t-1}\right), y_i^j\right)\right\|^2.$$ (16)

where $\nabla_{\theta_t^l} L\left(\varphi\left(x_i^j; \theta^{t-1}\right), y_i^j\right)$ is the gradient w.r.t. the pre-activation outputs of the last layer in a DNN. This upper bound is employed in lieu of the full gradient, enabling the implementation of our proposal.

Algorithm 1: **Improved Adaptive Sampling for Deep Learning**

1.   **Input:** $c_j = \{\{x_i, y_i\}_{i=1}^{N/k}\}_{j=i}^{k}$; epochs; $(\delta_{pbin}, \delta_q) \in (0,1)$; $\beta \in \mathbb{Z}^+$, batch size BS, No. of instances N

2.   **Initialize:** $gc[1, ..., k] \leftarrow \emptyset$; $P[p_1, p_2, ..., p_k] \sim \mathcal{U}$; $Q^j \left[q_1^j, q_2^j, ..., q_{|I_j|}^j\right] \sim \mathcal{U}$

            $t \leftarrow 0$; $l_{(1:N/k)}^{(1:k)} \leftarrow \infty$: l is a k–dimensional array to store loss values.

3.   **For** $epoch = 1$ **to** $epochs$ **do:**

4.   **For** $b = 1$ **to** N/BS **do:**

5.   **For** $s = 1$ **to** BS **do:**

6. $j \sim P$: Sample bin j according to (7).

7. $i \sim Q^j$: Sample instance i according to (14).

8. $l_i^j \leftarrow L(\varphi(x_i^j; \theta), y_i^j)$: Forward pass: compute the loss, store it in array l.

9. d^t : Compute the gradient using (5).

10. $\hat{G}_i$: Compute the gradient upper bound using (16).

11. $gc[j] \leftarrow sg[j] + \hat{G}_i$: Accumulate gradients of bin j

12. $gc[j] \leftarrow gc[j]/ Q^j[i]$: Divide the accumulated gradients by q_i^j

13.   **If** $(t \bmod \beta) = 0$ **then:**

14. $p_j \propto \sqrt{gc[j]}/N$: Re-compute p_j according to (7) $\forall j$.

15. $(p_j)^t \leftarrow \delta_p(p_j)^{t-1} + (1 - \delta_p)(p_j)^t$: Smooth current p_j using previous values.

16. $gc[1, ..., k] \leftarrow 0$

17.   **End if**

18. $t \leftarrow t + 1$

19.   **End for**

20. $d^b \leftarrow \sum_{r=1}^{BS} d^r /BS$: Compute the batch gradient.

21.   Update θ^t using d^b : Backward pass.

22. $q_i^j \propto l_i^j$: Re-compute q_i^j according to (14)

23. $(q_i^j)^t = \delta_q(q_i^j)^{t-1} + (1 - \delta_q)(q_i^j)^t$: Smooth current Q^j using previous values

24.   **End for**

25.   **End for**

26.   **Return:** optimized network parameters θ^*

The pseudocode of our proposal for improved adaptive sampling for training of DL models is given in **Algorithm 1**. During training, the probability distributions P and Q^j may tend to become zero for some bins or some instances, respectively. This behavior causes those bins and instances to never be selected again. To avoid such issues, P and Q^j are smoothed to mitigate the appearance of pronounced high and low values. This introduces two more hyper-parameters δ_p and δ_q, used to modulate the smoothing of P and Q^j respectively (see lines 15 and 23 of Algorithm 1).

4 Experimental Results

We investigate our proposed adaptive sampling on the standard MNIST dataset of hand-written digits (LeCun et al. [17]) with 60,000 training data points. We only conducted our experiments on training data (i.e., no validation or test data was used to evaluate the performance of the network). We used a CNN with two convolution and max-pooling layers, two fully connected (FC) layers, and ReLu activation for all the layers except for the last one (softmax activation, as part of the cost function). We employed Batch

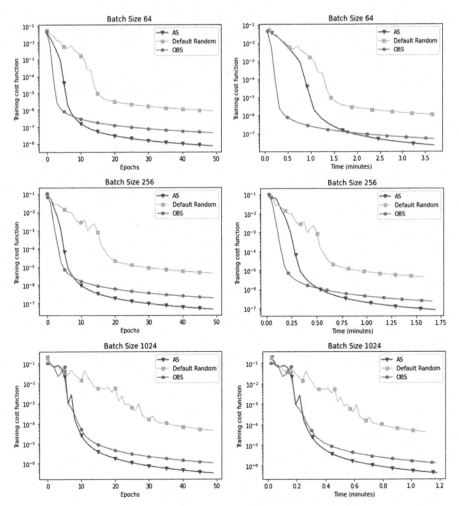

Fig. 1. Comparison of our proposed Adaptive Sampling (AS) vs SGD with uniform sampling (Default Random) and Online Batch Selection (OBS). Convergence curves of Adadelta (learning rate = 1.0, rho = 0.9), while training a CNN for classification of MNIST dataset. Curves shown are the average of the median over three runs.

Normalization on the convolutional layers, dropout of 0.5 on the first FC layer and data normalization. The cost function used was SoftMax cross-entropy loss. All experiments were implemented using the Python library PyTorch and executed on GPUs through Google Colab[1] notebooks. We evaluated our proposal in combination with two different optimizers: Adadelta [18] and Adam [20].

Experiments consisted in training our CNN for 50 epochs and reporting the average loss over three runs. For all the experiments C was set to be the set of class-labels. The hyper-parameters were set as follows: $\beta = 10$ to-ensure enough gradients accumulation

---

[1] https://colab.research.google.com/.

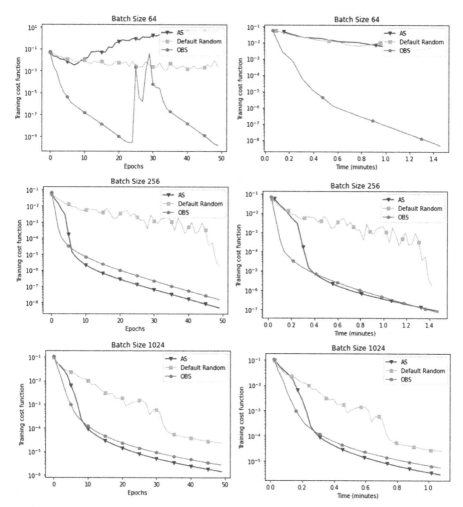

Fig. 2. Comparison of our proposed Adaptive Sampling (AS) vs SGD with uniform sampling (Default Random) and OBS. Convergence curves of Adam (learning rate $= 0.001$, $beta_1 = 0.9$, $beta_2 = 0.999$), while training a CNN for classification of MNIST

without saturating any bin; the smoothing hyper-parameters were adjusted using grid search, with $\delta_p \in (0, 1)$ and $\delta_q \in (0, 1)$; the optimum values obtained were $\delta_p = 0.9$ and $\delta_q = 0.1$. The final hyper-parameter to be set is the size of the mini-batches; we repeated the experiments with three commonly employed batch sizes of 64, 256 and 1024 training instances.

Results are shown in Fig. 1 (Adadelta), Fig. 2 (Adam) and. Our own method is referred to as *Adaptive Sampling* (AS) and is compared against two alternatives: the standard training algorithm, that samples data instances under a uniform distribution referred to as *Default Random*, and the proposal of Loshchilov & Hutter [4] called *Online Batch Selection* (OBS), which we consider a state of the art method to accelerate the training of CNNs. This latter algorithm requires one extra hyper-parameter and it is set to the optimal value reported in [4]: $r, s = 10^8$ from the beginning to the end of training.

5 Discussion

From Fig. 1 it can be observed that the cost function initially decreases faster with AS or OBS than with the default random sampling, which implies a faster convergence of the network parameters towards their optimum values. The most significant convergence occurs within the first 15 epochs (20 for default random); after that, the convergence rates of all three methods slow down, but by that time both AS and OBS have reached at least one order of magnitude below the cost value achieved by default random. This difference is maintained during the rest of the training process. From Fig. 2 it is observed that the cost-function value with AS diverges for a mini-batch size of 64, and reports a faster convergence for mini-batch sizes of 256 and 1024, showing the same behavior as in Fig. 1 with the Adadelta optimizer.

Comparing AS vs OBS in terms of training epochs (left column in Fig. 1) it can be seen that OBS is faster during the first five iterations (except for batch-size of 1024 in which case the two methods are quite similar) but then it slows down smoothly but dramatically. In contrast, AS does not slow down as significantly as OBS, so that by the tenth epoch AS has managed to overcome OBS in all three test scenarios and then maintains this advantage for the rest of the training. Thus, AS appears to be robust to the mini-batch size in combination with Adadelta and it tends to improve the asymptotic convergence over long periods of training.

One explanation for this behavior is found in the relationship between loss-values and gradient-norms. Katharopoulos & Fleuret have shown that small loss-values imply small gradients [11] and they also demonstrated that relatively large loss-values are not well correlated with gradient-norms [3]. Therefore, sampling strategies such as AS and OBS are more advantageous in the beginning of the training, when the losses exhibit large variance and the methods can be highly selective in order to minimize the gradient variance. When the loss-values get smaller as training progresses, the correlation between these and gradient-norms becomes higher, but the advantage of the methods is lost, since the variance decreases naturally.

Nevertheless AS with Adam optimizer presents a higher sensitivity to the mini-batch size. We conjecture that this is due to the probability distribution of the bins being concentrated in a few values for a mini-batch of a relatively small size. In future work we plan to investigate the precise causes of said observed behavior.

In terms of the computing time (right column in Fig. 1) a difference can be observed between the different batch-sizes tested: with a batch size of 64 instances, OBS is clearly faster than AS, but as the batch size is increased to 256 instances this advantage is reduced, and for a batch size of 1024 instances, the speed of both methods are practically the same. We conjecture that AS works well with larger batch-sizes because, as more information is available for each of the bins, the corresponding distribution becomes more stable.

It should be noted that independently of the relative differences between sampling methods, training requires more computing time with larger batch-sizes. However, in our experiments the increase is not very significant, and in the literature it has been suggested that increasing the batch-size can reduce the number of required parameter updates during training, consequently reducing training time [12], so at this point we consider this as an open issue to be further explored.

In theory, the selection of the side information of the instances could be any information just as long as it is informative enough to provide separability between the bins (which would typically correspond to the classes of a classification problem). For instance, Joseph et al. [13] have explored some measures of how informative are the instances; one of them is the entropy of the current model at training iteration.

Finally, we found that AS is highly sensitive to the values of the smoothing parameters. For the probability distribution P of the bins, we found that the optimum smoothing parameter δ_{pbin} is high in comparison with the smoothing parameter δ_q of the probability distributions Q^j of the instances. This can be explained because the cardinality of P is much smaller than the cardinality of each Q^j. For instance, on the MNIST dataset $|P| = 10$ because there are 10 classes in the dataset, while $|Q^j| = N/10$ ($N = 60{,}000$) for each of the j-th distributions. Consequently, the P distribution tends to become unstable due to the accumulation of very few values for each p_j, and a high value of the parameter δ_{pbin} is required to compensate this instability. On the other hand, for each Q^j the opposite happens, and the smoothing parameter δ_q required is smaller.

6 Conclusion and Future Work

A novel method to sample data in order to form mini batches for the training of DNNs has been described. This method is an improved adaptive sampling strategy designed to accelerate the training process, and is based on defining optimal distributions over data bins and instances to achieve a large reduction in the variance of the gradient-norms, which leads to faster convergence of the models. Our proposal was successful when compared against the typically used uniform sampling and also against OBS, which is a similar method in the state of the art. However, this paper represents only an initial study of AS schema for DL models. More advanced approaches might be explored in order to tackle harder classification problems such as those represented by the CIFAR-10 or CIFAR-100 datasets. In addition, some variations of the proposed sampling strategy can be easily implemented, such as switching between sampling w.r.t. the loss and the gradient-norm at different points during the training. These ideas are being considered for future work.

Acknowledgment. This work was partially supported by the National Council of Science and Technology (CONACYT) of Mexico, through Postgraduate Scholarship: 747189 (J. Ávalos) and Research Grants: CÁTEDRAS -2598 (A. Rojas) and CÁTEDRAS-7795 (S.I. Valdez).

References

1. Alom, M.Z., et al.: The history began from AlexNet: a comprehensive survey on deep learning approaches. arXiv:1803.01164 (2018)

2. Wang, L, et al.: Superneurons: dynamic GPU memory management for training deep neural networks. In: 23rd ACM SIGPLAN Symposium on Principles and Practice of Parallel Programming, pp. 41–53 (2018)
3. Katharopoulos, A., Fleuret, F.: Not all samples are created equal: deep learning with importance sampling. In: International Conference on Machine Learning, PMLR, pp. 2525–2534 (2018)
4. Loshchilov, I., Hutter, F.: Online batch selection for faster training of neural networks arXiv: 1511.06343 (2015)
5. Gopal, S.: Adaptive sampling for SGD by exploiting side information. In: International Conference on Machine Learning, PMLR, pp. 364–372 (2016)
6. Fan, Y., Tian, F., Qin, T., Bian, J., Liu, T.Y.: Learning what data to learn. arXiv:1702.08635 (2017)
7. Alain, G., Lamb, A., Sankar, C., Courville, A., Bengio, Y.: Variance reduction in SGD by distributed importance sampling. arXiv:1511.06481 (2015)
8. Zhao, P., Zhang, T.: Stochastic optimization with importance sampling for regularized loss minimization. In: International Conference on Machine Learning, PMLR, pp. 1–9 (2015)
9. Needell, D., Srebro, N., Ward, R.: Stochastic gradient descent, weighted sampling, and the randomized Kaczmarz algorithm. arXiv:1310.5715 (2013)
10. Schaul, T., Quan, J., Antonoglou, I., Silver, D.: Prioritized experience replay. arXiv:1511. 05952 (2015)
11. Katharopoulos, A., Fleuret, F.: Biased importance sampling for deep neural network training. arXiv:1706.00043 (2017)
12. Smith, S.L., Kindermans, P.J., Ying, C., Le, Q.V.: Don't decay the learning rate, increase the batch size. arXiv:1711.00489 (2017)
13. Joseph, K.J., Singh, K., Balasubramanian, V.N.: Submodular batch selection for training deep neural networks. arXiv:1906.08771 (2019)
14. Zhao, P., Zhang, T.: Accelerating minibatch stochastic gradient descent using stratified sampling. arXiv:1405.3080 (2014)
15. Wu, C.Y., Manmatha, R., Smola, A.J., Krahenbuhl, P.: Sampling matters in deep embedding learning. In: Proceedings of the IEEE International Conference on Computer Vision, pp. 2840–2848 (2017)
16. Bouchard, G., Trouillon, T., Perez, J., Gaidon, A.: Online learning to sample. arXiv:1506. 09016 (2015)
17. LeCun, Y., Bottou, L., Bengio, Y., Haffner, P.: Gradient-based learning applied to document recognition. Proc. IEEE 86(11), 2278–2324 (1998)
18. Zeiler, M.D.: ADADELTA: an adaptive learning rate method. arXiv:1212.5701.19 (2012)
19. He, K., Zhang, X., Ren, S., Sun, J.: Deep residual learning for image recognition. In: Proceedings of the IEEE Conference on Computer Vision and Pattern Recognition, pp. 770–778 (2016)
20. Kingma, D.P., Ba, J.: Adam: A method for stochastic optimization. arXiv:1412.6980 (2014)

Graph Representation for Learning the Traveling Salesman Problem

Omar Gutiérrez$^{(\boxtimes)}$, Erik Zamora, and Ricardo Menchaca

Instituto Politécnico Nacional - CIC,
Av. Juan de Dios Batiz S/N, Gustavo A. Madero, 07738 Mexico City, Mexico
ogutierrezd0800@alumno.ipn.mx, ezamorag@ipn.mx, ric@cic.ipn.mx

Abstract. Training deep learning models for solving the Travelling Salesman Problem (TSP) directly on large instances is computationally challenging. An approach to tackle large-scale TSPs is through identifying elements in the model or training procedure that promotes out-of-distribution (OoD) generalization, i.e., generalization to samples larger than those seen in training. The state-of-the-art TSP solvers based on Graph Neural Networks (GNNs) follow different strategies to represent the TSP instances as input graphs. In this paper, we conduct experiments comparing different graph representations finding features that lead to a better OoD generalization.

Keywords: Neural combinatorial optimization · Traveling salesman · Graph neural networks · NP-Hard

1 Introduction

Research on NP-hard combinatorial optimization problems such as the Traveling Salesman Problem (TSP) has been an active area among the scientific community due to its academic relevance and the large variety of industrial applications. Since there is no tractable way to solve these problems optimally at large scales, heuristics or approximation algorithms are the most common approaches to deal with NP-hard problems even when these methods do not guarantee optimal solutions.

In practice, solving TSP instances requires very specialized algorithms and knowledge; an example of this is the well-known state-of-the-art Concorde solver [2]. As an alternative, approximate NP-Hard problems with deep learning models that can learn directly from problem instances is a growing approach [13,16,25]. Recent papers [13,14,17] show similar results than Concorde when dealing with small TSPs (20, 50, or even 100 cities) but less competitive solutions for large-scale instances; moreover, training on large graphs from scratch is hugely time-consuming [12].

As a technique to scale up to large graphs, speed up the learning process or lead to better generalization on larger problems, [12–14] use k-nearest neighbors (k-NN) to incorporate additional information in the inputs graphs. This

© Springer Nature Switzerland AG 2021
E. Roman-Rangel et al. (Eds.): MCPR 2021, LNCS 12725, pp. 153–162, 2021.
https://doi.org/10.1007/978-3-030-77004-4_15

information is added to the representation by building a reduced graph with connections between the k-nearest nodes or embedding the neighborhood information in the complete graph's edge attributes. Some other strategies have been used to represent TSP instances as input graphs for a GNN, for example, using the distance matrix as edge features.

Guided by these ideas, we conduct experiments to compare different graph representations to find attributes that promote generalization. More specifically, the main contribution of this work is to show through empirical comparison which features in the graph constitute a better representation of the problem that lead models trained on small-scale TSP instances to generalize well on large problems.

The rest of the paper is structured as follows. In Sect. 2, we review some recent approaches to solve the TSP, later, in Sect. 3 we describe the problem, the model and the considered graph configurations. Finally, in Sect. 4, we address proposed experiments and discuss results.

2   Related Work

Earlier studies applying neural networks for the TSP include approaches using Hopfield networks [11], Elastic Nets [8] and Deformable Template models [1,9]. More recently, a nominal approach inspired by the advancements in sequence-to-sequence models [21] and attention mechanism [3] arise with the introduction of the Pointer Network [25]. In this model, an encoder-decoder architecture implemented with Long Short-Term Memory units (LSTMs) [10] uses an attention mechanism as a pointer to select at each time step a node of the input sequence as the output, building a TSP tour in an autoregressive way; the model was trained end-to-end in a supervised manner.

Following works in the area improved the obtained results in [25]. Milan et al. [18] incorporate the objective cost in the training procedure and Bello et al. [4] use the Pointer Network to parameterize the probability of a tour via the REINFORCE algorithm [26]. For solving the Vehicle Routing Problem, [19] also used Pointer Networks, however, they replaced the LSTM encoder by simple projections of the inputs and trained the model using policy gradient.

State-of-the-art approaches use graph neural networks [5,6,24] and multi-head attention mechanisms [23] as building blocks for encoder or encoder-decoder architectures. The model proposed by Khalil et al. [14] is trained with a combination of n-steps Q-learning [22] and Q-iteration first [20] to incrementally constructs a tour taking actions determined by a structure2vect graph embedding network [6]; additionally, to scale up to large instances, they build k-NN sparse graphs (with $k = 10$). Deudon et al. [7] use the encoder proposed in [23] and an autoregressive decoder with a pointing mechanism to generate a tour one node at a time; the model is trained via the REINFORCE algorithm taking the d-dimensional embeddings of the node coordinates as inputs.

In Kool et al. [16], a Graph Attention Network [24] encodes the d-dimensional representation of the node coordinates, and an attention-based decoder successively builds the solution; the model is trained end-to-end using the REIN-FORCE procedure with greedy rollout baseline.

Non-autoregressive models have also been studied, as instance, Joshi et al. [13] introduce a non-autoregressive approach by using Graph Convolutional Network (GCN) [5] that outputs an edge adjacency matrix denoting the probabilities of edges occurring on the TSP tour. The model is trained in a supervised manner with the output edge representations linked to the ground-truth TSP tour through a softmax output layer; during test time, the edge predictions are converted to a valid tour using beam search. One of the edge features used as input in this model is the k-NN graph that speeds up the learning process.

Joshi et al. [12] analyzed state-of-the-art end-to-end approaches for TSP to identify aspects that promote OoD generalization. As part of their experiments, they compared full graph training to sparse graph training based on k-NN heuristics, finding that even when both k-NN and $k\%$-NN ($n \times k\%$-NN with n being the number of nodes in the instance) lead to faster convergence on training instance sizes, only the last approach leads to better generalization on large problems than using full graphs.

Beyond [12] that explores k-NN based sparsification heuristics, this work compares different ways to represent TSP instances as input graphs for GNNs, analyzing features in these representations that promote generalization.

3 Methods

3.1 Problem Definition

We focus on the 2D Euclidean TSP. Given a set of city coordinates, the problem is to find the shortest possible route that visits each city exactly once and returns to the origin city. Formally, given a complete graph of n nodes in the two dimensional unit square $s = \{x_i\}_{i=1}^{n}$ with each $x_i \in [0,1]^2$, we aim to find an optimal permutation π over the nodes that minimizes the tour length:

$$L(\pi|s) = \sum_{i=1}^{n} \left\|x_{\pi_i} - x_{\pi_{i+1}}\right\|_2, \tag{1}$$

where $x_{\pi_i} = x_{\pi_{n+1}}$ and $\|\cdot\|_2$ denotes l_2 norm.

3.2 Model

To find elements that promote OoD generalization, Joshi et al. [12] explored recent state-of-the-art architectures and learning paradigms for learning large scale TSP. Based on these results, we take their proposed model which, in a high-level description, works as follows: the Graph Neural Network (GNN) encoder takes graph representation of the TSP instances as input and produces node embeddings. The attention decoder uses these embeddings along with the partial tour generated in previous time steps to produce the sequence π of nodes (predicted tour) one node at a time (Fig. 1). Details are explained below.

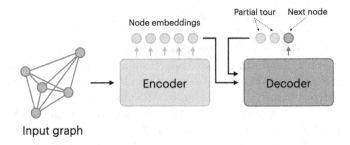

Fig. 1. High-level diagram of model architecture. The encoder receives an input instance of n nodes and produce node embeddings; next, at each time step $t \in \{1, ..., n\}$, the decoder uses these embeddings and the current partial tour to outputs the following node in the solution.

Encoder. An L-layers GNN takes the connections and the d-dimensional representation of the nodes and edges features that define a TSP instance (see Sect. 3.3). We compute the features at layer $\ell + 1$ following an edge gating message passing mechanism with max neighborhood aggregator:

$$h_i^{\ell+1} = h_i^\ell + ReLU\left(BN\left(U^\ell h_i^\ell + max_{j \in \mathcal{N}_i}\left(\sigma\left(e_{ij}^\ell\right) \odot V^\ell h_j^\ell\right)\right)\right), \quad (2)$$

$$e_{ij}^{\ell+1} = e_{ij}^\ell + ReLU\left(BN\left(A^\ell e_{ij}^\ell + B^\ell h_i^\ell + C^\ell h_j^\ell\right)\right), \quad (3)$$

where $h_i^\ell, e_{ij}^\ell \in \mathbb{R}^d$ are respectively the node and edge feature associated with node i and edge ij at layer ℓ; $U^\ell, V^\ell, A^\ell, B^\ell, C^\ell \in \mathbb{R}^{d \times d}$ are learnable parameters, ReLU refers to the rectified linear unit, BN stands for Batch Normalization layer, σ is the sigmoid function, $\mathcal{N}_i$ is the neighborhood of node i (determined by the connections of the graph), and $\odot$ represents the Hadamard product. Each layer has its own learneable parameters.

Decoder. Following [12], we use the autoregressive attention decoder introduced by Kool et al. [16]. At each time step $t \in \{1, ..., n\}$ the decoder builds a context vector h_c^t by concatenating the graph embedding $h_G = \frac{1}{n}\sum_{i=1}^{n} h_i^L$ and the embeddings of the first and last node in the partial tour (d-dimensional learned placeholders v^1 and v^f are used at time $t = 1$):

$$h_c^t = \begin{cases} h_c^t = \left[h_G; h_{\pi_1'}^L; h_{\pi_{t-1}'}^L\right], & t > 1 \\ h_c^t = \left[h_G; v^1; v^f\right], & t = 1, \end{cases} \quad (4)$$

where $[\cdot; \cdot; \cdot]$ represents the horizontal concatenation operator, and $\pi_{t'}'$ is the t'th element of the partial tour π' generated by the decoder at time $t' < t$.

The next step is computing a new context $\hat{h}_c^t$ via a M-headed Multi-Head Attention Mechanism (MHA) [23], with $M = 8$:

$$\hat{h}_c^t = \text{MAH}\left(Q = W_c h_c^t, K = \{h_1^L, ..., h_n^L\}, V = \{h_1^L, ..., h_n^L\}\right), \quad (5)$$

here Q, K, V, that stand for query, key, and value, respectively, are inputs to the MHA, and $W_c \in \mathbb{R}^{3d \times d}$ is a learnable parameter.

Finally, the compatibility $\hat{p}_{ij}$ between the context $\hat{h}_c^t$ and the embedding h_j is computed using a single-head attention mechanism:

$$
\hat{p}_{ij} =
\begin{cases}
C \cdot \tanh \left(\frac{\left(W_Q \hat{h}_c^t \right)^T \left(W_K h_j^L \right)}{\sqrt{d}} \right), & \text{if } j \neq \pi_{t'} \ \forall t' < t \\
-\infty, & \text{otherwise.}
\end{cases}
\tag{6}
$$

The compatibilities $\hat{p}_{ij}$ can be interpreted as unnormalized log-probability (log-its) for each edge e_{ij}; here, $i = \pi'_{t-1}$ is the last node in the current partial tour and j the possible next node in the solution. Visited nodes are masked (this is $\hat{p}_{ij} = -\infty$ if j is already in π') and results are clipped before masking to maintain the values within $[-C, C]$ ($C = 10$) [4,12,16]. The logits are converted to probabilities via a softmax over all edges.

Loss Function. Given the ground-truth TSP tour permutation π^*, at each step t, we minimize the cross-entropy loss between the predicted probability distribution over all edges e_{ij} and the next node in the ground-truth tour π_t^*.

Solution Search. We consider two approaches to building solutions, greedy solutions selecting at each step the most probable edge, and 128 beam search, which maintains the 128 most probable tours.

3.3   Input Graphs

A GNN receives a graph G of n nodes as input. We define G by three elements: a $n \times d_h$ node features matrix H, a $n \times n$ edge features matrix, and a connections matrix A (e.g. the $n \times n$ binary adjacency matrix); each row h_i of H is a d_h-dimensional node feature, while each entry $e_{i,j}$ of E is a d_e-dimensional edge feature. A basic way to represent a TSP instance as G is using the node coordinates as node features, the adjacency matrix of the complete TSP graph as connections, and an edge feature matrix where each e_{ij} is equal to 1 if the edge ij exists in the graph representation, i.e., if $A_{ij} = 1$, and a masked value otherwise (see Fig. 2). In our experiments we refer to this configuration as *full graph*.

In recent models, alternative graph configurations have been used; for instance, instead of complete graphs, [12–14] built k-NN sparse graphs. In the same way, additional information can be useful as node and edge features (e.g., distances between nodes).

Considering the state-of-the-art in deep learning approaches for solving the TSP, we focus this work on the graph configurations summarized in Table 1. In all cases the node coordinates are used as node features, complete graphs and 20%-NN graphs are $n \times n$ matrices with entries ij equal to one if the edge ij exists in the graph representation and zero otherwise, distance matrices are $n \times n$

matrices where each entry ij is the euclidean distance between the node i and j, and finally, to enforce graph structure, we masked the values A_{ij} and E_{ij} if the edge ij does not belong to the graph (when $A_{ij} = 0$). Following the empirical results shown in [12], we select $20\%-$NN graphs as our default graph reduction technique, i.e., connecting each node in the TSP to its $n \times k\%$-nearest neighbors. Figure 2 illustrates some graph configurations.

Table 1. Different TSP graph representations.

Graph name	Connections (A)	Edge features (E)
Full	Complete graph	Complete graph
Full-Dist	Complete graph	Distance matrix
Full-NN	Complete graph	20%-NN graph
NN	20%-NN graph	20%-NN graph
NN-Dist	20%-NN graph	Distance matrix

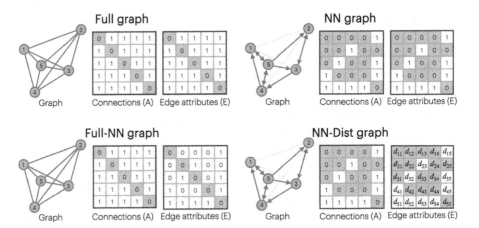

Fig. 2. Examples of input graph configurations. The n-nodes TSP instance is represented by a $n \times n$ matrix A (connections), a $n \times n$ matrix E (edge features) and a $n \times 2$ matrix V (node features) filled with the node coordinates (V is not showed). Shaded values are masked to enforce graph structure.

4 Experiments

4.1 Experimental Details

We conduct experiments to investigate the behavior of the different graph representations of TSP instances detailed in Table 1. Our analysis is mainly focused on identify graph configurations that promotes generalization beyond training size instances.

For each experiment, the model is trained using a particular graph representation as input; following [12], the model learn from small variable TSP graphs (20 to 50 nodes) and is tested on instances from 10 to 200 nodes. The results are compared against a non-learnt furthest insertion heuristic.

Dataset and Training. We use the first 128,000 samples of the training set provided by [12]. This dataset has Euclidean TSP instances with nodes drawn uniformly at random in the 2D unit square; at the same time, each sample i has n_i nodes with n_i sampled uniformly at random from 20 until 50 and groundtruth tours generated by the Concorde solver. In all the experiments, we trained the model for 10 epochs using Adam optimizer [15] with a fixed learning rate of $1e-4$, mini-batches of 128 graphs and clipping the L2 norm of the gradients to 1.0.

Model Hyperparameters. Across all experiments, we use the same model configuration: a 3-layers encoder with max aggregation function and Batch Normalization with learnable affine parameters using batch statistics; a 8-heads decoder with $tanh$ logits clipped to $C = 10$ [4,7]; and finally, we set to $d = 128$ the embedding/hidden dimensions in both encoder and decoder.

Evaluation. We follow the evaluation procedure described in [12], comparing experiments on a held-out test set of 25,600 TSP samples, consisting of 1,280 samples each of TSP instances with size 10, 20, 30, and so on until 200 nodes. As it was done in [12,13,16], we evaluate performance using the optimality gap w.r.t. the Concorde solver formulated as $\frac{1}{m} \sum_{i=1}^{m} \left(\frac{\hat{l}_i}{l_i} - 1 \right)$ where $\hat{l}_i$ is the ith predicted tour length, l_i the corresponding optimal solution and m the number of test instances. Each experiment was tested using greedy solutions and 128-width beam search.

4.2 Results

Results for greedy and beam search solutions are reported in Fig. 3 and Fig. 4, respectively. Both graphs show the optimality gap as the TSP size increase along with the 99% confidence interval.

Figure 3 indicates that, excluding the model trained with Full-NN graphs, all approaches have similar performance. In general, the NN graph is slightly better than the others. These results confirmed the work in [12], building 20%-NN

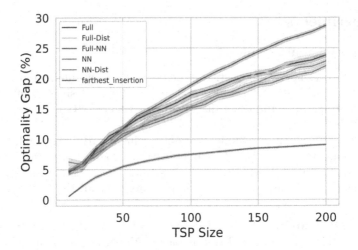

Fig. 3. Testing graph configurations with greedy decoding.

sparse graphs is a better choice than complete graphs to promote OoD generalization. Results also suggest that, in greedy solutions, using the distances in the
edge attributes is a good option for complete graphs but not for reduced graphs.
Results also show that despite graph configuration, the non-learned heuristic
outperforms the model's greedy solution.

Figure 4 illustrates that, whenever beam search is used, learning from complete graphs using 20%-NN as edge attributes (Full-NN graphs) produces worse
results than other graph configurations. In contrast with greedy solutions,
our experiments suggest that building 20%-NN reduced graphs with distance

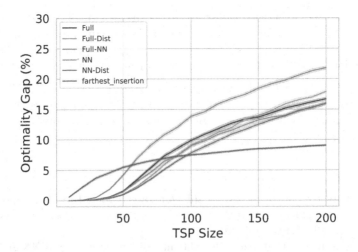

Fig. 4. Testing graph configurations with 128 beam search decoding.

attributes (NN-Dist) is in general the best option. Furthermore, it is clear that using NN-Dist graphs as inputs helps the model to get better performance than the farthest insertion heuristic with instances from 10 to 90 nodes even when the model was trained on instances with 20–50 nodes.

5 Conclusion

The state-of-the-art models based on GNNs for solving the TSP follow different strategies to represent the input graphs. Since training models directly on large TSP instances is computationally challenging, we performed a study comparing different approaches to define input graphs that promote generalization to instances larger than those seen in training.

In all cases, the baseline model was trained on small-scale instances (20 to 50 nodes) and tested on instances of size 10 to 200 using greedy solutions and beam search. The experiments support that the strategy followed to build the graph representation impacts the learning process; while some added features benefit the model, others drastically deteriorate performance. In general, if the solution is greedy, the model trained using 20%-NN reduced graphs (NN graphs) gets better performance across all TSP sizes. In contrast, if a beam search solution scheme is applied (which is the standard procedure in state-of-the-art models), 20%-NN graphs with the distance matrix used as edge attributes (NN-Dist graphs) are a better option. This last graph representation outperforms the farthest insertion heuristic for instances from 10 to 90 nodes.

Acknowledgement. R. Menchaca and E. Zamora would like to acknowledge the support provided by CIC-IPN in carrying out this research. This work was economically supported by SIP-IPN (grant numbers 20211096, 20210316). O. Gutiérrez acknowledges CONACYT for the scholarship granted towards pursuing his postgraduate studies.

References

1. Angeniol, B., Vaubois, G.D.L.C., Le Texier, J.Y.: Self-organizing feature maps and the travelling salesman problem. Neural Netw. **1**(4), 289–293 (1988)
2. Applegate, D., Bixby, R., Chvatal, V., Cook, W.: Concorde TSP solver (2006)
3. Bahdanau, D., Cho, K., Bengio, Y.: Neural machine translation by jointly learning to align and translate. arXiv preprint arXiv:1409.0473 (2014)
4. Bello, I., Pham, H., Le, Q.V., Norouzi, M., Bengio, S.: Neural combinatorial optimization with reinforcement learning. arXiv preprint arXiv:1611.09940 (2016)
5. Bresson, X., Laurent, T.: Residual gated graph convnets. arXiv preprint arXiv:1711.07553 (2017)
6. Dai, H., Dai, B., Song, L.: Discriminative embeddings of latent variable models for structured data. In: International Conference on Machine Learning, pp. 2702–2711 (2016)
7. Deudon, M., Cournut, P., Lacoste, A., Adulyasak, Y., Rousseau, L.-M.: Learning heuristics for the TSP by policy gradient. In: van Hoeve, W.-J. (ed.) CPAIOR 2018. LNCS, vol. 10848, pp. 170–181. Springer, Cham (2018). https://doi.org/10.1007/978-3-319-93031-2_12

8. Durbin, R., Willshaw, D.: An analogue approach to the travelling salesman problem using an elastic net method. Nature **326**(6114), 689–691 (1987)
9. Fort, J.: Solving a combinatorial problem via self-organizing process: an application of the Kohonen algorithm to the traveling salesman problem. Biol. Cybern. **59**(1), 33–40 (1988)
10. Hochreiter, S., Schmidhuber, J.: Long short-term memory. Neural Comput. **9**(8), 1735–1780 (1997)
11. Hopfield, J.J., Tank, D.W.: "neural" computation of decisions in optimization problems. Biol. Cybern. **52**(3), 141–152 (1985)
12. Joshi, C.K., Cappart, Q., Rousseau, L.M., Laurent, T., Bresson, X.: Learning TSP requires rethinking generalization. arXiv preprint arXiv:2006.07054 (2020)
13. Joshi, C.K., Laurent, T., Bresson, X.: An efficient graph convolutional network technique for the travelling salesman problem. arXiv preprint arXiv:1906.01227 (2019)
14. Khalil, E., Dai, H., Zhang, Y., Dilkina, B., Song, L.: Learning combinatorial optimization algorithms over graphs. In: Advances in Neural Information Processing Systems, pp. 6348–6358 (2017)
15. Kingma, D.P., Ba, J.: Adam: a method for stochastic optimization. arXiv preprint arXiv:1412.6980 (2014)
16. Kool, W., Van Hoof, H., Welling, M.: Attention, learn to solve routing problems! arXiv preprint arXiv:1803.08475 (2018)
17. Ma, Q., Ge, S., He, D., Thaker, D., Drori, I.: Combinatorial optimization by graph pointer networks and hierarchical reinforcement learning. arXiv preprint arXiv:1911.04936 (2019)
18. Milan, A., Rezatofighi, S., Garg, R., Dick, A., Reid, I.: Data-driven approximations to np-hard problems. In: Proceedings of the AAAI Conference on Artificial Intelligence, vol. 31 (2017)
19. Nazari, M., Oroojlooy, A., Snyder, L., Takác, M.: Reinforcement learning for solving the vehicle routing problem. In: Advances in Neural Information Processing Systems, pp. 9839–9849 (2018)
20. Riedmiller, M.: Neural fitted Q iteration – first experiences with a data efficient neural reinforcement learning method. In: Gama, J., Camacho, R., Brazdil, P.B., Jorge, A.M., Torgo, L. (eds.) ECML 2005. LNCS (LNAI), vol. 3720, pp. 317–328. Springer, Heidelberg (2005). https://doi.org/10.1007/11564096_32
21. Sutskever, I., Vinyals, O., Le, Q.V.: Sequence to sequence learning with neural networks. Adv. Neural Inf. Process. Syst. **27**, 3104–3112 (2014)
22. Sutton, R.S., Barto, A.G., et al.: Introduction to Reinforcement Learning, vol. 135. MIT press Cambridge (1998)
23. Vaswani, A., et al.: Attention is all you need. In: Advances in Neural Information Processing Systems, pp. 5998–6008 (2017)
24. Veličković, P., Cucurull, G., Casanova, A., Romero, A., Lio, P., Bengio, Y.: Graph attention networks. arXiv preprint arXiv:1710.10903 (2017)
25. Vinyals, O., Fortunato, M., Jaitly, N.: Pointer networks. Adv. Neural Inf. Process. Syst. **28**, 2692–2700 (2015)
26. Williams, R.J.: Simple statistical gradient-following algorithms for connectionist reinforcement learning. Mach. Learn. **8**(3–4), 229–256 (1992)

Satellite Imagery Classification Using Shallow and Deep Learning Approaches

Michelle Sainos-Vizuett$^{(\boxtimes)}$ⓘ and Irvin Hussein Lopez-Navaⓘ

Centro de Investigación Científica y de Educación Superior de Ensenada (CICESE),
22860 Ensenada, Baja California, Mexico
sainos@cicese.edu.mx, hussein@cicese.mx
https://www.cicese.edu.mx/

Abstract. Recent advances in remote sensing technology and high-resolution satellite imagery offer great possibilities for understanding the earth's surfaces. However, satellite image classification is a challenging problem due to the high variability inherent in satellite data. For this purpose, two learning approaches are proposed and compared for classifying a large-scale dataset including different types of land-use and land-cover surfaces (Eurosat). Traditional (shallow) machine learning models and deep learning models are built by using a set of features extracted from the satellite images for both approaches and using the RGB images for deep models. The best F1-score obtained by the shallow approach was 0.87, while for the deep approach it was 0.91. No significant difference was found in these results; however, significant improvements can be made by exploring the deep approach in greater depth.

Keywords: Satellite images · Satellite imagery classification · Image classification · Land use classification · Land cover classification · Remote sensing · Deep learning

1 Introduction

Recent advances in remote sensing technology and high-resolution satellite imagery offers great possibilities not only for understanding the earth's surfaces but also help in decision-making [19]. Satellite imagery classification is useful for a wide variety of applications such as urban planning or development, agriculture, disaster recovery, environmental impact tasks, among others. Satellite images commonly require processing to obtain high-level information, which implies segmenting and labeling them according to semantics [20]. For instance, land-use and land-cover represent physical land type or how a land is used, e.g., agriculture and buildings, respectively [8]. In addition, satellite image classification is a challenging problem due to the high variability inherent in satellite data [2]. This leads to high intra-class compactness, i.e. the images of the same class

The first author was supported by the Mexican National Council for Science and Technology (CONACYT), under the grant number 28602.

ⓒ Springer Nature Switzerland AG 2021
E. Roman-Rangel et al. (Eds.): MCPR 2021, LNCS 12725, pp. 163–172, 2021.
https://doi.org/10.1007/978-3-030-77004-4_16

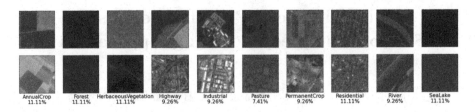

Fig. 1. Sample images of the 10 classes belonging to the EuroSat dataset.

can be very different, and there is low inter-class separability, i.e. the images of different classes can be confused with each other. Recently, the image classification task has been approached from two perspectives: (i) through the feature extraction process prior to being used in the construction of classification models, and (ii) automatic feature extraction for deep learning architectures. The first approach, shallow learning, can be further subdivided into supervised and unsupervised learning. Supervised learning, require carefully selected handcrafted features and substantial amounts of labeled data; on the other hand, purely unsupervised approaches are not able to learn the higher order dependencies inherent in the classification problem [2]. Both learning techniques have been used in the classification of satellite imagery [13,16]. The second approach, deep learning, is the state of the art in many classification tasks on satellite images since it provides a robust approach on the extraction of image features [21]. Overall, convolutional neural networks (CNN's) have great results on image classification tasks [10], however shallow learning approach is usually faster in the training and testing process. Whereas it cannot be claimed that deep learning is better than shallow learning on every problem, there has been evidence of a benefit when the task is complex enough, and there is enough data to capture that complexity [12]. This study aimed to answer the following research question: Is the shallow learning approach still competitive when classifying satellite imagery versus the deep learning approach?

2   Dataset

In order to classify satellite imagery based on models of both shallow and deep learning approaches, a large-scale dataset including different types of surfaces was selected[1]. The Eurosat dataset contains 27,000 labelled images that correspond to 10 different classes, as shown in Fig. 1. Notice that there are some classes that are similar to each other, for instance the elements of the class Highway are easily confused as Industrial or Residential. It can also be noted the high variability of images between the same classes. Each class corresponds to a different land-use or land-cover, ranging each class from 2000 to 3000 images; the proportion of instances is shown in Fig. 1. Land-use is defined as a series of operations on land with the intention to obtain products or benefits through

---

[1] https://github.com/phelber/eurosat

using land resources (e.g. permanent crop); and land-cover is defined as the vegetation or constructions which occur on the earth surface (e.g. industrial). The benchmark for this land-use and land-over classification is shown in [8], the average accuracy reached using a pre-trained CNN is 98.57%. The architecture used is the ResNet50 [7] that consist of 50 convolutional layers joined with a classifier. This model is known to be very effective in the image classification task, since it has been trained with robust datasets, such as ImageNet [5]. In contrast, the purpose of this study is to compare and evaluate traditional machine learning models with respect to deep learning models using a set of image features extracted from the satellite images for both approaches, and using the RGB images for deep learning. For the aim of this work, the dataset was divided using the hold-out validation technique (assigning 20% of the images to the test set and 80% to the training set). Furthermore, the training image set was divided in order to perform a 10-fold cross validation.

3   Feature Extraction

Imagery classification requires information that better discriminates between the classes, either automatically using the images or manually using specific features. The latter consists of extracting and selecting the most relevant features. Feature extraction step takes the distinct components from the images such as edges, corners, among others, which can be used to match the similarity for estimation of relative transformation between the images [14]. In this process the features extracted are added to a feature vector comprising both local and global features:

- Global color features (histogram of color). The main advantages of the color features is that they are relatively powerful in separating images from each other, they also are independent of the image size and orientation [14]. The color histogram analyzes every statistical color frequency in an image [1]. A major drawback for this feature is that is high-dimensional since extract the counts of the 256 intensity values of grey on every band of the image. Also, it is sensitive to noise, i.e., two different images with similar color distribution lead to similar histograms if they have the same exposure to light.
- Global texture features (Haralick texture). This kind of feature can be attributed to almost everything in nature, and can be extracted by computing the pixel statistics or finding the local pixel structures in original image domain. Gray Level Co-occurrence Matrix (GLCM) is a statistical method for examining texture features that consider the spatial relationship of pixels [14]. The statistical properties of the co-ocurrence matrices can serve as textural features. Haralick proposes 28 kinds of textural features each extracted from the GLCM. For this study we only use the first 13 features since the last features are normally considered to be unstable [4].
- Global shape features (Hu moments). Shape usually encodes simple geometrical forms such as straight lines with different directions. Hu [14], proposes seven properties related to connected regions that are invariant to rotation, scaling and translation.

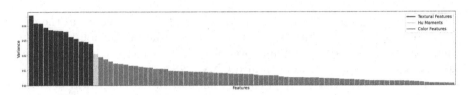

Fig. 2. The top 85 most relevant features. These features correspond to texture and color features mainly and Hu moments

- Histogram of oriented gradients (HOG). The HOG descriptor counts the number of occurrences of gradient orientation in a detection window [22]. It basically computes the horizontal and vertical directions of the image to obtain the gradient magnitudes and angles. Then the image is divided into small cells. The gradient magnitude is voted into different orientation bins and adjacent cells are grouped into blocks.

3.1   Feature Selection (FS)

After the extraction process, a feature vector with 3123 local and global features is computed from the training dataset. The next step is focused on discarding the less useful features for the classification task. There are three general classes of feature selection algorithms: filters, embedded, and wrapper algorithms. The wrapper methods rely on the information about feature relevance obtained from some classification method [9] and therefore may use deeper in-sight in data than filters. Figure 2 shows the 85 most important features according to the wrapper method. In this study we use Random Forest [3] and AdaBoost [6] algorithms to find the most relevant features. To choose the final set of features we selected the 85 features that match for both of the algorithms. These selected features have a cumulative variance of 97.49%. Figure 2 shows that the majority of the 85 features selected correspond to the histogram of color but the most important ones are from Haralick texture; there is also a Hu moment of high importance. There are no HOG descriptors in the top 85 because local features contain more variability and are highly in-homogeneous for images of the same class.

4   Imagery Classification

This section describes the proposed models for the classification of satellite imagery based on shallow learning (Sect. 4.1) and deep learning (Sect. 4.2).

4.1   Shallow Learning Approach

For this approach, ensemble algorithms were used due to the complexity of the task. Ensemble algorithms combine several weak learners to produce a better estimation on the classification [15]. Bagging methodologies (Random Forest) are especially good at reducing the high variance, whilst Boosting models

(AdaBoost) reduce high bias. The following models are built using the selected features described in Subsect. 3.1.

Random Forest (RF + FS). This model works as an ensemble classifier that produces many classification (CART)-like trees, where each tree is grown with a different bootstrapped sample of the training data, and approximately one third of the training data are left out in the construction of each tree [15]. This classifier is particularly good at handling high dimensional and non-normally distributed data, which makes it a great option for the image classification problem. The optimal number of learners converge around 100 trees according to an accuracy vs. number of learners analysis. The number of minimum levels of each tree is around 15 to achieve a high variance result for every decision tree.

AdaBoost (ADA + FS). Boosting is an approach of machine learning based on the idea of creating a highly accurate prediction rule by combining many relatively weak and inaccurate rules. AdaBoost classifier combines weak learners (CART trees) into a weighted voting machine. The AdaBoost algorithm of Freund and Schapire [6] was the first practical boosting algorithm. The optimal number of learners for this algorithm is around 150 according to an accuracy vs number of learners analysis. In contrast to the random forest model, in this boosting model we proposed the maximum number of levels for each tree to be 5 to ensure a high bias result for each decision tree.

4.2   Deep Learning Approach

For the deep learning approach we focused on using two different techniques: using the features extracted and selected in Subsect. 3.1 to feed a CNN, and using a pre-trained neural network model (ResNet50).

Convolutional Neural Network (CNN + FS). A CNN usually contains convolutional layers, pooling layers, batch normalizations, fully connected layers and, if the task is multi-class, a softmax layer. The convolutional and pooling layers are used for the feature extraction. The fully connected and softmax layers usually are regarded as the classifier. The feature extractor is connected to the classifier. According to [11], the design of a convolutional neural network often include: image pre-processing or feature extraction, selecting the activation function for each layer, normalizations between layers to avoid overfitting. In this case, the feature extraction and selection is done previously as specified in Sect. 3, i.e. the proposed neural network receives as input an array that contains the 85 features extracted. The model consists of a series of convolutional and dense layers as shown in Fig. 3(a). The model was trained for 200 epochs for each of the 10 folds. The convolutional layers employ a filter with a receptive field of 3×3, 1 or 2 pixel stride and 0 pixel padding. For the classifier, a dense layer was connected with 128 neurons to a softmax layer with 10 neurons (one for each class). The activation function used was ReLU [17] to reduce gradient diffusion. Dropout and batch normalization layers were used to reduce overfitting and local response normalization. As shown in Fig. 3(b), there is practically no overfitting in the learning curves.

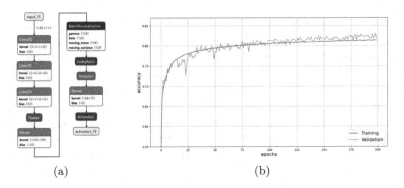

(a)   (b)

Fig. 3. CNN model: a) Configuration of the model; b) Learning curves of the model proposed from the training dataset.

Pre-trained ResNet50. Microsoft Residual Network model (ResNet) [7], tries to solve two main problems: vanishing gradient and degradation. The vanishing of the gradient is still an open problem which eventually leads the model to stop learning. Layers of a neural network learn high or low level features of the images while being trained. ResNet models use ReLU activations for a faster convergence. ResNet50 is a 50 residual layer network which has proven to be one of the most effective model for image classification. As a transfer learning strategy, a base network architecture is previously trained on a base dataset in order to adjust the weights and biases of that model. Once the feature extractor has been trained, the knowledge of this model (i.e. learned weights and biases) can be transferred to some other model to accomplish a similar task. This process works if the features are suitable for both base and target tasks [18]. ResNet models can take weeks to train on modern software so using pre-trained models have shown to be a great option both in computational cost and in performance for image classification tasks. For this work, we used the ResNet50 model pre-trained with the ImageNet training weights, and feeding the network with the images, unlike the network described in the previous Subsection. The model was trained 200 epochs per fold. Also, no data augmentation was considered to get a fair comparison against the former models.

5   Results

In order to evaluate the classification models a 10-fold cross validation strategy was used, using the 80% of the dataset for training. The testing scores were performed on the test dataset (the remaining 20%). Table 1 shows the performance of the four models in terms of average accuracy and average F1-score (testing set), computational time measured in minutes (training and testing sets) and AUC. Despite the ResNet50 model shows the best accuracy and F1-score it takes the most time for training (almost 5.2 h). Similarly, the AdaBoost model built with FS shows a similar accuracy and F1-score as ResNet50 but it takes

Table 1. Overall performance (standard deviation) of the models using the test set. Train times (min) with the FS includes the feature extraction of the 80 most relevant features and the classification times.

	Test accuracy	Test F1-score	Train time	Test time	AUC
RF + FS	0.86 (0.09)	0.86 (0.08)	93.0	0.03	0.92
ADA + FS	0.87 (0.10)	0.87 (0.09)	114.5	4.57	0.88
CNN + FS	0.80 (0.15)	0.83 (0.15)	231.4	0.01	0.92
ResNet50	0.91 (0.04)	0.91 (0.08)	312.5	0.91	0.94

significantly less time to train (1.9 h) than ResNet50. The Random forest model performs similar to AdaBoost but it's more efficient in computational time since it has the advantage of paralelization. Finally, the CNN using FS takes 3.85 h to train the models and has the worst average accuracy and F1-score above all the models. Table 2 shows the results (accuracy and F1-score) of each model per class. The class Highway has the lower performance scores for all classifiers. On the other hand, Forest and Sealake are the best classified among all the models. Random forest and Adaboost share similar metrics overall, in particular, SeaLake scores 0.98 of F1-measure from both shallow learning classifiers, which is the highest result of this study. The main difference between these two models is given by the computational cost on training and testing (see Table 1). In comparison to the above models, the CNN + FS shows a higher standard deviation for each metric. This means that it classifies certain classes very well and others very poorly, e.g. Annual Crop class scores 0.45 of F1-measure which is the lowest result of this study. Regarding the residual neural network model using the raw images (ResNet50), it has the highest values for central tendency and the lowest for dispersion, which indicates that it is the most robust model. Figure 4(a) shows the F1-score achieved by each model per class. Random Forest, AdaBoost and CNN using feature selection are slightly better at correctly classifying SeaLake, Annual Crop and Forest images than the ResNet50. In this regard, ResNet50 is much better at correctly classifying Highway, Herbaceous Vegetation, Industrial, Pasture, Permanent Crop and River. Additionally, Fig. 4(b) summarize the F1-score for the 10 classes allowing a comparison between the models. The CNN model using FS has higher variability of the F1-score over classes. On the other hand, the ResNet50 model using transfer learning shows lowest dispersion. The Random forest and AdaBoost model show a similar distribution. Finally, Fig. 5 shows the confusion matrices for the best shallow and deep learning models: AdaBoost and pre-trained ResNet50. In particular, Highway and River are the worst classified for AdaBoost. In fact, Highway class also performs poorly with Resnet50. As previously introduced in Fig. 1, Highway class has high intra-class variability and visually can be confused with Residential or even Industrial. The images from River class also contain crops of Highway and Pasture so it is comprehensive that the models confuse these classes. It is important to highlight that a large number of instances were misclassified as Annual Crop by ResNet50.

Table 2. Comparison of the models per class on the test dataset

Class	ADA + FS		RF + FS		CNN + FS		ResNet50	
	F1-Score	Acc	F1-Score	Acc	F1-Score	Acc	F1-Score	Acc
AnnualCrop	0.87	0.87	0.85	0.86	0.45	0.6	0.76	0.84
Forest	0.98	0.98	0.96	0.97	0.99	0.97	0.96	0.96
HerbaceousVegetation	0.9	0.87	0.86	0.85	0.86	0.76	0.95	0.92
Highway	0.68	0.69	0.7	0.66	0.71	0.54	0.87	0.84
Industrial	0.92	0.92	0.9	0.91	0.92	0.91	0.93	0.93
Pasture	0.79	0.82	0.79	0.81	0.84	0.83	0.91	0.91
PermanentCrop	0.78	0.79	0.77	0.78	0.82	0.69	0.88	0.88
Residential	0.96	0.96	0.94	0.95	0.92	0.94	0.94	0.95
River	0.75	0.74	0.76	0.74	0.78	0.7	0.9	0.88
SeaLake	0.98	0.98	0.98	0.97	0.97	0.97	0.97	0.93
Average	0.87	0.87	0.86	0.86	0.83	0.8	0.91	0.91
σ	0.10	0.09	0.08	0.09	0.15	0.15	0.08	0.04

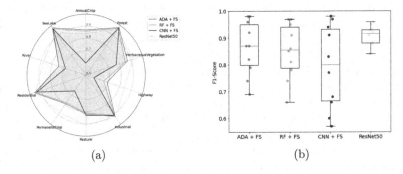

(a)   (b)

Fig. 4. Model comparisons: a) F1-score per class for each model; b) Variability comparison between models.

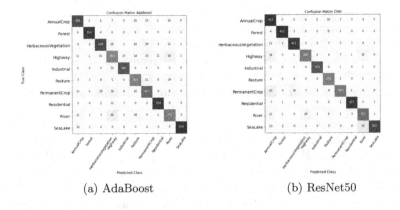

(a) AdaBoost   (b) ResNet50

Fig. 5. Confusion matrices of the best models tested over the test dataset.

6   Conclusions

Overall, ResNet50 outperforms the other models in the satellite imagery classification task in terms of average F1-score, average accuracy and lower variability. Otherwise, in terms of computational cost while training, the Random forest and AdaBoost models outperform the ResNet50. SeaLake, AnnualCrop and Forest classes are slightly better classified by AdaBoost, Random forest and CNN using feature selection. The reason of this behaviour is because the histogram of color represents the most important features to classify this type of images visually. ResNet50 is actually better classifying images with higher variability intra-class. Random forest and AdaBoost models (shallow learning) behaved similarly in terms of scores. The real difference between the two models is shown in the computational time of both training and test data. Random forest model outperforms any other in terms of computational speed. CNN using feature selection model had the lower performance out of all the models. In this work we did not achieve the state of the art of this task [8]. Possibly because we did not perform data augmentation to be able to compare these models as fairly as possible. The aim of this work was mainly to compare the shallow and deep learning approaches to show how the feature extraction and selection on image classification task is still relevant nowadays. Based on the results we still believe the shallow learning models allows to properly classify certain images, even better than techniques based on deep learning, even tough the results indicate that there are a large number of features that can be automatically extracted using deep learning approach. This last issue is important since for some applications it is practically impossible to determine which features may be appropriate to identify them in real-time, for example, the early detection of fires. Thereby, the next step is to explore in-depth architectures that allow combining the most important features found with the raw images, besides incorporating a data augmentation strategy.

References

1. Bagri, N., Johari, P.K.: A comparative study on feature extraction using texture and shape for content based image retrieval. Int. J. Adv. Sci. Technol. 80(4), 41–52 (2015)
2. Basu, S., Ganguly, S., Mukhopadhyay, S., DiBiano, R., Karki, M., Nemani, R.: DeepSat: a learning framework for satellite imagery. In: International Conference on Advances in Geographic Information Systems, pp. 1–10 (2015)
3. Breiman, L.: Random forests. Mach. Learn. 45(1), 5–32 (2001)
4. Coelho, L.P.: Mahotas: open source software for scriptable computer vision. J. Open Res. Softw. (2012)
5. Deng, J., Dong, W., Socher, R., Li, L.J., Li, K., Fei-Fei, L.: ImageNet: a large-scale hierarchical image database. In: 2009 IEEE Conference on Computer Vision and Pattern Recognition, pp. 248–255. IEEE (2009)
6. Freund, Y., Schapire, R.E.: A decision-theoretic generalization of on-line learning and an application to boosting. J. Comput. Syst. Sci. 55(1), 119–139 (1997)

7. He, K., Zhang, X., Ren, S., Sun, J.: Deep residual learning for image recognition. In: IEEE Conference on Computer Vision and Pattern Recognition, pp. 770–778 (2016)

8. Helber, P., Bischke, B., Dengel, A., Borth, D.: EuroSat: a novel dataset and deep learning benchmark for land use and land cover classification. IEEE J. Sel. Top. Appl. Earth Observ. Remote Sens. 12(7), 2217–2226 (2019)

9. Kohavi, R., John, G.H., et al.: Wrappers for feature subset selection. Artif. Intell. 97(1–2), 273–324 (1997)

10. Krizhevsky, A., Sutskever, I., Hinton, G.E.: ImageNet classification with deep convolutional neural networks. Commun. ACM 60(6), 84–90 (2017)

11. Lai, Z., Deng, H.: Medical image classification based on deep features extracted by deep model and statistic feature fusion with multilayer perceptron. Comput. Intell. Neurosci. 2018 (2018)

12. Larochelle, H., Bengio, Y., Louradour, J., Lamblin, P.: Exploring strategies for training deep neural networks. J. Mach. Learn. Res. 10(1) (2009)

13. Ma, L., Li, M., Ma, X., Cheng, L., Du, P., Liu, Y.: A review of supervised object-based land-cover image classification. ISPRS J. Photogramm. Remote. Sens. 130, 277–293 (2017)

14. Medhi, S., Ahmed, C., Gayan, R.: A study on feature extraction techniques in image processing. Int. J. Comput. Sci. Eng. 4(7), 89–93 (2016)

15. Millard, K., Richardson, M.: On the importance of training data sample selection in random forest image classification: a case study in peatland ecosystem mapping. Remote Sens. 7(7), 8489–8515 (2015)

16. Moya, L., Marval Perez, L.R., Mas, E., Adriano, B., Koshimura, S., Yamazaki, F.: Novel unsupervised classification of collapsed buildings using satellite imagery, hazard scenarios and fragility functions. Remote Sens. 10(2), 296 (2018)

17. Nair, V., Hinton, G.E.: Rectified linear units improve restricted Boltzmann machines. In: International Conference on Machine Learning, pp. 807–814 (2010)

18. Quattoni, A., Collins, M., Darrell, T.: Transfer learning for image classification with sparse prototype representations. In: IEEE Conference on Computer Vision and Pattern Recognition, pp. 1–8. IEEE (2008)

19. Verpoorter, C., Kutser, T., Seekell, D.A., Tranvik, L.J.: A global inventory of lakes based on high-resolution satellite imagery. Geophys. Res. Lett. 41(18), 6396–6402 (2014)

20. Yao, X., Han, J., Cheng, G., Qian, X., Guo, L.: Semantic annotation of high-resolution satellite images via weakly supervised learning. IEEE Trans. Geosci. Remote Sens. 54(6), 3660–3671 (2016)

21. Zhang, P., Ke, Y., Zhang, Z., Wang, M., Li, P., Zhang, S.: Urban land use and land cover classification using novel deep learning models based on high spatial resolution satellite imagery. Sensors 18(11), 3717 (2018)

22. Zhou, W., Gao, S., Zhang, L., Lou, X.: Histogram of oriented gradients feature extraction from raw Bayer pattern images. IEEE Trans. Circuits Syst. II Express Briefs 67(5), 946–950 (2020)

Skeletal Age Estimation from Hand Radiographs Using Ensemble Deep Learning

Divyan Hirasen, Verosha Pillay, Serestina Viriri$^{(\boxtimes)}$, and Mandlenkosi Gwetu

School of Mathematics, Statistics and Computer Science,
University of KwaZulu-Natal, Durban, South Africa
{viriris,gwetum}@ukzn.ac.za

Abstract. This paper presents experimental results obtained from using weakly tuned deep learning models as feature extraction mechanisms which are used to train regressor models for skeletal age estimation from hand radiographs of the RSNA Bone Age dataset. By leveraging transfer learning, deep learning models were initialised with the ImageNet dataset weights and then tuned for 5 epochs on the target RSNA Bone Age dataset. Thereafter, the deep learned models were used to extract features from the dataset to train various regressor models. The DenseNet201 combined with a Bayesian Ridge classifier obtained a MAE of 9.38. With the exploration of ensemble boosting and stacking, the performance improved to 8.66 months. These results suggest that weakly tuned deep learning models can be successfully used as feature extraction mechanisms with the advantage of not having to train the deep learning model excessively.

Keywords: Age estimation · Hand radiographs · Machine learning · Transfer learning · Convolutional neural network

1 Introduction

The method for assessing the bone age using left hand wrist radiographs is widely accepted due to its minimum radiation exposure, simplicity and choice of ossification centres for evaluation of maturity [5]. Any discrepancy between the chronological and assessed skeletal age of an individual can indicate abnormalities in the skeletal development [6]. Bone age assessment (BAA) methods usually start with taking a single X-ray image of the left hand, from the wrist to fingertips, as shown in Fig. 2 [3]. Bones in the X-ray image are compared with radiographs in a standardized atlas of bone development. The BAA considers three vital factors: The presence of primary and secondary centres of ossification, the development of both centres and lastly, the timing of the union of primary and secondary centres [4]. These bone age atlases are based on large numbers of radiographs collected from male and female individuals generally of the same ethnic group [3].

© Springer Nature Switzerland AG 2021
E. Roman-Rangel et al. (Eds.): MCPR 2021, LNCS 12725, pp. 173–183, 2021.
https://doi.org/10.1007/978-3-030-77004-4_17

BAA had been an ideal target for automated image evaluation since the quantity of radiographs in hospitals is increasing and with standardised reports containing clear information on gender and age labels. This combination is an appealing target for machine learning, as it sidesteps many labour-intensive pre-processing steps such as using Natural Language Processing (NLP) to process radiology reports and extract information to be used as labels. In the domain of medical imaging, convolutional neural networks (CNN) have been successfully applied on a rage of problems such as diabetic retinopathy screening [7], breast cancer histology image analysis [8] and bone disease prediction [10], to name a few. Furthermore, transfer learning-based approaches demonstrated performance improvements over custom deep learning methods since the lack of freely available hand radiographs to train models was compensated using transfer learning. The general implementation of a deep learning model is to be trained until a desirable accuracy rate is obtained while avoiding overfitting. This approach can potentially take up a large amount of time and, with the lack of openly available medical images for this problem, overfitting can become an issue. Moreover, the deep learning model itself is also used as a classifier.

This paper provides initial results obtained when deep learning models initilised on the ImageNet dataset weights and fine-tuned with only 5 epochs of training on a target RSNA Bone Age dataset of hand radiographs. Thereafter, the deep learned models are used as feature extraction mechanisms to train regressors for handling the task of classification. Boosting and stacking ensemble approaches are also applied to improve accuracy rates.

2   Transfer Learning

The goal of Transfer Learning is to adapt a classifier trained in a source domain D_S with learning task T_T with adequate samples to work effectively in a new target domain D_T which has its own learning task T_S and where the samples contain different distributions. In some cases, D_S and D_T may be similar in which case transfer learning models can be used while retaining the original layer weights. While in cases of D_S and D_T being different, fine-tuning of the respective model's hyperparameters can be done using D_T.

Creating labelled data is time consuming and expensive, so actively leveraging existing datasets is key. Traditional machine learning models learn patterns from a source training dataset and apply this knowledge to generalise from an unseen target dataset. With the use of transfer learning, models can continue the generalisation process of patterns already learnt from datasets with large amounts of training data. Transfer learning and generalisation are highly similar on a conceptual level as individuals can solve new tasks in an ad-hoc manner by using experiences from other situations. The primary distinction is that transfer learning transfers knowledge across tasks, instead of generalising within a specific task. Deep learning, especially in the case of supervised learning, requires large amounts of labelled data to perform effectively. Transfer learning is a viable approach to reducing the required size of training datasets for new target tasks, making it more applicable to real life scenarios where large amounts of labelled data is not easily available.

A domain can be represented mathematically as $D = (xP(X))$, where

- X is a feature space
- $P(X)$ is the edge probability distribution
- $X = \{x_1, x_2, ..., x_n\} \in X$

A task can be represented mathematically as $T = \{y, g(x)\}$, where

- y is the label space
- $g(x)$ is the prediction function, or conditional probability function $P(y|x)$

3   Ensemble Learning

Ensemble learning is a machine learning paradigm where multiple models, often called weak learners, are trained to solve the same problem and combined to get better results. The main hypothesis is that when weak models are correctly combined more accurate and robust models can be achieved.

There are three major kinds of meta-algorithms that aim at combining weak learners:

- Bagging, that often considers homogeneous weak learners, learns them independently from each other in parallel and combines them following some kind of deterministic averaging process
- Boosting, that often considers homogeneous weak learners and learns them sequentially in an adaptive way and combines them following a deterministic strategy
- Stacking, that often considers heterogeneous weak learners, learns them in parallel and combines them by training a meta-model to output a prediction based on the different weak model's predictions

Bagging will mainly focus at getting an ensemble model with less variance than its components whereas boosting and stacking will mainly try to produce strong models less biased than their components (even if variance can also be reduced). Bagging is the primary approach explored in this work with a final step of averaging and weighted averaging applied for ensemble.

4   Methods and Techniques

In the methodology represented in Fig. 1, the main goal is to integrate feature extraction done by deep learning models to train regressor, boosting and stacking models. Therefore, there are 2 main parts to the methodology. The first part is the feature extraction mechanism which makes use of transfer learning. In this part, deep learning models initialised on ImageNet dataset weights are fine-tuned for only 5 epochs on the RSNA Bone Age dataset. The fine-tuning of the model's makes use of bagging techniques as described previously. Thereafter, the fine-tuned models are used to produce a classification on observations in the dataset which is used as features for the second part of the methodology.

In the second part of the methodology, the features produced by the weakly-tuned deep learning model are used to train regressor models and produce classification results. These results are compared to boosting which is applied thereafter. Finally, stacking is applied and a Support Vector Regressor (SVR) is used as the meta-learner in the stacking ensemble process.

This methodology allows the assessment of weakly tuned deep learning models used primarily as feature extraction techniques and not directly in the classification mechanism.

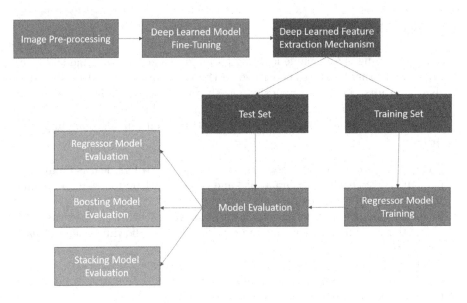

Fig. 1. The proposed framework for skeletal age estimation using ensemble deep learning.

4.1   Dataset

Precise skeletal age estimation requires a dataset which is both large and of high quality. Moreover, the dataset needs to be representative for each skeletal age which could be assessed. Most of the time datasets could be unevenly distributed, either in terms of gender or by age categories. These cases of uneven distribution can be solved by the implementation of data augmentation techniques to evenly distribute the dataset and increase its size. The RSNA dataset had skeletal hand radiographs of males and females in the range from 1 to 228 months. Table 1 provides gender information about the RSNA dataset.

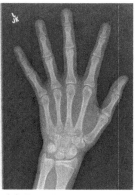 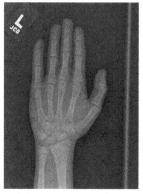 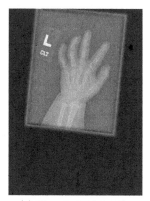

(a) Female 180 Months   (b) Male 120 Months   (c) Female 36 Months

Fig. 2. Hand radiograph samples from the RSNA bone age dataset

Table 1. The RSNA skeletal bone age dataset ranging from 1 to 228 months of age

Dataset	Size	Accessibility
RSNA challenge dataset (Male)	6 833	Public
RSNA challenge dataset (Female)	5 778	Public
Total	12 611	Public

4.2 Evaluation Protocols

Evaluation protocols determine the test and performance measures. Successful strategies are generally representative of the dataset population and independent of the specific training data being used [1]. Therefore, skeletal estimation techniques need to be validated using data which is unseen to the model in the attempt to reduce overfitting and improve the generalisation performance of the model, thus making it representative of a population. A popular strategy for classification is cross-validation. This strategy entails splitting the dataset into subsets of training and validation, which are used to train and validate the model respectively. The training and validation sets have consecutive turns to 'cross-over' for every learning iteration of the model. This allows the model to be evaluated then increase its performance preferably through each learning iteration.

In each validation iteration, the absolute error (AE) for an age estimate is given by 1:

$$AE = |a_k - \bar{a}_k| \tag{1}$$

where a_k is a of ground truth age and $\bar{a}_k$ is the respective estimate age. After all validation iterations are completed, the mean absolute error (MAE) can be defined as the average of all absolute errors. This is given by:

$$MAE = \frac{\sum_{k=1}^{n} |a_k - \bar{a}_k|}{n} \tag{2}$$

where n is the total number of instances ground truth and estimate age pairs. This performance metric is commonly used, but in terms of age estimation it is advantageous to gather the MAE within age groups rather than through the entire dataset. The MAE can be modified to fit this requirement. Suppose the dataset is split into j age groups, such that $D_s = a_1, a_2, ..., a_j$. Then the MAE for an age group is given by:

$$MAE_i = \frac{\sum_{k=1}^{n} |a_k - \bar{a}_k|}{n} \tag{3}$$

where n is all the images in age group i. The overall MAE can be found as a sum of the MAE is each age group. Such that:

$$MAE_{total} = \frac{\sum_{k=1}^{j} MAE_k}{j} \tag{4}$$

In statistics, mean absolute error (MAE) is a measure of difference between two continuous variables. It measures the average magnitude of the errors in a set of predictions, without considering their direction, where all individual differences have equal weight. RMSE is the standard deviation of the residuals, also known as prediction errors. Residuals are a measure of how far from the regression line data points are. In other words, the RMSE measures how spread out the residuals are or how concentrated the data is around the line of best fit. Root mean square error can be used for regression analysis to verify experimental results.

The RMSE is defined mathematically as:

$$RMSE = \sqrt{\frac{\sum_{i=1}^{n} |y_i - x_i|}{n}} \tag{5}$$

Both MAE and RMSE express average model prediction error in units of the variable of interest with the metrics ranging from 0 to ∞ and are indifferent to the direction of errors. The MAE and RMSE are negatively-oriented scores, which means lower values are better Taking the square root of the average squared errors has some interesting implications for RMSE. Since the errors are squared before they are averaged, the RMSE gives a relatively high weight to large errors. This means the RMSE should be more useful when large errors are particularly undesirable.

5   Results and Discussion

Following the methodology shown in Fig. 1, results are split and discussed in 3 main areas. The first area is the performance of regressor models which take in features extracted by the deep learned models and use that information for

Table 2. Model performance when boosting technique is applied

Model	Regressor	Evaluation		
		MSE	MAE	RMSE
DenseNet201	HistGradientBoostingRegressor	151.16	9.52	12.29
	GradientBoostingRegressor	146.19	9.31	12.09
VGG16	HistGradientBoostingRegressor	206.85	10.70	14.38
	GradientBoostingRegressor	203.03	10.56	14.24
ResNet50	HistGradientBoostingRegressor	231.84	11.39	15.22
	GradientBoostingRegressor	227.42	11.37	15.08
InceptionV3	HistGradientBoostingRegressor	617.12	19.40	24.84
	GradientBoostingRegressor	606.78	19.30	24.6

training and classification. The second area is the performance of the model when boosting is applied. Lastly, the performance of models when stacking ensemble is applied to the models which includes stacking of boosted models.

The deep learned models used for feature extraction were all pretrained on the ImageNet dataset. Thereafter, the weights of these models were altered by

Table 3. The table below describes regressor model performances when ensemble of deep learned models are used as feature extractors.

Model	Regressor	Evaluation		
		MSE	MAE	RMSE
DenseNet201 + VGG16	ExtraTreesRegressor	133.73	8.95	11.56
	RandomForestRegressor	138.09	9.13	11.75
	SVR	206.43	10.90	14.36
	BayesianRidge	136.68	9.01	11.69
	LassoLars	136.67	9.01	11.69
	PassiveAggressiveRegressor	244.98	12.75	15.65
	TheilSenRegressor	137.02	9.03	11.70
	LinearRegression	136.68	9.01	11.69
DN201 + VGG16 + IRNV2	ExtraTreesRegressor	134.15	9.03	11.58
	RandomForestRegressor	142.74	9.28	11.94
	SVR	650.79	20.31	25.51
	BayesianRidge	133.96	8.96	11.57
	LassoLars	133.93	8.96	11.57
	PassiveAggressiveRegressor	217.55	11.80	14.74
	TheilSenRegressor	137.19	9.06	11.71
	LinearRegression	133.93	8.96	11.57

Table 4. The following table shows model performance when Support Vector Regressor is used as a meta-learner for ensemble stacking.

Model	Regressor	Evaluation		
		MSE	MAE	RMSE
DenseNet201 + VGG16	ExtraTreesRegressor RandomForestRegressor HistGradientBoostingRegressor GradientBoostingRegressor	128.28	8.79	11.32
DenseNet201	ExtraTreesRegressor RandomForestRegressor HistGradientBoostingRegressor GradientBoostingRegressor	142.42	9.18	11.93
VGGG16	ExtraTreesRegressor RandomForestRegressor HistGradientBoostingRegressor GradientBoostingRegressor	184.02	9.94	13.56
VGG16 + DN201 + IRNV2	ExtraTreesRegressor RandomForestRegressor HistGradientBoostingRegressor	126.26	8.66	11.23

fine-tuning each model using the RSNA Bone Age dataset with only 5 epochs of training being allowed. Limiting the training epochs allows better evaluation of the ensemble techniques. All performance evaluations are represented in the 3 main metrics to allow comparison among current and future literature. These metrics are MAE, MSE and RMSE.

Table 5. The following table represents the performance improvements across the explored approaches.

Model	Regressor	Evaluation		
		MSE	MAE	RMSE
DenseNet201	–	160.83	9.96	12.68
VGG16 + DN201	Averaging	152.24	9.55	12.33
VGG16 + DN201 + IRNV2	Weighted 0.2/0.7/0.1	142.78	9.32	11.94
DenseNet201	BayesianRidge	147.51	9.38	12.14
DenseNet201 + VGG16	ExtraTreesRegressor	133.73	8.95	11.56
DenseNet201 + VGG16	GradientBoostingRegressor	133.52	8.97	11.55
VGG16 + DN201 + IRNV2	SVR Stacking	126.26	8.66	11.23
Weighted 0.2/0.7/0.1	ExtraTreesRegressor RandomForestRegressor HistGradientBoostingRegressor			

Table 6. Comparison of results obtained from literature indicate that the performance of weakly tuned model ensembling falls for feature extraction falls in range of other known approaches such as deep learning.

Method	Evaluation		
	MAE	MSE	RMSE
[2] VGG16	16.88	–	–
[2] VGG16	11.45	–	–
DenseNet201	9.96	160.83	12.68
VGG16 + DN201	9.55	152.24	12.33
[3] DL + Carpal	9.43	–	–
VGG16 + DN201 + IRNV2	9.32	142.78	11.94
GradientBoostingRegressor	8.97	133.52	11.55
ExtraTreesRegerssor	8.95	133.73	11.56
Stacking	8.66	126.26	11.23
[3] DL + Metacarpals	8.42	–	–
[3] DL + Hand	8.08	–	–
[2] VGG16	6.80	–	–
[9] Residual Learning	6.44	–	–

When boosting is applied the error rates achieved improves as seen in Table 2. Again, $DenseNet201$ performed as the best model for feature extraction, with boosting algorithms achieving improved MSe, MAE and RMSE of 146.19, 9.31 and 12.09 months respectively. Table 3 alters the feature extraction method and allows an ensemble of deep learned models to produce features which can be learned. In Table 3 we observe the ensemble feature extraction from the $DenseNet201$ and $VGG16$ models produce better results than previously achieved. The error rate improves and the best result is produced by tge Extra Trees Classifier which achieved a MSE, MAE and RMSE of 133.73, 8.95 and 11.56 months respectively. This is a much larger improvement in the results achieved than the previous techniques applied.

Table 4 combines some of the models used to produce a meta-learner, which in this case if a Support Vector Regressor. This method is known as stacking. Stacking is also combined with ensemble feature extraction. The error rates achieved improves and the best results are provided by features extracted by the $VGG16$, $DenseNet201$ and $Inception$ models which is used to train 3 regressors and finally stacked using a SVR. The achieved MSE, MAE and RMSE is 126.26, 8.66 and 11.23 months respectively.

Overall results achieved are compared in Table 5. In this table we can observe the improvement in classification as the mentioned techniques are applied, with previously basic ensemble techniques such as averaging and weighted average of deep learned models being use. The best performing deep learned model used for classification was the $DenseNet201$ which achieved a MSE, MAE and RMSE of 160.83, 9.96 and 12.68 months respectively. While when deep learned models are used for feature extraction and stacking of regressor models are used for classification, the best results achieved are a MSE, MAE and RMSE of 126.26, 8.66 and 11.23 months respectively. This is achieved keeping in mind that all deep learned models were initilised on the ImageNet dataset weights and fine tuned for only 5 epochs on the RSNA Bone Age dataset.

A literature comparison carried out in Table 6 shows that the results achieved using this methodology falls in range of other deep learning and transfer learning approaches used on the same dataset. The main difference is that other literature papers had trained the deep learned model fully and used it for classification, while in this methodology all deep learned models were only fine-tuned for 5 epochs.

6   Conclusion

In this paper we explored the issue of skeletal age estimation from hand radiographs, with specific insight to performance improvements using weakly fine-tuned deep learning models originally trained on the ImageNet dataset and thereafter used as feature extraction mechanism. These features were then used to train and predict skeletal ages within the RSNA Bona Age dataset. Multiple regressor models, boosting and stacking techniques were explored along with and ensemble of deep learning models for feature extraction being implemented. Using a *DenseNet*201 to train and test directly on the dataset after 5 epochs of training yielded a MSE, MAE and RMSE of 160.83, 9.96 and 12.68 months respectively. This was the best performing deep learning models after 5 epochs. Thereafter, the deep learning models were used foe feature extraction only and not for classification. When the training and stacking of regressor models from the features extracted from the deep learning models were implemented, the best MSE, MAE and RMSE achieved were 126.26, 8.66 and 11.23 months respectively.

References

1. Budka, M., Gabrys, B.: Density-preserving sampling: robust and efficient alternative to cross-validation for error estimation. IEEE Trans. Neural Netw. Learn. Syst. **24**(1), 22–34 (2013)
2. Castillo, J.C., Tong, Y., Zhao, J., Zhu, F.: RSNA bone-age detection using transfer learning and attention mapping, p. 5 (2018)
3. Iglovikov, V., Rakhlin, A., Kalinin, A., Shvets, A.: Pediatric Bone Age Assessment Using Deep Convolutional Neural Networks. arXiv:1712.05053 [cs], 11045:300–308 (2018)
4. Kattukaran, M.S., Abraham, A.: Bone age assessment using deep. Learning **9**(2), 4 (2018)
5. Pietka, E., Gertych, A., Pospiech, S., Cao, F., Huang, H.K., Gilsanz, V.: Computer-assisted bone age assessment: image preprocessing and epiphyseal/metaphyseal ROI extraction. IEEE Trans. Med. Imaging **20**(8), 715–729 (2001)

6. Poznanski, A.K., Garn, S.M., Nagy, J.M., Gall, J.C.: Metacarpophalangeal pattern profiles in the evaluation of skeletal malformations. Radiology **104**(1), 1–11 (1972)
7. Rakhlin, A: Diabetic Retinopathy detection through integration of Deep Learning classification framework. bioRxiv, June 2018
8. Rakhlin, A., Shvets, A., Iglovikov, V., Kalinin, A.: Deep convolutional neural networks for breast cancer histology image analysis. bioRxiv, April 2018
9. Souza, D., Oliveira, M.M.: End-to-end bone age assessment with residual learning. In: 2018 31st SIBGRAPI Conference on Graphics, Patterns and Images (SIBGRAPI), Parana, pp. 197–203. IEEE, October 2018
10. Tiulpin, A., Thevenot, J., Rahtu, E., Lehenkari, P., Saarakkala, S.: Automatic knee osteoarthritis diagnosis from plain radiographs: a deep learning-based approach. Sci. Rep. **8**(1) (2018)

Computer Vision

Quantifying Visual Similarity for Artistic Styles

Priscila Sánchez Santana[(✉)] and Edgar Roman-Rangel

Instituto Tecnológico Autónomo de México, ITAM, 01080 Mexico City, Mexico
{psanch35,edgar.roman}@itam.mx

Abstract. Determining the style or artistic movement to which a painter corresponds is a challenging and complicated problem because there are many factors that influence a painting, and these factors are of a qualitative nature, not a quantitative one. This work presents a methodology focused on the quantification of paintings via machine learning methods; we also perform a comparison between computer vision and machine learning techniques in order to understand the particularities and the functionalities of different methods.

Keywords: Computer vision · Deep learning · Artistic style

1 Introduction

Art is one of the most enigmatic and difficult disciplines that exist, because it is difficult to understand art in a numerical way; therefore, it requires new technological tools to find different solutions to the characterisation and the understanding of art. These tools can be provided by computer vision and machine learning techniques, which are used in this work to achieve quantitative analysis of similarity between art movements and artists.

The work presents a methodology designed to quantify the similarity among paintings belonging to different art movements and/or artists. We rely on two methods, one completely unsupervised and other one auto-supervised, to generate numerical representations of paintings and compare them to one another.

Our proposed methodology uses first the GIST descriptor [1], which was engineered for description of texture in images. Complementary, our method also makes use of convolutional autoencoders (CAE) [4], as they have proven able to learn robust image representations in an auto-supervised fashion [5]. Our results show that both methods properly characterize artistic styles, as they group images according to existing definitions made by art scholars [10].

2 Base Methods

This section surveys the base methods regarding image processing and neural networks which were used for our methodology. These methods are selected as image descriptors due to their relevance in the characterization problem and because of their importance in the computer vision and machine learning fields.

© Springer Nature Switzerland AG 2021
E. Roman-Rangel et al. (Eds.): MCPR 2021, LNCS 12725, pp. 187–197, 2021.
https://doi.org/10.1007/978-3-030-77004-4_18

2.1 GIST

This descriptor is a well-known way to characterize images exhibiting large amount of texture [1]. GIST has been proved to be the solution of the characterization of images based on the use of Gabor filters [6]. In addition, it has been successfully used to characterize paintings and for the classification of real from fake Van Goghs [2].

This method first preprocesses the input image, converting it to grayscale; in this way, the intensities are normalized and the contrast is scaled locally. The resulting image is then divided into a grid at various scales, and the response of each cell is calculated using a series of Gabor filters. All the responses of the cells are concatenated to form the characteristic vector of the image [1].

In other words, GIST provided a numerical description of the frequency components of an image, so that we could understand the qualitative features in a quantitative way.

2.2 Convolutional Autoencoders

Convolutional neural networks [3] are among the most successful methods for characterizing images; they are made up of convolutional filters which are learned through an iterative learning process [7,8]. Given their outstanding performance, they have become the standard solution to many problems in computer vision and image processing, including image classification and image description [9].

We use convolutional neural networks (with autoencoders), i.e., Convolutional Autoencoders (CAE) [4], as they can provide robust descriptors from the intermediate representation of the autoencoding process, also known as latent representation [5].

Autoencoders are convenient because they allow for the calculation of numerical descriptors in a self-monitoring way. Particularly, it is not required to know the label of its class, but rather the latent representation learned by the autoencoder, which can be used as the image descriptor [4].

3 Our Methodology

This section presents all the modules used during the design and the implementation of the different methods we use. It shows how the data was acquired, the methodology used, and the implementation of the methodology in each particular case of the modules herein presented.

3.1 Data

For all the data used in this work, no copyright is required, since they are freely distributed by the corresponding museums. In total, around 150 images were acquired per artistic movement. A total of 1556 images were collected in total, and they were distributed as shown in Fig. 1.

To gather our database, we acquired images available for download in three main museums:

- Art Institute of Chicago, Chicago, IL, United States,
- Musée d'Orsay, Paris, France,
- Met Museum, New York, NY, United States.

For this work, the sets of paintings were divided into classes. In total, there are 70 classes. Each class is identified by the combination of an artist and an art movement, as each artist can belong to different movements. The artists were chosen for being the foremost representatives of their time.

Furthermore, the visual similarity between styles and artistic movements were chosen for their historical moment, that is to say, that they were born from *Impressionism*, ending in the *Avant-garde*; all this was done to find not only an artistic development, but a historical timeline.

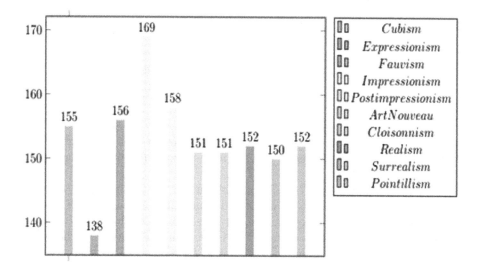

Fig. 1. Number of images per each artistic movement in our data base, which was collect from different online museums.

3.2 Methodology

Our general methodology is summarized in Fig. 2, where all the steps taken are presented. These steps are used for the two methods presented in this work. Even though the methodology was implemented in the same way for both GIST and CAE, some adjustments were made so that it fitted perfectly to the specific requirements of each individual method. Concretely, the second step: image representation is modular and can be adapted to work either with GIST or CAE.

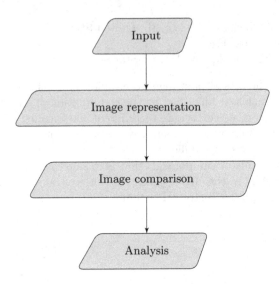

Fig. 2. Block diagram of our general methodology.

3.3 GIST

Images were processed in gray-scale format with a size of 255×255 pixels. The GIST descriptor [1] was computed for each image, using the approach presented in Sect. 2.1.

Once the characteristic vectors of each image is obtained, we use the Euclidean distance to compute the pairwise dissimilarity between pairs of images. Finally, for each pair of classes, we compute the average of the distance values among all elements from both classes. This is, we compute a metric of the *inter-class* distance. Note that when the two classes that are been compared correspond to the same class, this metric actually becomes the *intra-class* distance, i.e., the average distance among paintings of the same artist-style combination.

Given that our dataset is composed of 70 classes, the above described procedure results in a square matrix of size 70×70. The obtained matrix allows to see the distance of the n-th class against all other classes, and it has values across its diagonal that are close to zero because it corresponds to the n-th class compared to itself.

Due to the fact that we had many distances to compare, and that we needed to know which classes were the most similar and the most different between each other, we decided to specify a threshold of 0.83, this number was obtained empirically by doing manual verification. The threshold functioned as a filter because we could more easily group the classes between the ones that were more similar, the ones that were averagely similar, and the ones that were completely different.

After setting the threshold, we could discard some classes that were averagely similar, because we wanted to obtain two analyzes: the classes that were most similar to each other and those that have the least correlation with each other. The most different classes have a distance greater than 1, and the most similar ones, a distance close to zero.

3.4 CAE

For this method, we use our images at size of 128×128 pixels, as it was found to be the best size to avoid distorting the image. Given the learning nature of this method, and thus the need to validate its generalization performance, we divided our dataset randomly to obtain random training and test subsets. It was decided that the size of the test set was 0.33 of the initial set, and that the rest of the images were used for training. The total images distribution was 994 training images and 490 test images.

To obtain the description of the images, firstly, the convolutional model had to be defined to solve the problem. For this model, different filters were used so that the image was inserted into different layers, and in this way its characteristics could be obtained and it could be reconstructed in the most accurate way.

In the representation, the main characteristics of the image are the most important part. The process consists in the image entering the neural network, and passing through a filter; subsequently, the already filtered image is the input to another filter, and so on. In addition to obtaining the main characteristics of the images, the model also has the job of reconstructing them, this is not the main task of these natural networks, but it is useful to visualize the method.

Once the characteristic vectors were obtained, the distances between the images were calculated in a similar way to the GIST process, finishing with the computation of the average inter-class distance.

4   Results

4.1   GIST

The compared styles show similar brushstrokes, as well as floral themes, also the resemblance is also due to the time in which the movements were presented, since all the previously mentioned movements were born in response to Impressionism, unlike avant-gardes such as Cubism or Surrealism. In Table 1, the classes which are most similar to each other can be appreciated, that is, the ones which have the smallest distance on average. The distances can be in a range between 0 and 1.5. In the tables, it was decided to show only the five most similar to each other classes, since these are a reliable sample of how classes with the same art movement or the same artist are distributed.

Thanks to Table 1, it can be concluded that the largest distance is between Lacombe's Cloisonnism and Serusier's Cloisonnism. Despite belonging to the same movement, the artists have a significant difference in the use of colour and light, not to mention that the themes of the paintings are completely different.

Table 1. Classes with the shortest distance using the GIST image descriptor. Shortest distances in bold font.

Clase	Clase				
	Morisot-Im	Lacombe-Cl	Munch-Im	Serusier-Cl	Valtat-Fau
Morisot-Impressionism	0.31	**0.56**	**0.49**	0.61	0.60
Lacombe-Cloisonism	**0.56**	0.43	0.60	0.76	0.65
Munch-Impressionism	**0.49**	0.60	0.38	0.62	0.64
Serusier-Cloisonnism	0.61	0.76	0.62	0.48	0.74
Valtat-Fauvism	0.60	0.73	0.72	0.74	0.27

Similarly, it's noticeable that the smallest distance is found between Munch's Impressionism and Morisot's Impressionism. In Fig. 3, it can be seen that both artists used warm colors, represented similar scenarios, and shared the axis in terms of nature, light, and expression in their works, which translates into those being the classes with the shortest distance.

(a) Berthe Morisot (1872). Woman and Child on the Balcony. New York, Sammlung Ittleson.

(b) Edvard Munch(1890). Spring Evening on Karl Johann Street. Bergen, Billedgalleri.

Fig. 3. Examples of paintings by Morisot and Munch, both from the Impressionism. These images are examples of the most similar classes, on average, using GIST.

In Table 2, the most different classes are represented. Here, it can be found that the classes which are the most dissimilar correspond to Klimt-ArtNouveau, Klimt-Realism, and Matisse-Cubism. It is interesting to notice that Klimt and

Kandinsky seem to be, in general, somehow unique with respect to other artists and styles. Overall, here artists do not belong to a defined style, and each of them interprets styles in a different way.

Although they do share some characteristics, they also are independent movements, and scholars consider them to be *free*, which is why they are commonly known as vanguards. Likewise, they are movements harshly affected by the different wars that occurred, and that is why they also show different scenarios and techniques.

Table 2. Classes with largest distance using the GIST image descriptor. Largest distances in bold font.

Clase	Clase				
	Kandi-Exp	Klimt-AN	Klimt-Re	Matisse-Cub	Pic-Surr
Kandinsky-Expressionism	0.76	**1.49**	**1.43**	0.92	0.93
Klimt-ArtNouveau	**1.49**	0.11	0.20	**1.56**	0.98
Klimt-Realism	**1.43**	0.20	0.26	**1.49**	0.96
Matisse-Cubism	0.92	**1.56**	**1.49**	0.59	1.07
Picasso-Surrealism	0.90	0.98	0.96	0.97	0.96

The largest distance is between Klimt's Art-Nouveau and Matisse's Cubism. First of all, it should be noted that Klimt's style is unique, which means that not even the other artists belonging to the same movement are related to his style. This can be seen represented in the distances that his column presents in comparison with the others. In Fig. 4, the difference between the paintings can be appreciated, where it is shown that the styles of these two artists are completely different.

4.2 CAE

The same classes with the same paintings and artists were considered with this second method. The neural network was given all the images and subsequently

Table 3. Classes with shortest distance using CAE as image descriptor.

Clase	Clase				
	VanG-Postim	Monet-Impr	Mati-Fau	Gaug-Post	Seru-Clo
VanGogh-Postimpr	0.41	0.68	0.67	0.64	0.737
Monet-Impressionism	0.68	0.38	**0.58**	**0.55**	0.66
Matisse-Fauvism	**0.67**	**0.58**	0.50	**0.58**	0.76
Gauguin-Postimpr	**0.64**	**0.55**	**0.58**	0.45	0.73
Serusier-Cloisonnism	0.73	0.66	0.76	0.73	0.43

(a) Gustav Klimt (1901). Judith i. Viena, Österreichische Galerie.

(b) Henri Matisse (1914).Tête blanche et rose, Centre Georges Pompidou.

Fig. 4. Examples of paintings by Klimt-ArtNouveau and Matisse-Cubism. These images are examples of the most dissimilar classes, on average, using GIST.

the distances of each image against each image were obtained. Once the distances were acquired, they were grouped by class in order to derive the distances between classes.

In Table 3, the classes with the smallest distance between them can be seen. The movements are very similar to the ones obtained with GIST; although the artists are not the same, the movements are.

Similarly, it can be seen that the smallest distance is 0.59, which is between Monet's Impressionism and Gauguin's Post-Impressionism. Despite the fact that Monet's colours are darker, the technique is very similar. Both artists belong to movements that are very alike between each other, not only regarding the technique, but also with themes, since the themes of Post-Impressionism and of Impressionism are commonly landscapes, still lifes, flowers, etc. Likewise, both artists are known for their love of nature and colour.

The greatest distance within the classes with the smallest distance is 0.73, and this happens between Van Gogh's Post-Impressionism and Serusier's Cloisonnism, which is also a congruent result, since Van Gogh's style is quite characteristic and differs from the others to a great extent.

Similarly, within the movements which were mentioned as the most similar, Cloisonnism is the most different from these, since it was developed mostly by Gauguin outside of Europe; therefore, it deals with different topics and uses a peculiar technique.

Table 4. Classes with the largest distance using CAE as image descriptor.

Clase	Clase				
	Klimt-AN	Kandi-Exp	Pic-Surr	Msti-AN	Mati-Cub
Klimt-ArtNouveau	0.34	**0.87**	0.95	0.90	0.90
Kandinsky-Expressionism	**0.87**	0.27	**0.85**	0.83	**0.78**
Picasso-Surrealism	0.95	**0.85**	0.52	0.84	0.89
Mstislav-ArtNouveau	0.90	0.83	**0.84**	0.49	0.84
Matisse-Cubism	0.90	**0.78**	0.89	**0.84**	0.61

Table 4 shows the classes with the greatest distance. Here, the same behaviour as with GIST can be seen, since the classes in this table are cutting edge movements, also known as avant-garde movements. Unlike in Table 3, here there are also artists who repeat themselves: Klimt and Matisse. The difference is that here the greatest distance is between Klimt's Art-Nouveau and Picasso's Surrealism, which also fits, since Surrealism is one of the movements with fewer patterns within art, due to the fact that it relies only on the artist's imagination.

The smallest distance can be found between Kandisnky's Expressionism and Matisse's Cubism, as can be seen in Fig. 4. Although the styles are different, it can be seen that there is a certain similarity between the two artists: the lines

(a) Wassily Kandinsky (1903). The Singer. Lenbachhaus, Munich, Germany.

(b) Henri Matisse(1909-1917).Bathers by a River. Chicago, Art Institute of Chicago.

Fig. 5. Examples of paintings by Kandinsky and Matisse. These images are examples of the most similar classes, on average, using CAE.

are thick, the geometry is similar and the colours are dark. Therefore, it can be verified that of the most different classes, these are the most similar ones (Fig. 5).

Overall, our results show that both methods are able to group together images that belong to either the same artistic style, the same author, or both. The main difference between GIST and CAE is that the former prioritizes similarities in texture, while the later pays more attention to forms.

It is worth to mention that, since the results herein obtained are consistent with our predefined classes, which in turn are well studied by art scholars [10], this also implies that our proposed approach obtains results that are consistent with finding from the arts.

5   Conclusions

Throughout this work, two models of computational vision were designed for the characterization, identification and comparison of images to quantify the visual content of paintings, art movements, and specific styles of artists.

First, the GIST descriptor focuses entirely on the physical aspects of painting and its texture. Likewise, it was found was that the themes of the paintings were not really important for this method. On the other hand, Autoencoders identify shape characteristics, as it was common for them to identify paintings with similar themes. It associated nature with nature, portraits with portraits, etc.

The results also show what art historians have said for a long time: the importance and the evolution of art during the avant-garde movements, and how wars, poorness and crisis had importance on the art evolution making it more complex and unique [10].

Finally, it is shown that the tools used on this work can be modified to different types of program. This programs can be used to compare not only art movements, but styles, epochs, etc. Autoencoders and image descriptors are crucial to understand numerically what can only be artistically appreciated.

Acknowledgments. We thank the support of the Asociación Mexicana de Cultura A.C., in the realization of this research work.

References

1. Oliva, A., Torralba, A.: Modeling the shape of the scene: a holistic representation of the spatial envelope. Int. J. Comput. Vis. **42**, 145–175 (2001)
2. Lamberti, F., Sanna, A., Paravati, G.: Computer-assisted analysis of painting brushstrokes: digital image processing for unsupervised extraction of visible features from van Gogh's works. EURASIP J. Image Video Process. **2014**, Article no. 53 (2014)
3. Cireşan, D.C., Meier, U., Masci, J., Gambardella, L.M., Schmidhuber, J.: High-performance neural networks for visual object classification. arxiv:1102.0183 (2011)
4. Masci, J., Meier, U., Cireşan, D., Schmidhuber, J.: Stacked convolutional auto-encoders for hierarchical feature extraction. In: Honkela, T., Duch, W., Girolami, M., Kaski, S. (eds.) ICANN 2011. LNCS, vol. 6791, pp. 52–59. Springer, Heidelberg (2011). https://doi.org/10.1007/978-3-642-21735-7_7

5. Kingma, D.P., Welling, M.: Auto-encoding variational bayes. In: ICLR (2014)
6. Gonzalez, R.C., Woods, R.E.: Digital Image Processing, 3rd edn. Prentice Hall (2007)
7. LeCun, Y., et al.: Backpropagation applied to handwritten zip code recognition. Neural Comput. **1**(4), 541–551 (1989)
8. Goodfellow, I., Bengio, Y., Courville, A.: Deep Learning. MIT Press (2016)
9. Millstein, F.: Convolutional Neural Networks in Python. Create Space Independent Publishing Platform (2018)
10. Bürger, P., Shaw, M., Schulte-Sasse, J.: Theory of the Avant-garde. University of Minnesota Press (2016)

Automatic Classification of Zingiberales from RGB Images

Manuel G. Forero[1]([✉]) [ID], Carlos E. Beltrán[2] [ID], and Christian González-Santos[1] [ID]

[1] Semillero Lún, Facultad de Ingeniería, Universidad de Ibagué, Ibagué, Colombia
manuel.forero@unibague.edu.co,
christiansaulgonzalez@fedearroz.com.co
[2] Semillero Lún, Facultad de Ciencias Naturales y Matemáticas,
Universidad de Ibagué, Ibagué, Colombia
carlos.beltran@unibague.edu.co

Abstract. Colombia is the country with the largest number of plant species in the world. Within it, Zingiberaceae plays an important ecological role within ecosystems, acting as pioneers in the process of natural regeneration of vegetation and restoration of degraded soils. In addition, they maintain important coevolutionary relationships with other animal and plant species, becoming an important element within the complex web of life in the tropics. Manual classification is time consuming, expensive and requires experts who often have limited availability. To address these problems, three image classification methods SVM, KNN with Euclidean and intersection distances were used in this work. The database used for training, testing and validation of the methods comprises RGB images taken in the natural habitat of the Zingiberales, from their germination to their optimal cutting time. The images were pre-processed, making an adjustment of white balance, contrast and color temperature. To separate the Zingiberales from the background, a graphical segmentation technique using GrabCut was used. The descriptors were obtained using the technique known as BoW, finding that the number of visual words most suitable for classification was between 20 and 40. It was found that a better classification result was obtained by separating the flowers of a species into two subclasses, due to their different coloration. The best results were obtained with the KNN method, using the three closest neighbors, obtaining an accuracy of 97%.

Keywords: Zingiberales · Flower classification · Bag of words · Machine learning · K-means · SVM · KNN

1 Introduction

The Zingiberales (*Zingiberaceae*) as illustrated in Fig. 1 are perennial herbaceous plants, whose height varies from 70 cm, as in the Brachyantha zingiberaceae, to 10 m, as in the Rigid or Mariae zingiberaceae. The bracts are the most attractive part of a zingiberaceae, they are generally of primary or mixed colors. They are part of the zingiberales family and are known abroad as tropical exotic flowers, due to their variety of colors, shapes,

© Springer Nature Switzerland AG 2021
E. Roman-Rangel et al. (Eds.): MCPR 2021, LNCS 12725, pp. 198–206, 2021.
https://doi.org/10.1007/978-3-030-77004-4_19

sizes and long durability. They are found distributed between the tropics of Cancer and Capricorn and are typical, for the most part, of tropical and subtropical regions of Central and South America [1].

The Zingiberales are ornamental species that produce inflorescences highly appreciated in floriculture. The plants can be grown to produce cut flowers, or they can be planted in parks and gardens as part of landscaping. In addition to their inflorescences, Zingiberales produce useful foliage for various purposes and their rhizomes can be used for food or medicine [2–5].

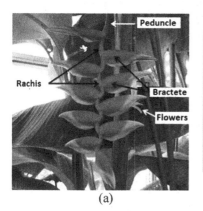 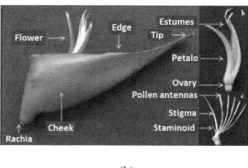

|(a)|(b)|

Fig. 1. Zingiberaceae *Rostrata* a) Complete inflorescence b) Cincinnati with the cincinal and floral bracts removed to show the flower at anthesis [6].

The Zingiberales, popularly known as platanillo, are grown in many regions of Colombia and the country is home to more than 70% of the varieties of the 250 known in Central and South America, which offers a comparative advantage over other countries such as the Philippines and Guinea, where they are also produced and exported [1].

Image processing and pattern recognition are being used in botanical applications. Thus, during the last years, interest in fields such as plant identification and characterization has increased significantly, being successfully used in their recognition. Thus, there are applications such as the PlantSnap program, which identifies Zingiberales, but without distinguishing each variety in particular [7]. For this reason, it is necessary to develop a technique that allows the classification or characterization of the Zingiberaceae independently of its flowering area, identifying its variety. Thus, this work aims to develop a new method that allows, through the use of image processing and pattern recognition techniques, to identify Zingiberales plant species such as: *Rostrata* (pendula), *Wagneriana red*, *Calathea Lutea* and *Ginger shampoo* (maracas), since these are some of the varieties are located in the center-west of the country, in the Andean region, which can become products of export of the Department, as occurs in other regions of Colombia and thus help in the study of the flora of the region, making a contribution to the national and international scientific community. Figure 2 shows photographs of the four species used in the study, taken ex situ from the flowering of Zingiberales at the University of Ibagué.

Fig. 2. Species of Zingiberales used in this work. a) *Rostrata* (pendula), b) *Wagneriana red*, c) *Calathea Lutea* and d) *Ginger shampoo* (maracas). (Color figure online)

Constant improvements in methods of description and image analysis have led to a growing interest in photo-based classification of plant species, a vital task for the study of biodiversity and ecological sensitivity. In recent years, various techniques have been proposed for the classification of plant species, a crucial task for the protection and conservation of biodiversity. One of the first known works in the area was developed in 1936 by Ronald Fisher who used four descriptors for the classification of three species of the Iris plant, using for its classification the method known as "Fisher's Linear Discriminant" [8]. Later, different studies have been made to identify plants and flowers using image processing and machine learning methods to eliminate noise, extract characteristics and classify them. Seeland and Rzanny used shape and color descriptors, and an SVM classifier for this purpose [9].

In 2014, as part of their participation in the LifeCLEF challenge, for plant identification, Issolah Mohamed et al. used the technique known as Bag of Words (BoW), extraction of points of interest using the SIFT method and a C-Support Vector Classification (C-SVC) method [10]. In Zingiberales, a statistical study was carried out in Mexico to characterize morphologically the wild species of the genus Zingiberales, by means of some qualitative and quantitative morphological descriptors. Although no specific techniques have been developed for Zingiberales classification, a statistical study was conducted in Mexico in 2017 to morphologically characterize eleven wild species of the genus Zingiberales, using 55 qualitative and quantitative morphological descriptors. Sixteen qualitative and twenty-three quantitative morphological descriptors were studied. Fourteen inflorescence (bract) descriptors were the most important, followed by plant (11), leaf (8), seed (3), fruit (2) and flower (1) [11].

2 Materials

To develop the method, 40 ex situ photographs, from germination to flowering, of each variety of Zingiberaceae studied were acquired, as shown in Fig. 3. The images were acquired in RAW format with a Canon 7D 18 megapixel camera and using a Canon

EF 100mm f/2.8 USM macro lens. The photographs were acquired using an ISO 100 sensitivity to minimize noise amplification. The aperture was set at f/11 or smaller to bring the entire flower into focus and to maintain proper illumination, preventing underexposure or overexposure of the photos. Finally, the shutter speed was set to 1/8 s and a shutter release cable was used during acquisition to prevent camera shake. The best illumination was in natural light, without direct exposure to the sun, in the morning hours.

Fig. 3. Image acquisition method.

The techniques were written in Python 3.7, using the sklearn and openCV libraries, and developed on a computer processor Intel® Xeon (R) CPU E5-2650 v4 2.20 GHz with 16 GB of RAM, running on Linux-Ubuntu 16.04 LTS operating system.

3 Methods

Initially the images were calibrated, to look for each color to remain identical in the different photographs. For this purpose, the color chart presented in Fig. 4 was used and the adjustment protocol established by the chart manufacturer was followed [12].

Fig. 4. Chart used to adjust the colour.

Once the color was matched, each image was segmented using a semi-automatic technique known as GrabCut. This is an iterative algorithm, which combines statistics and graph cutting to achieve a detailed two-dimensional segmentation [13]. GrabCut consists of two phases. The first stage is a semi-automatic segmentation where only the user is required to draw a bounding box around the foreground. The second requires user interaction to provide more point inputs from the foreground and background to improve the quality of the segmentation.

As the images have a resolution of 3648 × 5472, their processing is very time consuming. Since neighboring pixels are highly correlated, each image has a large number of redundant values and can be reduced in size without noticeably affecting the information. Therefore, the images were resampled at a much lower resolution of 120 × 320, as illustrated in Fig. 5.

(a)   (b)

Fig. 5. Zingiberaceae sample image. a) Segmentation result. b) Subsampling result (120 × 320 pixels).

To identify each zingiberaceae species, the color information of the bractea was used, since, according to the statistical study conducted by Arrazate et al. [11], this part of the plant allows the best classification results. A BoW model was used to characterize the colors of the bractea, constructing a visual histogram of characteristic words of each species of zingiberaceae. Since the appropriate number of visual words to represent the spathe or inflorescences is unknown, a study was conducted to determine it. To this end, a sweep was done by selecting from 10 to 100 words in increments of ten to determine the best representation of the floral spathe using color descriptors and the K-means method was used to group the samples and find the visual words.

Two classification techniques KNN and SVM were evaluated, varying their parameters, seeking to find those that deliver better accuracy. For this purpose, 60% of the samples were used for training, 20% for fitting tests and 20% for data validation. These parameters are shown in Table 1.

Table 1. Evaluated parameters of KNN and SVM classifiers.

Classifier	Parameters	Range
KNN	• Neighbors number	➢ 1 to 29 in increments of 1.
	• Distance type	➢ Euclidian. ➢ Intersection.
SVM	• Kernel • LIBLINEAR	➢ Kernel lineal. ➢ Kernel rbf: Gamma in 0,7. ➢ Kernel poly: of 0 to 9 in increments of 1.

As can be seen in Table 2, the highest accuracy, 93.7%, was achieved by the KNN classifier, with K = 1 using Euclidean distance and 30 visual words, and also with K = 1, using intersection distance and 40 visual words. The SVM classifier did not allow reaching the same accuracy, being only 91% in the best case.

Table 2. Maximum accuracy values obtained with the KNN and SVM classifiers.

Clusters number		10	20	30	40	50	60	70	80	90	100
Classifier	Parameters										
KNN	K=1	88	91	94	91	91	91	91	91	91	91
	Intersection	78	88	91	94	91	91	91	91	91	91
SVM	Lineal	84	91	91	91	91	91	91	91	91	91
	Poly	84	91	91	91	91	91	91	91	91	91

To improve the results, the characteristics of the misclassified samples were observed to determine the cause of the error. As shown in Table 3, only two *Calathea Lutea* inflorescences were misclassified with both 1-NN classifiers. For this reason, all samples of this species were studied to find the possible causes of the error, finding that they have two different color tones, yellow and greenish, which is due to the fact that the flower changes its shade according to its exposure to the sun, being more yellow the flowers that are more exposed to solar radiation, as illustrated in the examples in Fig. 6. This is due to the coloring effects produced by the presence of a substance called anthocyanin, which is activated by the incidence of the sun on the plant, causing changes in the color shade to be present. This variation was seen only in this flower and, therefore, it was divided into two subclasses for proper identification.

Table 3. Confusion matrix obtained with the 1NN classifier with the test samples.

	Rostrata	*Wagneriana*	*Calathea Lutea*	*Ginger shampoo*
Rostrata	8	0	0	0
Wagneriana	0	8	0	0
Calathea Lutea	2	0	6	0
Ginger shampoo	0	0	0	8

(a)   (b)

Fig. 6. Color change of Zingiberaceae *Calathea Lutea* flower spat under different solar radiation conditions. a) Growth in the shade. b) Growth in the sun.

Thus, the KNN classification method was selected, the SVM was dismissed and the *Calatea Lutea* class was subdivided into two, selecting the elements of each subclass according to their coloring using the k-means method. Then, the KNN method was evaluated again with different parameters to find the most accurate one.

4   Results

To validate the method, the classifiers with the parameters that provided the best accuracy, shown in Table 4, were used. As can be seen, the highest accuracy, 97%, was obtained with the KNN classifier, using 7 neighbors and 20 to 40 clusters. Although the comparison between histograms of BoW feature words is normally performed using the intersection distance, the best result was obtained using the Euclidean distance. Although there is still an error in the classification of a Zingiberaceae *Rostrata*, this is lower. A significant contribution of the proposed method is that regardless of the growth stage of the flowering spathe, the correct classification of each zingiberaceae variety was achieved in 97%, where the color and shape of the flowering spathe vary significantly. As can be observed in the Table 5, a spathe of *Rostrata* is still identified as *Wagneriana Red*, which is due to the fact that these two species have similar colors. These results could be improved by expanding the database, allowing to find better visual words or also by considering the spatial position of the colors within the spathe.

Table 4. Classification results obtained with the KNN method.

| # de clusters | | 20 | 30 | 40 | 70 |
Classifier	Parameters				
KNN	Euclidian K=7	97	97	97	-
	Intersection	-	84	-	91

Table 5. Confusion matrix obtained with Euclidean Distance and K = 7 classifier with the test samples.

	Rostrata	Wagneriana	Calathea Lutea	Ginger Shampoo
Rostrata	7	1	0	0
Wagneriana	0	8	0	0
Calathea Lutea	0	0	8	0
Ginger Shampoo	0	0	0	8

5 Conclusions

Zingiberaceae is a plant with a high commercial interest, since it is exported to Europe and the United States by Latin American and African countries. For its correct management, it is necessary to develop classification techniques, since it allows setting guidelines and can be used for its differentiation and propagation. Likewise, to design new cultural attentions for its harvest, conservation, storage and commercialization, since it provides knowledge that can be used to promote the study of the genus, to exploit it in a sustained way, conserving this phylogenetic resource in the country. Likewise, it guarantees the grower the homogeneity of the flowering rods at the optimum moment of cutting, since the automatic classification allows monitoring the growth, flowering and uniform quality of each one of these varieties. For this purpose, a new method for the classification of Zingiberales was presented in this work. This method requires a quick intervention of the user to segment the floral spathe from the bottom. For the classification, flower spathes were sampled from germination to the optimal cutting stage, which allowed the identification of four varieties of zingiberaceae with an accuracy of 97%, independent of their growth stage, making it robust to changes in coloration and shape throughout the growth of each flower spathe for each variety. Thus, the database consisting of 40 bracts of each variety of Zingiberaceae, allows the development of classification techniques to recognize each species at any point of its flowering.

Blossom images are affected by the ambient illumination present during acquisition. Therefore, it is necessary to use calibration tables to uniform the flower color under different illumination conditions.

The color analysis of the floral spathe determined that the different varieties of Zingiberales can have different shades, depending on their exposure to the sun, and therefore can be subdivided into several subclasses, allowing a significant improvement in the varieties' identification.

BoW is an effective method for text classification and very little used for obtaining descriptors in flower images. In this work, a method that makes use of this technique to obtain the most discriminating color characteristics of each variety was presented. It was found that between 20 to 40 visual words are sufficient for the correct classification of the four species of Zingiberales studied here, obtaining the best results with the KNN classifier, finding the seven nearest neighbors, with an accuracy of 97%. Although the BoW technique is usually used with intersection distance, the best results were obtained using Euclidean distance. These results will facilitate the identification of the Zingiberales varieties existing in the national territory and extend to the classification of other kinds of flowers and other varieties that are distinguished mainly by their color. It is also a valuable contribution to growers who will be able to recognize the variety regardless of its growth stage.

References

1. Turriago, K.: Heliconias (2014). https://encolombia.com/economia/agroindustria/floricult ura/floriculturandina_heliconias/.
2. Jerez, E.: El cultivo de las heliconias. Cultiv. Trop. **28**, 29–35 (2007)
3. Gómez-Merino, F., Trejo-Téllez, L.I., Garcia-Albarado, J.C., Perez Sato, J.A.: Diversity, distribution and propagation of heliconias, vol. 11, pp. 33–40, August 2018
4. Alarcón, C., Juan, P., Martinez, D.M., Salazar-Ospina, A.: In vitro porpagation of Heliconia curtispatha P, plant used against snakebite by some rural communities of the colombian region of Uraba. Vitae, **18**(3), 271–278 (2011). https://www.scielo.org.co/scielo.php?script=sci_art text&pid=S0121-40042011000300005&lng=en&nrm=iso&tlng=es
5. Kress, J., Betancur, J.: A new species of Heliconia (Heliconiaceae) from the Chocó region of Colombia, Instituto de Ciencias Naturales, Facultad de Ciencias-Universidad Nacional de Colombia, vol. 31, no. 1 (2009)
6. Perdomo, T.: Heliconia: características, hábitat, reproducción y cultivo. https://www.lifeder. com/heliconia/
7. Ralls, E.: PlantSnap. Telluride (2017)
8. Fisher, R.: The use of multiple measurements in taxonomic problems. Ann. Eugen. **7**(Part II), 179–188 (1936). https://onlinelibrary.wiley.com/doi/epdf/10.1111/j.1469-1809.1936.tb0 2137.x
9. Seeland, M., Rzanny, M., Alaqraa, N., Wäldchen, J., Mäder, P.: Plant species classification using flower images—A comparative study of local feature representations. PLoS One **12**(2), e0170629 (2017)
10. Issolah, M., Lingrand, D., Precioso, F.: Plant species recognition using bag-of-word with SVM classifier in the context of the LifeCLEF challenge (2014)
11. Avendaño-Arrazate, C., et al.: Morphological characterization in wild species of Heliconias (Heliconia spp) in Mexico. Am. J. Plant Sci. **8**, 1210–1223 (2017). https://doi.org/10.4236/ ajps.2017.86080
12. Bayarri, N.: Calibra tu cámara: tarjetas de calibración de color, la herramienta definitiva. Accesorios de fotografía, Consejos y Tutoriales (2019). https://blog.foto24.com/calibra-cam ara-tarjetas-calibracion-color-la-herramienta-definitiva/
13. Rother, C., Kolmogorov, V., Blake, A.: 'GrabCut': interactive foreground extraction using iterated graph cuts. In: ACM SIGGRAPH 2004 Papers, pp. 309–314 (2004). https://doi.org/ 10.1145/1186562.1015720

Classification of Rail Welding Defects Based on the Bag of Visual Words Approach

Mohale Molefe[1,2] and Jules-Raymond Tapamo[1(✉)] (iD)

[1] University of KwaZulu Natal, Durban, South Africa
mohale.molefe@transnet.net
[2] Transnet Freight Rail, Johannesburg, South Africa
tapamoj@ukzn.ac.za

Abstract. Railway transportation is one of the safest modes of transportation commonly used to transport heavy freight. Rails are the most critical and maintenance demanding component of the railway infrastructure. Rails are usually welded together during the installation process to form a continuous railway line using the thermite welding process. However, thermite welding is prone to the formation of defects on the welded rails, thus the weld joint is usually inspected. Radiography is the widely used Non-Destructive Testing method to inspect the weld joint for possible defects which could have occurred during the welding process. However, the detection and classification of defects from the generated radiography images is done manually by a trained radiography expert. Furthermore, the process is lengthy, costly and subjective even if conducted by a trained expert. This work presents an automated defect detection and classification method based on the Bag of Visual Words approach where the Speeded Up Robust Feature is used as the low-level feature descriptor. A Support Vector Machine is used as the classifier. The proposed method achieved the average classification accuracy of 94.60%.

Keywords: Railway transportation · Thermite welding · Bag of visual words · Support vector machine

1 Introduction

Railway transportation plays an essential role in developing the world economy, and it is considered the safest transportation mode compared to other means of transportation. As a system, the railway infrastructure is complex and multi-disciplinary. It comprises systems such as tunnels, bridges, earthworks and track structure. Track structure is the most fundamental railway infrastructure system. Its primary purpose is to provide guidance to the train wheels and absorb

---

Supported by Transnet Freight Rail.

E. Roman-Rangel et al. (Eds.): MCPR 2021, LNCS 12725, pp. 207–218, 2021.
https://doi.org/10.1007/978-3-030-77004-4_20

dynamic load induced by the train motion. The track structure comprises components such as rails, sleepers, ballast and fasteners.

Rails are the most critical and maintenance demanding component of the track structure as they are in direct contact with the train wheels. Rails are manufactured in sections, and therefore require to be joined together during the installation process. The widely used joining method is the thermite welding process. Also known as the aluminothermic welding, thermite welding offers a fast, mobile and inexpensive way of permanently joining two sections of rails. It is an exothermic welding process characterised by the chemical reaction between iron oxide and aluminium to produce a superheated molten iron which fuses with the rails to form a weld joint. Thermite welding is prone to the formation of welding defects on the generated weld joint. Thus, it is essential to inspect the weld joint for quality assurance purposes.

Several Non-Destructive Testing (NDT) methods are available to inspect the weld joint for possible welding defects. These include Acoustic Emission (EM), Eddy Current (EC), Ultrasonic Testing (UT) and Radiography Testing (RT). RT is the commonly used NDT method as it allows radiography experts to visually identify different types of welding defects from the generated images. However, the process of detecting and classifying the welding defects using human expertise is not acceptable due to low efficiency, lack of objectivity, high false alarm rate and lengthy turnaround times. Studies indicate that most of the train derailments are directly linked to the rail breaks resulting from a crack which initiated from a welding defect [11]. Thus, there is a considerable demand by the railway industry for development of a computer vision systems that can detect and classify defects automatically.

Recently, computer vision technologies have been studied for a wide range of applications in the railway industry. Some of the successful applications include the development of the automatic rail surface defect detection [5,7] and rail fastener monitoring frameworks [3,10]. However, Most of these frameworks are based on global and local feature extraction techniques [2,6,8,9]. Global features are computed by considering the entire image. Global features are attractive because they yield a compact representation of images where each image is represented by a single feature vector in a high dimensional feature space. However, global features are not invariant to image transformations such as scale, rotation and viewpoint. Furthermore, global features are sensitive to clutter and occlusion [4].

The limitations of global features are addressed by local features which find interesting characteristic of the image content despite significant changes in illumination, occlusion, viewpoint and clutter. Local feature extraction techniques involve two steps; keypoint detection and description. Keypoint detection aim at finding keypoints that are invariant to significant image transformations. Subsequently, the keypoint description step aims to construct a feature vector that describes the local content of each detected keypoint. However, local feature extraction methods generally yield many descriptor vectors representing a single image. Thus the classification results are significantly impacted by outliers.

Mid-level feature extraction methods combine a set of features extracted by local feature extraction techniques into a global image representation. The advantage is that the final feature vector is global yet invariant to various image transformations. The most popular mid-level feature extraction method is the Bag of Visual Words (BoVW) approach which forms a global image feature by grouping a set of descriptor vectors based on the similarity measure. To the best of authors knowledge, little research work exists in the literature for the classification of rail welding defects based on the mid-level image representation. In this work, the method based on the Speeded Up Robust Features (SURF) descriptor and BoVW approach is proposed to extract defect features in thermite weld joint images. The features formed by the BoVW approach are used to train and validate the Support Vector Machine (SVM) classifier.

2   Materials and Methods

This work proposes an automatic classification of thermite weld defects based on four steps. Weld joint images are initially enhanced to improve image quality. This is followed by extracting local features using the SURF descriptor. Then, the extracted features are passed on to the BoVW approach where the codebook is constructed, and each image in the dataset is presented by a global feature vector. This global feature vector is a count of how many times each codeword appears in the image. The formed vectors are fed into the SVM classifier. Test feature vectors are then classified each into a feature vector related to a defect-less weld or having one of the following defects; wormholes, shrinkage cavities and inclusions.

2.1   Feature Extraction

Keypoint extraction using the SURF descriptor is broken down into four steps; keypoint detection, keypoint localisation, orientation assignment and keypoint description.

Keypoint Detection. The SURF descriptor uses the Hessian matrix to determine the location and scale of the potential keypoints. For a given point $c = (x, y)$ at Gaussian scale σ in an octave, the Hessian matrix $H(c, \sigma)$ is defined as:

$$H(c, \sigma) = \begin{bmatrix} L_{xx}(c, \sigma) & L_{xy}(c, \sigma) \\ L_{xy}(c, \sigma) & L_{yy}(c, \sigma) \end{bmatrix} \tag{1}$$

where $L_{xx}(c, \sigma)$, $L_{yy}(c, \sigma)$ and $L_{xy}(c, \sigma)$ are the convolutions of Gaussian second-order derivatives with image I at point c in x, y and xy direction respectively. The determinant of Hessian matrix at this location is then defined as [1]:

$$det(H_{app}) = D_{xx}D_{yy} - (0.9D_{xy})^2 \tag{2}$$

where D_{xx}, D_{yy} and D_{xy} are the approximations of the Gaussian second-order derivatives in x, y and xy directions respectively.

The SURF algorithm uses responses of box filters to approximate these three derivatives in respective directions. The box filter responses are calculated using the integral images. In an integral image, any pixel's value is the sum of the pixel values above and to the left of the same pixel in the original image. The integral image I_{int} computed from image I can be calculated as:

$$\sum I_{int} = \sum_{x' \leq x, y' \leq y} I(x', y') \tag{3}$$

Keypoint Localisation. Some keypoints detected from the keypoint detection step are week and unstable and therefore needs to be eliminated. This is achieved in the keypoint localisation steps. Keypoint localisation is achieved in three stages; In the first stage, all keypoints are tested against a fixed threshold value called the $minHessian$. Keypoints above this value are accepted and passed on to the next stage; otherwise, keypoints are discarded. The second stage performs non-maxima suppression across the $3 \times 3 \times 3$ neighbourhood. Every keypoint is compared to 26 neighbouring pixels, 9 in the scale below and above it and 8 in the current scale. A keypoint is considered a strong keypoint if its value is greater or smaller than all its neighbouring pixels. The last stage is to determine the accurate position and scale of each keypoint. This is achieved by fitting a 3D quadratic function around every keypoint neighbourhood; the value obtained is selected as a sub-pixel and sub-scale location. The function is approximated by the Taylor expansion of the scale-space function with the keypoints (from stage 2) as the origin. The Taylor expansion is defined as [1]:

$$D(z) = D + \frac{\partial D^T}{\partial z} z + \frac{1}{2} z^T \frac{\partial^2 D}{\partial z^2} z \tag{4}$$

Orientation Assignment. The previous steps' output are keypoints that are scale-invariant and localised to a sub-pixel accuracy in terms of (x, y, σ). The orientation assignment step aims to add rotation invariant to the keypoints from the previous step. Orientation assignment is achieved in two steps. First, a circular region of radius 6σ is taken around every keypoint, then within this region, Haar wavelets responses of size 4σ are computed in x and y directions. The obtained responses are then weighted using a Gaussian kernel with its centre at a location of a keypoint and plotted as a vector points in x and y coordinates. In the second step, a window of size $\pi/3$ is rotated around the keypoints, pixels inside this window are summed up, and the most dominant results are assigned as the orientation of keypoints.

Keypoint Description. The keypoint description step constructs a feature vector for each keypoint [1]. It places a square region centred around every keypoint and oriented along the direction of the dominant orientation obtained from the previous step. This region is divided into 4×4 sub-regions, and for each sub-region, Haar wavelet responses are computed at 5×5 regular spaced sample points. The x and y wavelet responses denoted by dx and dy respectively are calculated and summed up to yield the first two values of the feature vector. The last two features are the absolute values of the responses $|d_x|$ and $|d_y|$. Thus for each sub-region, a vector is four-dimensional given as:

$$v = (\sum d_x, \sum d_y, \sum |d_x|, \sum |d_y|) \tag{5}$$

The final feature vector for every keypoint is a 64 dimensional feature vector computed by concatenating vectors from 4×4 sub-regions. Algorithm 1 presents the steps used to extract features using the SURF descriptor.

Algorithm 1. Keypoint detection and description using SURF

Require: Weld joint images from training and test dataset
Output: Keypoint descriptor vectors per image

1: **for** each image I in the dataset **do**
2:     Calculate integral image I_{int} using Eq. 3.
3:     Construct scale space.
4:     **for** each pixel in I_{int} **do**
5:         Calculate D_{xx}, D_{yy}, D_{xy} using box filters.
6:         Calculate the Hessian determinant $H_{(c,\sigma)}$ using Eq. 2.
7:         **if** $H_{(c,\sigma)} \geq minHessian$ **then**
8:             Store as a potential keypoint.
9:         **end if**
10:     **end for**
11:     **for** each potential keypoint **do**
12:         Perform non-maxima suppression in $3 \times 3 \times 3$ neighbourhood.
13:         Find sub-pixel and scale location using Eq. 4.
14:         Assign orientation.
15:         Construct a square region centred around a keypoint.
16:         Divide into 4×4 sub-regions.
17:         **for** each sub region **do**
18:             Calculate a keypoint descriptor vector using Eq. 5.
19:         **end for**
20:         Concatenate and store a keypoint vector.
21:     **end for**
22: **end for**

2.2 Bag of Visual Words

The SURF descriptor produces many descriptor vectors for each image. The BoVW approach aims to represent each image using only a single feature vector. BoVW is achieved in three steps. Codebook construction, coding and pooling. As shown in Fig. 1, the codebook is constructed by grouping together the keypoint descriptors from the training dataset that are similar, and each group represents a visual word or a codeword. Coding and pooling represent every image in the dataset as a global feature vector which is a count of the number of times each codeword appears on an image.

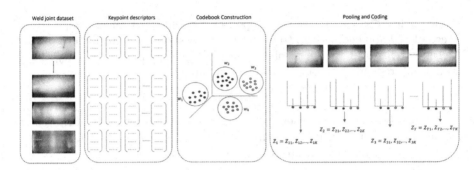

Fig. 1. Bag of Visual Words process

Codebook Construction. In the codebook construction step, all the keypoint descriptor vectors from the training dataset are clustered together, and each cluster represents a codeword. Let $V = \{v_j \mid j = 1, 2, ..., N\}$ be a set of unordered keypoint descriptors extracted from the training dataset where $v_j \in \mathbb{R}^D$ is a keypoint descriptor vector and N is the total number of keypoint descriptors. In this work, the K-means clustering algorithm is used to construct the codebook. This is done by clustering the N keypoint descriptor vectors into K clusters. The output from K-means clustering is then a codebook defined as: $C = \{c_k | k = 1, 2, ..., K\}$ where $c_k \in \mathbb{R}^D$.

Coding. The coding step aims to represent every image in the dataset in terms of the codebook elements (codewords). The coding step can be modelled using the function f defined as:

$$f : \mathbb{R}^D \longrightarrow \mathbb{R}^K$$

$$v_j \longrightarrow \beta_j \tag{6}$$

where $\beta_j = \{(\beta_{k,j}) | k = 1..., K\}$ maps a descriptor vector v_j into the closest codeword c_k in the codebook according to the following hard coding equation.

$$\beta_{k,j} = \begin{cases} 1, & \text{if } k = \arg\min_{k \in \{1...,K\}} \|v_j - c_k\|_2^2 \\ 0, & \text{otherwise} \end{cases} \tag{7}$$

where $\beta_{k,j}$ is the kth component of the encoded vector β_j.

Pooling. The final step in the BoVW approach is to construct a vector z that provides a global description of an image. This vector is a count of how many times each codeword appears on a given image. The idea of the pooling step is to concatenate and add all the elements of the encoded descriptor vector for every keypoint on an image. Thus given an image with the total number of n descriptors, the kth component of vector z is calculated as:

$$z_k = \sum_{j=1}^{n} \beta_{k,j} \tag{8}$$

Algorithm 2 summarises the steps used to construct the codebook and to form a global feature vector for every image in the dataset using the BoVW approach.

Algorithm 2. Feature extraction using BoVW

Require: Keypoint descriptor vectors from training and test dataset
Output: Global feature vector per image
1: Store the training descriptor vectors into a dictionary V.
2: Randomly choose K number of descriptor vectors from V to form codeword centres.
3: **while** codeword centres are unchanged **do**
4:     Allocate each descriptor vector to the nearest codeword centre.
5:     Replace codeword centres with the mean of the descriptor vectors in their codewords.
6: **end while**
7: Form a codebook C with K number of codewords.
8: **for** every image I in the dataset **do**
9:     **for** every descriptor vector in I **do**
10:         Assign to the nearest codeword in C using Eq. 6.
11:     **end for**
12:     Form a histogram feature vector z using Eq. 8.
13: **end for**

2.3   Feature Classification

Features extracted by the BoVW approach are used as inputs to train and validate the SVM classifier. The SVM classifier then classifies the test features into one of the following classes; defect-less, wormholes, shrinkage cavities and inclusions.

Support Vector Machine is one of the widely used algorithms for a classification task. Initially formulated for binary classification problems, SVM soon expanded for use with multiclass problems through one vs one and one vs all formulations. SVM can be understood by considering a classification task consisting of two classes. Let $((z_1, y_1, ..., (z_n, y_n))$ be the training dataset where z_i are the feature vectors and $y \in (-1, +1)$ are the corresponding class labels; Then, the main idea of the SVM is to construct a hyperplane that separates the two distinct classes with largest possible margin. Feature vectors from the test dataset are then assigned a class label depending on their relative position from the constructed hyperplane. It turns out that the margin which must be maximised between the vectors closest to the hyperplane is expressed as distance $d = 2/||w||$. SVM then maximises the distance d, by solving the primal optimization problem defined as:

$$\min \frac{1}{2}||w||^2 \quad \text{subject to } y_i(w.z_i + b) \geq +1 \text{ for } i = 1, 2, ..., n \qquad (9)$$

where w is the vector constrained to be perpendicular to the hyperplane and b is the bias term. The optimization problem of Eq. 9 is solved by introducing Lagrangian's formulation, which solves the minima or maxima of any function without having to worry about the constraints. It introduces new Lagrangian multiplier α_i for each constraint, and the minimization problem of Eq. 9 becomes:

$$L = \frac{1}{2}||w||^2 - \sum_{i=1}^{l} \alpha_i y_i (z_i w_i + b) + \sum_{i=1}^{l} \alpha_i \tag{10}$$

The partial derivatives of Eq. 10 with respect to w and b yields $w = \sum_{i=1} \alpha_i y_i z_i$ and $\sum_{i=1} \alpha_i y_i = 0$ respectively. Substituting these two equations to Eq. 10 yields the dual SVM defined as.

$$L = \sum_i \alpha_i - \frac{1}{2} \sum_i \sum_j \alpha_i \alpha_j y_i y_j (z_i \cdot z_j) \text{ subject to } \sum_{i=1} \alpha_i y_i = 0 \text{ and } \alpha_i \geq 0 \tag{11}$$

The dual optimization problem is solved by the Sequential Minimal Optimization (SMO), and it yields the coefficients of α_i. The samples with $\alpha_i > 0$ are called the support vectors. Only the support vectors affect the solution of the SVM problem, hence only the support vectors are needed to express the solution of the vector w. The decision rule for classification of the new, unseen feature vector x is therefore defined as: $f(x) = \sum_i^M y_i \alpha_i (z_i^T \cdot x) + b$. The predicted class label of vector x is then determined by the sign of the decision function $f(x)$.

The formulation of non-linear SVM is also possible for instances where feature vectors cannot be separated linearly. Non-linear SVM transforms the feature vectors from the current feature space to a high dimensional feature space χ where they can be separated. The transformation requires the dot product between any pairs of samples to be computed in χ (i.e. $\phi(z_i) \cdot \phi(z_j)$). This transformation is computationally expensive, thus kernel functions are used. A kernel function F that corresponds to the dot product in χ is defined as: $F(z_i, z_j) = \phi(z_i) \cdot \phi(z_j)$, thus only F is needed for computing the dot product without mapping into a high dimensional feature space. This work uses the non-linear SVM and the Radial Basis Function (RBF) kernel defined as: $F(z_i, z_j) = \exp(\frac{||z_i - z_j||^2}{2\sigma^2})$ is used as a kenel function, where σ is the kernel width. The dual problem of Eq. 12 then becomes:

$$L = \sum_i \alpha_i - \frac{1}{2} \sum_i \sum_j \alpha_i \alpha_j y_i y_j (F(z_i \cdot z_j)) \text{ subject to } \sum_{i=1} \alpha_i y_i = 0 \text{ and } \alpha_i \geq 0 \tag{12}$$

This work uses the one vs one SVM classifier for multiclass classification, where two pairs of classes are trained at a time, yielding a total of $D(D-1)$ classifiers where D is the total number of classes. A test feature vector is assigned to a class label with a majority vote. Algorithm 3 gives the steps involved in the classification of weld joint images using the non linear SVM classifier.

Algorithm 3. Feature classification using SVM

Require: Feature vectors from training and test dataset.

Output: Class label for each feature vector in the test dataset.

1: Train a one vs one SVM model
2: **for** any pair of classes y_i and y_j **do**
3:    Map the feature vectors into a high dimensional feature space using RBF kernel.
4:    Obtain a separating hyperplane by minimizing Eq. 12.
5: **end for**
6: **for** each feature vector z in the test dataset **do**
7:    Assign to class label with the majority vote.
8: **end for**

3   Experimental Results and Discussion

3.1   Dataset Description

The dataset used to conduct experiments in this work consists of 300 weld joint images collected from the Transnet welding department. The dataset represents a defect-less class and three welding defect types: wormholes, shrinkage cavities and inclusions. Each class consist of 75 images, and Fig. 2 depicts the weld joint sample image for each class.

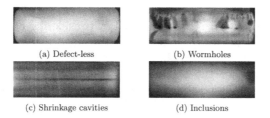

(a) Defect-less   (b) Wormholes

(c) Shrinkage cavities   (d) Inclusions

Fig. 2. Weld joint image per each class

3.2   Feature Extraction

Weld joint images were initially enhanced using the Contrast Limited Histogram Equalization technique to improve the image quality and to make defects more visible. The detection and description of keypoints from the enhanced images was achieved using the SURF descriptor according to the steps listed by Algorithm 1. The $minHessian$ value for filtering the unstable keypoints was chosen to be 500. The BoVW method was then applied on the keypoint descriptors to learn the codebook and to represent every image in the dataset as a global feature vector as explained by Algorithm 2. For codebook construction, the K-means clustering algorithm was applied to the randomly sampled keypoint descriptors. The codebook was constructed at increasing number of codewords ranging from 200 to 2000 in order to obtain the optimal codebook size.

3.3 Defect Classification

The feature vectors formed by the BoVW approach were used to train and validate the SVM classifier. The five fold cross-validation method was used due to a limited dataset, and for each fold, 240 feature vectors (60 per class) were used to train the classifier while 60 (15 per class) were used for test purposes. The value of the RBF kernel width $\sigma = 8$ was used in all the experiments. Table 1 shows the classification accuracy achieved by the SVM classifier for each fold at varying codebook size.

Table 1. Classification accuracies over folds

		Codebook size									
		200	400	600	800	1000	1200	1400	1600	1800	2000
Accuracies	Fold 1	76.66	91.66	75.00	95.00	90.66	91.66	95.00	91.66	90.67	90.00
	Fold 2	88.33	88.33	81.66	90.00	95.00	90.00	**96.66**	92.09	88.33	88.33
	Fold 3	88.33	88.33	81.66	90.00	95.00	90.00	**96.66**	92.09	88.33	88.33
	Fold 4	85.00	86.66	85.00	88.33	88.33	95.00	93.00	95.00	92.09	93.33
	Fold 5	83.66	85.00	88.33	88.33	90.00	90.00	93.33	92.09	90.67	88.33
	Average	84.06	87.33	83.03	90.33	90.80	91.66	94.60	93.17	91.89	89.98

The results of Table 1 can be interpreted by considering Fig. 3 which depicts classification accuracies for each fold and their average at varying codebook size. It can be observed that the classification accuracy increases with an increase in the codebook size for the first 1400 codewords. Afterwards, the accuracy decreases linearly from 1400 to 2000 codewords. Therefore, the highest classification accuracy achieved by the proposed method is 94.60% and the optimal codebook size is 1400 codewords.

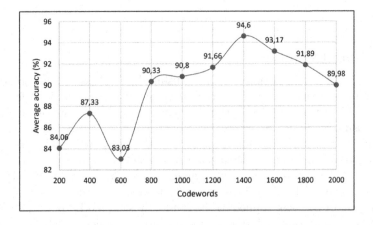

Fig. 3. Average classification accuracy at varying codebook size

4   Conclusion

In this paper, a method for classification of thermite weld defect based on mid-level image representation was proposed. Keypoint descriptors were detected by the SURF descriptor. Then, the BoVW method was applied to the detected keypoints to construct the codebook and to form a global feature vector for every image. Features were then used as inputs to train and validate the SVM classifier based on the five fold cross-validation method. The codebook size was varied in order to understand its impact on the classification accuracy, and the highest classification accuracy was obtained at a codebook size of 1400 codewords. Even though the dataset used in this work is limited and not publicly available; The obtained results will serve as a foundation for further research on the topic. Future work will involve gathering more weld joint image dataset and implementing a classification method based on the state of the art Deep learning approaches.

References

1. Bay, H., Tuytelaars, T., Van Gool, L.: SURF: speeded up robust features. In: Leonardis, A., Bischof, H., Pinz, A. (eds.) ECCV 2006. LNCS, vol. 3951, pp. 404–417. Springer, Heidelberg (2006). https://doi.org/10.1007/11744023_32
2. Gao, E., Gao, Q., Chen, J.: The welding region extraction technology based on HOG and SVM. In: 2017 7th International Conference on Education, Management, Computer and Society (EMCS 2017), pp. 1292–1295. Atlantis Press (2017)
3. Gibert, X., Patel, V.M., Chellappa, R.: Robust fastener detection for autonomous visual railway track inspection. In: 2015 IEEE Winter Conference on Applications of Computer Vision, pp. 694–701. IEEE (2015)
4. Ibrahim, A.S., Youssef, A.E., Abbott, A.L.: Global vs. local features for gender identification using Arabic and English handwriting. In: 2014 IEEE International Symposium on Signal Processing and Information Technology (ISSPIT), pp. 000155–000160. IEEE (2014)
5. Liu, Y., Fan, L., Zhang, S.: Exploration of rail defects detection system. In: 2018 5th International Conference on Information Science and Control Engineering (ICISCE), pp. 1118–1122. IEEE (2018)
6. Mekhalfa, F., Nacereddine, N.: Multiclass classification of weld defects in radiographic images based on support vector machines. In: 2014 Tenth International Conference on Signal-Image Technology and Internet-Based Systems, pp. 1–6. IEEE (2014)
7. Min, Y., Xiao, B., Dang, J., Yue, B., Cheng, T.: Real time detection system for rail surface defects based on machine vision. EURASIP J. Image Video Process. **2018**(1), 1–11 (2018). https://doi.org/10.1186/s13640-017-0241-y
8. Shao, J., Shi, H., Du, D., Wang, L., Cao, H.: Automatic weld defect detection in real-time x-ray images based on support vector machine. In: 2011 4th International Congress on Image and Signal Processing, vol. 4, pp. 1842–1846. IEEE (2011)
9. Valavanis, I., Kosmopoulos, D.: Multiclass defect detection and classification in weld radiographic images using geometric and texture features. Expert Syst. Appl. **37**(12), 7606–7614 (2010)

10. Wei, X., Yang, Z., Liu, Y., Wei, D., Jia, L., Li, Y.: Railway track fastener defect detection based on image processing and deep learning techniques: a comparative study. Eng. Appl. Artif. Intell. **80**, 66–81 (2019)
11. Zhao, J., Chan, A.H.C., Stirling, A.B.: Risk analysis of derailment induced by rail breaks-a probabilistic approach. In: RAMS 2006, Annual Reliability and Maintainability Symposium, pp. 486–491. IEEE (2006)

Fast Background Subtraction and Graph Cut for Thermal Pedestrian Detection

Oluwakorede M. Oluyide, Jules-Raymond Tapamo$^{(\boxtimes)}$ (iD), and Tom Walingo

Discipline of Electrical, Electronic and Computer Engineering, School of Engineering,
University of KwaZulu-Natal, Durban 4000, South Africa
213554623@stu.ukzn.ac.za, {tapamoj,walingo}@ukzn.ac.za

Abstract. Most studies in pedestrian detection from surveillance videos focus on analysing footage from visible image cameras which require external light and are sensitive to illumination changes. The presence or absence of external light determines the possibility of monitoring a scene while variations in illumination determines the degree of detection accuracy. In this paper, pedestrian detection is performed on thermal (infrared) images using a Graph-based background-subtraction technique. First, to address the limitation of thermal images such as polarity changes and halo around objects of extreme temperatures, motion is used as leverage in generating a reliable background which allows for candidate region extraction for further processing. Second, to address the limitations of automatic detection methods in the presence of multiple objects and absence of sharp edges, interactive Graph Cut is used to perform the final labelling of the valid candidate regions. Experiments on the all-inclusive benchmark dataset of thermal imagery from the Ohio State University (OSU) shows the effectiveness of the proposed method.

Keywords: Pedestrian detection · Thermal images · Background subtraction · Graph Cut

1 Introduction

In the last two decades, human behaviour analysis has attracted the interest of many researchers, because given the global rising security need [7], such systems have numerous advantages and applications. There is an equally rising demand for proactive video surveillance systems (VSS) which can function in a persistent - 24/7 - manner [9,17]. However, this is a difficult task for visible light camera VSS because their performance depends on the presence of external light and the images produced are subject to problems of over-, under- or non-uniform illumination, shadows or too many fine details which can hinder accurate video analysis. Thermal (infrared) cameras have been considered an alternative to visible light cameras since they do not require external light but depend on the heat (infrared) energy emitted from objects, thus functioning in a persistent manner. They, also, have the added advantage of being able to see through fog, smoke and vegetation.

© Springer Nature Switzerland AG 2021
E. Roman-Rangel et al. (Eds.): MCPR 2021, LNCS 12725, pp. 219–228, 2021.
https://doi.org/10.1007/978-3-030-77004-4_21

Ideally, there should be little difficulty detecting a person from a thermal footage because the temperature of human beings is higher than the surrounding environment and should appear very distinct from the background. However, thermal sensors detect only the amount of heat energy emitted from objects and different factors arising from either the physical properties of the materials present in the scene or weather condition affect how much heat energy is detected. Furthermore, ferroelectric thermal cameras, in particular, suffer from handicaps such as low signal-to-noise ratio, halos which appear around very hot or very cold objects and polarity changes from white hot to black hot.

The advantage of the proposed method is its adaptability to the wide range of intensity variation for the following reasons. Firstly, detecting motion in images does not depend on the intensity value itself but on the change in value. Secondly, the appearance model to perform binary labelling is built directly from each image using information from selected pixels called seeds.

The rest of the paper is organised as follows. A review of related works is presented in Sect. 3. The details of the proposed method are provided in Sect. 3. The experimental results and analysis is presented in Sect. 4. Section 5 concludes the paper and presents future work.

2   Related Works

Significant research efforts have been directed at detecting people in thermal videos. Majority of the works put forward in literature favour unsupervised methods. There are generally two stages in this category - generate likely pedestrian candidates and separate the pedestrians from non-pedestrians through validation. Davis and Sharma [4] proposed a contour-based background subtraction technique to detect people in thermal imagery. Rajkumar and Mouli [15] proposed a method for detecting pedestrians comprising of a background subtraction model, high-boost filtering and local adaptive thresholding. Jeon et al. [10] fused the result of the background subtraction - pixel difference image - with the edge pixel information for each video frame to detect the pedestrians. Jeyabharathi and Dejay [11] proposed a method for detection based on Reflectional Symmetrical Patterns (RPS). The frame differencing used in this work inspired its use in the proposed method. However, while they [11] require two difference frames from every three consecutive video frames to construct a background model, the proposed method requires only two consecutive frames from the whole video to generate a suitable background image.

Several other methods combine unsupervised candidate generation with supervised validation. Davis and Keck [3] proposed a two-stage template based method consisting of a fast screening procedure to hypothesize pedestrian location in the image and an AdaBoost classification step with adaptive filters to separate the best pedestrian candidates from the remaining non-person foreground objects detected in the first stage. Rajkumar and Mouli [16] included a preprocessing step which combines both mean filtering and Laplacian of Gaussian (LoG) filtering to suppress the background and enhance the pedestrians. Candidate generation is done thereafter using morphological processing and local thresholding. Histogram of Oriented Gradients (HOG) and Local Directional Pattern (LDP) features are then extracted from the images and used to train a Support Vector Machine (SVM) classifier to recognise the pedestrians. They posit that designing new features and classifiers will lead to better results.

Some research efforts have made use of supervised methods for the whole process of detecting pedestrian. A general scenario for such methods involves cropping out or delineating the pedestrians manually rather than generating them, extracting features, training a classifier to detect pedestrians and then testing it. Li et al. [13] proposed a novel mid-level feature descriptor called Covariance Matrix Map (CMM) created from Steering Kernel Regression (SKR) to capture local pixel structure in thermal images. The CMM is then fed into SVM to train a discriminative classifier useful for pedestrian detection. Li et al. [12] create a feature vector from a combination of HOG and geometric features which are fed into a linear SVM for binary - object/non-object - classification.

Following the related works, this work considers a mix of unsupervised method and semi-supervised method for candidate generation and validation respectively. To the best of our knowledge, none of the methods at the moment make use of semi - supervised methods. Similarly, while Graph Cut has been tested on various grayscale images, such as in [5,14], it has not been tested in the thermal (infrared) domain. Consequently, this paper introduces Graph Cut optimisation into the domain and uses a fast background subtraction method to provide prior knowledge to guide the labelling result for effective pedestrian detection.

3 Proposed Method

The first stage of the proposed algorithm is to generate candidates for validation which involves obtaining a background image from any two consecutive video frames in a particular video and by subtracting the background from all the frames in that video. The second stage is the validation and final labelling of the candidates generated from the first step using Graph Cut. The Graph Cut framework used is based on [2]. The overall structure is shown in Fig. 1.

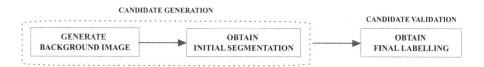

Fig. 1. Overview of the proposed method

3.1 Candidate Generation Using Fast Background Subtraction

Temporal (frame) differencing is popular in tracking algorithms as it detects moving objects [6]. It is used in this study for the purpose of obtaining a background image as it provides a simple and easy way to detect the moving pixels by taking the absolute pixel intensity difference between any two consecutive video frames. As mentioned in Sect. 2, the proposed method requires only two consecutive frames from the whole video to generate a suitable background image. Therefore, any, and only, two consecutive frames can be chosen from the whole video.

Given $(I_n)_{0 \leq n \leq N_f-1}$ a sequence of N_f images from a video, the pixel-wise absolute difference between any two frames I_f and I_{f+1} yields the difference $\mathcal{D}_f$, defined as

$$\mathcal{D}_f = |I_f - I_{f+1}| \tag{1}$$

The final background image $\mathcal{B}$ is defined as

$$\mathcal{B} = (\mathcal{D}_f + I_f^c)^c \tag{2}$$

where I^c denotes the pixel-wise inversion of each value of an image I, and $I + J$ denotes the pixel-wise sum of pixels values of images I and J. The operation $\mathcal{D}_f + I_f^c$ has the effect of cancelling out the moving pixels in the fth frame.

The candidates for validation are then obtained from background subtraction. The absolute difference between the background image and each video frame yields a sequence of N_f images $(\mathcal{Q}_n)_{0 \leq n \leq N_f-1}$ containing the extracted candidates. For each frame I_p, the process is defined as

$$\mathcal{Q}_p = |\mathcal{B} - I_p| \quad 0 \leq p < N_f-1 \tag{3}$$

Algorithm 1 summarises the steps of generation of candidate images.

Algorithm 1: Candidate Generation

Input: Sequence of N_f images$(I_n)_{0 \leq n \leq N_f-1}$
Output: Sequence of N_f images$(\mathcal{C}_n)_{0 \leq n \leq N_f-1}$

comment: pick any frame I_f from sequence $(I_n)_{0 \leq n \leq N_f-1}$
1. Compute $\mathcal{D}_f$ using Eq. 1
2. Output background image $\mathcal{B}$ using Eq. 2

comment: for all the frames in sequence $(I_n)_{0 \leq n \leq N_f-1}$
3. **for** $p \leftarrow 0$ **to** N_f-1
    do Generate the candidates using Eq. 3
4. **end for**

3.2 Candidate Validation Using Graph Cut

This stage of the proposed method validates the candidates generated and performs the final labelling with Graph Cut. The task of validation is posed as a binary labelling problem where labels are assigned to objects based on observed data. The labelling problem is defined formally as a function $f : P \to L$ where P is an image with a set of pixels $p = 1, 2, ..., n$ and L represents the set of l possible labels. For a problem with n pixels and l labels, the search space of possible labels for the mapping function f is of size l^n thus requiring efficient algorithms to search for an optimal solution.

Let $\mathcal{L} = ('0', '1')$ be the set of possible labels assigned to a pixel corresponding to the pedestrians and background respectively. Let h_y be a binary vector whose components specify label assignments to pixels y in $\mathcal{Y}$. Each h_y is taken from $\mathcal{L}$. The labelling of $\mathcal{Y}$ over $\mathcal{L}$ is a function $h : \mathcal{Y} \to \mathcal{L}$ that minimizes the energy

$$E(h) = \sum_{y \in \mathbf{Y}} D_y(h_y) + \sum_{\{y,z\} \in \mathbf{N}} S_{y,z}(h_y, h_z) \cdot \delta(h_y \neq h_z) \qquad (4)$$

where $D(h)$ is the *regional term* which incorporates appearance information and $S(h)$ is the *boundary term* as it incorporates the boundary information between two neighbouring pixels. Details of $D(h)$ and $S(h)$ are provided in Sect. 3.2.

To implement graph cut, a graph $\mathcal{G} = \langle \mathcal{V}, \mathcal{E} \rangle$ is constructed over an image $\mathcal{Y}$ with set of pixels y. $\mathcal{V}$ is the set of vertices which correspond to the pixels of the image. $\mathcal{E}$ is the set of edges connecting the vertices. In addition to the image's pixels, two vertices called terminals, source s and sink t, connect pixels which absolutely belong to the object of interest and the background respectively. The placement of edges between the vertices is determined by a neighbourhood system $\mathcal{N}$, which is the set of all (unordered) pairs $\{y, z\}$ of neighbouring pixels in $\mathcal{Y}$. Each edge $e \in \mathcal{E}$ is assigned a non-negative weight w_e. A cut $\mathcal{C}$ is a subset of edges $\mathcal{C} \subset \mathcal{E}$ removed from $\mathcal{G}$ which partitions $\mathcal{V}$ into two disjoint sets S and $T = \mathcal{V} - S$ such that $s \in S$ and $t \in T$. The cost of the cut $\mathcal{C}$ is the sum of its edge weights:

$$\mathcal{C} = \sum_{e \in \mathbf{C}} w_e \qquad (5)$$

The minimum cut separating the two terminals is the cut with the minimum cost. The Max-flow/Mincut algorithm in [1] is used to minimize the energy in Eq. 4 to produces the final labelling on the original image.

Image Modelling
Due to low signal-to-noise ratio of infrared images, it is non-trivial to construct reliable image models. As the candidate generation stage has eliminated most of the background, each image's histogram has been greatly simplified and pedestrian pixels are easier to detect. Therefore, after generating $(\mathcal{Q}_n)_{0 \leq n \leq N_f - 1}$ (defined in Eq. 3), the user selects pixels that definitely belong to the pedestrian and the background to model the probability distribution for the region term $D_y(h_y)$ and to guide the final labelling for each image. These pixels, called hard constraints or seeds, are denoted as $\mathcal{P}$ and $\mathcal{B}$ respectively;

$$\forall y \in \mathcal{P} : h_y = (\text{"ped"})$$
$$\forall y \in \mathcal{B} : h_y = (\text{"obj"})$$

where y and h_y are as defined in Eq. 4.

$D_y(h_y)$ in Eq. 4 calculates the cost of assigning a label to a pixel and assigns penalties to each pixel for belonging to the "object" (pedestrians) and the "background". The value assigned reflects how each pixel fits into the histogram of the object and background. If label h_y is likely for a pixel, then $D_y(h_y)$ should be small and vice versa. Therefore, these penalties, $D_y(\text{"ped"})$ and $D_y(\text{"bkg"})$ are calculated as negative log-likelihoods motivated by MAP-MRF formulations [2,8] as follows.

$$
\begin{aligned}
D_y(\text{"ped"}) &= -\ln \Pr(\mathcal{Y}_y | \textbf{"ped"}) \\
D_y(\text{"bkg"}) &= -\ln \Pr(\mathcal{Y}_y | \textbf{"bkg"})
\end{aligned}
\tag{6}
$$

$S_{y,z}(h_y, h_z)$ in Eq. 4 calculates the cost of assigning different labels between neighbouring pixels y and z and assigns penalties to discontinuities between them. A boundary exists when two adjacent pixels are assigned different labels, thus $S_{y,z}$ is a sum over two adjacent pixels y and z. The higher the similarity of the pixels, the higher the penalty assigned. A lower penalty ensures that those links are included in cut $\mathcal{C}$ described in Sect. 3.2. The function given in Eq. 7 is used to compute the penalties and penalizes a lot for dissimilarities between pixel intensity values. It works under the assumption that pixels in very close proximity to each other with similar intensities most likely belong to the same class while pixels with dissimilar intensity values most likely belong to different classes. It also assumes that pixel pairs with dissimilar intensity values are usually at the borders of segments in the image.

$$
S_{y,z} = \exp\left(\frac{(y-z)^2}{2\sigma^2}\right)
\tag{7}
$$

where y and z represent neighbouring pixel pairs and σ is the variance of the video frame under consideration.

Table 1. Detection Results of the Proposed Method

	Session										
	1	2	3	4	5	6	7	8	9	10	1–10
#People	91	100	101	109	101	97	94	99	95	97	984
#TP	85	100	84	109	97	93	90	93	95	89	932
#FP	0	2	3	0	1	0	1	0	0	0	7
Sensitivity	.93	.97	.83	1.0	.96	.96	.96	.94	1.0	.92	.95
PPV	1.0	.98	.97	1.0	.99	1.0	.99	1.0	1.0	1.0	.99

4   Experimental Results

The performance of the proposed method is tested on a benchmark collection of 360×240 pixel thermal images [3] of the walking intersection and street of

Table 2. Comparison of True Positive (TP) and False Positive (FP) values between the proposed method and other methods

Session (#Ped)	#TP							#FP						
	[3]	[13]	[12]	[18]	[16]	[19]	Ours	[3]	[13]	[12]	[18]	[16]	[19]	Ours
1 (91)	88	89	78	**90**	87	77	85	0	0	2	0	5	3	0
2 (100)	94	**100**	95	95	96	99	97	0	0	3	0	14	2	2
3 (101)	**101**	91	70	**101**	83	64	84	1	0	13	1	27	90	3
4 (109)	107	108	**109**	108	**109**	107	**109**	1	0	10	0	18	7	0
5 (101)	90	99	91	95	**100**	97	97	0	0	6	0	13	16	1
6 (97)	93	**97**	88	94	94	92	93	0	0	2	0	2	8	0
7 (94)	92	**94**	64	93	86	78	90	0	0	2	0	4	8	1
8 (99)	75	**99**	82	80	97	89	93	1	3	0	1	3	8	0
9 (95)	**95**	94	91	**95**	**95**	91	**95**	0	0	9	0	2	4	0
10 (97)	**95**	90	77	**95**	94	91	89	3	1	0	3	8	18	0
1–10 (984)	930	961	845	946	941	885	932	6	4	47	5	96	164	7

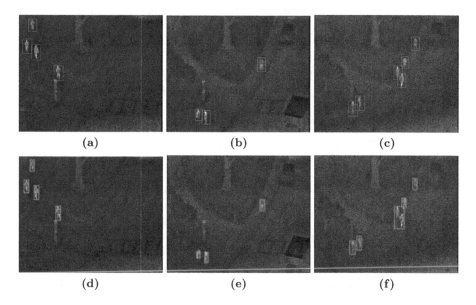

Fig. 2. Results showing the visual performance of the proposed method. (a)-(c) Ground Truth (d)-(f) Results of Proposed Method

the Ohio State University captured during both day and night over many days under a variety of environmental conditions. 10 sessions were captured using Raytheon 300D thermal sensor with 75mm lens camera mounted on an eight storey building numbering a total of 284 frames each having an average of 3–4 people.

The performance of the proposed method is evaluated using four quantitative measures namely. False Positive (FP), True Positive (TP), Sensitivity and Positive Predictive Value (PPV). FP calculates the number of detections that are not pedestrians. TP calculates the number of detections that are pedestrians. Sensitivity measures the pedestrian detection rate while PPV measures the false positive detection rate. Sensitivity and PPV are given in 8 and 9

$$\text{Sensitivity} = \frac{\text{True Positives (TP)}}{\text{Total No. of People}} \tag{8}$$

$$\text{PPV} = \left(1 - \frac{\text{False Positives (FP)}}{\text{Total No. of People}}\right) \tag{9}$$

The total number of pedestrians in the database is 984. The proposed method detected 932 pedestrians (TP) and 7 non-pedestrians (FP) thus achieving a overall Sensitivity of .95 and a (PPV) of .99. The performance breakdown of the proposed method on each of the sessions is shown in Table 1. In Fig. 2, it can be seen that the proposed method is successful when pedestrians are not very close to each other. It is not robust against overlapping pedestrians.

The performance of the Proposed Method with regards to the number of True Positives (#TP) and False Positives (#FP) is also shown in comparison with other pedestrian detection methods in Table 2. As there is an element of user intervention in the proposed method, the works chosen for comparison also have an element of user intervention in the form of manually delineating or demarcating regions which belong to pedestrians for extracting features and training discriminative classifiers. In the Table 2, the method(s) achieving the highest TP and FP score in each session is(are) highlighted in bold.

5   Conclusion

In this paper, a novel algorithm incorporating a fast background method and Graph Cut has been proposed which has several advantages. First, it introduces the powerful Graph Cut framework which guarantees an exact solution to binary labelling problems into the thermal imaging domain. To the best of our knowledge, this is its first application in the thermal domain. Second, it puts forward a fast background subtraction technique which uses motion as leverage and only requires the use of any two consecutive frames in the image to generate the likely candidates for validation. The background detection method put forward in this study is meant to provide an initial segmentation to guide the final Graph Cut labelling without adding high computational overhead. Therefore, the shortcomings in the initial results during the candidate generation stage are expected to be rectified in the candidate validation stage. Third, it introduces a semi-automatic method into the thermal imaging domain. Although this is a preliminary work, the approach produced good Sensitivity and high Positive Predictive Values (PPV) comparable with the those in the literature when tested on a wide variety of thermal imagery. Further work needs to be done to improve its performance especially in the area of overlapping pedestrians.

References

1. Boykov, Y., Kolmogorov, V.: An experimental comparison of min-cut/max-flow algorithms for energy minimization in vision. IEEE Trans. Pattern Anal. Mach. Intell. **26**(9), 1124–1137 (2004)
2. Boykov, Y., Jolly, M.P.: Interactive graph cuts for optimal boundary and region segmentation of objects in N-D images. In: Proceedings of the Eighth IEEE International Conference on Computer Vision, ICCV 2001, vol. 1, pp. 105–112 (2001)
3. Davis, J.W., Keck, M.A.: A two-stage template approach to person detection in thermal imagery. In: Proceedings of the Seventh IEEE Workshop on Applications of Computer Science. WACV/MOTION 2005 (2005)
4. Davis, J.W., Sharma, V.: Robust background-subtraction for person detection in thermal imagery. In: IEEE Workshop on Object Tracking and Classification Beyond the Visible Spectrum (2004)
5. Funka-Lea, G., et al.: Automatic heart isolation for CT coronary visualization using Graph-Cuts. In: 3rd IEEE International Symposium on Biomedical Imaging: Nano to Macro, ISBI 2006, pp. 614–617 (2006)
6. Gawande, U., Hajari, K., Golhar, Y.: Pedestrian detection and tracking in video surveillance system: issues, comprehensive review, and challenges. In: Recent Trends in Computational Intelligence (2020)
7. Gowsikhaa, D., Abirami, S., Baskaran, R.: Automated human behavior analysis from surveillance videos: a survey. Artif. Intell. Rev. **42**(4), 747–765 (2012). https://doi.org/10.1007/s10462-012-9341-3
8. Greig, D.M., Porteous, B.T., Seheult, A.H.: Exact maximum a posteriori estimation for binary images. J. R. Stat. Soc. Ser. B (Methodol.) **51**(2), 271–279 (1989)
9. Hampapur, A., Brown, L., Connell, J., Pankanti, S., Senior, A., Tian, Y.: Smart surveillance: applications, technologies and implications. In: Fourth International Conference on Information, Communications and Signal Processing 2003 and the Fourth Pacific Rim Conference on Multimedia, Proceedings of the Joint, vol. 2, pp. 1133–1138 (2003)
10. Jeon, E.S., et al.: Human detection based on the generation of a background image by using a far-infrared light camera. Sensors **15**, 6763–6787 (2015)
11. Jeyabharathi, D.: Dejey: efficient background subtraction for thermal images using reflectional symmetry pattern (RSP). Multimed. Tools Appl. **77**(17), 22567–22586 (2018). https://doi.org/10.1007/s11042-018-6220-1
12. Li, W., Zheng, D., Zhao, T., Yang, M.: An effective approach to pedestrian detection in thermal imagery. In: 2012 8th International Conference on Natural Computation, pp. 325–329 (2012)
13. Li, Z., Qiang, W., Zhang, J., Geers, G.: SKRWM based descriptor for pedestrian detection in thermal images. In: 2011 IEEE 13th International Workshop on Multimedia Signal Processing, pp. 1–6 (2011)
14. Oluyide, O.M., Tapamo, J.R., Viriri, S.: Automatic lung segmentation based on graph cut using a distance constrained energy. IET Comput. Vis. **12**, 609–615 (2018)
15. Soundrapandiyan, R., Mouli, C.: Adaptive pedestrian detection in infrared images using background subtraction and local thresholding. Procedia Comput. Sci. **58**, 706–713 (2015)
16. Soundrapandiyan, R., Mouli, C.P.: An approach to adaptive pedestrian detection and classification in infrared images based on human visual mechanism and support vector machine. Arab. J. Sci. Eng. **43**, 3951–3963 (2018). https://doi.org/10.1007/s13369-017-2642-8

17. Webster, C.W.R.: CCTV policy in the UK: reconsidering the evidence base. Surveill. Soc. **6**(1), 10–22 (2009)
18. Wu, D., Wang, J., Liu, W., Cao, J., Zhou, Z.: An effective method for human detection using far-infrared images. In: 2017 First International Conference on Electronics Instrumentation Information Systems (EIIS), pp. 1–4 (2017)
19. Zhao, Y., Cheng, J., Zhou, W., Zhang, C., Pan, X.: Infrared pedestrian detection with converted temperature map. In: 2019 Asia-Pacific Signal and Information Processing Association Annual Summit and Conference (APSIPA ASC), pp. 2025–2031 (2019)

Image Processing and Analysis

Development of a Method for Identifying People by Processing Digital Images from Handprint

Victor A. Tuesta-Monteza[1]([✉]) [iD], Barny N. Cespedes-Ordoñez[1]([✉]) [iD],
Heber I. Mejia-Cabrera[1]([✉]) [iD], and Manuel G. Forero[2]([✉]) [iD]

[1] LABSIS, Grupo TIAP, Universidad Señor de Sipán, Pimentel, Perú
{vtuesta,ordonezb,hmejiac}@crece.uss.edu.pe
[2] Semillero Lún, Grupo D+Tec, Facultad de Ingeniería,
Universidad de Ibagué, Ibagué, Colombia
manuel.forero@unibague.edu.co

Abstract. Fingerprint recognition methods present problems due to the fact that some prints are blurred or have changes due to the activities carried out with the hands by some people. In addition, these identification methods can be violated by using false fingerprints or other devices. Therefore, it is necessary to develop more reliable methods. For this purpose, a handprint-based identification method is presented in this paper. A database was built with the right handprints of 100 construction workers. The method comprises an image pre-processing and a classification stage based on deep learning. Six neural networks were compared VGG16, VG19, ResNet50, MobileNetV2, Xception and DenseNet121. The best results were obtained with the RestNet50 network, achieving 99% accuracy, followed by Xception with 97%. Showing the reliability of the proposed technique.

Keywords: Hand print · Palmprint · Convolutional Neural Networks · Biometrics · Security system · ResNEt50 · Xception

1 Introduction

The identification of persons has been a constant concern for society. Therefore, several methods have been developed to confirm the identity of a subject, from the issue of documents, through the use of credentials, to the biometric characteristics that ensure the unequivocal identification of an individual. Biometrics is a technique that uses one or more physical and non-transferable characteristics of people to achieve a more efficient identification. However, these methods are also targets of attacks, such as the cloning of fingerprints for illegal use. In 2014, the BBC published an article about the cloning of the fingerprints of the German Minister of Defense, the note narrates that in the speech presented by Jan Krissler at the convention of the Chaos Computer Club, a European community of hackers, he performed such a feat using a simple photograph taken during a public appearance of the Minister [1]. In the face of these threats, hardware-based solutions were developed to prevent access to systems using fake fingerprints made of

© Springer Nature Switzerland AG 2021
E. Roman-Rangel et al. (Eds.): MCPR 2021, LNCS 12725, pp. 231–239, 2021.
https://doi.org/10.1007/978-3-030-77004-4_22

latex, plastic, rubber, etc. called LFD - Live Finger Detection technology, but they are very expensive to implement.

According to Sancho [2] biometric authentication is the verification of the identity of individuals by means of biological data which are obtained from biological features of people, by means of a device and software. In this way, the authentication process makes it possible to confirm or discard the individual's identity. The main biometric systems found in the literature are based on fingerprint, iris, voice, face and hand contour recognition, being fingerprint and voice systems the most frequently used and for this reason the most frequently attempted to be breached or hacked. In addition, an identification problem that occurs in some apartment construction companies in the city of Lima, Peru, which perform attendance control by identifying workers through biometric equipment based on their fingerprints, is the difficulty of identifying them correctly. This is due to the fact that the prints are notably affected by the mistreatment produced by the daily work, causing multiple negative markings and the delay of the entrance of the personnel to the work site, bringing as a consequence the dissatisfaction and delay in their daily assigned tasks. Several works have been conducted for palmprint-based person identification. Gopal et al. performed a multimodal personal authentication system using palm print, dorsal hand vein pattern and palm phalanges impression using 500 images of 50 persons. They used the K nearest neighbors method as a classifier and obtained an accuracy of 99.00% [3]. El-Tarhouni et. al. proposed to use multispectral images of the hand, combining pyramidal oriented gradient histograms, a variant of the Local Binary Pattern (LBP) and a probabilistic LDA classifier using Euclidean distance, obtaining an accuracy of 99.17%, 98.33%, 99.34% and 98.77% for the blue, green, red and NIR spectra, respectively [4]. Poonam Poonia et al. implemented five feature extraction algorithms Mean, AAD (Average Absolute Deviation), GMF (Gaussian Membership Function), SIFT (Scale Invariant Feature Transformation) and SURF (Accelerated Robust Feature) and SVM (Support Vector Machine) and KNN (K-Nearest Neighbor) classifiers, obtaining a correct recognition rate (CRR) of 99.56% and 97.95% for the IIT-Delhi and PolyU palmprint database, with the SURF descriptors. Subsequently, this same group proposed the use of a non-invertible palmprint template to store the relative geometric orientation information of physiological fingerprint features, obtaining a correct recognition rate (CRR) and equal error rate (EER) of 95.4% and 0.37%, respectively. Mejia et al. employed a database consisting of 750 palm images of 50 people, using 15 images for training and the remaining for testing. They proposed a background elimination method and compared three convolutional neural networks, finding that the VGG 16 network allowed 100% accuracy [5]. Akhoundzadeh et al. obtained coarse and fine scale features using the SURF method. The coarse scale was employed for general categorization and the fine scale for obtaining gradient histogram features. Classification was performed using sparse coding for the classification feature matrices obtaining a recognition rate of approximately 99.85% [6]. New works using new sources of identification have been developed recently, which seeks to identify people by finger veins using CNN, achieving an identification rate of 94% [7]. Similarly, Yazhao Li et al. proposed a biometric identification method using electrocardiogram (ECG) signals with cascade convolutional neural networks, achieving an average identification rate of 94% [8].

The aforementioned works do not include images of the handprint strongly affected by cracks and deformations produced by daily work in construction or mining, deteriorating the characteristics of the hand used for identification. Also, the methods developed have not been evaluated with this type of images. Therefore, this research presents a new method for the identification of people with palm prints affected by intense manual labor, using digital image processing and convolutional neural networks.

2   Material and Method

2.1   Material

For the development of the research, a dataset was constructed consisting of 300 the right handprint images of 100 civil construction workers, 3 per person, who due to their work suffer mistreatment of their hands, causing damage to their fingerprints and hand palms. Due to the health crisis caused by the SARS-CoV-2 virus, a biosecurity protocol was implemented for the acquisition of samples and to prevent the spread of the disease. The protocol consists of a series of rules: Use of personal protective equipment, consisting of facemasks and hand disinfection with medical alcohol.

a   b

Fig. 1. a) Application of medical alcohol to a research participant, b) Scanned hand of a participant.

For the images acquisition, a protocol was established to ensure that their quality was the best possible and that they were obtained under the same light and background conditions. For this purpose, a structure was built, as shown in Fig. 1 and whose details are shown in Fig. 2. A cardboard box 40 cm long, 20 cm wide and 30 cm high was used for the construction of the structure. These measurements were established, since it is larger than the acquisition device, an Epson scanner model L220, which is 38 cm long, 18 cm wide and 20 cm high inside the box, leaving a 10 cm clearance so that the user can comfortably insert his hand through a hole. The box was internally covered with black cardboard to avoid reflections on the cardboard. The hole size was sufficient to avoid the light entering from the outside during the acquisition. The sheet size and scanner resolution were set to find good quality images. The color samples were then acquired in A4 size with a resolution of 300 ppi, obtaining images of 2481 × 3509 pixels, as shown in Fig. 3.

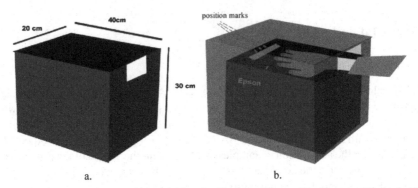

Fig. 2. Structure used for sample acquisition. a. Cardboard box to block external light. b. Hand location for acquisition.

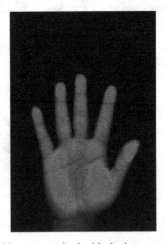

Fig. 3. Right hand image acquired with the image acquisition protocol.

The software was developed in an Intel Corel I7-6700H (R) CPU 2.60 GHz × 8, 8 GB RAM, NVidia GTX 960M 4 GB × 64, operating on Windows 10. The software was written in Python 3.7 using the NumPy, Matplotlib and OpenCV2 libraries.

2.2   Method

As can be seen in Fig. 3, the details of the subject's hand are clearly distinguishable. Since the resolution is very high, and the pixels are highly correlated with each other, the image size was reduced, observing that the details were maintained, thus reducing the computation time in the classification process.

To separate the region of interest, i.e., the hand, from the rest of the image, a segmentation process was performed. Since color is not important during this stage, images were converted to gray levels, as shown in Fig. 4. Then, each image is smoothed with a Gaussian filter, strong enough (sigma = 2.5) to reduce noise, uniformizing the hand and background, as shown in Fig. 5.

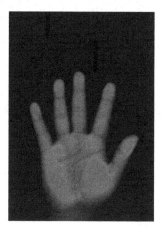

Fig. 4. Monochrome image of the hand.

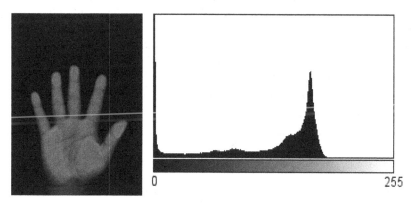

0   255

Fig. 5. Image of the smoothed channel with a Gaussian filter (sigma = 2.5) and its corresponding histogram.

Since the image consists only of the hand and the background, the typical histogram, as shown in Fig. 5, is characterized by being a bimodal one where the modes follow a Gaussian distribution. For this reason, the Otsu thresholding method was used for segmentation. Then, the resulting image was processed with a morphological aperture filter, and then closed to eliminate the remaining noise in the background, and to close the gulfs that could have been left in the hand. The holes were then filled. Finally, the bounding box of each hand was found, and the largest bounding box among all the hands was chosen as the standard dimension of all images. Each binarized image thus obtained was used as a mask to obtain the image of the color hand of standard size given by the largest bounding box. These images were used as input for each neural network used for the learning process (Fig. 6).

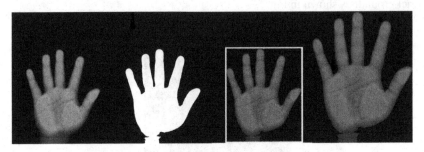

Fig. 6. Steps to choose the new method of identifying people.

Two of the three images of each subject's hand were used for training and the remaining one to evaluate the method. Twenty-six architectures found in the literature were ranked according to their results in the classification of biometric data, selecting the six best: VGG16, MobileNetV2, VGG19, Xception, ResNet50, DenseNet121, which were used for the recognition of subjects according to their handprint, as shown in Fig. 7. The pre-learnt weights were used to initialize the networks and tuned using the palm images. It is worth noting that each network converged to a solution, while this did not happen when the background removal step was suppressed by using a mask in the pre-processing phase, even though cropped samples were used, showing the usefulness of this step. To perform the learning, the resulting color images were resized to the dimensions accepted by each network. Thus, they were reduced to 224 × 224 pixels for networks VGG16, VGG19, ResNet50, DenseNet121 and to 260 × 260 for MobileNetV2 and Xception.

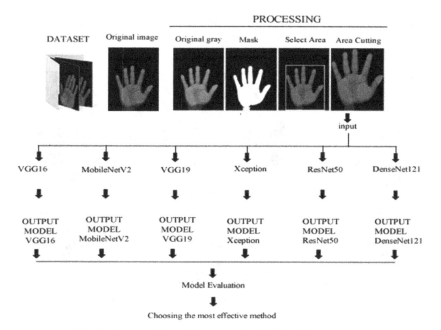

Fig. 7. Steps to choose the new method of identifying people.

3   Results and Discussions

Table 1 shows the accuracy and training time results obtained with each classifier. The ResNet50 neural network identified 99% of the subjects, having only failed to correctly find one of the persons.

Table 1. Performance of convolutional network architectures in handprint recognition.

Convolutional Network architecture	Response time	Precision	Accuracy	Recall
VGG16	2616321 ms	0,668	0,75	0,75
MobileNetV2	2316234 ms	0,925	0,95	0,95
VGG19	2516453 ms	0,648	0,73	0,73
Xception	2816345 ms	0,955	0,97	0,97
ResNet50	2716442 ms	0,985	0,99	0,99
DenseNet121	2616321 ms	0,668	0,75	0,75

Figure 8 shows the hand of the incorrectly identified subject and the one with which it was misidentified. As can be seen, there is a great similarity between them. The network that followed in performance was Xception, correctly identifying 97 of the subjects. The other networks did not perform as well, identifying at most 77 subjects. It is worth noting that the ResNEt50 network used smaller images as input than Xception, showing that the image size did not affect the quality of the classification (Fig. 9).

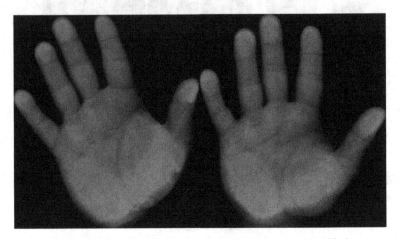

Fig. 8. Images of the handprints that were incorrectly identified.

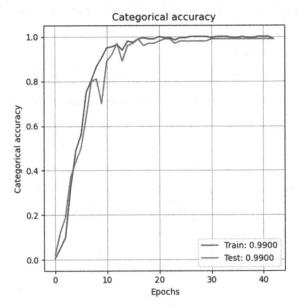

Fig. 9. Learning curve of the RESNET 50 convolutional network architecture.

4 Conclusions

The identification of people is currently of great importance. Several biometric systems have been implemented, among them the most used is based on the fingerprint. However, when fingerprints deteriorate due to the heavy work performed with the hands, this technique is inaccurate. For this reason, a technique based on handprint detection was presented in this work. Initially, an acquisition protocol was developed to obtain good quality images with a scanner. A database of the right hand of 100 construction workers was built. The identification technique comprises two stages. In the first, a mask is obtained to eliminate the background and retain only the region of interest. The resulting image is classified by a convolutional neural network to identify the subject. Six network architectures were evaluated, obtaining the best accuracy with ResNet50, correctly identifying 99 out of a total of 100 subjects, followed by Xception with 97% accuracy. Without the first step the networks did not converge, showing its importance to obtain good results.

References

1. Broadcasting Corporation British «BBC new». https://www.bbc.com/news/technology-306 23611. Accessed 04 Feb 2021
2. Sancho, C.: Breve Historia de la inteligencia artificial, Revista de Occidente, España (2018)
3. Gopal, G., Srivasta, S., Bhardwaj, S., Bhargava, S.: Fusion of palm-phalanges print with palmprint and dorsal hand vein. Appl. Soft Comput. **47**, 12–20 (2016)
4. El-Tarhouni, W., Boubchir, L., Elbendak, M., Bouridane, A.: Multispectral Palmprint Recognition Using Pascal Coefficients-Based LBP and PHOG Descriptors with Random Sampling. Springer, no. 21, p. 2 (2019). https://doi.org/10.1007/s00521-017-3092-7
5. Poonia, P., Ajmera, P.K., Bhalerao, A.: Palm-print recognition based on scale invariant features. In: IEEE 16th India Council International Conference. Indicon, pp. 1–4 (2019)
6. Akhoundzadeh, P., Ebrahimnezhad, H., Mirjalily, G.: Palm print recognition using modified local features based on sparse. In: 27th Iranian Conference on Electrical Engineering, Iranian, Iran, pp. 1429–1433 (2019)
7. Poonia, P., Ajmera, P.K., Shende, V.: Palmprint recognition using robust template matching. Proc. Comput. Sci. **167**, 727–736 (2020)
8. Li, Y., Pang, Y., Wang, Y., Xuelong, L.: Toward improving ECG biometric identification using cascaded convolutional neural networks. Neurocomputing **391**, 83–95 (2020)

Finding the Optimal Bit-Quad Patterns for Computing the Euler Number of 2D Binary Images Using Simulated Annealing

Wilfrido Gómez-Flores[1]([✉]) [iD], Humberto Sossa[2,3] [iD], and Fernando Arce[4] [iD]

[1] Centro de Investigación y de Estudios Avanzados del IPN,
Unidad Tamaulipas, Ciudad Victoria, Tamaulipas, Mexico
wgomez@cinvestav.mx
[2] Instituto Politécnico Nacional, Centro de Investigación en Computación,
07738 Mexico City, Mexico
[3] Tecnológico de Monterrey, Escuela de Ingeniería y Ciencias,
Zapopan, Jalisco, Mexico
[4] Centro de Investigaciones en Óptica A. C., León, Guanajuato, Mexico

Abstract. This paper presents an automatic method for obtaining formulas to calculate the Euler number in 2D binary images. This problem is addressed as a combinatorial optimization problem, where specific bit-quad patterns are optimally combined. An algorithm based on simulated annealing is devised to find optimal expressions to compute the Euler number, considering 4- and 8-connectivity. The proposed approach found the complete family of expressions using three bit-quad patterns that correctly estimate the Euler number. Besides, another 58 new expressions are found that use more than three bit-quads. Hence, the proposed method can obtain automatically explainable formulas of the Euler number, and it can be potentially extended to other image representations.

Keywords: Euler number · Bit-quad patterns · Combinatorial optimization · Simulated annealing · Explainability

1 Introduction

In computer vision tasks, calculating numerical features to describe the objects' nature is a necessary step. It is well known that such features should be invariant to image transformations and discriminant between different classes [2].

Generally, features for object recognition are designed through human engineering, based on the designer's intuition and expertise. These kinds of features are usually named hand-crafted features. Commonly, these features have the property of explainability; that is, a human being can understand the meaning of all the parts that make up the calculation of a feature [1]. However, the design of invariant and discriminant hand-crafted features can take a long time to trial different operator combinations to obtain a satisfactory result.

© Springer Nature Switzerland AG 2021
E. Roman-Rangel et al. (Eds.): MCPR 2021, LNCS 12725, pp. 240–250, 2021.
https://doi.org/10.1007/978-3-030-77004-4_23

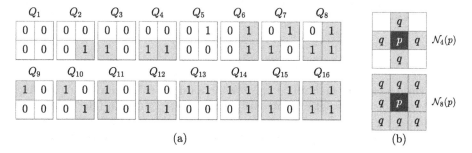

(a)   (b)

Fig. 1. (a) The 16 bit-quad patterns for computing the Euler number. (b) Two 1-valued pixels, p and q, are 4- and 8-connected if $q \in \mathcal{N}_4(p)$ and $q \in \mathcal{N}_8(p)$, respectively, where p is the central pixel of the neighborhood $\mathcal{N}$.

Although artificial intelligence-based methods for automatic feature extraction have become popular (e.g., deep neural networks), the lack of explainability is emerging as their critical deficiency. Hence, explainability is recognized nowadays as one of the main research fields in Artificial Intelligence [8].

In particular, the Euler number is a topological feature defined as [2]

$$e = c - h, \tag{1}$$

where c is the number of connected components, and h is the number of holes in the image. The Euler number is invariant under linear and nonlinear geometric transformations of the image. Hence, the Euler number has been used in many image analysis, computer vision, and object recognition applications [6,7,10].

Several approaches have been developed to compute the Euler number in 2D binary images, $I(x, y) \in \{0, 1\}$, where bit-quad-based algorithms are widely used to count specific bit-quad patterns in the image. Figure 1(a) shows the complete family of 16 bit-quad patterns, considering 0-pixels as the background and 1-pixels as the foreground (i.e., connected components).

Assuming that the digital image is composed of squared cells (Fig. 1(b)), the most well-known expressions to compute the Euler number using bit-quads in 4-connectivity (e_4) and 8-connectivity (e_8) were proposed by Gray [3]:

$$e_4 = (\#Q_\mathcal{A} - \#Q_\mathcal{B} + 2\#Q_\mathcal{C})/4, \tag{2}$$

$$e_8 = (\#Q_\mathcal{A} - \#Q_\mathcal{B} - 2\#Q_\mathcal{C})/4, \tag{3}$$

where $Q_\mathcal{A} = \{Q_2, Q_3, Q_5, Q_9\}$, $Q_\mathcal{B} = \{Q_8, Q_{12}, Q_{14}, Q_{15}\}$, and $Q_\mathcal{C} = \{Q_7, Q_{10}\}$, and the operator $\#$ counts the number of times that the elements of the bit-quad set $Q_{\{\cdot\}}$ appear in an input image. Notice that Gray's formulas use ten bit-quad patterns, making the Euler number calculation computationally inefficient.

Later, Sossa et al. demonstrated by mathematical induction that three bit-quad patterns are enough to compute the Euler number, reaching the following formulas [9]:

$$e_4 = \#Q_9 + \#Q_{10} - \#Q_{15}, \tag{4}$$

$$e_8 = -\#Q_7 + \#Q_9 - \#Q_{15}. \tag{5}$$

Likewise, Lin et al. proposed another set of formulas [5]:

$$e_4 = \#Q_2 - \#Q_8 + \#Q_{10}, \tag{6}$$
$$e_8 = \#Q_2 - \#Q_7 - \#Q_8. \tag{7}$$

All the expressions mentioned above were obtained using human engineering by analyzing distinct solutions manually. Nevertheless, one can infer that other expressions can still be undiscovered. Hence, to automatically find other new expressions for the Euler number calculation, it can be approached as an optimization problem, in which a search space is explored to find optimal solutions.

In this paper, an automatic method based on simulated annealing (SA) is proposed to find new formulas for calculating the Euler number in 2D binary images, considering 4- and 8-connectivity. The goal is to demonstrate the feasibility to automatically create new features that preserve the property of explainability, which means "saying" new formulas to compute, in this case, the Euler number as proof of concept.

2   Proposed Approach

2.1   Optimization Problem

The bit-quad-based Euler number can be expressed by the linear combination

$$e = z_1 \cdot \#Q_1 + z_2 \cdot \#Q_2 + \ldots + z_{16} \cdot \#Q_{16}, \tag{8}$$

where $\mathbf{z} = [z_1, z_2, \ldots, z_{16}]$ defines a solution of bit-quad patterns combination, such that the jth coefficient $z_j \in \{-1, 0, +1\}$.

A feasible solution $\mathbf{z}$ is tested on an image dataset during an optimization procedure where each sample has its correct Euler number. In this sense, let $X = \{\mathbf{x}_1, \mathbf{x}_2, \ldots, \mathbf{x}_n\}$ be an image dataset with n observations described by bit-quads, where each sample is a vector defined by $\mathbf{x} = [\#Q_1, \#Q_2, \ldots, \#Q_{16}]^T$, which is associated with an actual Euler number $e \in \mathbb{Z}$ to form the couple $(\mathbf{x}, e)_i$, for $i = 1, \ldots, n$.

The optimal solution is the vector $\mathbf{z}^*$ for which the dot product $e = \mathbf{x} \cdot \mathbf{z}^*$ provides the correct Euler number for every sample in the image dataset X. For instance, (4) can be expressed in terms of the following optimal solution:

$$\mathbf{z}^* = [0, 0, 0, 0, 0, 0, 0, 0, +1, +1, 0, 0, 0, 0, -1, 0].$$

The total number of potential solutions that should be tested to find the optimal combination of bit-quads is $\sum_{k=1}^{q} \binom{q}{k} \cdot 2^k$, where q is the total number of bit-quad patterns. Thus, for the 16 bit-quads in Fig. 1, the total number of potential solutions is about 43×10^6, which is computationally expensive to evaluate. Therefore, using the dataset X, the problem of finding the optimal combination of bit-quads can be formulated as

$$\begin{aligned} &\text{minimize } f(\mathbf{z}), \\ &\text{such that } z_j \in \{-1, 0, +1\}, \quad j = 1, \ldots, 16, \end{aligned} \tag{9}$$

where the objective function $f(\cdot)$ is the error rate defined as

$$\epsilon_{\mathbf{z}} = \frac{1}{n} \sum_{i=1}^{n} \mathbf{1}_{e_i}(\hat{e}_i^{\mathbf{z}}), \quad \text{with} \quad \mathbf{1}_e(\hat{e}) = \begin{cases} 1, & e \neq \hat{e}, \\ 0, & \text{otherwise}, \end{cases} \tag{10}$$

where $\hat{e}_i^{\mathbf{z}}$ is the predicted Euler number of the ith image using the solution $\mathbf{z}$. For the optimal solution $\mathbf{z}^*$, the error rate is zero.

2.2   Finding the Optimal Bit-Quad Patterns Using SA

SA is a stochastic local search method for global combinatorial optimization, allowing gradual convergence to a near-optimal solution. SA performs a sequence of moves from a current solution to a better one according to specific transition rules while occasionally accepting some uphill solutions to guarantee diversity in the domain exploration and avoid getting caught at local optima. The optimization process is managed by a cooling schedule that controls the number of iterations [4]. Thus, SA is adequate to find the optimal combination of bit-quad patterns to create an expression for computing the Euler number.

Algorithm 1 shows the pseudocode for finding the optimal bit-quad patterns using SA. The initial solution $\mathbf{z}_0$ (line 4) is generated as follows:

$$z_{0j} = [2 \cdot \mathcal{U}(0,1) - 1], \quad j = 1, \ldots, 16, \tag{11}$$

where $[\cdot]$ is the rounding function, and $\mathcal{U}(0,1)$ is a random number in the range $(0,1)$ drawn from a uniform distribution. The perturbation function to create a new state $\mathbf{z}'$ from $\mathbf{z}$ (line 8) is shown in Algorithm 2. Notice that some elements of $\mathbf{z}$ are randomly perturbed in the range $[-1,1]$. The Euler number is predicted by performing the dot product between $\mathbf{z}$ and $\mathbf{x}$ (line 9), which is equivalent to evaluating (8). The error rates of solutions $\mathbf{z}$ and $\mathbf{z}'$ are measured using (10) (line 10).

While the search space is explored, it is possible to find different solutions with an error rate of zero (i.e., optimal solutions). However, it is desirable to obtain solutions with zero error and a reduced number of bit-quads. Hence, the following rule is implemented to save the best solution so far (line 16): Save solution $\mathbf{z}$ if its error is less than the current best solution $\mathbf{z}^*$, or save solution $\mathbf{z}$ if its error is equal to the current best solution $\mathbf{z}^*$ and it has more zeros. For counting the zeros in $\mathbf{z}$, the following indicator function is used:

$$\mathbf{1}_0(z) = \begin{cases} 1, & z = 0, \\ 0, & \text{otherwise}. \end{cases} \tag{12}$$

Lastly, because the lowest number of bit-quads to compute the Euler number is three, then Algorithm 1 halts if the optimal solution $\mathbf{z}^*$ has 13 zeros (line 18).

Algorithm 1. Proposed approach based on SA.

---

input: Image dataset $(\mathbf{x}, e)_i$, $i = 1, \ldots, n$
1: $t \leftarrow 5$ // Initial temperature
2: $t_{\min} \leftarrow 1 \times 10^{-6}$ // Final temperature
3: $l_{\max} \leftarrow 100$ // Number of iterations at each temperature t
4: $\mathbf{z} \leftarrow \mathbf{z}_0$ // Generate initial solution
5: $\mathbf{z}^* \leftarrow \mathbf{z}$, $\epsilon^* \leftarrow \epsilon_{\mathbf{z}}$ // Save best solution and lowest error
6: **repeat**
7:     **for** $l \leftarrow 1$ **to** $l_{\max}$ **do**
8:         Generate a new solution $\mathbf{z}'$ by perturbing $\mathbf{z}$ // Algorithm 2
9:         $\begin{cases} \hat{e}_i^{\mathbf{z}} \leftarrow \mathbf{x}_i \cdot \mathbf{z}, \ \forall i \\ \hat{e}_i^{\mathbf{z}'} \leftarrow \mathbf{x}_i \cdot \mathbf{z}', \ \forall i \end{cases}$ // Predict Euler numbers
10:         $\Delta\epsilon = \epsilon_{\mathbf{z}'} - \epsilon_{\mathbf{z}}$ // Compute error rate difference
11:         **if** $\Delta\epsilon < 0$ **then**
12:             $\mathbf{z} \leftarrow \mathbf{z}'$, $\epsilon_{\mathbf{z}} \leftarrow \epsilon_{\mathbf{z}'}$ // Accept the new solution
13:         **else**
14:             **if** $\exp(-\Delta\epsilon/t) > \mathcal{U}(0, 1)$ **then**
15:                 $\mathbf{z} \leftarrow \mathbf{z}'$, $\epsilon_{\mathbf{z}} \leftarrow \epsilon_{\mathbf{z}'}$ // Accept with some probability
16:         **if** $\left(\epsilon_{\mathbf{z}} < \epsilon^*\right) \vee \left(\left(\epsilon_{\mathbf{z}} = \epsilon^*\right) \wedge \left(\sum_{j=1}^{16} \mathbf{1}_0(z_j) > \sum_{j=1}^{16} \mathbf{1}_0(z_j^*)\right)\right)$ **then**
17:             $\mathbf{z}^* \leftarrow \mathbf{z}$, $\epsilon^* \leftarrow \epsilon_{\mathbf{z}}$ // Save best solution so far
18:         **if** $\left(\epsilon^* = 0\right) \wedge \left(\sum_{j=1}^{16} \mathbf{1}_0(z_j^*) = 13\right)$ **then**
19:             **return**
20:     $t \leftarrow t/(1 + 0.01t)$ // Decrease temperature
21: **until** $t < t_{\min}$
output: Best solution $\mathbf{z}^*$

Algorithm 2. Perturbation function.

Input: Solution $\mathbf{z}$
1: $\mathbf{z}' \leftarrow \mathbf{z}$
2: **for** $i \leftarrow 1$ **to** 16 **do**
3:     **if** $\mathcal{U}(0, 1) > 0.5$ // Perturb ith position
4:         **if** $z_i > 0$
5:             $z_i' \leftarrow [\mathcal{U}(0, 1) - 1]$ // Random integer number in the range $[-1, 0]$
6:         **else if** $z_i < 0$
7:             $z_i' \leftarrow [\mathcal{U}(0, 1)]$ // Random integer number in the range $[0, 1]$
8:         **else**
9:             $z_i' \leftarrow [2 \cdot \mathcal{U}(0, 1) - 1]$ // Random integer number in the range $[-1, 1]$
Output: Perturbed solution $\mathbf{z}'$

2.3 Experimental Setup

A training dataset with $11,500$ binary images of size 96×96 was used during the SA-based search procedure to measure the error rate. For each training image, it was calculated the reference Euler number for 4- and 8-connectivity using Gray's formulas in Eqs. 2 and 3, respectively. The calculated Euler numbers were in the range $[-20, 23]$.

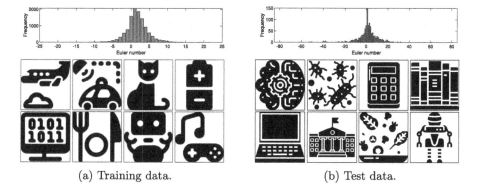

(a) Training data.   (b) Test data.

Fig. 2. Top: Distribution of Euler numbers for 8-connectivity. A similar behavior is obtained for 4-connectivity. Bottom: Examples of 2D binary images. The image negatives are shown for illustrative purposes.

For evaluating the correctness of the expressions found to compute the Euler number, an independent test set with $1,122$ binary images (256×256 pixels) was used. For every test image, the reference Euler number for 4- and 8-connectivity was calculated using Gray's formulas. The calculated Euler numbers were in the range $[-85, 61]$, which is broader than the Euler numbers in the training set, aiming to assess the generalization of the found expression outside the known range. Figure 2 shows examples of training and test binary images.

Because the SA algorithm is a stochastic search procedure, 100 independent experiments were run. At each experiment, $10,000$ samples from the entire training set were drawn randomly. The goal is to verify if the proposed approach can converge to the optimal solution with variations in the training set. The found optimal solutions to compute the Euler number were evaluated in the test set, and the error rate was measured.

3   Results

Table 1 summarizes the eight optimal expressions composed of three bit-quads for computing the Euler found by SA. The third column shows the number of times that the proposed method found each expression over 100 experiments. Notice that four expressions already reported in the literature were found, as well as four new expressions. This result reveals the proposed approach's capability to find expressions made by human engineering and create new ones. The eight expressions in Table 1 attained an error rate of zero on the test set for all the 100 experiments. It is worth mentioning that the four expressions for each

Table 1. The optimal combination of three bit-quads for computing the Euler number found by SA on the training dataset. Symbol '•' marks expressions that were reported in the literature.

Expression	Bit-quad patterns			Times found
4-connectivity				
$\#Q_5 + \#Q_7 - \#Q_{14}$	$\left(\begin{smallmatrix}0&1\\0&0\end{smallmatrix}\right)$	$\left(\begin{smallmatrix}0&1\\1&0\end{smallmatrix}\right)$	$\left(\begin{smallmatrix}1&1\\0&1\end{smallmatrix}\right)$	23
$\#Q_3 + \#Q_7 - \#Q_{12}$	$\left(\begin{smallmatrix}0&0\\1&0\end{smallmatrix}\right)$	$\left(\begin{smallmatrix}0&1\\1&0\end{smallmatrix}\right)$	$\left(\begin{smallmatrix}1&0\\1&1\end{smallmatrix}\right)$	23
$\#Q_2 + \#Q_{10} - \#Q_8$	$\left(\begin{smallmatrix}0&0\\0&1\end{smallmatrix}\right)$	$\left(\begin{smallmatrix}1&0\\0&1\end{smallmatrix}\right)$	$\left(\begin{smallmatrix}0&1\\1&1\end{smallmatrix}\right)$	23•
$\#Q_9 + \#Q_{10} - \#Q_{15}$	$\left(\begin{smallmatrix}1&0\\0&0\end{smallmatrix}\right)$	$\left(\begin{smallmatrix}1&0\\0&1\end{smallmatrix}\right)$	$\left(\begin{smallmatrix}1&1\\1&0\end{smallmatrix}\right)$	31•
8-connectivity				
$\#Q_9 - \#Q_7 - \#Q_{15}$	$\left(\begin{smallmatrix}1&0\\0&0\end{smallmatrix}\right)$	$\left(\begin{smallmatrix}0&1\\1&0\end{smallmatrix}\right)$	$\left(\begin{smallmatrix}1&1\\1&0\end{smallmatrix}\right)$	28•
$\#Q_2 - \#Q_7 - \#Q_8$	$\left(\begin{smallmatrix}0&0\\0&1\end{smallmatrix}\right)$	$\left(\begin{smallmatrix}0&1\\1&0\end{smallmatrix}\right)$	$\left(\begin{smallmatrix}0&1\\1&1\end{smallmatrix}\right)$	30•
$\#Q_3 - \#Q_{10} - \#Q_{12}$	$\left(\begin{smallmatrix}0&0\\1&0\end{smallmatrix}\right)$	$\left(\begin{smallmatrix}1&0\\0&1\end{smallmatrix}\right)$	$\left(\begin{smallmatrix}1&0\\1&1\end{smallmatrix}\right)$	20
$\#Q_5 - \#Q_{10} - \#Q_{14}$	$\left(\begin{smallmatrix}0&1\\0&0\end{smallmatrix}\right)$	$\left(\begin{smallmatrix}1&0\\0&1\end{smallmatrix}\right)$	$\left(\begin{smallmatrix}1&1\\0&1\end{smallmatrix}\right)$	22

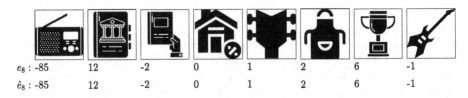

e_8 : -85	12	-2	0	1	2	6	-1
$\hat{e}_8$: -85	12	-2	0	1	2	6	-1

Fig. 3. Euler numbers calculated on test images. The reference value e_8 is calculated with Gray's formula in (3), and the estimated value is calculated with the new expression $\hat{e}_8 = \#Q_3 - \#Q_{10} - \#Q_{12}$.

connectivity type represent the complete set of optimal combinations of three bit-quad patterns. Figure 3 shows examples of the Euler number calculated on test images using the new expression $\hat{e}_8 = \#Q_3 - \#Q_{10} - \#Q_{12}$. Notice that for all cases the correct value of the Euler number was obtained.

Figure 4 shows an example of a test image composed of one connected component and four holes, giving an Euler number of -3. After applying different linear and nonlinear geometric transformations to the original image, the new expression $\hat{e}_8 = \#Q_5 - \#Q_{10} - \#Q_{14}$ correctly estimates the Euler number.

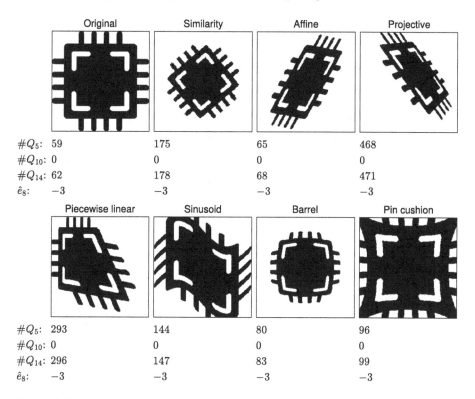

Original	Similarity	Affine	Projective

$\#Q_5$: 59   175   65   468
$\#Q_{10}$: 0   0   0   0
$\#Q_{14}$: 62   178   68   471
$\hat{e}_8$: -3 -3 -3 -3

Piecewise linear	Sinusoid	Barrel	Pin cushion

$\#Q_5$: 293   144   80   96
$\#Q_{10}$: 0   0   0   0
$\#Q_{14}$: 296   147   83   99
$\hat{e}_8$: -3 -3 -3 -3

Fig. 4. Euler numbers calculated on a test image under distinct linear and nonlinear geometric transformations. The estimated value of the Euler number is calculated with the new expression $\hat{e}_8 = \#Q_5 - \#Q_{10} - \#Q_{14}$.

For computational efficiency purposes, Algorithm 1 was designed to output an expression with three bit-quad patterns. However, other optimal solutions for computing the Euler number can be found during the optimization procedure before finding the final solution, as shown in Table 2. In the 4- and 8-connected cases, there were found 30 and 28 new expressions, respectively. Nevertheless, optimal solutions with more than three bit-quads can be considered local optima from the viewpoint of multiobjective optimization, where both the error rate and the number of bit-quad patterns are minimized. Although the proposed approach is based on global optimization, the implemented rule for selecting the best solution helps obtain expressions with the lowest number of bit-quads.

Table 2. Optimal solutions with more than three bit-quad patterns. For clarity, the operator '#' is omitted.

4-connectivity	8-connectivity
$-Q_2 + Q_3 - Q_6 + Q_7 + Q_9 + Q_{11} - Q_{14}$	$-Q_3 - Q_4 + Q_5 - Q_7 - Q_8 + Q_9 + Q_{13}$
$-Q_3 - Q_4 + Q_5 - Q_8 + Q_9 + Q_{10} + Q_{13}$	$+Q_3 - Q_5 - Q_6 - Q_7 - Q_8 + Q_9 + Q_{11}$
$-Q_2 - Q_4 + Q_5 + Q_7 + Q_9 - Q_{12} + Q_{13}$	$+Q_2 - Q_3 + Q_5 + Q_6 - Q_7 - Q_{11} - Q_{15}$
$+Q_2 + Q_5 + Q_6 + Q_7 - Q_9 - Q_{11} - Q_{12}$	$+Q_2 + Q_3 - Q_5 - Q_7 - Q_8 - Q_{12} + Q_{14}$
$+Q_2 + Q_3 + Q_4 + Q_7 - Q_9 - Q_{13} - Q_{14}$	$+Q_2 - Q_3 + Q_5 - Q_7 - Q_8 + Q_{12} - Q_{14}$
$+Q_3 - Q_5 - Q_6 - Q_8 + Q_9 + Q_{10} + Q_{11}$	$-Q_2 - Q_4 + Q_5 + Q_9 - Q_{10} - Q_{12} + Q_{13}$
$+Q_2 + Q_5 + Q_7 - Q_8 - Q_9 - Q_{14} + Q_{15}$	$-Q_3 + Q_5 - Q_7 + Q_9 + Q_{12} - Q_{14} - Q_{15}$
$+Q_2 + Q_3 + Q_7 - Q_8 - Q_9 - Q_{12} + Q_{15}$	$-Q_2 + Q_3 + Q_8 + Q_9 - Q_{10} + Q_{11} - Q_{15}$
$-Q_2 + Q_3 + Q_7 + Q_8 + Q_9 - Q_{12} - Q_{15}$	$-Q_6 - Q_7 - Q_8 + Q_9 + Q_{11} + Q_{12} - Q_{14}$
$-Q_2 + Q_5 + Q_7 + Q_8 + Q_9 - Q_{14} - Q_{15}$	$+Q_2 + Q_3 - Q_8 - Q_9 - Q_{10} - Q_{12} + Q_{15}$
$-Q_4 + Q_5 + Q_7 - Q_8 - Q_{12} + Q_{13} + Q_{15}$	$+Q_2 + Q_3 + Q_4 - Q_9 - Q_{10} - Q_{12} - Q_{14}$
$+Q_2 - Q_3 + Q_5 + Q_6 + Q_{10} - Q_{11} - Q_{15}$	$-Q_2 + Q_5 + Q_8 + Q_9 - Q_{10} - Q_{14} - Q_{15}$
$+Q_3 + Q_4 + Q_7 + Q_8 - Q_{13} - Q_{14} - Q_{15}$	$+Q_3 - Q_5 - Q_7 + Q_9 - Q_{12} + Q_{14} - Q_{15}$
$+Q_2 + Q_3 + Q_4 - Q_5 + Q_{10} - Q_{13} - Q_{15}$	$-Q_4 - Q_7 - Q_8 + Q_9 - Q_{12} + Q_{13} + Q_{14}$
$+Q_2 + Q_3 - Q_5 - Q_8 + Q_{10} - Q_{12} + Q_{14}$	$+Q_2 + Q_5 + Q_6 - Q_9 - Q_{10} - Q_{11} - Q_{12}$
$+Q_5 + Q_6 + Q_7 + Q_8 - Q_{11} - Q_{12} - Q_{15}$	$+Q_2 + Q_5 - Q_8 - Q_9 - Q_{10} - Q_{14} + Q_{15}$
$+Q_2 - Q_3 + Q_5 - Q_8 + Q_{10} + Q_{12} - Q_{14}$	$-Q_2 + Q_3 - Q_8 + Q_9 - Q_{10} + Q_{11} - Q_{14}$
$+Q_3 - Q_6 + Q_7 - Q_8 + Q_{11} - Q_{14} + Q_{15}$	$+Q_2 + Q_6 - Q_7 - Q_{11} - Q_{12} + Q_{14} - Q_{15}$
$-Q_4 - Q_8 + Q_9 + Q_{10} - Q_{12} + Q_{13} + Q_{14}$	$+Q_5 + Q_6 + Q_8 - Q_{10} - Q_{11} - Q_{12} - Q_{15}$
$-Q_3 + Q_5 + Q_9 + Q_{10} + Q_{12} - Q_{14} - Q_{15}$	$-Q_4 + Q_5 - Q_8 - Q_{10} - Q_{12} + Q_{13} + Q_{15}$
$+Q_3 - Q_5 + Q_9 + Q_{10} - Q_{12} + Q_{14} - Q_{15}$	$+Q_3 + Q_4 + Q_8 - Q_{10} - Q_{13} - Q_{14} - Q_{15}$
$-Q_6 - Q_8 + Q_9 + Q_{10} + Q_{11} + Q_{12} - Q_{14}$	$+Q_2 + Q_4 - Q_7 + Q_{12} - Q_{13} - Q_{14} - Q_{15}$
$+Q_2 + Q_4 + Q_{10} + Q_{12} - Q_{13} - Q_{14} - Q_{15}$	$+Q_3 - Q_6 - Q_8 - Q_{10} + Q_{11} - Q_{14} + Q_{15}$
$+Q_2 + Q_6 + Q_{10} - Q_{11} - Q_{12} + Q_{14} - Q_{15}$	$+Q_2 - Q_3 - Q_4 + Q_5 + Q_6 - Q_7 - Q_8 - Q_{11} - Q_{12} + Q_{13} + Q_{14}$
$-Q_2 - Q_4 + Q_5 - Q_6 + Q_7 - Q_8 + Q_9 + Q_{11} + Q_{13} - Q_{14} + Q_{15}$	$-Q_2 + Q_3 - Q_4 - Q_6 - Q_8 + Q_9 - Q_{10} + Q_{11} - Q_{12} + Q_{13} + Q_{15}$
$+Q_2 + Q_4 + Q_5 + Q_6 + Q_7 + Q_8 - Q_9 - Q_{11} - Q_{13} - Q_{14} - Q_{15}$	$-Q_3 - Q_4 + Q_5 + Q_6 - Q_7 + Q_9 - Q_{11} - Q_{12} + Q_{13} + Q_{14} - Q_{15}$
$-Q_2 + Q_3 - Q_4 - Q_6 + Q_7 - Q_8 + Q_9 + Q_{11} - Q_{12} + Q_{13} + Q_{15}$	$-Q_2 - Q_4 + Q_5 - Q_6 - Q_8 + Q_9 - Q_{10} + Q_{11} + Q_{13} - Q_{14} + Q_{15}$
$+Q_2 - Q_3 - Q_4 + Q_5 + Q_6 - Q_8 + Q_{10} - Q_{11} - Q_{12} + Q_{13} + Q_{14}$	
$+Q_3 + Q_4 - Q_5 - Q_6 + Q_9 + Q_{10} + Q_{11} + Q_{12} - Q_{13} - Q_{14} - Q_{15}$	
$-Q_3 - Q_4 + Q_5 + Q_6 + Q_9 + Q_{10} - Q_{11} - Q_{12} + Q_{13} + Q_{14} - Q_{15}$	

4   Conclusions

One of the current research directions in computer vision is automatic feature learning through Artificial Intelligence techniques, such as convolutional neural networks. This learning paradigm has reduced human intervention, impacting the time required to manually design invariant and discriminant features. However, learned features lack explainability, which is the property of explaining what is happening such that a human can understand it. Therefore, the automatic design of explainable features is an open research field.

For automatically designing explainable features, a feasible way is to search for the best combination of known basic operators, leading to a mathematical expression that can be understood by a human. In this work, we take the Euler number as a proof of concept since it is an important topological feature that can be computed by combining specific bit-quad patterns.

We proposed using simulated annealing to find the optimal combination of bit-quads for the Euler number calculation. The experimental results revealed that the proposed method found the complete family of expressions that use three bit-quads in 4- and 8-connectivity. There were found four new expressions with three bit-quads (the least amount possible) to calculate the Euler number and obtained the expressions that had been reported in the literature designed by human engineering. We demonstrated that the new expressions are invariant to linear and nonlinear geometric transformations of the image, a fundamental property of the Euler number.

Besides, 58 new expressions were found to calculate the Euler number for 4- and 8-connectivity correctly. Although these 58 expressions are valid, they could be considered computationally inefficient since they are composed of more than three bit-quad patterns. Nevertheless, we reported them with the purpose of demonstrating that the proposed approach can create new expressions understandable by humans.

The satisfactory performance of the proposed approach is because of the conjunction of two main factors. The first one is using simple operators, i.e., bit-quads, whose operation is easily understood. The second factor is the optimization method to combine the bit-quads so that the Euler number calculation can be computed correctly.

Due to these promising results, future work considers extending the proposed method to discover new formulas by optimally combining bit-octos to estimate the Euler number of 3D binary images. Moreover, other image representations different from bit-quad patterns can be explored. This research direction implies discovering explainable features for binary and grayscale images that are useful for image classification problems. Also, other combinatorial optimization methods and population-based metaheuristics will be investigated.

Acknowledgements. The authors would like to thank the Cinvestav-IPN, Centro de Investigaciones en Óptica A.C., and Instituto Politécnico Nacional for the economic support under projects: FidSC2018/145 (Fondo SEP-Cinvestav), 20200630 and 20210788 (SIP-IPN), 65 (Frontiers of Science, CONACYT), 6005 (FORDECYT-PRONACES, CONACYT) to undertake this research.

References

1. Doshi-Velez, F., Kim, B.: Considerations for evaluation and generalization in interpretable machine learning. In: Escalante, H.J., et al. (eds.) Explainable and Interpretable Models in Computer Vision and Machine Learning. TSSCML, pp. 3–17. Springer, Cham (2018). https://doi.org/10.1007/978-3-319-98131-4_1
2. Gonzalez, R.C., Woods, R.E.: Digital Image Processing, 4 edn. Pearson (2018)
3. Gray, S.B.: Local properties of binary images in two dimensions. IEEE Trans. Comput. C **20**(5), 551–561 (1971)
4. Kirkpatrick, S., Gelatt, C.D., Vecchi, M.P.: Optimization by simulated annealing. Science **220**(4598), 671–680 (1983)
5. Lin, X., Ji, J., Gu, Y.: The Euler number study of image and its application. In: 2nd IEEE Conference on Industrial Electronics and Applications, pp. 910–912 (2007)
6. Maji, P., Chatterjee, S., Chakraborty, S., Kausar, N., Samanta, S., Dey, N.: Effect of Euler number as a feature in gender recognition system from offline handwritten signature using neural networks. In: 2nd International Conference on Computing for Sustainable Global Development, pp. 1869–1873 (2015)
7. Matsuoka, Y.R., Sandoval, G.A.R., Say, L.P.Q., Teng, J.S.Y., Acula, D.D.: Enhanced intelligent character recognition (ICR) approach using diagonal feature extraction and Euler number as classifier with modified one-pixel width character

segmentation algorithm. In: International Conference on Platform Technology and Service, pp. 1–6 (2018)

8. Rudin, C.: Stop explaining black box machine learning models for high stakes decisions and use interpretable models instead. Nat. Mach. Intell. **1**, 206–2015 (2019)

9. Sossa-Azuela, J.H., Carreón-Torres, Á.A., Santiago-Montero, R., Bribiesca-Correa, E., Petrilli-Barceló, A.: Efficient computation of the Euler number of a 2-D binary image. In: Sidorov, G., Herrera-Alcántara, O. (eds.) MICAI 2016. LNCS (LNAI), vol. 10061, pp. 401–413. Springer, Cham (2017). https://doi.org/10.1007/978-3-319-62434-1_33

10. Zhang, Q., Wang, L., Yu, J.H., Zhang, M.: Segmentation-based Euler number with multi-levels for image feature description. Proc. Comput. Sci. **111**, 245–251 (2017)

Perceptual and Pixel-Wise Information for Visual Novelty Detection

Miguel A. Palacios-Alonso$^{(\boxtimes)}$, Hugo Jair Escalante, and L. Enrique Sucar

Department of Computer Science, Instituto Nacional de Astrofísica,
Óptica y Electrónica, 72840 Puebla, Mexico
{mpalacio,hugojair,esucar}@inaoep.mx

Abstract. Novelty detection is a process of identifying if new data does
not belong to the previously observed patterns; this is important in
several applications such as medical diagnosis and autonomous driving, where wrongly identifying a novel pattern could be catastrophic.
We focus on the problem of novelty detection in images based on deep
learning (DL) techniques. DL based models are trained through an optimization process in which a loss function is minimized. For visual novelty
detection, this loss function must be able to capture in a scalar value the
visual properties of the *normal* samples, usually the mean square error
(MSE). While satisfactory performance has been obtained with this formulation, it is often complicated for a single loss function to capture all
of the relevant information to discriminate novelty from normality. In
this paper we propose novel reconstruction loss that combines pixel-wise
and perceptual information. Its performance is experimentally evaluated
using generative adversarial networks (GANs), and compared against
autoencoders based on MSE, showing superior performance. Additionally, we present an application to novelty detection in X-Ray images,
which is relevant for current work con COVID diagnosis.

Keywords: Novelty detection · Deep learning · Autoencoders ·
Generative adversarial networks

1 Introduction

The novelty term was introduced by Pavlov [19] in a psycho-physiology study
about the orienting reflex. In this study, novel is an unknown or unexpected
stimuli that generates a response in humans and animals. From the modeling
point of view, novelty detection is a process of identifying if new data does not
belong to the previously observed patterns. Consequently, explicit information
on the *target* is not available during the training phase.

Novelty detection has been studied with a wide diversity of approaches
including Bayesian and neural network based [17]. It is a problem closely related
to outlier detection and anomaly detection. Practical applications have been

© Springer Nature Switzerland AG 2021
E. Roman-Rangel et al. (Eds.): MCPR 2021, LNCS 12725, pp. 251–260, 2021.
https://doi.org/10.1007/978-3-030-77004-4_24

studied in different domains. Some of these applications include network intrusion [7], autonomous driving [2], video surveillance [23], and medical applications [5], among others.

We are particularly interested in novelty detection in images, which is important in several applications such as medical diagnosis and autonomous driving. In this context, deep learning based methods have gained popularity because of their capability to abstract information contained in large visual datasets. However, while this capability depends on the availability of data, novelty detection is an unsupervised task, hence no information from the target is available. Therefore, these capabilities cannot be directly exploited by traditional classification architectures for the case of novelty detection. Nevertheless, developments in deep learning have shown the potential of autoencoders and Generative Adversarial Networks (GANs) as a framework for novelty detection [1,4,16,18,21]. The main reason is that novelty detection can be modeled as a one class classifier in which only normal data is available. Hence, the generative capabilities of GANs and autoencoders can be used as a means of capturing normality.

In general, deep learning based models are trained through an optimization process in which a loss function is minimized. This function is the prediction error of the model whose design/selection depends on the type of data. Design or selection of this function can be a challenging problem because the loss function must capture in a scalar value the desired behavior of the model in the particular domain. It is difficult for a single loss function to capture all of the relevant information to discriminate novelty from normality.

In this paper we propose novel reconstruction loss that combines pixel-wise and perceptual information in order to abstract the visual properties of images, which are integrated via a weighted linear combination. Its performance is experimentally evaluated using generative adversarial networks (GANs), and compared against autoencoders based on the Mean Square Error (MSE), showing superior performance. Additionally, we present an application to novelty detection in X-Ray images, which is relevant for current work on COVID diagnosis. The main contribution of our work lies in the fact that it is the first one that combines specific complimentary loss functions in a single model for the novelty detection task.

The remainder of this paper is organized as follows. The next section provides an overview of related work. The architecture and the proposed loss function are described in Sect. 3. The experiments and quantitative comparisons are described in Sect. 4. Finally, conclusions are presented in Sect. 5.

2   Related Work

Although different techniques have been proposed for novelty detection, in this brief review we focus on novelty detection in images based on deep learning. Deep learning methods have gained popularity because of the capability of these models to extract data features which can be used in end-to-end solutions, providing very good results in several areas. Recently, generative models like autoencoders and GANs have been studied as mechanisms that provide a framework for novelty detection. The self-supervised capabilities of these types of models allows the design of one class classification solutions [10].

In general, an autoencoder aims to reproduce the input in the output. As novelty detection considers normal data for training, it is expected higher error reconstructions for novel samples. So, the error reconstruction can be used as a novelty signal. In [1], the encoding capability of an autoencoder is used for mapping an image into features. These features are used for clustering using a density clustering-based technique. Chen et al. [4] proposed an autoencoder model for the detection of novel visual scenarios in vision-based self-driving systems. Visual Back Propagation [3] is used to compute activation maps that are presented to the autoencoder. The Similarity Structural Index is used as a loss function and error reconstruction is used as novelty measure. Amini et al. [2] model the uncertainty about the environment in which a full-scale autonomous car navigates. Variance of each latent variable of a variational autoencoder trained for heading prediction and the L_1 norm are used for modeling uncertainty.

On the other hand, GANs provide also a convenient framework for novelty detection. The capability of GANs to generate synthetic 'novel' samples during early stages of training can be used as partial knowledge about novelty data. Also, the discriminator provides feedback about the level of normality/novelty both in training and testing phases. A study about GANs for novelty detection is presented in [21]. A comparison with PCA is analyzed showing competitive results on MNIST [6] and industrial monitoring datasets. In [16], the authors proposed OCGAN, a model based on a denoising variational autoencoder that aims to constraint the latent distribution in order to represent normal data only. The strategy considers an adversarial training phase with a latent discriminator. Motivated by encoder and GAN capabilities, methods that exploit/complement capabilities of these models have been proposed. An adversarial approach is presented by [18]. The modeling is based on a GAN in which the generator subnetwork is a convolutional autoencoder. The discriminator's output is used as a novelty measure.

Along with the deep architecture design, the selection/design of a function that captures the properties of data is required. In particular, to capture the complexity and semantic information contained in images by a single value can be a challenging task. Most of the state of the art considers the MSE as loss function. However, for complex visual scenarios and novelty detection requirements this measure may not correctly capture the properties of the images required to discriminate novelty. In contrast with previous work, we propose a GAN-based model for visual novelty detection in which a weighted combination of pixel-wise and structural measures are considered as the loss function.

3 Novelty Detection Method

For visual novelty detection, we adopt a model that uses a Generative Adversarial Network (GAN) approach. A GAN [9] is based on a theoretic game scenario in which two sub-networks compete one against the other. A generator, G, produces samples $\tilde{x} = G(z, \theta_G)$. Where z is a latent variable and θ_G are the parameters of G. A second network, the discriminator, D, tries to distinguish between fake and real samples. The output of this model is the probability that the input is (or not) real. Consequently, the Generator and Discriminator are learned with a loss function formulated as follows:

$$\mathcal{L}_{adv} = \min_G \max_D (\mathbb{E}_{X \sim p_t}[log(D(X, \theta_D))]) + \mathbb{E}_{Z \sim p_z}[log(1 - D(G(Z, \theta_G)))]) \quad (1)$$

where Z is the latent space, p_t the distribution of the data, p_z the latent space distribution and θ_D the discriminator's parameters.

It is worth pointing out that the standard generator G in Eq. 1 can be an autoencoder model [18]. As a result of this integration, a GAN can be able to generate samples from specific inputs instead of noise. Hence, this model provides a framework for novelty detection in which the inputs are the normal samples.

3.1   Architecture

As proposed by [18], we use a GAN-based approach with a convolutional denoising autoencoder as the generator. A general overview of the model is shown in Fig. 1. In the training phase, samples, X, from normal data are presented to G. Reconstructions produced by G and normal samples are inputs to D. Thus, the generator tries to produce normal samples, while the discriminator tries to identify normal samples.

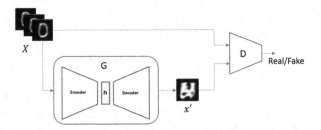

Fig. 1. A novelty detector based on a GAN architecture. As proposed by Sabokrou et al. [18], a convolutional autoencoder is used as the Generator.

Figure 2 shows the architecture of the Generator and Discriminator sub-networks. The generator is a convolutional denoising autoencoder with 4 convolutional layers (encoder) with Leaky-ReLU activations and 5 deconvolutional layers (decoder), 3 of these layers with ReLU activations and the last layer with sigmoid activation. The discriminator has 4 convolutional layers, 1 flatten layer and a final node with sigmoid activation.

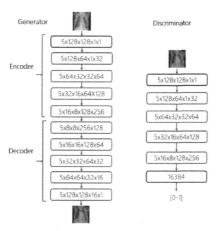

Fig. 2. Generator and discriminator architectures. Blue rectangles are convolutional layers and black rectangles are input layer in case of generator and input/flatten layers for the Discriminator. Considering *width = height* for kernels, inputs and outputs, parameters are indicated as: kernel size x input size x output size x input channels x output channels.

3.2   Loss Function

As mentioned before, in the GAN learning phase the generator tries to generate real samples and the discriminator tries to identify fake samples, i.e., samples produced by the generator. This interaction is captured by the L_{adv} function. In addition to this function, we introduced a second component, the specific loss function for the autoencoder that is in charge of capturing visual properties contained in images. This component consist of a weighted linear combination of two elements, the Mean Square Error and the Similarity Structural Index.

Mean Square Error. The Mean Square Error (MSE) is used to measure the pixel-wise difference between the images x and y. In this context, x is the input and y the reconstruction.

$$\mathcal{L}_{MSE} = \frac{1}{n} \sum_{1}^{n} (x_i - y_i)^2 \qquad (2)$$

Structural Similarity Index. The Structural Similarity Index (SSI) is a perceptual measure that quantifies similarity between two images considering luminance, contrast and structural information [22].

$$\mathcal{L}_{SSI} = l(x,y)^\alpha c(x,y)^\beta s(x,y)^\gamma \qquad (3)$$

where $l(x,y)$ is the luminance component, $c(x,y)$ is the contrast component and $s(x,y)$ is the structural component. These components compute the correlation between two samples based on average, variance and co-variance, respectively. α, β and γ are weight factors.

MSE is a well-known metric that measures the average of the squares of the errors. Because its simplicity, it has been used in several generative approaches. However, for image comparison pixel-wise difference could not be able to abstract all the visual information. So, the SSI is used to complement the loss function used for the generator in the GAN framework. The generator loss is defined as follows:

$$\mathcal{L}_G = \alpha\mathcal{L}_{SSI} + (1-\alpha)\mathcal{L}_{MSE} \tag{4}$$

Consequently, L_G loss is a combined function that goes beyond distances in image space and can capture perceptual properties, α is a weight factor (determined experimentally). The complete loss of the model is defined as:

$$\mathcal{L} = \mathcal{L}_{adv} + \mathcal{L}_G \tag{5}$$

Thus, two main elements guide the optimization process: the L_G loss function that favors capturing features in a pixel-wise and perceptual level, and the adversarial design (L_{adv}) that aims to promote the generalization of the method.

4   Experiments

We evaluated the performance of the model in terms of Area Under the Curve (AUC) for the MNIST and radiography datasets. We used the proposed L_G loss function in the generator. For the adversarial loss L_{adv} we used the Binary Cross Entropy [8] in both generator and discriminator. During training we used RMSprop optimizer [20], a learning rate of 0.001, a batch size of 128, a maximum of 100 epochs, and the proposed L_G loss function with $\alpha = 0.5$ in all experiments. Unlike [18], we used L_G as the novelty measure in the test phase. As the model has been trained with normal data, higher reconstruction errors are expected for novel samples compared to normal samples.

A baseline convolutional autoencoder is used for quantitative comparison. During training, L_{MSE} is used as loss function and as a novelty measure in the test phase. The Adam optimizer [13] is used with a learning rate of 0.003.

4.1   Datasets

MNIST. This dataset [6] includes images of handwritten digits (0–9). Data used for training is considered the normal set. In this way, 10 experiments are executed in which each of the ten digits is considered as the normal set, and all other categories as novelty. Each experiment consists of 5 training/test phases. For testing, we used 630 samples as normal data and 630 samples as novel.

Radiography. This data includes several high dimensional datasets, thorax [12], hand [11], breast [14] and brain [15] X-ray images (see Fig. 3). All samples are resized to 128×128 pixels. For this dataset, only thorax X-ray images are considered as normal, and all other types of X-rays as novelty. We evaluated the model in this dataset as part of a Covid diagnosis system in which a verification step was required. Only thorax radiographies must be considered for Covid diagnosis; otherwise should be rejected.

Fig. 3. Some samples of the thorax, brain, breast and hand X-ray images used in the experiments.

4.2   Autoencoder

As a baseline model, we used a convolutional autoencoder. The hidden representation is a 128-channel feature map of 8×8. The version used for the autoencoder experiments is shown in Fig. 4. A max pooling layer is used after each convolutional layer of the encoder. ReLU activations are used in 8 convolutional layers and the final layer uses a sigmoid activation.

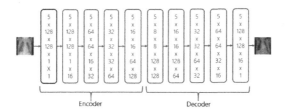

Fig. 4. Architecture of the baseline convolutional autoencoder

4.3   Results

Table 1 summarizes the results for the MNIST data in terms of the AUC computed from 5 training/testing phases for every digit. The AUC is computed based on the L_G errors of the test set. From the MNIST test data, 630 samples were selected as normal and 630 samples as novel. For novel samples, 70 instances of each digit different to target are selected. Autoencoder and GAN models were adjusted in order to support the dimension of the MNIST samples and corresponding experiments were executed. In 9 of the 10 digits the GAN-based model with L_G loss obtains a higher AUC, in one case there is a tie.

Table 2 reports the AUCs obtained considering the GAN and autoencoder models in 5 training/test phases for the radiography dataset. In this experiment, 600 thorax radiographies are the normal set, and 600 hand, brain and breast samples are the novel set. Novel set contains 200 samples of each novel category. Although the AUCs are closer, also the GAN with L_G loss shows a better performance.

Table 1. Comparison of the proposed model and an autoencoder for the MNIST dataset. Average AUCs and standard deviations computed from 5 training/testing phases for each category. Categories different to normal class are used as novel samples.

Model	0	1	2	3	4
Ours	**0.95 ± 0.0091**	0.99 ± 0.0005	**0.82 ± 0.0101**	**0.83 ± 0.0221**	**0.89 ± 0.0130**
AE	0.83 ± 0.0241	0.99 ± 0.0005	0.68 ± 0.0161	0.75 ± 0.004	0.79 ± 0.014
Model	5	6	7	8	9
Ours	**0.79 ± 0.0197**	**0.95 ± 0.005**	**0.91 ± 0.0135**	**0.88 ± 0.0356**	**0.93 ± 0.0062**
AE	0.68 ± 0.007	0.79 ± 0.016	0.89 ± 0.0069	0.63 ± 0.0361	0.79 ± 0.0141

4.4   Discussion

As reported, the GAN-based method overcomes the autoencoder in all the tested scenarios. The adversarial setting and the informative L_G loss provide a dual feedback that helps to improve the model during the optimization process. On the other hand, since the main task is related to discriminative reconstructions, an interesting finding is that the performance of the model does not require a high quality reconstruction. Even though the GAN based model significantly outperforms the autoencoder, the autoencoder's reconstructions are visually more closer to the real samples. More specifically, the GAN learns a type of template which is unrealistic but at the same time more representative of the normal data (see Fig. 5). It can be observed the even in the case of the novel image, the GAN produces almost the same output as for the normal images.

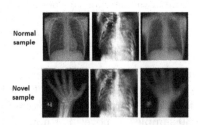

Fig. 5. Reconstruction examples. The first column shows the input, column 2 the reconstructions of the GAN, and column 3 the reconstructions of the autoencoder.

Table 2. AUC for novelty detection with the proposed model vs. a MSE-based autoencoder for the radiography dataset. It shows five executions with thorax as normal data.

Model	AUC1	AUC2	AUC3	AUC4	AUC5	Average
Ours	**0.9954**	**0.9985**	**0.9934**	**0.9965**	**0.9978**	**0.9959 ± 0.0022**
AE	0.9622	0.9405	0.9477	0.9265	0.9406	0.9388 ± 0.0088

5 Conclusion

A novelty detection method based on a GAN architecture has been proposed. The method uses a loss function that includes pixel-wise and structural information in the generator optimization process. Experiments were conducted on MNIST and radiography datasets. The experimental results on two different datasets show that the performance of the GAN model with the proposed loss function overcomes a baseline autoencoder in terms of AUC. Future work considers the integration of additional measures at the feature level and experiments with datasets with more perceptual information.

References

1. Amarbayasgalan, T., Jargalsaikhan, B., Ryu, K.H.: Unsupervised novelty detection using deep autoencoders with density based clustering. Appl. Sci. **8**(9), 1468 (2018)
2. Amini, A., Schwarting, W., Rosman, G., Araki, B., Karaman, S., Rus, D.: Variational autoencoder for end-to-end control of autonomous driving with novelty detection and training de-biasing. In: 2018 IEEE/RSJ International Conference on Intelligent Robots and Systems (IROS), pp. 568–575, October 2018
3. Bojarski, M., et al.: Visualbackprop: efficient visualization of CNNs for autonomous driving. In: 2018 IEEE International Conference on Robotics and Automation (ICRA), pp. 4701–4708 (2018)
4. Chen, V., Yoon, M., Shao, Z.: Novelty detection via network saliency in visual-based deep learning. CoRR abs/1906.03685 (2019)
5. Cichosz, P., et al.: Novelty detection for breast cancer image classification. In: Romaniuk, R.S. (ed.) Photonics Applications in Astronomy, Communications, Industry, and High-Energy Physics Experiments 2016. vol. 10031, pp. 861–872. International Society for Optics and Photonics, SPIE (2016)
6. Deng, L.: The MNIST database of handwritten digit images for machine learning research [best of the web]. IEEE Signal Process. Mag. **29**(6), 141–142 (2012)
7. Ferrag, M.A., Maglaras, L., Moschoyiannis, S., Janicke, H.: Deep learning for cyber security intrusion detection: approaches, datasets, and comparative study. J. Inf. Secur. Appl. **50**, 102419 (2020)
8. Goodfellow, I., Bengio, Y., Courville, A.: Deep Learning. The MIT Press (2016)
9. Goodfellow, I.J., et al.: Generative adversarial networks (2014)
10. Hadsell, R., Chopra, S., LeCun, Y.: Dimensionality reduction by learning an invariant mapping. In: 2006 IEEE Computer Society Conference on Computer Vision and Pattern Recognition (CVPR 2006), vol. 2, pp. 1735–1742 (2006)

11. Halabi, S.S., et al.: The RSNA pediatric bone age machine learning challenge. Radiology **290**(2), 498–503 (2019). pMID: 30480490
12. Kermany, D.S., et al.: Identifying medical diagnoses and treatable diseases by image-based deep learning. Cell **172**(5), 1122–1131.e9 (2018)
13. Kingma, D.P., Ba, J.: Adam: a method for stochastic optimization (2017)
14. Lekamlage, C.D., Afzal, F., Westerberg, E., Cheddad, A.: Mini-DDSM: Mammography-Based Automatic Age Estimation, pp. 1–6. Association for Computing Machinery, New York (2020)
15. Menze, B.H., et al.: The multimodal brain tumor image segmentation benchmark (BRATS). IEEE Trans. Med. Imaging **34**(10), 1993–2024 (2015)
16. Perera, P., Nallapati, R., Xiang, B.: Ocgan: one-class novelty detection using GANs with constrained latent representations. In: The IEEE Conference on Computer Vision and Pattern Recognition (CVPR), June 2019
17. Pimentel, M.A., Clifton, D.A., Clifton, L., Tarassenko, L.: A review of novelty detection. Signal Process. **99**, 215–249 (2014)
18. Sabokrou, M., Khalooei, M., Fathy, M., Adeli, E.: Adversarially learned one-class classifier for novelty detection. In: 2018 IEEE/CVF Conference on Computer Vision and Pattern Recognition, pp. 3379–3388 (2018)
19. Sokolov, E.N.: Higher nervous functions: the orienting reflex. Ann. Rev. Physiol. **25**(1), 545–580 (1963). pMID: 13977960
20. Tieleman, T., Hinton, G.: Lecture 6.5–RmsProp: divide the gradient by a running average of its recent magnitude. COURSERA: Neural Networks for Machine Learning (2012)
21. Huan-gang Wang, Xin Li, T.Z.: Generative adversarial network based novelty detection using minimized reconstruction error. Front. Inf. Technol. Electron. Eng. **19**(1), 116 (2018)
22. Wang, Z., Bovik, A.C., Sheikh, H.R., Simoncelli, E.P.: Image quality assessment: from error visibility to structural similarity. IEEE Trans. Image Process. **13**(4), 600–612 (2004)
23. Zhou, J.T., Du, J., Zhu, H., Peng, X., Liu, Y., Goh, R.S.M.: Anomalynet: an anomaly detection network for video surveillance. IEEE Trans. Inf. Forensics Secur. **14**(10), 2537–2550 (2019)

Multi-core Median Redescending M-Estimator for Impulsive Denoising in Color Images

Dante Mújica-Vargas[1]([✉]), Arturo Rendón-Castro[1], Manuel Matuz-Cruz[2], and Christian Garcia-Aquino[1]

[1] Tecnológico Nacional de México-CENIDET, Cuernavaca-Morelos, Mexico
`dante.mv@cenidet.tecnm.mx`
[2] Tecnológico Nacional de México-ITTapachula, Tapachula-Chiapas, Mexico

Abstract. In this paper, to reduce impulsive noise in color images we propose an extension of the Median Redescending M-Estimator. For that purpose, a multitasking approach was developed such as a multi-core processing in order to reduce in parallel the noise on R, G and B color channels. With this paradigm, an acceleration up to three times can be guaranteed compared to the sequential paradigm, while having the ability to reduce corrupted data up to densities of 80% of fixed-value and 40% of random-value impulsive noises, guaranteeing the preservation of edges. The effectiveness of our proposal is verified by quantitative and qualitative results.

1 Introduction

The acquisition or transmission of digitized images through digital communication channels inherently brings the incorporation of noise. Usually this corrupted information is modeled as an additive, multiplicative or impulsive noise. In this research paper, we concentrate on the impulsive denoising on color images. The state-of-the-art suggests that this type of noise has been commonly modeled such as salt and pepper impulse or random impulse. Two aspects that must be satisfied regardless of the type of noise are the suppression of atypical information while avoiding destroying the fine details of the images. To ensure better performance in the high-level processing tasks of digital image processing or computer vision, images need to be noise-free with a high visual quality.

In the literature interesting methods to filter impulse noise have been introduced; more specifically: in [1], an Adaptive Fuzzy Filter based on Histogram Estimation (AFHE) was proposed; in which, the size of the processing window was adapted based on local noise densities using fuzzy based criterion. In [2], an Adaptive Interpolation-based Impulse Noise Removal (AIBINR) algorithm was proposed, with the merit of developing parametric self-tuning. A Modified Cascaded Filter (MCF) was submitted in [3], this consisted of a cascading connection of Decision-based Median Filters and Un-symmetric Trimmed-Mean

© Springer Nature Switzerland AG 2021
E. Roman-Rangel et al. (Eds.): MCPR 2021, LNCS 12725, pp. 261–271, 2021.
https://doi.org/10.1007/978-3-030-77004-4_25

Filters. A Spatially Adaptive Image Denoising via Enhanced Noise Detection method (SAID-END) was reported in [4], in this proposal the denoising was achieved using a two-stage sequential algorithm, the first stage ensured accurate noise estimation by eliminating over and under detection of noisy pixels. The second stage performed image restoration by considering non-noisy pixels in estimation of the original pixel value. A Difference Based Median Filter Method (DBMF) was issued in [5], it introduced the difference method and generates a difference image by subtracting the image processed using median filter from the original, according to the difference image, it was extracted the position of the noise pixels, and then replaced the intensity values with the corresponding median filter results. In [6], a family of switching filters designed for the impulsive noise removal in color images was analyzed. A self-tuning version of the newly introduced Fast Adaptive Switching Trimmed Arithmetic Mean Filter (FAS-TAMF) was introduced in [7], the major virtue of the self-tuning FASTAMF was its adaptability to noise density. In [8], a Fuzzy C- Means (FCM) clustering had been incorporated with Fuzzy-Support Vector Machine (FSVM) classifier for classification of noisy and non-noisy pixels in removal of impulse noise from color images.

An in-depth analysis of the aforementioned proposals permits disclosure that some of them were variations of median and trimmed mean filters, other ones were based on the fuzzy paradigm or hybrid techniques. Some relevant aspects that can be highlighted are: (1) these omit the concept of impulse detectors, (2) most of them were focused simply in suppressing the impulses, without considering the magnitude reduction of the atypical pixels, (3) some consider algorithmic acceleration through specialized devices such as FPGAs or GPUs, (4) most of them were tested exclusively on images corrupted with fixed-value impulse noise. To compensate these aspects, we consider our previous manuscript [9], and we extend its performance to filter color images, we exploit the computing capacity of multi-core processors that are very common today. In addition, we retain the use of a pulse estimator, which are useful to avoid subjecting noise-free pixels to the filtering process incessantly, so as not to smooth or destroy the fine details of the images. Although the proposal was originally to suppress fixed-value impulsive noise, experimental results show that it can reduce random-value impulsive noise up to densities of 40%.

An outline of the remainder of the paper is as follows. In Sect. 2, a brief discussion about the Median Redescending M-Estimator is presented. The suggested upgrading is described in Sect. 3. Section 4 reports the experimental results of our scheme, as well as the comparisons with other state-of-art methods. The conclusion and the next effort are drawn in Sect. 5.

2   Median Redescending M-Estimator

As it was established in [9], the Median Redescending M-Estimator develops detection and suppression of impulsive noise on gray-scale images. At the impulse noise detector stage, the algorithm analyzes in local way each pixel $\hat{x}$ with respect to its vectorized neighborhood $\overrightarrow{h}$, this vector was obtained from a sliding square window w with size of $n \times n$ pixels and centered at (i, j). To consider $\hat{x}$ as an impulse the detector identified if it had the minimum and maximum value in $\overrightarrow{h}$. So as not to fall into false detections a second condition was considered, this analyzed the variability among all the pixels of $\overrightarrow{h}$, by means of the median of the absolute deviations around the median $mad(\overrightarrow{h})$. Mathematically this detector was formulated in the following way:

$$\left(\left(\min(\overrightarrow{h}) < \hat{x} \right) \wedge \left(\hat{x} < \max(\overrightarrow{h}) \right) \right) \wedge \left(mad(\overrightarrow{h}) < 0.5 \right), \tag{1}$$

the threshold 0.5 was obtained by experimentation. At the impulse noise suppressor stage, in the first instance an improved Redescending M-Estimators was formulated in terms of the absolute deviations around the median, i.e.:

$$\psi_{(r)}(\overrightarrow{h}) = \left\{ \psi(\overrightarrow{h}_i) = 0 \,\forall\, \left| \overrightarrow{h}_i - \text{median}\left\{ \overrightarrow{h} \right\} \right| \geq r \right\}, \tag{2}$$

where the r is a threshold that bounds for the influence function in the range $0 < r < \infty$, $\overrightarrow{h}_i$ is the ith element of the vector $\overrightarrow{h}$ and $\text{median}\left\{ \overrightarrow{h} \right\}$ calculates the median value of this vector. The Redescending M-Estimators were designed to vanish outside of central region, their working logic implies that the very central observations receive the maximum weight, if they depart from the center, their weights are declined, and when they reach specified bounds, their function ψ-function becomes 0. Based on (2), in [9] Simple-Cut, Andrew's Sine, Tukey Biweight, Hampel's Three Part Redescending and Insha enhanced influence function were stated. Taking into account that the best experimental results where obtained with Hampel's Three Part Redescending, in this paper that function is taken up again:

$$\psi(\overrightarrow{h}) = \begin{cases} \overrightarrow{h}_i & 0 \leq \left| \overrightarrow{h}_i - \text{median}\left\{ \overrightarrow{h} \right\} \right| < \alpha \\ \alpha \cdot \text{sgn}(\overrightarrow{h}_i) & \alpha \leq \left| \overrightarrow{h}_i - \text{median}\left\{ \overrightarrow{h} \right\} \right| < \beta \\ \alpha \cdot \dfrac{r - |\overrightarrow{h}_i|}{r - \beta} \cdot \text{sgn}(\overrightarrow{h}_i) & \beta \leq \left| \overrightarrow{h}_i - \text{median}\left\{ \overrightarrow{h} \right\} \right| < r \\ 0 & r \leq \left| \overrightarrow{h}_i - \text{median}\left\{ \overrightarrow{h} \right\} \right| \end{cases}, \tag{3}$$

where r, α and β thresholds are computed adaptively using the neighborhood information taking into account the homogeneity of the elements in $\overrightarrow{h}$, i.e.: $r = 1.483 \cdot \text{median} \left(\left| \overrightarrow{h}_i - \text{median}\left\{ \overrightarrow{h} \right\} \right| \right)$, $\alpha = 0.05 \cdot r$ and $\beta = 0.95 \cdot r$. In this regard, it can be argued that this algorithm is adaptive and therefore does not require tuning of any parameter. As can be noted from (3) last condition assigns zero values, in order to not consider these elements, just $\psi(\overrightarrow{h}) > 0$ elements are considered, which are identified as $\tilde{\psi}(\overrightarrow{h})$. Finally, to obtain an estimate of a noiseless pixel, expression (3) was introduced into the Median-Estimator by following manner:

$$\tilde{\mu}_{MM} = \begin{cases} \tilde{\psi}\left(\overrightarrow{h}_{\left(\frac{n+1}{2}\right)}\right) & \text{if } n \text{ is odd} \\ \frac{1}{2} \cdot \left(\tilde{\psi}\left(\overrightarrow{h}_{\left(\frac{n}{2}\right)}\right) + \tilde{\psi}\left(\overrightarrow{h}_{\left(\frac{n+1}{2}\right)}\right)\right) & \text{if } n \text{ is even} \end{cases}, \qquad (4)$$

where n was a parameter that depends on the quantity of selected elements.

3   Proposed Denoising Scheme

A successful an intuitive proposal to remove impulsive noise in RGB color images involves forking them into the R, G and B channels, and then developing the noise suppression on each of these; subsequently, they must be combined to make up the color image. Traditionally, filtering for each channel is carried out sequentially, resulting in increased runtime, especially when working with large images degraded with high-density noise. To effectively solve these issues, in this paper it is proposed the scheme depicted in Fig. 1; where in parallel mode, a Median Redescending M-Estimator removes the impulsive noise on each R, G and B channels. With which it is guaranteed that instead of increasing the computational cost three times, it will be reduced three times.

As can be seen in the flowchart, the proposal consists of a heterogeneous architecture, with two sequential processes developed by the master core, and a parallel process where three tasks are developed simultaneously by three different cores. This parallel processing is based on shared memory between multiple cores enabled by the OpenMP Application Program Interface, this API is ideally suited to investigate the parallelization potential of sequential code or to speed up trivially parallelizable algorithms within a short period of time, as it is shown in Listing 1. In detail, in the first sequential region, the master core reads the image, separates the three color channels, and configures the parallel region to filter each of the image channels simultaneously.

```
1  # pragma omp parallel shared(rows, cols)
2  {
3  # pragma omp sections
4  {
5  # pragma omp section
6  mu_mmR(r, rows, cols);
7  # pragma omp section
8  mu_mmG(g, rows, cols);
9  # pragma omp section
10  mu_mmB(b, rows, cols);
11  }
12  }
```

Listing 1.1. Multitasking parallel processing

In the parallel region, each core performs the following processes: take a sliding window w of size 3×3 on the image, obtain the central pixel $\hat{x}$, transform the matrix w into a vector $\overrightarrow{h}$ and compute the minimum, maximum as well as the median of the absolute deviations around the median. These values are used by the pulse detector (1), if the conditions are satisfied, then the central pixel $\hat{x}$ is considered noise-free and is assigned as the filter output $\tilde{\mu}_{MM} \leftarrow \hat{x}$. Otherwise the pixel of interest should be filtered, considering its spatial information, in the first instance all the pixels of the vector are analyzed by the Redescending M-Estimator $\psi(\vec{h})$ in order to reduce the contribution of all the data degraded by noise. Data greater than zero are selected such as $\tilde{\psi}(\vec{h})$; then, they are used by the median to estimate a noise-free approximation by means of $\tilde{\mu}_{MM}\left(\tilde{\psi}(\vec{h})\right)$. Depending on the satisfied condition $\tilde{\mu}_{MM}$ can take the value of the central pixel or the estimated noise-free value. Once each pair of cores relive the above processes, the parallel region is finalized by the master core, and in the second sequential regions this combines the noise-free components into the restored RGB image Y.

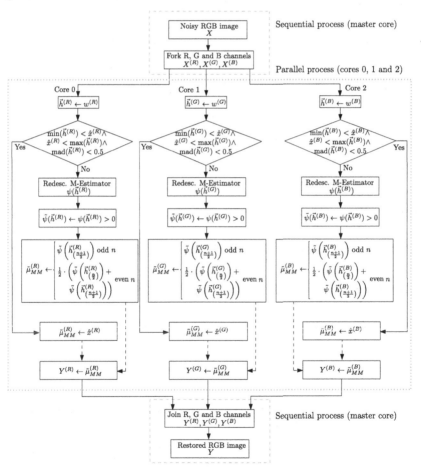

Fig. 1. Flowchart of proposed Multi-core Median Redescending M-Estimator.

4   Experimental Results

The performance and robustness of the proposed scheme is validated through two experiments, using conventional test images such as Lena, Baboon, Monarch, Pool, Kodim15 and Kodim23. The proposed scheme was programmed in C language using the OpenMP API 4.5, as well as an Intel(R) Core(TM) processor i7-4720HQ CPU @2.60 GHz with 4 cores and 16 GB of RAM memory. The comparative methods for ease were implemented on MATLAB.

4.1   Metrics

To determine the algorithmic acceleration performed by the parallel algorithm with respect to sequential one, it can be quantified using the Runtime ratio (RR), given by the following expression:

$$Runtime\ ratio = \frac{Rt_s}{Rt_p}, \tag{5}$$

where Rt_s and Rt_p stand for runtime of the sequential and parallel algorithms, respectively. Meanwhile, the noise suppressing quality was quantified by using the Peak Signal-to-Noise Ratio (PSNR) [10] and Structural Similarity Index (SSIM) [11]; while, to quantify the preservation of the fine details of the image the Mean Absolute Error (MAE) [10] was considered. These three metrics can be determined from the following expressions:

$$PSNR = 10 \cdot log \left[\frac{(max(x(i,j)))^2}{MSE} \right], \tag{6}$$

where MSE is the Mean Quadratic Error and is determined by:

$$MSE = \frac{1}{M \cdot N} \sum_{i=1}^{M} \sum_{j=1}^{N} [x(i,j) - \hat{e}(i,j)]^2, \tag{7}$$

where $M \cdot N$ represents the size of the images that are being analyzed, $x(i,j)$ is the original image and $\hat{e}(i,j)$ is the improved image. The SSIM metric in a simplified form is calculated by the following expression:

$$SSIM(x,y) = \frac{(2\mu_x\mu_y + C_1) \cdot (2\sigma_{xy} + C_2)}{(\mu_x^2\mu_y^2 + C_1) \cdot (\sigma_x^2 + \sigma_y^2 + C_2)}, \tag{8}$$

where x is the original image, y is the refined image, μ_x and μ_y the luminance values, σ_x and σ_y are the contrast values, C_1 and C_2 are two constant values. On the other hand, MAE can be computed by:

$$MAE = \frac{1}{M \cdot N} \sum_{i=1}^{M} \sum_{j=1}^{N} [x(i,j) - \hat{e}(i,j)], \tag{9}$$

4.2   Runtime Versus Image Size

In the first experiment, the runtime of sequential and parallel Median Redescending M-Estimator was quantified in order to quantify the ratio of the algorithmic acceleration. For that purpose, Lena image was scaled to 512×512, 1024×1024, 2048×2048, 4096×4096 and 8192×8192 sizes, and each image was corrupted with $0 \leq \%$ Noise density ≤ 80 of fixed-value impulsive noise, with increments of 2%.

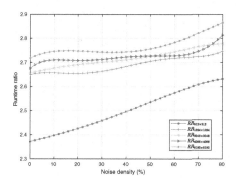

Fig. 2. Runtime ratio for different noise densities and image sizes.

As it is shown in Fig. 2, the Runtime ratio increases depending on noise density and image size; more specifically: $2.372 \leq RR_{512 \times 512} \leq 2.632$, $2.649 \leq RR_{1024 \times 1024} \leq 2.747$, $2.656 \leq RR_{2048 \times 2048} \leq 2.777$, $2.675 \leq RR_{4096 \times 4096} \leq 2.814$ and $2.718 \leq RR_{8192 \times 8192} \leq 2.865$. In an ideal case, in this experiment $RR \approx 3$, since the filtering is done by three cores. However, keep in mind that each core may require its own processing time, the master core must synchronize all processes and close the parallel region. In this sense, these invisible tasks for the user contribute to the final processing time.

4.3   Quantitative Noise Suppression Evaluation

In the second experiment, the performances of the proposed method (McMRM-E), as well as the comparative algorithms MCF [3], FASTAMF [7], FSVM [8] and AFHE [1] were quantified in terms of the metrics $PSNR$, $SSIM$ and MAE. The Baboon, Monarch, Pool, Kodim15 and Kodim23 images, with a size of 512×512 pixels were considered in this experiment. Each one of them was degraded with $0 \leq \%$ Noise density ≤ 80 of fixed-value impulsive noise, with increments of 2%. As well as, $0 \leq \%$ Noise density ≤ 60 of random-value impulsive noise, with the same interval of increments.

To illustrate the average performance with respect to fixed-impulsive noise, Figs. 3a, 3c and 3e can be considered. In relation to PSNR metric: $24.35 \leq$ MCF ≤ 35.71, $21.84 \leq$ FASTAMF ≤ 35.8, $24.35 \leq$ FSVM ≤ 35.71, $25.39 \leq$

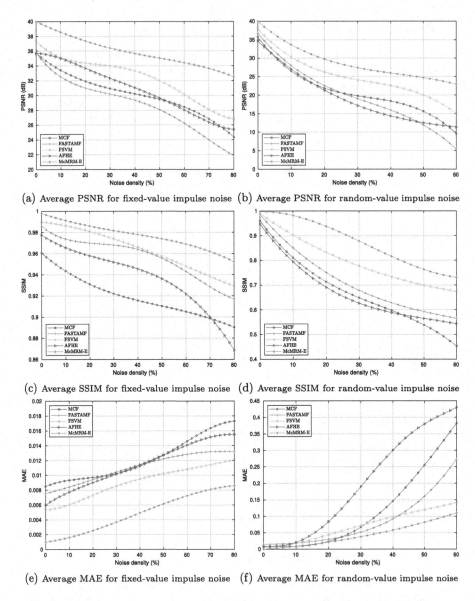

(a) Average PSNR for fixed-value impulse noise (b) Average PSNR for random-value impulse noise

(c) Average SSIM for fixed-value impulse noise (d) Average SSIM for random-value impulse noise

(e) Average MAE for fixed-value impulse noise (f) Average MAE for random-value impulse noise

Fig. 3. Average performance by the proposed and competing algorithms.

AFHE $\leq$ 35.70 and 32.5 $\leq$ McMRM $-$ E $\leq$ 39.96, these results are evidence that the proposed scheme had a superior result of $PSNR \approx 3.56$ dB compared to the closest method. For SSIM metric: $0.890 \leq$ MCF ≤ 0.960, $0.917 \leq$ FASTAMF ≤ 0.986, $0.929 \leq$ FSVM ≤ 0.990, $0.868 \leq$ AFHE ≤ 0.977 and $0.952 \leq$ McMRM $-$ E ≤ 0.998, where it is evident that McMRM $-$ E had $SSIM \gtrsim 0.0133$ than FSVM. Meanwhile, for MAE metric: $0.0085 \leq$

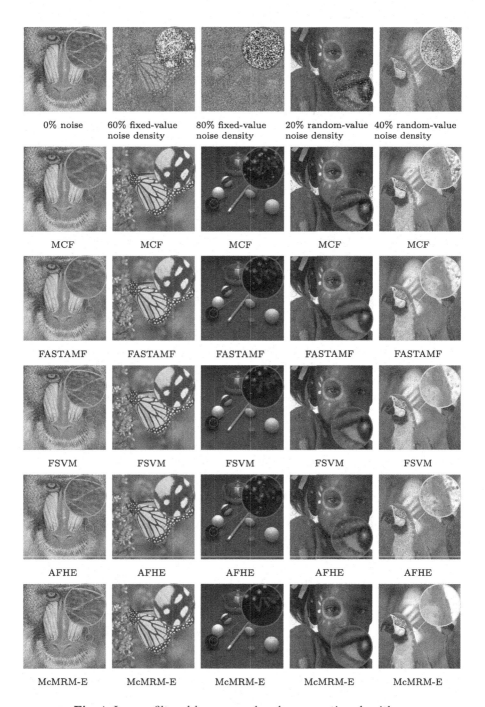

Fig. 4. Images filtered by proposed and comparative algorithms.

MĆF $\leq$ 0.0173, 0.0075 $\leq$ FASTAMF $\leq$ 0.0132, 0.0054 $\leq$ FSVM $\leq$ 0.0121, 0.006 $\leq$ AFHE $\leq$ 0.0155 and 0.0009 $\leq$ McMRM $-$ E $\leq$ 0.0085, for this metric, proposed method had $MAE \lesssim 0.004174$ than FSVM.

On the other side, Figs. 3b, 3d and 3f depict the ability to reduce random-value impulsive noise of all evaluated algorithms. In particular for PSNR metric: 9.587 $\leq$ MCF $\leq$ 35.780, 5.402 $\leq$ MCF $\leq$ 36.811, 15.020 $\leq$ MCF $\leq$ 38.009, 11.341 $\leq$ MCF $\leq$ 34.759 and 22.941 $\leq$ MCF $\leq$ 39.988. It is necessary to emphasize that this type of noise affects the performance of all algorithms, which is noticeable as the noise density increases. In spite of that, our proposal had better performance than comparative algorithms, with $PSNR \approx 3.84$ dB compared to the closest method. For Structural Similarity Index: 0.452 $\leq$ MCF $\leq$ 0.961, 0.565 $\leq$ FASTAMF $\leq$ 0.986, 0.673 $\leq$ FSVM $\leq$ 0.990, 0.543 $\leq$ AFHE $\leq$ 0.948 and 0.731 $\leq$ McMRM $-$ E $\leq$ 0.998, McMRM $-$ E had $SSIM \gtrsim 0.077$ than FSVM (this one was designed to filter random-value impulsive noise). Finally, Mean Absolute Error exposes an increase in the destruction of fine image detail by comparative algorithms, i.e.: 0.0079 $\leq$ MCF $\leq$ 0.3827, 0.0150 $\leq$ FASTAMF $\leq$ 0.2737, 0.0054 $\leq$ FSVM $\leq$ 0.1414, 0.008 $\leq$ AFHE $\leq$ 0.4304, while $1.8e - 05 \leq$ McMRM $-$ E $\leq$ 0.1101, which guarantees that the proposed method tends to preserve the fine details of the filtered images.

Figure 4 helps to ratify and illustrate the quantitative results obtained. In the first instance, the Baboon image was used, this test image is widely-used, since it has appeal because of its distinctive mix of colors, textures, and it contains some regions that can be considered as noise. In this sense, the image was not corrupted, the zoom-in regions reveal that the whiskers are smoothed with MCF and FASTAMF, while FSVM and AFHE degraded some pixels, proposed method was able to preserve with greater fidelity. Images Monarch and Pool were corrupted with fixed-value impulsive noise, in this case all algorithms were tolerant to those noise densities; however, the comparative methods affected the borders of the regions of interest compared to the proposed method. Ultimately, Kodim15 and Kodim23 images were degraded with random-value impulsive noise, despite being lower densities, this type of noise affected to a greater extent the performance of the comparative methods, as well as the edges of the images. Nevertheless, McMRM-E method was able to filter this type of noise with the highest performance and best edge preservation.

5   Conclusion and Future Work

In this article, a scheme for impulsive noise suppression was presented, which was able to process both the fixed-value and random-value types. The proposal was based on robust estimators; particularly, Redescending M-Estimator and Median-Estimator. With this fusion it can be guaranteed that the scheme is capable of reducing densities of 80% of impulsive noise with a fixed-value and 40% of noise with a random-value. To speed up the processing time of the proposed method, algorithmic parallelization was made using the OpenMP API; whereupon, the algorithmic acceleration was $2.372 \lesssim RR \lesssim 2.865$, which is a contribution when real-time image processing is required. As future work, other hardware alternatives such as GPUs and FPGAs can be considered. Furthermore, it is convenient to provide the proposed scheme with the ability to treat multiplicative and additive noises.

Acknowledgements. The authors thank to CONACYT, as well as TecNM-CENIDET for their financial support through the project "Controlador Difuso para ajuste de coeficientes de rigidez de un modelo deformable para simulación en tiempo real de los tejidos del hígado humano".

References

1. Roy, A., Manam, L., Laskar, R.H.: Removal of 'salt & pepper'noise from color images using adaptive fuzzy technique based on histogram estimation. Multimedia Tools Appl. 1–23 (2020)
2. Gökcen, A., Kalyoncu, C.: Real-time impulse noise removal. J. Real-Time Image Proc. **17**(3), 459–469 (2018). https://doi.org/10.1007/s11554-018-0791-y
3. Karthik, B., Krishna Kumar, T., Vijayaragavan, S.P., Sriram, M.: Removal of high density salt and pepper noise in color image through modified cascaded filter. J. Ambient. Intell. Humaniz. Comput. **12**(3), 3901–3908 (2020). https://doi.org/10.1007/s12652-020-01737-1
4. Singh, A., Sethi, G., Kalra, G.: Spatially adaptive image denoising via enhanced noise detection method for grayscale and color images. IEEE Access **8**, 112985–113002 (2020)
5. Ma, C., Lv, X., Ao, J.: Difference based median filter for removal of random value impulse noise in images. Multimedia Tools Appl. **78**(1), 1131–1148 (2018). https://doi.org/10.1007/s11042-018-6442-2
6. Malinski, L., Smolka, B.: Fast adaptive switching technique of impulsive noise removal in color images. J. Real-Time Image Proc. **16**(4), 1077–1098 (2016). https://doi.org/10.1007/s11554-016-0599-6
7. Malinski, L., Smolka, B.: Self-tuning fast adaptive algorithm for impulsive noise suppression in color images. J. Real-Time Image Proc. **17**(4), 1067–1087 (2019). https://doi.org/10.1007/s11554-019-00853-2
8. Roy, A., Laskar, R.H.: Fuzzy SVM based fuzzy adaptive filter for denoising impulse noise from color images. Multimedia Tools Appl. **78**, 1785–1804 (2019)
9. Mújica-Vargas, D., Gallegos-Funes, F.J., de Jesús Rubio, J., Pacheco, J.: Impulsive noise filtering using a median redescending m-estimator. Intell. Data Anal. **21**, 739–754 (2017)
10. Mújica-Vargas, D., de Jesús Rubio, J., Kinani, J.M.V., Gallegos-Funes, F.J.: An efficient nonlinear approach for removing fixed-value impulse noise from grayscale images. J. Real-Time Image Proc. **14**(3), 617–633 (2017). https://doi.org/10.1007/s11554-017-0746-8
11. Wang, Z., Simoncelli, E.P., Bovik, A.C.: Multiscale structural similarity for image quality assessment. In: The Thrity-Seventh Asilomar Conference on Signals, Systems & Computers, vol. 2, pp. 1398–1402. IEEE (2003)

A Comparative Study of 3D Plant Modeling Systems Based on Low-Cost 2D LiDAR and Kinect

Harold Murcia(✉) ⒾⒹ, David Sanabria, Dehyro Méndez ⒾⒹ, and Manuel G. Forero ⒾⒹ

Universidad de Ibagué, Ibagué-Tolima 730002, Colombia
{harold.murcia,manuel.forero}@unibague.edu.co,
{2420141016,2d20191003}@estudiantesunibague.edu.co

Abstract. Morphological information of plants is an essential resource for different agricultural machine vision applications, which can be obtained from 3D models through reconstruction algorithms. Three dimensional modeling of a plant is an XYZ spatial representation used to determine its physical parameters from, for example, a point cloud. Currently two low-cost methods have gained popularity in terms of 3D object reconstructions in 360° employing rotating platforms, based on 2D LiDAR and Kinect. In this paper, these two techniques are compared by getting a 3D model of a *Dracaena braunii* specie and evaluating their performance. The results are shown in terms of their accuracy and time consumption using a Kinect V1 and a LiDAR URG-04LX-UG01, a well-performance low-cost scanning rangefinder from Hokuyo manufacturer. In terms of error calculation, the Kinect-based system probed to be more accurate than the LiDAR-based, with an error less than 20% in all plant measurements. In addition, the point cloud density reached with Kinect was approximately four times higher than with LiDAR. But, acquisition and processing time was about twice than LiDAR system.

Keywords: Low-cost · Phenotyping · LiDAR · Kinect · Point clouds · 3D modeling

1 Introduction

The importance of plant phenotyping, i.e. the determination of plant structures and morphological parameters is widely recognized among researchers from different scientific fields. Phenotyping platforms are necessary to allow the determination of plant features and the formulation of genomic models for plant breeding. An appropriate plant surface sampling, with a convenient resolution of the 3D modeling, leads to different morphological measurements such as leaf area and angle, and plant topology. The requirements for real-time responses to post-processing data are an important task in different perception fields. Therefore, in recent years, a new generation of 3D sensors has appeared, known as depth

© Springer Nature Switzerland AG 2021
E. Roman-Rangel et al. (Eds.): MCPR 2021, LNCS 12725, pp. 272–281, 2021.
https://doi.org/10.1007/978-3-030-77004-4_26

cameras, which main advantage is the rapid acquisition of depth images. Some of them are based on structured light emission sensors, such as the Microsoft Kinect or Asus Xtion, and others on laser scanning sensors, using what is known as Time of Flight (ToF) technology, representing a revolution in 3D imaging due to its performance offered at a low cost. ToF allows getting distances by measuring phase difference between the modulated signal emitted and received with a specific wavelength. LiDAR devices are based on ToF and its use in phenotyping applications is not entirely new. However, its application has not yet been fully explored. LiDAR-based techniques are popular in field and laboratory applications, given their wide resistance to dust, robustness to changing lighting conditions, wide measurement range, fast time response and ease of deployment.

Besides, they are suitable for 3D plant and foliage reconstruction, a fundamental factor in obtaining characteristic plant models and their monitoring over time. The use of LiDAR technology in the phenotyping process includes the measurement of density and volume in plants and crops for the estimation of different parameters such as height, biomass, leaf indices, etc. [10,16]. LiDAR sensors are frequently chosen, in a large number of applications, to provide range data, such as plant differentiation by height and pattern, automatic identification of stem and leaf organs using point clouds obtained from the 3D scanning of barley and other cereals, according to their geometric shapes and histograms. They are also used to create virtual plants and tree models on large-scale phenotyping platforms. The 3D models obtained with LiDAR sensors can also be merged with visual information to generate geometric and multispectral models that allow developing more complete phenotyping processes, and also new classification and automatic processing techniques used for pest and disease control, irrigation, fertilization and plant stress, among others.

Kinect devices introduced by Microsoft (version V1 and V2) as an interface to track body position for Xbox videogame consoles have gained popularity in engineering and robotics applications [12]. One of its main advantages is its low cost compared to other sensors. Kinect sensors cost about 0.1% of commercial research LiDAR systems. The Kinect projects a pattern of points using an infrared laser on the scene of interest. The target is captured by an infrared camera and aligned with the image obtained from a standard one. In this way, the Kinect produces a point cloud with XYZRGB dimensions in a distance range from 0.5 to 4 m approximately. Compared to version 1, the Kinect V2 has improved characteristics like higher video resolution of 1920×1080 pixels, data transfer rate of 30 fps, field of view of $70° \times 60°$ and better signal to noise ratio in daylight scenes [1]. Given the recent interest in this type of work and the absence of comparative technical studies between these types of sensors, the aim of this work is to present and compare two methods for 3D plant modeling from a point cloud. The following section summarizes the basics of ToF perception and briefly reviews the literature dealing with the generation of plant point clouds. Section 3 describes the elements and methods used. Finally, Sects. 4 and 5 present the experimental results and conclusions.

2   Related Work

Although the state-of-the-art mentions the generation of 3D models using multivision systems, these are not included among those that provide depth clues and require a neutral background, easily separable from the object due to its strong contrast, to facilitate better segmentation [11]. Several 3D reconstruction applications based on 2D LiDAR sensors have been developed in the literature. Most of them are installed on mobile platforms for outdoor applications that present high-quality results after a camera calibration process [2,5,8,9]. However, some equipments are used indoors for phenotyping purposes. Wang et al. [14] reported accurate results in an indoor environment with a lower-cost RP-LiDAR laser scanner integrated into a mobile proximal detection system. Thapa et al. [13] proposed a scanning system consisting of a SICK LMS511 LIDAR and a 360° rotating platform. Panjvani et al. [7] presented a LIDAR system based on a SICK LMS400 device integrated in a linear moving platform for leaf feature extraction. Unfortunately, most of them are based on expensive sensors, which are not easily accessible to many users.

Therefore, several approaches have been developed for the reconstruction of 3D models using low-cost sensors such as Kinect, in particular for plant phenotyping. Li et al. [3] introduced a method to segment leaves without occlusions from three different types of 3D image platforms: stereo cameras, a Kinect V2 sensor and a multi-vision stereo camera in a mobile phone, scanning four types of plants. The technique included the automatic estimation of morphological features such as area, length and width of the leaf. Point coverage rate between 87% and 99% and accuracy of almost 100% were obtained in all cases. McCormick et al. [5] developed a semiautomatic image acquisition and processing pipeline for shoot segmentation of a sorghum variety. For each plant, a series of 12 depth and RGB images were acquired and the resulting point clouds were processed to segmented meshes. Image-based measurements like shoot and leaf height, surface area, leaf width and angle were well correlated with manual measurements. Root-Mean-Square Difference (RMSD) coefficient of variation for the measurements ranged from 0.07 to 0.3 within the same range as real values. Yamamoto et al. [15] employed a method to extract a 3D model and evaluate volume and diameter for fruits and vegetables. Both Kinect V1 and V2 were used to create 111 3D models. Depth and color information were processed and several features of 3D models were examined using an open-source software. Both model shapes were similar to the real fruit. However, they were slightly different from each other. The Kinect V2 model had a more uneven shape because of noise from the TOF sensor. The accuracy of the fruit volume estimate and the largest diameter was 93% and 86% respectively, with Kinect V2. Liu et al. [4] identified different kind of fruits and leaves using RealSense F200 and Kinect V1 depth sensors. The RealSense F200 has a color and an infrared cameras and an infrared laser projector. 120 depth data samples were collected from one plant, placed in 64 different positions modified manually and from different angles. Results showed that little occlusion and low adhesion brought the fruit recognition rate up to 80–100%. Different species with occlusions had a lower detection rate.

3   Materials and Methods

Two experiments were carried out to produce a three-dimensional point cloud of plants. The first experiment was done with a Kinect V1 sensor and the second was based on a 2D LiDAR device. The basic principle of both scanners is optical depth measurement. The three-dimensional modeling system consisted of a depth sensor placed on a fixed tripod, a rotating disk moved by a stepper motor, a drive motor, a power source, and a computer used to control it, as shown in Fig. 1a. The modeling methods were written in Python 3.7 language on an Intel Core i5 7th Gen 2.5 GHz with 8 GB of RAM to control the turntable under Ubuntu 16.04 OS and using Open3d [17] library for 3D point cloud registration process. The computer system was connected via USB to an Arduino Nano, which controlled a stepper motor through a driver V44A3967. The disk angle was estimated with an open-loop counter algorithm, which returned the position to the master system every time it moved. Geometrical information from the depth sensor (LiDAR 2D or Kinect) was acquired using a ROS (Robot Operating System) environment with a Kinetic version, once the initial and final angles and angular steps were configured. The obtained point clouds were stored in LASer format and visualized using the free access software CloudCompare. The stepper motor used in the rotating platform shown in Fig. 1b had a torque of 9.4 kg/cm, a gearbox with a ratio of 100:1 and an angular speed between 1.2 to 3.6 RPM. The motor, which was adapted to a mechanism by a worm, had the capacity to move every 0.36°. The worm wheel had 26 teeth and a transmission ratio of 36:1, which increased the torque system and angular resolution, resulting in the following final mechanical characteristics: torque of 300 kg/cm, a gearbox of 3600:1 and the ability to move the disc every 0.01°. However, the final angular speed was reduced to a range of 0.033–0.1 RPM. The turntable was modeled in SolidWorks 2018. For the experimental setup a plant of the species *Dracaena braunii* was scanned, with an approximate height of 0.8 m measured from the base of the pot to the top of the plant, in a controlled environment using white artificial light.

3.1   LiDAR Modeling

This experiment was based on a 2D LiDAR sensor URG-04LX-UG01, one of the simplest of the manufacturer Hokuyo. Basically, the laser emits an infrared beam on a rotating mirror, which changes its direction, illuminating a specific region of the scene. The reflected light is then used to determine the distance to the target. The main specifications of the scanner are shown in Table 1. The acquisition protocol and the software used were based on an earlier version developed by Murcia et al. [6]. They presented a methodology for the calibration and reconstruction process of the same sensor and motor unit. However, in this work, a new kinematic model was established for the developed platform system.

Kinematic Model. The purpose of the kinematic model is to acquire a 3D initial coordinate P_i to a reference coordinate frame P_o located in the center of

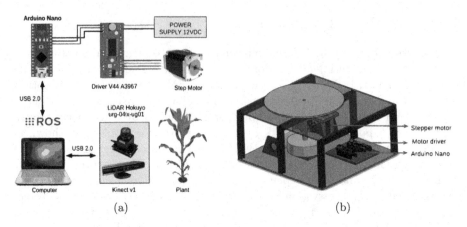

Fig. 1. Main components of the scanning system: (a) functional diagram; (b) representation of the used rotating platform and its main components.

Table 1. Main specifications of the 2D LiDAR sensor URG-04LX-UG01.

Feature	Hokuyo URG-04LX-UG01
Measurement distance	20 to 5600 mm
Resolution	1 mm
Scan angle	240°
Angular resolution	0.36° (360°/1024 steps)
Accuracy	± 30 mm (For distance above < 10000 mm)
Scanning time	100 ms/scan
Power source	5 VDC ± 5% (USB Bus Power)

the disk for relative LiDAR detection. The final 3D point cloud in P_o is representated in a XYZ space as a function of LiDAR horizontal angle θ and radial distance γ, as well as the disk angle β and system constant parameters, which represent the distances between the sensor and the target. The transformation matrix $T_p = R_z * T$ in 3D space was obtained using homogeneous coordinates by means of a $[4 \times 4]$ dimensional matrix. Where T is a translation transformation with three parameters t_x, t_y and t_z, which represent the respective translations of P_o along X, Y, Z axes and Rz is a rotation matrix around Z axis (yaw). Each one of these matrices is described below. Thus, the final XYZ reconstruction of the studied plant was calculated with a three-frame transformation based on T_p as shown below:

$$T = \begin{bmatrix} 1 & 0 & 0 & t_x \\ 0 & 1 & 0 & t_y \\ 0 & 0 & 1 & t_z \\ 0 & 0 & 0 & 1 \end{bmatrix}, R_z = \begin{bmatrix} cos(\gamma) & -sin(\gamma) & 0 & 0 \\ sin(\gamma) & cos(\gamma) & 0 & 0 \\ 0 & 0 & 1 & 0 \\ 0 & 0 & 0 & 1 \end{bmatrix} \tag{1}$$

$$P_o = T * R_z * P_i \Rightarrow P_i = \begin{bmatrix} r * cos(\theta) \\ 0 \\ r * sin(\theta) \\ 1 \end{bmatrix} \tag{2}$$

P_i is represented as an input XYZ matrix with dimensions $[4\mathrm{x}m]$, where m is the number of samples or points. Where r is a range vector of m samples obtained from a LiDAR ROS node, which represent the measurement of each LiDAR angle θ_i.

3.2   Kinect Modeling

The main technical characteristics of the Kinect sensor are the resolutions of its color and depth cameras: 320×240 pixels and 640×480 pixels respectively. The TOF camera has a depth range of 0.5 to 3.5 m. It was mounted at a height of 1.5 m with a horizontal view at an angle of less than 27°. The camera's horizontal and vertical fields of view are 57° and 43° respectively and the sampling rate is 30 fps. The Kinect sensor was mounted on the same tripod used by the LiDAR platform. The data capture process took approximately 1 h and 40 min and 361 point clouds were obtained.

Point Cloud pre-processing. Initially, the algorithm pre-processed the data in four stages: Down-sampling, statistical removal of points, outliers removal, and estimation of normal vectors. Voxel downsampling function uses a regular voxel mesh to create a uniformly reduced point cloud. The algorithm works in two steps: Points are grouped into voxels. Each occupied voxel generates an exact point by averaging all the points within it. The statistical outlier removal function is a filter that eliminates points that are farther away from their neighbors compared to the point cloud average. A function of the standard deviation of those average distances is established as a threshold level. The lower this number, the more aggressive the filter will be. The radius outlier removal function is a filter that eliminates points that have few neighbors on a given sphere around them, by setting the minimum number of points on the sphere and the radius of the sphere that will be used to count the neighbors. Finally, the function to estimate normals finds adjacent points and calculates the principal axis of the adjacent points using analysis of covariance.

ICP Algorithm. Once the point clouds were pre-processed, they were merged into a single one, also unifying the framework of reference. For this purpose, the point-to-plane ICP (Iterative Closest Points) algorithm was used, which minimizes the Root-Mean-Square-Error RMSE between the transformed point clouds. After fusion, new outliers may appear. To remove them, a point optimization method was performed based on the neighboring nodes and the voxel size. This step also reduces possible false alignments between edges and, avoid duplication and excess points. The ICP algorithm requires a number of parameters to be tuned. The setting values found are: The voxel size for sample reduction should be 0.001 or less to improve performance. The threshold of the recording edge should be 0.006 or less, the search radius equal to 0.5 cm and maximum of neighbors equal to 100. The number of iterations of the fixed ICP in 5 for greater efficiency. Although the point cloud range is not required for processing, it is included to determine the fitting error between the point clouds.

4   Results

Figure 2 shows a frontal and top view of the resulting 3D point cloud. 3D representation had a density of 558639 points and the whole acquisition and processing took about 1.25 h, with no color information. Figures 3a and 3b show a frontal view of the resulting 3D point cloud. Unlike the reconstruction done by LiDAR, the Kinect includes dimensions of color information (Red, Green and Blue, RGB) in the acquired data. The final 3D reconstruction had 2230527 points. The registration algorithm took 45 min meanwhile the complete procedure took about 2.5 h.

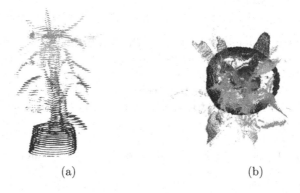

(a)   (b)

Fig. 2. Reconstructed 3D plant point cloud with Hokuyo URG-04LX-UG01 using a color scale based on altitude: a) side view of point cloud, b) top view of point cloud.

4.1   3D Modeling Comparison

Both methods were tested in the same laboratory conditions using the same rotating platform and acquisition software. The comparative results are summarized in Table 2. As was expected, experiment carried out with Kinect presented a higher point density and processing time regarding the procedure with LiDAR. A second comparison was performed to determine an error estimation in four measurements of the plant called A, B, C, D as shown in Fig. 3c according to Eq. 3.

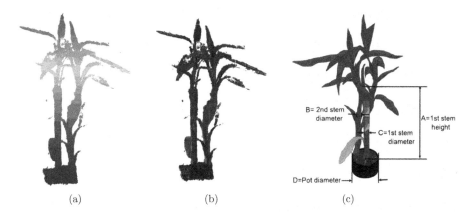

(a)   (b)   (c)

Fig. 3. (a) side view of reconstructed 3D point cloud with Kinect using a color scale based on altitude. (b) side view of reconstructed 3D point cloud with Kinect using color information. (c) Illustration of manual plant measurements: (A) Height of the first stem. (B) Diameter of the second stem, (C) Diameter of the first stem (D) Pot diameter.

Table 2. Comparative features of generated point clouds.

Feature	Kinect V1	URG-04LX-UG01
Number of points	2230527	558639
Acquisition time [s]	6000	4530
Processing time [s]	2735	4
Color	Yes	No

$$error[\%] = \left| \frac{X - W}{W} \right| \tag{3}$$

where X is the software measurement from 3D point cloud using point picking tool in CloudCompare and W is the real measurement obtained in the laboratory, called reference. Table 3 shows the measurement obtained from each point cloud and the error calculated in each case.

As can be observed on Table 2, the acquisition and processing time was almost double in the Kinect-based system compared to the LiDAR one. This was mainly due to the fact that the Kinect takes longer to acquire the data, in addition to simultaneously obtaining the color information. In this case, the number of points in the acquired point clouds was exactly four times higher than that obtained with LiDAR. The acquisition rates measured in points per second for the Kinect and LiDAR systems were 255 points/s and 123 points/s respectively. Thus, the Kinect, despite requiring more time, was more than twice as fast as LiDAR in acquiring relevant plant data. According to the results in Table 3, the Kinect-based system had the highest accuracy, as the error found in

Table 3. Error calculation from point clouds and manual measurements.

Measurements		Kinect V1		URG-04LX-UG01	
Letter	Ref. [mm]	meas. [mm]	Error[%]	meas. [mm]	Error [%]
A	280	308.54	10.19	246.83	23.86
B	14	16.79	19.92	23.09	64.92
C	15	15.55	3.66	22.99	53.26
D	131	117.3	10.45	210.13	60.40

the plant parameter measurements was lower than with LiDAR. In both cases, the largest error occurred with the B parameter. This error was due to the characteristic occlusions of the plant architecture making it difficult to correctly acquire the points in that particular part of the plant.

5   Conclusions

In this paper, two low-cost three-dimensional modeling of the plant based on rotating platform and depth sensors are presented. Two point cloud reconstruction experiments based on 2D LiDAR and Kinect V1 were performed. The Kinect procedure presented better results, in terms of point cloud density and rendering quality, due to the color information used. However, acquisition and processing times were longer than those of 2D LiDAR. Results using Hokuyo URG-04LX-UG01 showed a point cloud acquisition without color or intensity information that required less time. Employing the open source software CloudCompare, the 3D point clouds obtained with LiDAR were filtered to reduce noise. On the other hand, the lowest error was achieved with the Kinect sensor, so it turned out to be the most suitable system for accuracy. In addition, the LiDAR stage required a kinematic model, so a characterization of the data was necessary to determine the model parameters, which could introduce distortions in the point clouds if they were far from the real values. The acquisition data and reconstruction codes, as well as the LAS files obtained, are available online at https://github.com/HaroldMurcia/plant_reconstruction.git. As future work, the improvement of the 3D reconstruction results using the LiDAR system by introducing a new sensor with better technical characteristics, such as divergence angle, resolution, signal-to-noise ratio and fusion techniques between digital cameras and LiDAR, is proposed.

Acknowledgment. This work was funded by the OMICAS program: Optimización Multiescala In-silico de Cultivos Agrícolas Sostenibles (Infraestructura y validación en Arroz y Caña de Azúcar), anchored at the Pontificia Universidad Javeriana in Cali and funded within the Colombian Scientific Ecosystem by The World Bank, the Colombian Ministry of Science, Technology and Innovation, the Colombian Ministry of Education, the Colombian Ministry of Industry and Tourism, and ICETEX, under grant FP44842-217-2018 and OMICAS Award ID: 792-61187.

References

1. Corti, A., Giancola, S., Mainetti, G., Sala, R.: A metrological characterization of the Kinect V2 time-of-flight camera. Robot. Autonomous Syst. **75**, 584–594 (2016)
2. Guo, Q., et al.: Crop 3D—a LiDAR based platform for 3D high-throughput crop phenotyping. Sci. China Life Sci. **61**, 328–339 (2018)
3. Li, D., et al.: An overlapping-free leaf segmentation method for plant point clouds. IEEE Access **7**, 129054–129070 (2019)
4. Liu, J., et al.: Experiments and analysis of close-shot identification of on-branch citrus fruit with realsense. Sensors **18**(5) (2018)
5. McCormick, R.F., Truong, S.K., Mullet, J.E.: 3D sorghum reconstructions from depth images identify QTL regulating shoot architecture. Plant Physiol. **172**(2), 823–834 (2016)
6. Murcia, H.F., Monroy, M.F., Mora, L.F.: 3D scene reconstruction based on a 2D moving LiDAR. In: Florez, H., Diaz, C., Chavarriaga, J. (eds.) ICAI 2018. CCIS, vol. 942, pp. 295–308. Springer, Cham (2018). https://doi.org/10.1007/978-3-030-01535-0_22
7. Panjvani, K., Dinh, A.V., Wahid, K.A.: LiDARPheno - a low-cost LiDAR-based 3D scanning system for leaf morphological trait extraction. Front. Plant Sci. (2019)
8. Paulus, S.: Measuring crops in 3D: using geometry for plant phenotyping (2019)
9. Rosell-Polo, J.R., et al.: Advances in structured light sensors applications in precision agriculture and livestock farming. Adv. Agron. **133**, 71–112 (2015)
10. Saeys, W., et al.: Estimation of the crop density of small grains using LiDAR sensors. Biosyst. Eng. (2009)
11. Santos, T.T., Koenigkan, L.V., Barbedo, J.G.A., Rodrigues, G.C.: 3D plant modeling: Localization, mapping and segmentation for plant phenotyping using a single hand-held camera. In: Agapito, L., Bronstein, M., Rother, C. (eds.) ECCV 2014. LNCS, vol. 8928. Springer, Heidelberg (2015). https://doi.org/10.1007/978-3-319-16220-1_18
12. Spoliansky, R., et al.: Development of automatic body condition scoring using a low-cost 3-dimensional kinect camera. J. Dairy Sci. (2016)
13. Thapa, S., Zhu, F., Walia, H., Yu, H., Ge, Y.: A novel LiDAR-Based instrument for high-throughput, 3D measurement of morphological traits in maize and sorghum. Sensors (Switzerland) (2018)
14. Wang, H., Lin, Y., Wang, Z., Yao, Y., Zhang, Y., Wu, L.: Validation of a low-cost 2D laser scanner in development of a more-affordable mobile terrestrial proximal sensing system for 3D plant structure phenotyping in indoor environment. Comput. Electron. Agric. **140**, 180–189 (2017)
15. Yamamoto, S., et al.: 3D reconstruction of apple fruits using consumer-grade RGB-depth sensor. Eng. Agric. Environ. Food **11**(4), 159–168 (2018)
16. Zhang, L., Grift, T.E.: A LIDAR-based crop height measurement system for Miscanthus giganteus. Comput. Electron. Agric. **85**, 70–76 (2012)
17. Zhou, Q.Y., Park, J., Koltun, V.: Open3D: A modern library for 3D data processing. arXiv:1801.09847 (2018)

Evaluation of Denoising Algorithms for Source Camera Linking

Diego Azael Salazar⬤, Ana Elena Ramirez-Rodriguez⬤, Mariko Nakano$^{(\boxtimes)}$⬤,
Manuel Cedillo-Hernandez⬤, and Hector Perez-Meana⬤

Mechanical and Electrical Engineering School, Instituto Politecnico Nacional,
04440 Coyoacan, Mexico City, Mexico
mnakano@ipn.mx

Abstract. In the source camera linking (SCL) tasks, a large number of images taken by the same camera is not available, then forensic investigation must be carried out using only residual noises extracted from each natural image without any knowledge about their source camera. Therefore, an efficient denoising algorithm and/or noise enhancement function are required to estimate accurately Sensor Pattern Noise (SPN). In this paper we provide a systematic evaluation of common-used denoising algorithms with different parameters under a SCL task. The denoising algorithms considered are locally adaptive window-based denoising and the Block-matching 3D (BM3D) denoising. The SCL task used for evaluation is image clustering based on their source camera, in which we construct three sets with natural images taken by 5, 10 and 15 different source cameras. Linkage clustering algorithm with Ward modality is applied to group the images by their source camera. The experimental results show that the BM3D denoising with standard (σ) deviation of 5 provides the best performance. Said method achieved a clustering accuracy of 98%, 96% and 85% for 5, 10 and 15 cameras respectively.

Keywords: Photo Response Non-Uniformity (PRNU) · Sensor Pattern Noise (SPN) · Source camera linking · Denoising · SPN enhancement · Hierarchical clustering

1 Introduction

In the digital photo forensic, the Photo Response Non-Uniformity (PRNU) provides an important clue for diverse investigations. The PRNU is an invisible weak signal that slightly modifies the pixel values of the captured image. Because the PRNU is caused by imperfection in sensor fabrication and inhomogeneity of the silicon wafers [1], it can be considered as a deterministic sensor pattern noise (SPN) and then as a unique fingerprint of each device. If a large number of images taken by the same camera is available [1], the PRNU can be estimated efficiently using averaging [2] or Maximum Likelihood Estimation (MLE) method [3]. Once the SPN´s of several cameras are estimated, the source camera of a specific image in question can be identified, computing a normalized correlation between the SPNs and the residual noise extracted from the image. This task

© Springer Nature Switzerland AG 2021
E. Roman-Rangel et al. (Eds.): MCPR 2021, LNCS 12725, pp. 282–291, 2021.
https://doi.org/10.1007/978-3-030-77004-4_27

is known as source camera identification (SCI) and until now several efficient methods have been proposed by researchers [1–4].

However, in many real scenarios of the digital forensics, neither cameras nor enough number of images taken by the same camera are available. For example, a forensic investigator who is attempting to link suspected social medias profiles to some other crime related profile or platform, the evidence available to prove this link is limited to the images published in the different sources but does not have any knowledge about the source devices of these images [5]. When some website related to criminal cases, such as a child pornography, is detected, the number of cameras involved in the crime is an important issue for the digital forensics [5]. This challenging task is called source camera linking (SCL), in which residual noises extracted from each image are only resource to carry out the forensic investigation.

In the SCL task, an efficient denoising algorithm is essential to obtain good performance. However, almost all denoising algorithms also suppress details of image scene, such as edges and textures. As the consequence of its inefficient denoising process, the extracted SPN is heavily contaminated by the image scene and then a reliable camera linking cannot be attained. To reduce the contamination in the SPN, several enhancement methods have been proposed. Gupta and Tiwari provided an extensive evaluation of denoising and enhancement algorithms for SCI task, in which source cameras are available [6]. As far as our knowledge, until now systematical evaluation for SCL task has not been performed. The SCL tasks must be carried out under the absence of any knowledge about source of images.

In this paper, we provide an evaluation using two representative wavelet-based denoising algorithms [7, 8] and the SPN enhancer [9] under the SCL task. In the color filter array (CFA) interpolation, the green channel contains more original pixel values compared with other two channels (red and blue). So, we also compared performance using the green channel and using all three channels. As the SCL task, we used a hierarchical clustering algorithm to group images by their source camera.

The rest of the paper is organized as follows: In Sect. 2, we provide the background and several basic concepts used in this paper, and the experimental results together with our observation are described in Sect. 3. Finally, in Sect. 4 we conclude our work.

2 Background

In this section, we provide some basic concepts about the SPN estimation, denoising algorithms and the SPN enhancers.

2.1 SPN Estimation for SCI and SCL Tasks

The sensor pattern noise (SPN) is composed of the Fixed Pattern Noise (FPN) and the PRNU. The FPN is additive noise, which depends on physical condition when an image is captured, such as temperature and camera exposure time, while the PRNU is multiplicative noise caused by the sensor imperfection [3], which is dominant part of the SPN. When a large number of flat-field images, such as blue-sky images, are available for a camera 'c', the PRNU K_c can be estimated using averaging method given by (1) or MLE given by (2) [3, 4].

$$\widehat{K}_c = \frac{1}{M} \sum_{i=1}^{M} R_i \tag{1}$$

$$\widehat{K}_c = \frac{1}{M} \sum_{i=1}^{M} \left[\frac{I_i}{\sum_{i=1}^{M} I_i^2} \right] R_i \tag{2}$$

where I_i is i-th flat-field image taken by camera 'c', M is number of all available flat-field images and R_i is i-th residual noise, which is obtained by denoising function f.

$$R_i = I_i - f(I_i) \tag{3}$$

When M is large (for example $M = 100$), the PRNU can be estimated accurately [3, 4]. In the source camera identification (SCI) task, the source camera of a specific query image I_q is identified using normalized correlation $\rho_{c,q} = corr\left(R_q, I_q \widehat{K}_c\right)$, between residual noise of I_q and scaled PRNU $I_q \widehat{K}_c$, where $R_q = I_q - f(I_q)$ and $\widehat{K}_c$ is the estimated PRNU of the camera 'c'. The correlation value $\rho_{c,q}$ is compared with a threshold value Th_{SCI} to determine if the camera c is source of the image I_q or not.

In the source camera linking (SCL) task, a normalized correlation between residual noises of the natural images I_{q1}, I_{q2}, is calculated. If $\rho_{q1,q2} = corr\left(R_{q1}, R_{q2}\right)$ is larger than a predetermined threshold Th_{SCL} then we can consider that the images I_{q1}, I_{q2} are taken by the same camera. Obviously in the SCL task, the SNP is not estimated accurately, then the correlation value $\rho_{q1,q2}$ depends strongly on performance of the denoising function f.

2.2 Denoising Algorithms and SPN Enhancer

In the SCI and SCL tasks, two denoising functions have been used commonly, which are locally adaptive window-based denoising [7] and the Block-matching 3D (BM3D) denoising based on collaborative filter [8]. Both algorithms operate in wavelet domain. In [7], four-level wavelet decomposition is applied to the image, and noise-free high-pass sub-bands are estimated from noisy high-pass sub-bands using maximum likelihood estimator. While, in BM3D several 2D blocks with similar image scene, such as edges and texture, are stacked to form 3D block. A 3D filter is applied to each 3D block to attenuate noise, which is unrelated to image scene [8]. The BM3D denoising shows better conservation of the scene details compared with [7], although textured components of the image are still eliminated or attenuated as noise components, then the estimated SPN still contains image scene details.

To reduce further the contamination caused by image detailed scene in the SPN, several SPN-enhancement functions have been proposed [9]. The enhancement functions are based on the observation that the magnitude of real SPN is generally small compared with scene details of the image. So, noise with larger magnitude is attenuated applying enhancement function. We evaluate a SPN-enhancement function proposed in [9], which is expressed by (4).

$$n_e(i, j) = \begin{cases} e^{\frac{-0.5n^2(i,j)}{\alpha}}, & \text{if } 0 \le n(i, j) \\ -e^{\frac{-0.5n^2(i,j)}{\alpha}}, & \text{otherwise} \end{cases} \tag{4}$$

where $\alpha = 7.0$. Figure 1 shows the enhancement function given by (4).

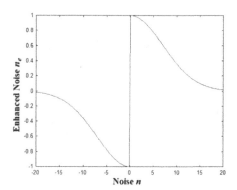

Fig. 1. SPN enhancement function [9].

3 Experimental Results

3.1 Parameter Selection for Denoising Algorithm

As mentioned above, in the Source Camera Linking (SCL) tasks, there are only natural images without any information about their source camera. Here, natural image means common photographs published in social networks or in some public/private web site. To obtain a good performance in the SCL tasks, a precise estimation of the SPN from images is indispensable and then an appropriate selection of denoising algorithm together with the SPN enhancement function is required for success in SCL tasks.

Two denoising algorithms used in the evaluation are denoted as $\{Mihcak, BM3D\}$, which are proposed in [7] and [8], respectively. Both algorithms require a standard deviation of the SPN σ_n as input parameter. According to the suggestion provided in [7, 8], we used $\sigma_n \in \{2, 3\}$ for *Mihcak* and $\sigma_n \in \{4, 5\}$ for *BM3D*. Table 1 indicates some principal experiments which are combinations of denoising algorithms and enhancement function under different values of σ_n and type of the color-channels used to apply denoising. As the color channel, we considered green channel and gray scale image obtained using three color channels.

To select a denoising algorithm and their appropriate parameters, we calculate two types of correlation values, the first one is the correlation between SPNs extracted from two images taken by the same device, which is demoted as ρ_{same}. The second one is correlation between SPNs of two images taken by the different devices, which is denoted as ρ_{diff}. In this experiment, we used in total 600 images taken by four devices, which are "Iphone11" by Apple, "Ipad Air (3rd generation)", "Redmi Note 8 pro" by Xiaomi and "JKM-LX3" by Huawei. Using each device, we took 150 natural images.

Finally, a ratio *Ratio* between average of ρ_{same} and average of ρ_{diff} using 600 images is calculated by

$$Ratio = \frac{\frac{1}{M_1}\sum_{i=1}^{M_1} \rho_{same}^{(i)}}{\frac{1}{M_2}\sum_{j=1}^{M_2} \rho_{diff}^{(j)}} \qquad (5)$$

where $\rho_{same}^{(i)}$ is the correlation value between SPNs extracted from the *i-th* pair of images taken by the same device, which is given by $\rho_{same} = corr\left(R_{q1}, R_{q2}\right), I_{q1}, I_{q2} \in C$, and M_1 is the number of image pairs of the same device, then $M_1 = 4 \times \binom{2}{150}$. While $\rho_{diff}^{(i)}$ is the correlation value between SPNs extracted from the *i-th* pair of images taken by the different devices, which is given by $\rho_{diff} = corr\left(R_{q1}, R_{q2}\right), I_{q1}, I_{q2} \notin C$ and M_2 is number of pairs of images, being $M_2 = \binom{2}{600} - M_1$. The larger *Ratio* indicates better method, because we expect that the SPNs extracted from images of the same device present large correlation, while the correlation between SPNs from the images taken by the different devices is small. Figure 3 shows the ratio R of 12 SPN extraction methods given by Table 1. From the figure, BM3D denoising algorithm under $\sigma = 4$ together with enhancement function given by (4) provides best performance, following by the method 6 with $\sigma = 5$.

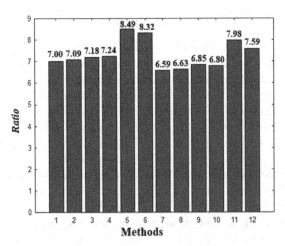

Fig. 2. The ratio R between average of ρ_{same} and average of ρ_{diff}.

Table 1. Experimental evaluation methods

Method	Denoising algorithm	Enhancement function	σ	Color channel
1	*BM3D*	No	4	Green
2	*BM3D*	No	5	Green
3	*BM3D*	No	4	Gray
4	*BM3D*	*No*	5	*Gray*
5	**BM3D**	**Equation (4)**	**4**	**Gray**
6	*BM3D*	Equation (4)	5	Gray
7	*Mihcak*	No	2	Green
8	*Mihcak*	No	3	Green
9	*Mihcak*	*No*	2	*Gray*
10	*Mihcak*	No	3	Gray
11	*Mihcak*	Equation (4)	2	Gray
12	*Mihcak*	Equation (4)	3	Gray

3.2 Evaluation in Image Clustering by Source Camera

Table 2. Device descriptions used for image classification.

Camera ID	Make	Model	Source
40D	Canon	EOS 400D digital	Flickr
90D	Canon	EOS 90D	Flickr
A105	Samsung	SM-A105M	Personal
A3	ZTE	Blade A3 2020	Personal
Apple11	Apple	iPhone 11	Personal
G331	Sony	G3313	Personal
Ipad22	Apple	iPad Air (3rd generation)	Personal
J411	Samsung	SM-J410G	Personal
J4	Samsung	SM-J410G	Personal
LGar	LG Electronics	LGMS210	Personal
M1	Olympus	E-M1MarkII	Flickr
Red8	Xiami	Redmi Note 8 Pro	Personal
SMJ1	Samsung	SM-J111M	Personal
SMP5	Samsung	SM-P580	Personal
T290	Samsung	SM-T290	Personal
XRed8	Xiaomi	Redmi 8	Personal
X	Apple	iPhone X	Flickr
Y9	Huawei	JKM-LX3	Personal

In this section, we further evaluate three methods with relatively better performance obtained in the previous section. These three methods are 4, 5 and 9. This selection allows us to compare two denoising algorithms: *BM3D* (method 4) and Mihcak (method 9) and the effectiveness of use of SPN enhancer given by (4): without enhancer (method 4) and with enhancer (method 5).

A more realistic SCL task is considered for the evaluation of these three methods, then we selected image clustering based on their source cameras. The Linkage with Ward method is selected as clustering algorithm, which is unsupervised hierarchical algorithm [10]. We selected the Ward method to calculate distance between any two clusters, because in general the Ward method provides a better clustering performance, compared with other methods such as single, complex, average, and centroid methods, [11]. In this experiment, we used 180 images taken by 18 cameras (10 images per camera). The brief description of each device is given by Table 2. The camera ID will be used in the performance comparison of three denoising methods. It is worth noting that two smartphones with the same model (J411 and J4) are used for evaluation. From 180 images, three sets with different number of cameras are constructed. The Table 3 indicates Camara IDs that compose three sets. Figure 3 shows some images used in the experiments.

Table 3. Three sets of images used for evaluation of three denoising methods.

Sets	Camera-ID used in each set
Set-1 (5 cameras)	Ipad22, Red8, SMJ1, X, Y9
Set-2 (10 cameras)	G331, J4, J411, LGar, Red8, SMJ1, SMP5, T290, XRed8, Y9
Set-3 (15 cameras)	40D, 90D, A3, Apple11, Ipadd22, J4, J411, LGar, M1, Red8, SMJ1, SMP5, T290, X, Y9

Fig. 3. Some images used for experiments.

Using the Set-1 with 50 images taken by 5 different devices, the Set-2 with 100 images from 10 devices and the Set-3 with 150 images from 15 devices, shown in the Table 3, we evaluated two denoising methods: *Mihcak* and *BM3D* (method 4 and method

9). Figure 4 shows confusion matrices obtained by the linkage clustering after applying these denoising methods to images.

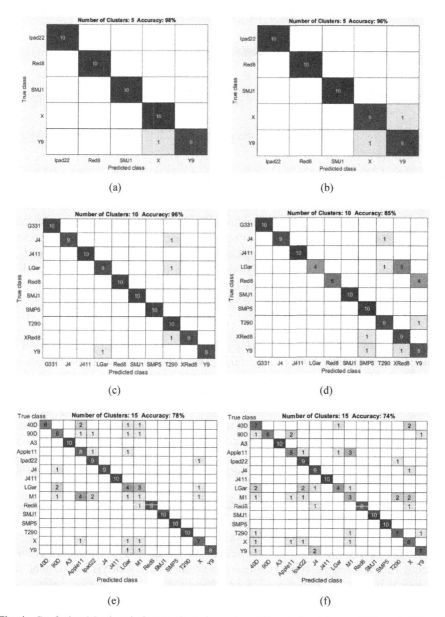

(a)   (b)

(c)   (d)

(e)   (f)

Fig. 4. Confusion Matrices in image clustering using different denoising methods and different number of cameras. (a), (c) and (e) *BM3D* denoising (method 4), (b), (d) and (f) *Mihcak* denoising (method 9)

Table 4 shows the accuracy comparison of two denoising methods (4 and 9 in Table 1) and BM3D denoising with enhancer (method 5).

Table 4. Accuracy comparison in image clustering task.

	Number of cameras		
	5	10	15
Method 4	98%	96%	85%
Method 9	96%	78%	74%
Method 5	92%	74%	67.3%

From Fig. 4 and Table 4, we can observe that the method 4, which is BM3D denoising method applying gray-scale image under $\sigma = 5$, provides better clustering results in image sets of different number of cameras used. The method 5, which is *BM3D* denoising together with the enhance function given by (4) cannot improve the clustering performance, although the ratio *Ratio* between average correlations given by (5) presents highest value as shown in Fig. 2. The principal reason of this situation can be the fact that the enhancing function attenuates also some PRNU components. In general, the *BM3D* denoising provides a better performance than *Mihcak* denoising algorithm.

4   Conclusions

In this paper, we evaluated two denoising algorithms with different parameters for the Source Camera Linking (SCL) tasks. Firstly, we evaluated several combinations of parameters of denoising algorithms, such as standard deviation of the SPN σ, color-channel of image to which the denoising algorithms are applied and use of enhancement function as postprocessing. To evaluate different conditions of the denoising algorithm, we introduced a metric, which is a ratio between the average correlation value for images taken by the same camera and that for images taken by the different cameras. In this evaluation, we obtained the method 5, which is a combination of BM3D denoising and enhancing algorithm given by (4) under $\sigma = 4$ in gray-scale image, provides best performance.

To evaluate the performance of denoising algorithms with different parameters for more realistic SCL task, image clustering by the SPN using Linkage algorithm is selected. The linkage is unsupervised clustering algorithm, which construct a hierarchical structure called Dendrogram. We prepared three sets of images taken by 5,10 and 15 different cameras. The experimental results indicate that the method 4, which is BM3D denoising with $\sigma = 4$ in gray-scale images, without enhancement, provides better performance. The confusion matrix and accuracy comparison show that this method provides fairly good performance, even if the image set is constructed from 15 different cameras and two of them are the same model.

As future work, we will analyze and propose an efficient image preprocessing to improve accuracy of the SPN estimation for more realistic scenarios of the SCL tasks, such as user profile linking using highly compressed images.

References

1. Farid, H.: Photo Forensics, 1st edn. The MIT Press, Cambridge (2016)
2. Lukas, J., Fridrich, J., Goljan, M.: Digital camera identification from sensor pattern noise. IEEE Trans. Inf. Forensics Secur. 1(2), 205–214 (2006)
3. Chen, M., Fridrich, J., Goljan, M., Lukas, J.: Determining image origin and integrity using sensor noise. IEEE Trans. Inf. Forensics Secur. 3(1), 74–90 (2008)
4. Li, R., Li, C.-T., Guan, Y.: Inference of compact representation of sensor fingerprint for source camera identification. Pattern Recogn. 74, 556–567 (2018)
5. Valsesia, D., Coluccia, G., Bianchi, T., Magli, E.: User authetication via PRNU-based physical unclonable functions. IEEE Trans. Inf. Forensics Secur. 12(8), 1941–1956 (2008)
6. Gupta, B., Tiwari, M.: An empirical cross-validation of denoising filters for PRNU extraction. Forensic Sci. Int. 292, 110–114 (2018)
7. Mihcak, K., Kozintsev, I., Ramchandran, K.: Spatially adaptive statistical modeling of wavelet image coefficients and its application to denoising. In: IEEE International Conference Acoustics, Speech, Signal processing, Phoenix, AZ, vol. 6, pp. 3253–3256 (1999)
8. Dobov, K., Foi, A., Katkovnik, V., Egiazarian, K.: Image denoising by sparse 3-D thansform-domain collaborative filtering. IEEE Trans. Image Process. 16(8), 2080–2095 (2007)
9. Li, C.-T.: source camera identification using enhanced sensor pattern noise. IEEE Trans. Inf. Forensics Secur. 5(2), 280–287 (2010)
10. Duda, R., Hart, P., Stork, D.: Pattern Classification, 2nd edn. John Wiley and Sons, Canada (2001)
11. de Amorim, R.C.: Feature relevance in ward's hierarchical clustering using the Lp norm. J. Classif. 32, 46–62 (2015)

Texture Based Supervised Learning for Crater-Like Structures Recognition Using ALOS/PALSAR Images

Nancy Jimenez-Martinez[1,2] [ID], Raquel Diaz-Hernandez[1(✉)],
Marius Ramirez-Cardona[3], and Leopoldo Altamirano-Robles[1]

[1] Instituto Nacional de Astrofísica, Óptica y Electrónica (INAOE), Sta. Ma. Tonantzintla,
San Andrés Cholula, Puebla 72840, México
{nancyjm,rdiaz,raqueld,robles}@inaoep.mx
[2] Cátedras Conacyt, Av. Insurgentes 1582, Crédito Constructor, Alcaldía Benito Juárez,
Ciudad de México 03940, México
[3] Área Académica de Ciencias de la Tierra y Materiales, Universidad Autónoma del Estado de
Hidalgo (UAEH), Ciudad del Conocimiento, Col. Carboneras,
Mineral de la Reforma, Hidalgo 42784, México
mariusr@uaeh.edu.mx

Abstract. Meteorite impacts participated in the formation of the Solar System
and continue to modify the planetary surfaces, originating a structure present in
all of them, the craters. Terrestrial craters are abundant, geological and biological
significant structures and are related to large mineral ores. The Earth impact record
continues to be deciphered, currently 190 terrestrial impact structures have been
confirmed, and it is estimated that several hundred remain to be discovered. One
of the techniques to detect a crater candidate site is Remote Sensing, however it
is a difficult task, due to the large information that must be processed, the lack of
discriminant features for crater and non-crater regions and appropriated methods
to recognize them. We propose an approach to identify meteorite impact structures, based on textural features of ALOS/PALSAR grayscale radar images, using
supervised automatic learning. For this, the quotient of HV and HH polarimetric
bands of these images was calculated. The resulting images were segmented by
global thresholding to generate two sets of training samples: structure type and
regions type of craters and non-craters, with them different kinds of classifiers
(Bayesian, Fuzzy, Genetics, Bagging, and Boost) were trained, getting accuracy
between 81 to 99% for craters identification.

Keywords: Crater recognition · Classification · Textural analysis

1 Introduction

Impact craters are a geomorphological feature present in all celestial bodies of the Solar
System; automatic crater identification has been the object of study to determine their
age and evolution and to obtain information on topics such as shock wave propagation,

© Springer Nature Switzerland AG 2021
E. Roman-Rangel et al. (Eds.): MCPR 2021, LNCS 12725, pp. 292–301, 2021.
https://doi.org/10.1007/978-3-030-77004-4_28

crater mechanics, physical conditions and impact melt formation, environmental and biological effects and the flow of impacts over geological time. Although it is not possible to classify a structure as an impact crater using only remote sensing technology, it is helpful to implement a detailed field study in the potential areas to be analyzed. Machine Learning has enhanced the recognition of impact craters on Earth in remotely sensed imagery; in this sense, learning can be supervised [1] or non-supervised [2–5].

In this paper, we propose a method applied to remote sensing to classify candidate crater sites. Crater recognition in remotely sensed imagery can be considered as a particular case of object detection in images, and is a critical task in computer vision because of the craters lack distinctive features [6]. Our method is based on grey-scale texture features for images of ALOS PALSAR. The images were first pre-processed to remove the inherited speckle noise, then the ratio of the HH/HV polarization was calculated. The resulting images were processed using histogram threshold segmentation, obtaining crater and non-crater samples sets, at the same time of each set structure-type and regions-type samples were created. With these sets and types samples we built the learning and test datasets that were used in the training and validation of Bayesian, Fuzzy, Genetic, Bagging and Boost Classifiers.

Western Desert in Egypt were chosen to test the effectiveness of our method of classifying impact structures, because a large number of circular structures of both meteoric (Oasis and BP) and volcanic origin (El-Baz Crater structure) have been found there. The contribution of this study is also that without using topographic data, good results are obtained in the classification of impact structures by applying the textural features of radar images to discriminate between different geological structures, in this case between craters and non-craters.

2 Materials and Methods

Impact craters and volcanic structures samples were selected from four databases: The Earth Impact Database, The Collapse Caldera Worldwide Database, the Smithsonian Institution National Museum of Natural History Global Volcanism Program and finally the Volcano Table of the Oregon State University [7–10]. Among them, only those with diameter ≥ 1 km were chosen, then, we made a random choice and a total of 82 samples were obtained: 38 are craters and 44 non-craters (calderas, stratovolcanoes, volcanic crater-lakes, complex and shield volcanoes, and one mountain). Both half, for craters and non-craters (i.e. 19 craters 10% of the total terrestrial craters and 22 non-craters), were used for training; the remaining samples for testing.

The training and testing samples were built from the ALOS (Advanced Land Observing Satellite), PALSAR L-band (Phased Array type L-Band Synthetic Aperture Radar) global 25 m mosaic data, created by the Japan Aerospace Exploration Agency (JAXA) [11]. We used 138 HH and HV polarization pairs of ALOS/PALSAR L-band images, the low frequency of L-band penetrates the vegetation or dry soils, enables detection of eroded or buried meteoritic structures [12]. From them, Regions of Interest (ROI's) were extracted and used to build mosaics. First, the ROI's images were pre-processed using the MeanSP [13] filter to reduce the inherited speckle effect, suppress extreme gray values (white and black dots) in radar images.

The second step in the pre-processing stage consisted in the enhancement of the structures of interest (impact and volcanic); for this purpose, a common practice in SAR imagery is to use linear operations (sums and differences) or band ratios between the polarimetry images. The ratio in Eq. (1) enhances the contrast between features of interest and reduces the influence of environmental effects (e.g. surface brightness, topographical slopes, appearance, shadows and seasonal changes) present in the image [12]. Accordingly, Eq. (1) was the best option to be applied in the identification of craters.

$$ratio_1 = \frac{HV}{HH} \tag{1}$$

Band ratios images were segmented using a global threshold [13], thereby generating the structure-type samples set, where craters and non-craters were obtained as only one geomorphological structure. So, we got 82 training samples (38 craters and 44 non-craters), which were also used as unlabeled test samples.

Connected components of 82 structure-type samples were computed. A total of 2997 Region-type samples of craters and non-craters were obtained with the connection operation, where 1499 were taken for training and the others for testing. The main difference between two sets of samples is that the region-type represents crater or no-crater in a group of "pieces" (regions) whereas the structure-type is the geoform as a single region.

Texture is a property that represents the surface and structure of an image and can be defined as an entity of mutually related and grouped pixels; this group of pixels is called texels or primitive textures. The textural analysis of SAR images increases the accuracy of the classification [14–16], as well as the optimization of the automatic identification. There are four approaches to textural analysis: structural, syntactic, statistical and hybrid. In this work, we applied statistical textural analysis, using first and second order statistics. Accordingly, 18 first-order histogram-based features were calculated: Anisotropy, Entropy, Mean, Deviation, Ra, Rb, Phi, Min, Max, Range, Plane Deviation, Fuzzy Entropy, Fuzzy Perimeter, MRow, MCol, Alpha, Beta and Mean1 and the calculation of the following second-order statistical features: Energy, Correlation, Local Homogeneity and Contrast [11]. To determine the biggest differentiation rate between craters and non-craters sets of samples, we calculated the discriminative power distance (dd) on the basis of Fisher's discriminative distance [17]:

$$dd = \frac{\mu_1 - \mu_2}{\sqrt{\sigma_1^2 + \sigma_2^2}} \tag{2}$$

where:

μ_1 is the mean of the textural features of craters.
μ_2 is the mean of the textural features of non-craters.
σ_1^2 is the variance of the textural features of craters.
σ_2^2 is the variance of the textural features of non-craters.

For the classification model training phase, we chose all the statistical textural features with a value of dd greater than 1.5 accordingly with the good results in other Radar images texture classification studies [17]. The algorithms analyzed for the classification were: AdaBoostM1, Bagging, BayesNet with genetic search, Fuzzy NN, Fuzzy Ownership NN, Fuzzy Quick Rules, Genetic Programming and Naive Bayes [18–24], all of them are available in Weka [25]. The classifiers were evaluated using the well-known statistical measures of the performance of a binary classification test (i.e. sensitivity, specificity, precision); the pre-processing and processing of training and testing data extracted from ALOS/PALSAR images were validated in the same way. The classifier model with the best performance was selected and applied to unlabeled structures located in various sites of the Western Desert in Egypt. This area represents a big challenge because, as it happens in all over the central-eastern Sahara (Eastern Libya, North-western Sudan and northern Chad), there are a large number of circular landforms with two possible sources: meteoritic impacts or volcanic processes [26, 27]. Figure 1 shows a flowchart of the methodology used in this work.

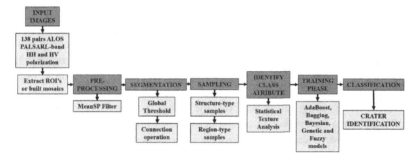

Fig. 1. Flowchart of the method applied in this work.

3 Results and Analysis

An example of the pair of ALOS/PALSAR radar images used to obtain the band ratio is shown in Fig. 2. Figure 2a shows the corrected (filtered) image of the L-band with the HH polarization, Fig. 2b contains the same band but with the HV polarization and finally, Fig. 2c is the image resulting from the Eq. (1) of these two polarizations.

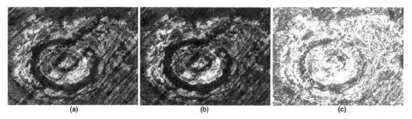

Fig. 2. ALOS/PALSAR images of the Aorounga Crater in Chad. (a) Radar image of the HH band. (b) Radar image of the HV band. (c) Result of band ratio (HH/HV).

The resulting images were segmented by the global threshold (Fig. 3a) to generate two sets of samples: one is structure-type and the other is region-type. Corresponding examples of the samples obtained are shown in Figs. 3b and 3c.

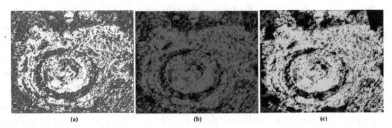

(a)   (b)   (c)

Fig. 3. Training samples: (a) Contour of the segmented structure by the global threshold; (b) Structure-type sample of Aorounga impact crater in Chad; (c) Regions-type sample of Aorounga impact crater in Chad.

False Positive Rate FPR (specificity), True Positive Rate TPR (sensitivity), was calculated and then the ROC graph is plotted (Fig. 4), each classifier is represented by a point (FPR, TPR). The ROC Graph is a technique very useful to visualize, organize, compare and select a classification algorithm. As can be seen in Fig. 4a and 4b, all classifiers fall in the upper left area, above the dotted red line, very close to the point [0, 1]. This scenario means that an almost perfect classification was performed. When using regions-type samples, Bagging classifier is the closest to the point [0, 1] (Fig. 4a).

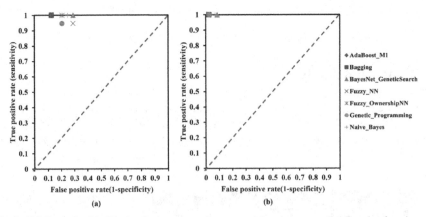

(a)   (b)

Fig. 4. ROC graph. (a) Graph of structures of craters and non-craters. (b) Graph of regions of craters and non-craters.

As seen in Fig. 5, all classifiers have sensitivity higher than 90%, which means that each and every one of them identifies all or most of the craters. Moreover, Specificity presents values less than 80%, as it is in the case of the Naive Bayes to classify structures-type samples of non-craters.

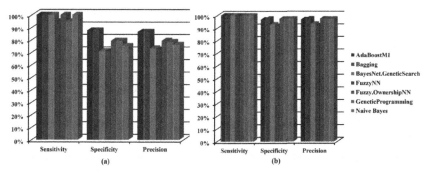

Fig. 5. Statistical measures of the performance of a binary classification test. (a) Classification of structure-type samples. (b) Classification of region-type samples.

Finally, to validate the extraction and delineation method of the training and testing samples (segmentation) and get the performance and absolute quality classification, we calculated the Quality Assessment Factors. Table 1 shows the results of the four factors: Branching Factor (B), Miss Factor (M), Detection Percentage (D) and Quality Percentage (Q).

Table 1. Quality assesment factors

Classifier	Sample type	Crater				Non-crater			
		B	Q	D	M	B	Q	D	M
AdaBoostM1	Structure	0,16	86	100	0	0	88	88	0,14
	Regions	0,03	100	97	0	0	97	97	0,03
Bagging	Structure	0,16	86	100	0	0	88	88	0,14
	Regions	0,02	100	98	0	0	98	98	0,02
BayesNet.GeneticSearch	Structure	0,37	73	100	0	0	71	71	0,41
	Regions	0,09	100	92	0	0	91	91	0,09
FuzzyNN	Structure	0,39	69	95	0,06	0,06	68	71	0,41
	Regions	0,03	100	98	0	0	97	97	0,03
Fuzzy.OwnershipNN	Structure	0,26	79	100	0	0	79	79	0,26
	Regions	0,03	100	97	0	0	97	97	0,03
GeneticProgramming	Structure	0,28	75	95	0,06	0,05	76	79	0,26
	Regions	0,03	100	98	0	0	97	97	0,03
NaiveBayes	Structure	0,32	76	100	0	0	75	75	0,33
	Regions	0,07	100	94	0	0	93	93	0,07

3.1 Testing on Impact Craters and Circular Geoforms in the Western Desert in Egypt

20 unlabeled sites of the Western Desert of Egypt were classified using the model with the best performance i.e. Bagging algorithm. These areas represent a major challenge because there are a large number of circular landforms with two possible sources: meteoritic impacts or volcanic processes [26, 27].

Figure 6 shows the area where Oasis (24°34'N, 24°24'E) and Kebira (24.40°N, 24.58°E) structures are located, Oasis is a confirmed impact structure. Moreover, Kebira was proposed by El-Baz and Ghoneim as a possible meteoritic crater and probable Libyan Desert Glass source [28], however, in a recent numerical modeling study they propose the LDG formation can be related with meteorite impact with or without crater formation [29].

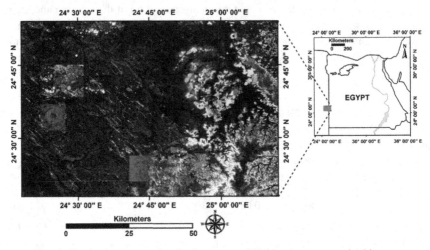

Fig. 6. Regions-type samples Oasis crater and Kebira structure are in this area.

The result of the classification of the regions-type testing samples is presented in Fig. 7. From the classification in Fig. 7, it is apparent that the classifier succeeded in labeling Oasis as crater, also correctly classified the northeast regions of the Oasis as no-crater because they are volcanic origin structures, the labeling of Kebira suggests is a crater.

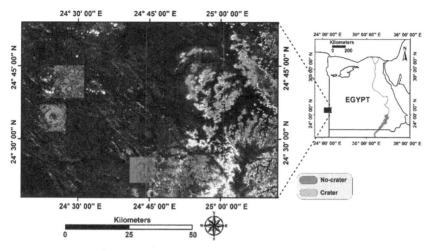

Fig. 7. Result of classification of Kebira and Oasis.

4 Discussion

Remote sensing does not provide an infallible criterion for crater recognition but, it is possible to delineate candidate crater areas from satellite or radar data. In this work ALOS PALSAR image analysis is a crucial step to delineate and extract impact and volcanic training samples because ensures the efficient computation and successful choice of discriminative features between structures types classified.

A notable study in automatic terrestrial craters detection is proposed in [2] they implement a group of routines in a user-friendly interface system, the goal is the same as our research i.e. identify impact and volcanic structures, but the image analysis is different, while for them is not significant the images enhancement phase to us, the pre-processing is a crucial stage. A limiting factor of any supervised method is the crater candidate detection in comparison to unsupervised methods such as in Portugal et al. [3], that using SRTM and ASTER digital elevation models modify the Hough transform, through a semblance operation. This method may be useful to identify structures with missing pieces. This last point coincides with the present method, because the algorithm better qualified (Bagging algorithm) is trained to identify regions of craters (and "parts" of craters). This algorithm is also an alternative to detect crater candidates using a supervised method.

Bruzzone et al. and Earl et al. [4, 5] implemented a Radial Consistency based algorithm, into a terrestrial crater detection prototype, this method identifies the majority of test and training samples. Nevertheless, when images like ALOS PALSAR are used without topographic data, is more difficult to discriminate between craters and non-craters, this is the major contribution of the present work, that can discriminate, with good detection percentage, the nature of the impact and volcanic structures.

5 Conclusions

A novel method for the processing of ALOS/PALSAR radar images to identify impact craters and volcanic structures was successfully developed and applied. The approach presented can use classification algorithms as diverse as AdaBoost, Bagging, Bayesian, Fuzzy, and Genetics based. We could obtain an accuracy and precision average of 80% and 90%, respectively, but in the case of Bagging up to 99%.

The performance obtained from all classifiers is in the range from good to excellent. This assessment is based on all the statistical measures that were applied to corroborate this performance. It can be concluded that the pre-processing and processing of radar images is determinant in the ability of these algorithms to correctly classify craters and non-craters.

References

1. KrØgli, S.O., Dypvik, H., Etzelmüller, B.: Automatic detection of circular depressions in digital elevation data in the search for potential Norweigian impact structures. Norwegian J. Geol./Norsk Geologisk Forening **87**, 157–166 (2007)
2. de Alburquerque Aráujo, A., Hadad, R., Pereira Martins, P.J.: Identification of patterns in satellite imagery: circular forms. In: Dougherty, E.R., Astola, J.T., (eds.) Nonlinear Image Processing and Pattern Analysis XII, vol. 4304, pp. 25–35. SPIE-International Society for Optical Engine (2001). https://doi.org/10.1117/12.424989
3. Portugal, R.S., de Souza Filho, C.R.: Automatic crater detection using DEM and circular coherency analysis - a case study on South American craters. In: 67th Annual Meteoritical Society Meeting on Proceedings, Rio de Janeiro, Brazil, no. 5096 (2004)
4. Bruzzone, L., Lizzi, L., Marchetti, P.G., Earl, J., Milnes, M.: Recognition and detection of impact craters from EO products. In: Proceedings of the Conference "ESA-EUSC 2004", ESA Publications Division, Madrid, Spain (2004)
5. Earl, J., Chicarro, A., Koeberl, C., Marchetti, P.G., Milnes, M.: Automatic recognition of crater-like structures in terrestrial and planetary images. In: 36th Annual Lunar and Planetary Science Conference, League City, Texas, USA, p. 1319 (2005)
6. Liu, S., Ding, W., Gao, F., Stepinski, T.F.: Adaptive selective learning for automatic identification of sub-kilometer craters. Neurocomputing **92**, 78–87 (2012)
7. Earth Impact Database. https://www.passc.net/EarthImpactDatabase, Accessed 1 Jan 2018.
8. The collapse caldera worldwide database. https://www.gvb-csic.es/CCDB/, Accessed 1 Jan 2018
9. Smithsonian Institution-Global Volcanism Program. https://volcano.si.edu/, Accessed Jan 2018
10. Volcano Table-Volcano World-Oregon State University. https://volcano.oregonstate.edu/volcano_table, Accessed 1 Jan 2018
11. Global PALSAR-2/PALSAR/JERS-1 Mosaic and Forest/Non-Forest map. https://www.eorc.jaxa.jp/ALOS/en/palsar_fnf/data/index.htm, Accessed 1 Dec 2017
12. Simental, E., Guthrie, V., Blundell, S.B.: Polarimetry band ratios, decompositions, and statistics for terrain characterization. In: Global Priorities in Land Remote Sensing on Proceedings of the Pecora, vol. 16, pp. 23–27. American Society for Photogrammetry and Remote Sensing, Sioux Falls (2005)
13. MVTec Halcon 10.0, version 2014; MVTec software GmbH. https://www.mvtec.com

14. van Gasselt, S., Kim, J., Choi, Yun-Soo., Kim, J.: The Oasis impact structure, Libya: geological characteristics from ALOS PALSAR-2 data interpretation. Earth Planets Space **69**(1), 1–12 (2017). https://doi.org/10.1186/s40623-017-0620-8
15. Thapa, R.B., Watanabe, M., Motohka, T., Shimada, M.: Potential of high-resolution ALOS–PALSAR mosaic texture for aboveground forest carbon tracking in tropical region. Remote Sens. Environ. **160**, 122–133 (2015)
16. Rakwatin, P., Longépé, N., Isoguchi, O., Shimada, M., Uryu, Y., Takeuchi, W.: Using multi-scale texture information from ALOS PALSAR to map tropical forest. Int. J. Remote Sens. **33**(24), 7727–7746 (2012)
17. Singh, M., Kaur, G.: SAR image classification using PCA and texture analysis. In: International Conference on Advances in Information Technology and Mobile Communication Proceedings, pp. 435–439. Springer, Heidelberg (2011)
18. Freund, Y., Schapire, R.E.: Experiments with a new boosting algorithm. In: Saitta, L., Kaufmann, M. (eds.) 13th International Conference on Machine Learning, vol. 96, pp. 148–156 (1996)
19. Breiman, L.: Bagging predictors. Mach. Learn. **24**(2), 123–140 (1996)
20. Aha, D.W., Kibler, D., Albert, M.K.: Instance-based learning algorithms. Mach. Learn. **6**(1), 37–66 (1991)
21. Jensen, R., Cornelis, C.: A new approach to fuzzy-rough nearest neighbor classification. In: Chan, C.C., Grzymala-Busse, J.W., Ziarko, W.P. (eds.) 6th International Conference, RSCTC, pp. 310–319. Springer, New York (2008)
22. Koza, J.R.: Genetic Programming: On the Programming of Computers by Means of Natural Selection. MIT Press, New York (1992)
23. Banzhaf, W., Nordin, P., Keller, R.E., Francone, F.D.: Genetic Programming: An Introduction: On the Automatic Evolution of Computer Programs and Its Applications. Morgan Kaufmann Publishers Inc., San Francisco (1998)
24. John, G.H., Langley, P.: Estimating continuous distributions in bayesian classifiers. In: Besnard, P., Hanks, S. (eds.) Uncertainty in Artificial intelligence 1995, pp. 338–345 (1995)
25. Waikato Environment for Knowledge Analysis (WEKA), Version 3.6.12: The University of Waikato, Machine Learning Group at the University of Waikato (2014). https://www.cs.waikato.ac.nz/ml/weka/downloading.html
26. Abate, B., Koeberl, C., Kruger, F.J., Underwood Jr., J.R.: BP and oasis impact structures, libya, and their relation to libyan desert glass. In Dressler, B.C., Sharpton, V.L. (eds.) Large Meteorite Impacts and Planetary Evolution II, pp. 177–192. Geological Society of America Inc. (1999)
27. Orti, L., Di Martino, M., Morelli, M., Cigolini, C., Pandeli, E., Buzzigoli, A.: Non-impact origin of the crater-like structures in the Gilf Kebir area (Egypt): Implications for the geology of Eastern Sahara. Meteorit. Planet. Sci. **43**(10), 1629–1639 (2008)
28. El-Baz, F., Ghoneim, E.: Largest crater shape in the Great Sahara revealed by multispectral images and radar data. Int. J. Remote Sens. **28**(2), 451–458 (2007)
29. Svetsov, V., Shuvalov, V., Kosarev, I.: Formation of Libyan desert glass: numerical simulations of melting of silica due to radiation from near-surface airbursts. Meteorit. Planet. Sci. **55**(4), 895–910 (2020)

Medical Applications of Pattern Recognition

A Comparison Study of EEG Signals Classifiers for Inter-subject Generalization

Carlos Emiliano Solórzano-Espíndola[1]([✉]) [iD], Humberto Sossa[1,2] [iD], and Erik Zamora[1] [iD]

[1] Instituto Politécnico Nacional - CIC,
Av. Juan de Dios Batiz S/N, Gustavo A. Madero, 07738 Mexico City, Mexico
csolorzanoe1200@alumno.ipn.mx, hsossa@cic.ipn.mx, ezamorag@ipn.mx
[2] Tecnológico de Monterrey,
Campus Guadalajara. Av. Gral. Ramón Corona 2514, 45138 Zapopan, Jalisco, Mexico

Abstract. Brain-computer interfaces are a promising technology for applications ranging from rehabilitation to video-games. A common problem for these systems is the ability to classify correctly signals corresponding to different subjects, as a consequence these systems are trained individually for each person. In this paper several classification methods, along with regularization methods, are compared, to establish a baseline for common datasets in the motor imagery paradigm for intra-subject classification and measure how they influence inter-subject classification.

Keywords: BCI · EEG · Motor imagery · Classification · Inter-subject

1 Introduction

Brain-computer interfaces (BCI) aim to translate activity from the brain recorded with different sensors [9]. The system outputs a command that can interact with a mechanical, like a wheelchair, or virtual, like a computer pointer device. The applications of this technology are then evident in many fields, especially in healthcare and rehabilitation. Allowing people with disabilities to interact in a more friendly manner with their surrounding environment [9].

For the recording of the signals, it is important to consider that different sections of the brain are related to specifics phenomena. That is why the recordings possess temporal and spatial resolution [15]. The activity and patterns from the brain are obtained using different technologies with different ranges of resolutions and susceptibilities to noise. Some of the most accurate BCI systems are achieved *invasive* methods, they require surgery to place the recording device, like Electrocorticography (ECoG) or implants [10].

Electroencephalography (EEG) is one of the most common methods as it is relatively simple, requires less subject preparation, and has a high temporal resolution. As EEG electrodes are exposed, they sense different sources of noise, both from the subject's body and from the environment [11].

© Springer Nature Switzerland AG 2021
E. Roman-Rangel et al. (Eds.): MCPR 2021, LNCS 12725, pp. 305–315, 2021.
https://doi.org/10.1007/978-3-030-77004-4_29

To correctly translate the brain activity into a command, the system follows a processing pipeline. Considering that the signals are obtained through EEG recording, the pipeline includes steps to filter noise-related components, extract relevant information or *features*, and finally use statistical and machine learning methods to discern the correct command output [4].

BCIs work according to a paradigm of the type of events that the signal represents. Some of these paradigms require that the system's pipeline is fit for a specific subject, which requires collecting training data for each possible user and increases the time and cost of the project. The data variability may be attributed to several factors, like fatigue, adaptation to the task, and differences in the development of motor control [13].

A review of several classical and newer approaches for the classification of EEG-based BCIs is presented in [8], including some of the current challenges that this field needs to overcome. For the problem of inter-subject variability, adaptive methods [5,14] and transfer learning [12] have been proposed to obtain subject-independent features and reduce the amount of data needed for the training. In this work, we describe and evaluate the performance of unmodified methods for the intra and inter-subject classification tasks in the motor imagery paradigm.

2   Fundamentals of Motor Imagery

The motor cortex in the brain is the area that displays more changes in wave patterns related to the execution of voluntary movements by muscles, excluding eye movements. There is evidence that this area of the brain can also react to the planning or see a different subject executing the action [17].

Motor imagery-based BCIs refers to the systems that allow identifying brain activity when the subject imagines a movement and translate it into a command [8]. The setup commonly involves recording with an EEG device using mainly the C_3, C_z and C_4 electrodes, following the 10-20 system, along with adjacent electrodes to filter out noise to cover the region of the motor cortex.

The filtering of the signal can be divided mainly in frequency-based filtering, which removes components outside the frequency band of interest, and spatial-based filtering, which remove noise components that are similar in adjacent areas of the brain [7].

According to the paradigm that the BCI follows, the last two steps are fitted using a training subset of the data. In many paradigms, including motor imagery, the feature extraction and classification steps suffer from high inter-subject variability [8,13]. Thus, the last stages of the pipeline are fitted for each person using the respective training subset.

2.1   Feature Extraction

A complex system, such as the brain, is composed of an ensemble of components to perform a task. Even when such elements are simple, the interactions between them arise non-linear phenomena that are not explained as an aggregate of these. To study these systems we extract *features* that capture some of these non-linearities and use them to characterize some event of interest and discard the redundant information [7]. These features are often proposed by previous knowledge in the field.

Such features also help the system by reducing the dimension of the input to the classifier models, as many of them can suffer the effects of the *curse of dimensionality* by inadequately exploring the feature space resulting in a classifier with a low *generalization* capability.

CSP. Common spatial patterns (CSP) is a supervised decomposition method that aims to find spatial filters that also allow extracting features [16]. The resulting filters are applied to the signal, and the new channels increase the variance for events of a certain class while reducing the variance for other classes.

The new channels z_j are formed by linearly weighing each original channel at the same time step n as $z_j[n] = \sum w_{ij} \cdot c_i[n]$. The filters w_j are calculated by, first calculating the averaged covariance matrices P_1 and P_2 over trials for each class, and then solving the joint diagonalization problem $W^T P_1 W = D_1, W^T P_2 W = D_2$ of both matrices with an equality constraint $D_1 + D_2 = I$. The resulting elements of $W = \{w_1, w_2, ...w_n\}$ are the filters where usually only a subset of the most relevant, weighted by the associated eigenvalues in the diagonal matrix D_1, are used for extracting features. Lastly the variance, or log variance, in each resulting filtered channel $Var(w_1^T X)$ can be taken as the features that represent the signal.

Filter Bank CSP. Filter bank CSP (FBCSP) is another method for feature extraction and a variation of CSP. As the brainwaves are the result of many independent processes in the brain, activity is present on different frequency bands at the same time. FBCSP uses a set of frequency filters for some specific frequency bands and then calculates again the CSP filters on the resulting signals [8]. The dimension of the feature vector will be the number of both types of filters multiplied.

Riemmanian Methods. The CSP-based methods require calculating an average covariance matrix P_i for each class to optimize spatial filters for the classification. In contrast, Riemannian methods use the covariance matrices considering their properties as symmetric positive definite matrices (SPD) for each trial and map it to a manifold to measure the similarity from one matrix to another. For example calculating the norm on the tangent space of a matrix P as $\langle S_1, S_2 \rangle_P = Tr(S_1 P^{-1} S_2 P^{-1})$, where P_1, S_1 and S_2 are SPD matrices. In this work, we use an approach called *tangent space mapping* which allows mapping to an euclidean space where the *tangent vectors* w.r.t P_G, the Riemannian mean of the whole training set, that represent the matrices as the feature vectors [2].

2.2   Classification

Classifier models are the last step in the processing pipeline for BCIs as they return an estimation of the intended command [8]. They are mathematical functions $f : \phi(X) \rightarrow Y$ that map the features $\phi(X) \in \mathbb{R}^D$ that represents a signal sample, or a window of the former, to an output $y \in \mathbb{R}^k$, where k is the possible number of output commands for the system.

The classifier partitions the feature space and assigns each region to a determined class. As some classifiers can produce only one hyperplane, an approach of one-vs-rest (OvR) is used, resulting in an ensemble of k classifiers f_i, the resulting class will be given by $\arg\max_i(f_1(x), ..., f_k(x))$.

To approximate the parameters, the models require a *learning rule*, which is an algorithm or heuristic that will use the observed data to estimate the best parameters for the task in a process that we refer as *training*. Even for the same model and observations, the rules find different solutions according to their assumptions and *hyperparamters*.

Linear Classifiers. The simplest models for classification are the linear classifiers. These classifiers obtain a hyperplane defined in Eq. 1 as a linear combination of the input features multiplied by the β_i parameters and a bias term. The function f acts as a threshold, if an observation X falls below or above the hyperplane it is assigned to the corresponding class.

$$\hat{y} = f\left(\sum_i \beta_i \phi_i(X) + \beta_0\right) \tag{1}$$

Linear discriminant analysis (LDA), support vector machines (SVM), and logistic regression (LR) are examples of linear classifiers that have been used previously for BCIs [8]. Their training methods can be found in [6].

Random Forest. A decision tree divides the feature space by proposing thresholds on the features values such that the resulting leaves have a high purity to their assigned class. A measure of purity is $GINI = \sum_{k=1}^{K} \hat{p}_{mk}(1 - \hat{p}_{mk})$, where p_{mk} is the probability of a leaf m to belong to the class k. One problem is that this training procedure results in a high bias towards the training data. Random forest (RF) trains several decision trees such that each one only observes a subset of the training data represented without all the features. The predictions of the resulting trees are then averaged to obtain a final prediction of the estimated class.

Multilayer Perceptron. A multi layer perceptron (MLP) is composed of several artificial neurons disposed in layers [1], where each neuron has the same structure of a linear classifier defined in Eq. 1, as each neuron in the same layer has an equal number of weights, the output of a layer can be represented as $A^i = f(A^{i-1}W^i + b^i)$, where $W \in \mathbb{R}^{D \times M^i}$ is the matrix of weights, where D is the dimension of the features or the previous layer output, and M, the number of neurons in layer i. The output of one layer then becomes the input for the next one A^{i+1}, until a final activation is reached.

The function f can be any non-linear differentiable function as the training is done by the *backpropagation* algorithm, which requires a differentiable loss function and a differentiable model to update the parameters using the gradient w.r.t the expected loss.

3   Methods

3.1   Experiments

A dataset in motor imagery has associated, besides the labels of training or testing, information about which subject the trial belongs. Signals are recorded on different days for each person, which will be referenced on the dataset as sessions or runs. The proposed experiments aim to answer questions about the generalization capabilities of the classifiers among subjects in the motor imagery framework by dividing four datasets in different ways for training and testing of the models.

The two experiments make a direct comparison of the same models for the intra-subject and inter-subject classification. In both cases, a classifier only sees the data from one subject during the training. In the first experiment, the classifiers use the train-test data split shown on Table 1 for the same subject, establishing a baseline for the classifiers in the framework for BCIs as intra-subject classification performance. In the second experiment, the classifiers learn from both the train and test subsets of one subject. The data from the remaining subjects are used as the test data to estimate the inter-subject classification performance.

3.2   Fitting the Classifiers

The best hyper-parameters for each model are estimated with a 5-fold cross-validation split. A set of proposed hyper-parameters, including regularization techniques, corresponding to each of the classifiers are tested through this method. The cross-validation uses the training sets for the corresponding experiment and calculates an average score across all the subjects. Once found, the models are re-trained using the whole training set for each case, and the training and test scores are reported.

For the feature extraction stage, the methods of CSP and Filter Bank CSP are fitted with the training set. For the classifiers using CSP, the number of components is a hyper-parameter for the cross-validation scheme to be estimated between 4 to 8 CSP components. In the case of FBCSP, the number of features is set to 4 for each frequency band.

Data. The datasets are from the BNCI Horizon project [3], all of which contain EEG signals from motor imagery recordings and are shown in the Table 1. The datasets contain between 9 to 12 subjects and at least two sessions or runs per subject with an equal amount of examples of each command. Using those sessions the datasets can be divided into train and test subsets.

Pre-processing. All the available EEG channels are included for each one of the datasets. The pre-processing step is limited bandpass filtering using a 16th order Butterworth filter for the range of 8 35 Hz, to help reduce the noise. Followed by scaling of the signals so that 90% of the signal is within the range between -1 to 1, using the 0.5 to the 0.95 percentile values.

Table 1. Datasets from the BNCI Horizon project used for the experiments.

Dataset	Subjects	Commands	Channels	Train	Test
1 : 001-2014	9	4	22	Session 0	Session 1
2 : 002-2014	14	2	15	Runs 0-4	Runs 5-7
3 : 004-2014	9	2	3	Sessions 0-2	Sessions 3-4
4 : 001-2015	12	2	13	Session A	Session B

4   Experimental Results

4.1   Experiment 1: Intra-subject Classification

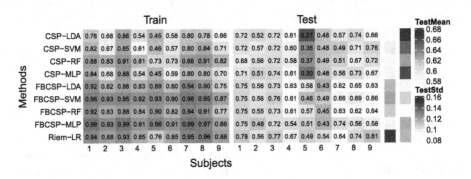

Fig. 1. Accuracy using the best found models for the dataset 1 on the experiment 1.

The first experiment shows tendencies for each one of the datasets for both the methods and the subjects. This can be mainly seen in Fig. 1 where a heatmap for the resulting accuracies on dataset 1. The MLP with FBSCP features achieves some of the highest training accuracies, but low test accuracies. Although the classifier with the lowest average test accuracy is LDA with CSP features, it has a close performance to other methods, except for the accuracy on subject 5. The best model on average was a logistic regression with Riemmanian features, and subject 3 achieved the best intra-subject generalization (Fig. 2).

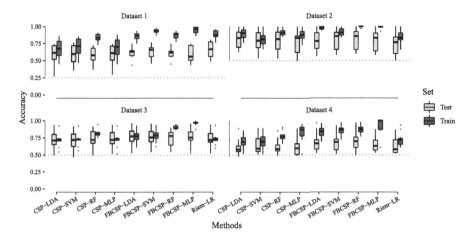

Fig. 2. Distribution of accuracies for each model in experiment 1.

On the Table 2 the average accuracies for the methods on each datasets is shown. The performance of the algorithms vary heavily depending on which dataset has been used. The logistic regression with Riemannian features had the best performance for the first dataset, but has the lowest accuracy on the second dataset. In general, the algorithms with CSP features achieve lower accuracy when compared with FBCSP, using a t test statistic a p-value of 6.144e−06 is returned when comparing the difference between one method to the other for the same classifiers along all the datasets.

Table 2. Average accuracy across subjects for the proposed algorithms on the experiment 1.

| | Dataset 1 | | Dataset 2 | | Dataset 3 | | Dataset 4 | |
	Train	Test	Train	Test	Train	Test	Train	Test
CSP-LDA	0.682	0.588	0.897	0.802	0.716	0.723	0.695	0.610
CSP-SVM	0.705	0.600	0.817	0.780	0.723	0.721	0.701	0.638
CSP-RF	0.833	0.589	0.914	0.793	0.816	0.731	0.772	0.620
CSP-MLP	0.699	0.590	0.873	0.762	0.719	0.735	0.826	0.612
FBCSP-LDA	0.857	0.621	0.976	0.782	0.769	**0.762**	0.841	0.684
FBCSP-SVM	0.933	0.628	0.916	0.803	0.781	0.754	0.860	0.682
FBCSP-RF	0.867	0.615	0.997	**0.808**	0.902	0.744	0.872	**0.693**
FBCSP-MLP	0.948	0.589	0.989	0.788	0.963	0.758	0.933	0.653
Riem-LR	0.890	**0.667**	0.845	0.742	0.734	0.735	0.728	0.633
Average	0.824	0.610	0.91	0.784	0.791	0.740	0.803	0.647

4.2   Experiment 2: Inter-subject Classification

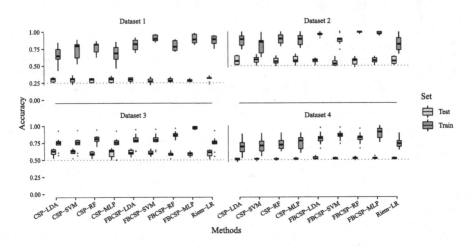

Fig. 3. Distribution of accuracies for each model in experiment 2.

On the second experiment, whose results are in Fig. 3 and Table 3, most of the test accuracy values are relatively low when compared with experiment 1 and closer to the values given by a random classifier. Except for the first dataset, the best classifiers are no longer the same for this task as in the previous experiments. Dataset 1 has the lowest average as expected from having four classes, however, the remaining dataset averages order does not correspond to their order in the previous experiment. Another thing to point out is that the two classifiers using the CSP features achieved the best accuracy this time. Using a t-test to verify if CSP methods get better results than FBCSP now returns a p-value of 0.013, which can be considered as moderate evidence of better performance.

As the test accuracy on the second experiments are relatively low, they are still on average above that of a random classifier level (RC), t-test is used to measure this difference. To measure the predictive power of each model from the first experiment with the corresponding model of the second experiment a linear regression was performed for to each dataset. The test and regression metrics can be seen at Table 4 with varying results, where only the models on the first dataset show evidence of related performance for the two tasks.

Table 3. Average accuracy across subjects for the proposed algorithms on the experiment 2.

	Dataset 1		Dataset 2		Dataset 3		Dataset 4	
	Train	Test	Train	Test	Train	Test	Train	Test
CSP-LDA	0.666	0.303	0.885	0.580	0.741	0.618	0.698	0.510
CSP-SVM	0.734	0.298	0.808	**0.586**	0.746	**0.621**	0.710	0.514
CSP-RF	0.769	0.289	0.894	0.572	0.805	0.590	0.733	0.511
CSP-MLP	0.680	0.300	0.878	0.585	0.724	0.606	0.757	0.515
FBCSP-LDA	0.801	0.299	0.962	0.570	0.786	0.610	0.813	**0.524**
FBCSP-SVM	0.909	0.283	0.883	0.541	0.789	0.607	0.854	0.520
FBCSP-RF	0.794	0.291	0.990	0.561	0.867	0.584	0.816	0.519
FBCSP-MLP	0.895	0.287	0.974	0.574	0.972	0.590	0.885	0.523
Riem-LR	0.874	**0.311**	0.816	0.573	0.745	0.598	0.746	0.519
Average	0.791	0.296	0.899	0.571	0.797	0.603	0.779	0.517

Table 4. Metrics for the tests performed on the classifiers results.

	Dataset 1	Dataset 2	Dataset 3	Dataset 4
RC t-test p	2.2e−16	2.2e−16	2.2e−16	2.2e−16
Regression R^2	0.153	0.0395	−0.011	−0.004
Regression p	0.0001694	0.0336	0.7713	0.4451

5   Conclusion

BCIs presents challenges for the accurate classification of more than one subject. In order to make the BCIs a technology available to the public, with an acceptable performance accuracy, the need for training data coming from the user should be reduced as the task of collecting a sufficient amount of training examples can be time expensive.

The results from the second experiment show that even though most of the models can classify above the level of a random classifier for subjects not previously seen, the accuracy is still too low to be used for practical purposes.

From the results, it can also be seen that there seems to be no relation to the performance of a model for the intra-subject task to the inter-subject classification task. This may be as a result of the feature extraction step, which in all these cases use the spatial information of the signals for each subject that may cause a bias towards that specific subject, this may be addressed with modifications to make the feature extraction support multi-modal data. This also evidence that even if the current methods work well for the intra-subject task, they may not perform as well for inter-subject generalization and the need to develop new methods.

Acknowledgement. H. Sossa and E. Zamora would like to acknowledge the support provided by CIC-IPN in carrying out this research. This work was economically supported by SIP-IPN (grant numbers 20200651, 20210316 and 20210788), CONACYT Fronteras de la Ciencia 65 and FORDECYT-PRONACES 60055. CE Solórzano-Espíndola acknowledges CONACYT for the scholarship granted towards pursuing his postgraduate studies.

References

1. Arce, F., Zamora, E., Hernández, G., Antelis, J.M., Sossa, H.: Recognizing motor imagery tasks using deep multi-layer perceptrons. In: Perner, P. (ed.) MLDM 2018. LNCS (LNAI), vol. 10935, pp. 468–482. Springer, Cham (2018). https://doi.org/10.1007/978-3-319-96133-0_35

2. Barachant, A., Bonnet, S., Congedo, M., Jutten, C.: Multiclass brain-computer interface classification by Riemannian geometry. IEEE Trans. Biomed. Eng. **59**(4), 920–928 (2012)

3. Brunner, C., et al.: BNCI Horizon 2020: towards a roadmap for the BCI community. Brain-Comput. Interfaces **2**(1), 1–10 (2015)

4. Nam, C.S., Nijholt, A., Lotte, F.: Brain–Computer Interfaces Handbook, vol. 73. Taylor & Francis, CRC Press, Boca Raton (2018) (2018)

5. Costa, A.P., Møller, J.S., Iversen, H.K., Puthusserypady, S.: An adaptive CSP filter to investigate user independence in a 3-class MI-BCI paradigm. Comput. Biol. Med. **103**(September), 24–33 (2018)

6. Hastie, T., Tibshirani, R., Friedman, J.: The Elements of Statistical Learning. SSS. Springer, New York (2009). https://doi.org/10.1007/978-0-387-84858-7

7. Hu, L., Zhang, Z. (eds.): EEG Signal Processing and Feature Extraction. Springer, Singapore (2019). https://doi.org/10.1007/978-981-13-9113-2

8. Lotte, F., et al.: A review of classification algorithms for EEG-based brain-computer interfaces: a 10 year update. J. Neural Eng. **15**(3), 031005 (2018)

9. Major, T.C., Conrad, J.M.: A survey of brain computer interfaces and their applications. In: IEEE SOUTHEASTCON 2014, pp. 1–8 (2014)

10. Miller, K.J., Hermes, D., Staff, N.P.: The current state of electrocorticography-based brain-computer interfaces. Neurosurg. Focus **49**(1), 1–8 (2020)

11. Minguillon, J., Lopez-Gordo, M.A., Pelayo, F.: Trends in EEG-BCI for daily-life: requirements for artifact removal. Biomed. Signal Process. Control **31**, 407–418 (2017)

12. Ozdenizci, O., Wang, Y., Koike-Akino, T., Erdogmus, D.: Transfer learning in brain-computer interfaces with adversarial variational autoencoders. In: International IEEE/EMBS Conference on Neural Engineering, NER, vol. 2019-March, pp. 207–210. IEEE, March 2019

13. Saha, S., Baumert, M.: Intra- and inter-subject variability in EEG-based sensorimotor brain computer interface: a review. Front. Comput. Neurosci. **13**(January), 1–8 (2020)

14. Schonleitner, F.M., Otter, L., Ehrlich, S.K., Cheng, G.: A comparative study on adaptive subject-independent classification models for zero-calibration error-potential decoding. In: 2019 IEEE International Conference on Cyborg and Bionic Systems, CBS 2019, pp. 85–90, no. September. IEEE, September 2019

15. Tiwari, N., Edla, D.R., Dodia, S., Bablani, A.: Brain computer interface: a comprehensive survey. Biol. Inspired Cogn. Architect. **26**(October), 118–129 (2018)

16. Virgilio Gonzalez, C.D., Sossa Azuela, J.H., Rubio Espino, E., Ponce Ponce, V.H.: Classification of motor imagery EEG signals with CSP filtering through neural networks models. In: Batyrshin, I., Martínez-Villaseñor, M.L., Ponce Espinosa, H.E. (eds.) MICAI 2018. LNCS (LNAI), vol. 11288, pp. 123–135. Springer, Cham (2018). https://doi.org/10.1007/978-3-030-04491-6_10
17. Yin, S., Liu, Y., Ding, M.: Amplitude of sensorimotor mu rhythm is correlated with BOLD from multiple brain regions: a simultaneous EEG-fMRI study. Front. Hum. Neurosci. **10**(July), 1–12 (2016)

COVID-19 Related Pneumonia Detection in Lung Ultrasound

Michael Stiven Ramirez Campos[1,2]([envelope]) [ORCID], Santiago Saavedra Bautista[1] [ORCID],
Jose Vicente Alzate Guerrero[1] [ORCID], Sandra Cancino Suárez[1] [ORCID],
and Juan M. López López[1] [ORCID]

[1] Semillero PROMISE, Escuela Colombiana de Ingeniería Julio Garavito,
Av. Cra. 40 N 205-59, Bogotá, D.C., Colombia
semillero.promise@escuelaing.edu.co
[2] Universidad del Rosario, Ak. 24 No. 63C-69, Bogota, D.C, Colombia
https://www.escuelaing.edu.co

Abstract. Accurate diagnosis plays an important role in the current public health situation caused by the Covid-19 outbreak. Ultrasound images offer some advantages over other imaging techniques due to their lowers costs; however, to the authors' knowledge, these type of images have not received as much attention as the other methods. This article describes a set of novel features for Covid-19 detection from lung ultrasound scans, obtained from the Pocovid database described in [3]. Two simultaneous approaches were considered: analysis and segmentation of the pleura, and highlighting of information from frame sequences through PCA and ICA. The proposed features were tested using machine learning models, achieving an average accuracy of 0.9, which considering the interpretability of the features and the complexity of the classification models used, is a good result.

Keywords: Covid-19 · ICA · Pleura segmentation · PCA · Pneumonia · Machine learning

1 Introduction

Lung ultrasound represents a diagnostic technique that has proven to be highly effective in detecting and monitoring lung conditions such as pneumonia and other similar infections. This technique has important advantages over conventional radiology due to its low cost, the wide availability of ultrasound scanners in health care centers, the fact that it is a non-invasive and innocuous technique, and that it can be performed at the point of care without having to mobilize the patient [4]. The aforementioned advantages make lung ultrasound a valuable tool in the management of patients with Covid-19, thanks to the evidence of specific patterns of the disease that can be observed with this technique [11]. Currently, different automatic detection algorithms have been developed using digital image processing along with machine learning and deep learning models, specifically

© Springer Nature Switzerland AG 2021
E. Roman-Rangel et al. (Eds.): MCPR 2021, LNCS 12725, pp. 316–324, 2021.
https://doi.org/10.1007/978-3-030-77004-4_30

for the detection of Covid-19 from lung ultrasound scans. Some of these studies implemented convolutional neural networks (CNN) yielding remarkable results such as [3], where a 3-class (pneumonia, Covid-19, and healthy) classification algorithm, named Pocovid, is proposed with an accuracy of 89%, and [8], where a probability score for Covid-19 is estimated for lung ultrasound videos, obtaining an accuracy of 97%. Likewise, other types of medical imaging techniques have been used in conjunction with deep learning algorithms for the automatic detection of Covid-19; some of these studies include conventional chest X-ray along with CNN and histogram oriented gradient (HOG) as in [2], and computed tomography scans with pre-trained CNN like the one used in [1], obtaining accuracies of 98% and 90% respectively.

This document details a novel set of relevant features, based on the morphology of pleura for Covid-19 detection in lung ultrasound scans, along with a test performed with a set of machine learning models. Moreover, dimensionality reduction techniques like Principal Component Analysis (PCA) and Independent Component Analysis (ICA) were used for the extraction of characteristic patterns of lung ultrasound scans. An accuracy of 99% was achieved for a Random Forest model, which overcomes previous results [3,8]. Novel features exhibited a high correlation with Covid-19 and may be useful to improve diagnostics and treatments.

2   Methods and Materials

2.1   Database

The videos used in the present project were obtained from the database described in [3]. 124 videos (18230 frames) of lung ultrasound scans taken with convex probe were used where 51 videos are labeled as COVID, 26 as pneumonia and 47 as regular (healthy controls).

2.2   Pleural Processing

There are 18230 images obtained from the cropped videos. The first step was to convert all images to grayscale, in order to facilitate the operations that were performed in the processing and feature extraction stage. Taking into account that speckle noise is the typical noise in ultrasound images, an anisotropic diffusion filter was used to remove such noise [7]. In addition, a contrast enhancement was applied.

After the steps described above, the upper 35% of the image was removed, because it is in that region of the image where the pleura is usually found. Once the upper part of the image is removed, a gamma contrast adjustment is again applied to better differentiate the pleura. Next, a white hat morphology operator with a rectangular structuring element is used. A binarization follows the previous step, using Otsu's method. Since the goal of this first step is to extract pleural features from each of the images, two iterations were performed

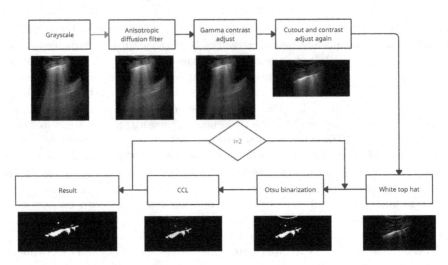

Fig. 1. Block diagram corresponding to the digital processing applied to the ultrasound video frames.

using connected-component labeling to find connected regions and again applying Otsu's method(Fig. 1).

A dataframe was generated with the most relevant characteristics of the pleura (area, convex area, eccentricity, length of the major axis, length of the minor axis, perimeter, Euler number, equivalent diameter, solidity) discarding those regions with an area of less than 49 pixels. To homogenize the data, the characteristics of each of the segmented regions were averaged. In this phase, 1044 images were discarded (5.72% of the total data) because the algorithm did not detect the presence of pleura. It is important to clarify that the images obtained are the frames that make up the videos described above, therefore, it is normal that in some frames the pleura cannot be detected due to the change generated from frame to frame during the recording.

2.3 Pleural Continuity

The continuity of the pleura in lung ultrasound images is a feature of great relevance [6], therefore it is important to detect this parameter individually with respect to the rest of the features. Once the final segmentation of the pleura was obtained (Fig. 1), we proceeded to perform a skeletonization of this segmentation in order to have a topological representation of the structure of the pleura. Then, a connected-component labeling (CCL) [10] was used, with 8-connected neighborhood, so that the skeleton was considered by the algorithm as a connected region (Fig. 2) and thus to extract some features such as the dimensions of the bounding box, the perimeter, major axis length, minor axis length, and solidity. These features allowed to establish a threshold of values to determine whether a pleura is continuous, non-continuous or not detected.

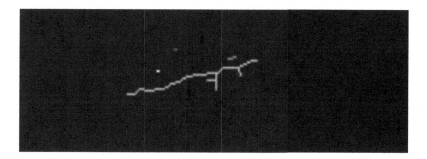

Fig. 2. Segmented pleural skeleton.

2.4 Principal Component Analysis (PCA) and Independent Component Analysis (ICA) for Ultrasound Feature Extraction

Due to the fact that the samples available for the development of the algorithm were videos, it was decided to generate additional features besides the ones previously obtained from the pleura, in order to take into account the relationship between the different frames composing each video. For this purpose, the statistical techniques PCA [9] and ICA [5] were used for dimensionality reduction as shown in Fig. 3. First, an array containing the frame sequence of each video was generated to subsequently estimate the covariance matrix of this array. From this matrix, the eigenvalues and eigenvectors were calculated, which made it possible to determine an optimal number of components through the explained variance of the data set; in this case, the optimal number chosen was six components which describe 98.7% of the variance in the frame sequence. Then, dimensionality reduction was performed to generate six new frames describing the principal components of each video, which on average were composed of 100 frames each. Finally, the ICA technique was applied to the frames obtained using the FastICA algorithm to identify the statistically independent components of each video [5].

Having obtained a new set of PCA and ICA frames for each video, we proceeded to calculate the difference between the original frames and the components obtained, to compute the percentage of pixels corresponding to the regions of interest (B lines, A lines, consolidations, pleural line, etc.), through segmentation by Otsu's method. Thus, these white pixel percentages for each component are added as additional features to those previously obtained from the pleura.

2.5 Statistical Analysis and Classification

A descriptive statistical analysis was computed in order to observe which features could offer a better discriminant power (see Fig. 4).

Five machine learning models (Random Forest, SVM, KNN, Decision Trees and Logistic Regression) were used to classify the database obtained in three classes: Covid, pneumonia and regular (healthy).

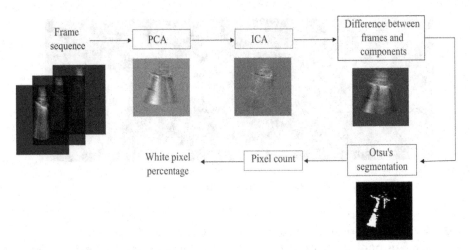

Fig. 3. Feature extraction with PCA and ICA

Table 1. Performance of Machine Learning Models

Model	Test accuracy	Class	Specificity	Sensitivity	Precision	F1-score	Recall
Random Forest		Covid	0.99	0.99	0.99	0.99	0.99
	0.99	Pneumonia	0.99	0.98	0.99	0.98	0.99
		Regular	0.99	0.99	1.00	1.00	1.00
SVM		Covid	0.98	0.99	0.98	0.99	0.99
	0.98	Pneumonia	0.99	0.94	0.98	0.97	0.95
		Regular	0.98	0.99	0.99	0.99	0.99
KNN		Covid	0.99	0.98	0.99	0.99	0.99
	0.98	Pneumonia	0.99	0.96	0.98	0.97	0.98
		Regular	0.98	0.98	0.98	0.99	0.99
Decision Tree		Covid	0.98	0.97	0.97	0.97	0.98
	0.96	Pneumonia	0.98	0.90	0.92	0.91	0.90
		Regular	0.98	0.97	0.97	0.97	0.97
Logistic Regression CV	0.77	Covid	0.84	0.79	0.77	0.78	0.79
		Pneumonia	0.95	0.36	0.6	0.46	0.37
		Regular	0.78	0.90	0.81	0.85	0.90

3   Results

After the computation of all the features, a data set was organized and the 5 machine learning models described above were trained, obtaining accuracies higher than 0.9 in 4 of the 5 models selected. Table 1 shows the report of each of the 5 models and the value of the metrics related to each of the classes.

As can be seen in Table 1, the model with the best performance was Random Forest with a very small margin with respect to SVM. The accuracy of SVM for

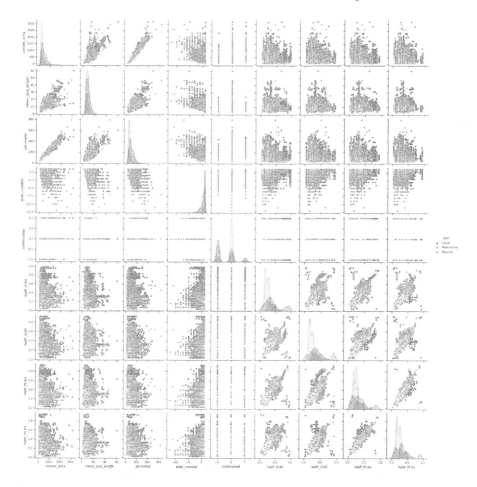

Fig. 4. Pairwise relationships between the characteristics that are part of the data set

the training set was 0.9977 and for the test set was 0.9846, while Random Forest obtained 1 for the training set and 0.9937 for the test set.

4   Discussion of Results

A novel set of features for lung ultrasound images were proposed and tested for Covid-19 pneumonia detection. Those features were based on the knowledge about pleura area when affected with pneumonia and the relationship between frames in the ultrasound recordings [12].

On the other hand, PCA and ICA highlighted information across the frames forming the ultrasound videos, providing a way to obtain information not only from individual static images but from the whole sequences. The application of these multivariate techniques, to the knowledge of the authors, is novel for classification tasks. Other authors [3,8] have analyzed frames individually.

We have not used convolutional neural networks, because the available database was small in comparison to those used in deep learning models. In addition, when working with videos, it is possible to have redundant information across frames and, since one of our goals was to provide a better interpretability of the features, we decided to test them in simpler machine learning models. It should be noted that, compared to other studies that have also used lung ultrasound scans for Covid-19 detection, we obtained a considerably better performance: the Pocovid-net neural network described in [3] has an accuracy of 89%, and the scoring algorithm developed in [8] presents an accuracy of 97%. In

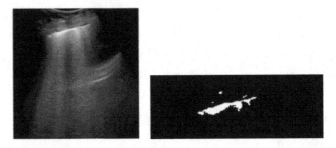

Fig. 5. Example of an ultrasound scan showing a continuous pleural line, before and after image processing (pleural detection).

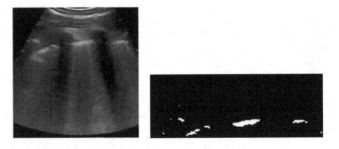

Fig. 6. Example of an ultrasound scan showing a discontinuous pleural line, before and after image processing (pleural detection).

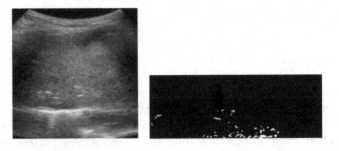

Fig. 7. Example of an ultrasound where no pleural line is evident.

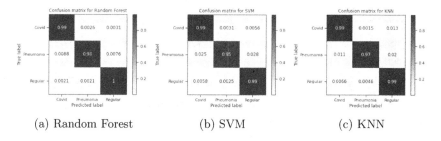

| | (a) Random Forest | (b) SVM | (c) KNN |

Fig. 8. Confusion matrices for the 3 models are superior in performance to the similar studies previously mentioned.

this article, we were able to obtain higher performance metrics than the previously described for three of the five machine learning models tested (Figs. 5, 6, 7 and 8).

5 Conclusion

The main goal of the study was achieved: novel relevant features for Covid-19 detection on lung ultrasound scans were extracted and tested using five machine learning models. Those features have a high degree of interpretability since they take into account the morphological attributes of the pleura, the characteristic patterns of lung ultrasound scans, as well as the relation between the frames of each video. The obtained performance metrics were considerably better to the ones described in [3] and [8], despite the fact that no neural networks were used in the algorithm proposed in this paper. Four of the five tested models accomplished an accuracy higher than 90%. These techniques for feature extraction may provide relevant information that can increase the performance of other artificial vision tasks in different contexts.

References

1. Abdar, A.K., Sadjadi, S.M., Soltanian-Zadeh, H., Bashirgonbadi, A., Naghibi, M.: Automatic detection of coronavirus (COVID-19) from chest CT images using VGG16-based deep-learning. In: 27th National and 5th International Iranian Conference of Biomedical Engineering, ICBME 2020, November 2020, pp. 212–216 (2020). https://doi.org/10.1109/ICBME51989.2020.9319326
2. Alam, N.A.A., Ahsan, M., Based, M.A., Haider, J., Kowalski, M.: COVID-19 detection from chest X-ray images using feature fusion and deep learning. Sensors **21**(4), 1480 (2021). https://doi.org/10.3390/s21041480, https://www.mdpi.com/1424-8220/21/4/1480
3. Born, J., et al.: POCOVID-net: automatic detection of COVID-19 from a new lung ultrasound imaging dataset (POCUS). arXiv (2020)
4. Gehmacher, O., Mathis, G., Kopf, A., Scheier, M.: Ultrasound imaging of pneumonia. Ultrasound Med. Biol. **21**(9), 1119–1122 (1995). https://doi.org/10.1016/0301-5629(95)02003-9

5. Hyvärinen, A., Oja, E.: Independent component analysis: algorithms and applications. Neural Netw. **13**(4–5), 411–430 (2000). https://doi.org/10.1016/S0893-6080(00)00026-5, https://linkinghub.elsevier.com/retrieve/pii/S0893608000000265

6. Peng, Q.Y., Wang, X.T., Zhang, L.N.: Findings of lung ultrasonography of novel corona virus pneumonia during the 2019–2020 epidemic. Intensive Care Med. **46**(5), 849–850 (2020). https://doi.org/10.1007/s00134-020-05996-6

7. Perona, P., Malik, J.: Scale-space and edge detection using anisotropic diffusion. IEEE Trans. Pattern Anal. Mach. Intell. **12**(7), 629–639 (1990). https://doi.org/10.1109/34.56205, http://ieeexplore.ieee.org/document/56205/

8. Roy, S., et al.: Deep learning for classification and localization of COVID-19 markers in point-of-care lung ultrasound. IEEE Trans. Med. Imaging **39**(8), 2676–2687 (2020). https://doi.org/10.1109/TMI.2020.2994459

9. Shalizi, C.R.: Principal components analysis. In: Advanced Data Anlysis from an Elementary Point of View, pp. 2940–2949 (2008). https://doi.org/10.1016/B978-008045405-4.00538-3

10. Shapiro, L.G.: Connected Component Labeling and Adjacency Graph Construction, pp. 1–30 (1996). https://doi.org/10.1016/S0923-0459(96)80011-5, https://linkinghub.elsevier.com/retrieve/pii/S0923045996800115

11. Smith, M.J., Hayward, S.A., Innes, S.M., Miller, A.S.: Point-of-care lung ultrasound in patients with COVID-19 - a narrative review. Anaesthesia **75**(8), 1096–1104 (2020). https://doi.org/10.1111/anae.15082

12. Vetrugno, L., et al.: Our Italian experience using lung ultrasound for identification, grading and serial follow-up of severity of lung involvement for management of patients with COVID-19. Echocardiography **37**(4), 625–627 (2020). https://doi.org/10.1111/echo.14664

Breastfeeding and Caries. A Relationship Analysis to Develop a Computer-Assisted Diagnosis Using Random Forest

Laura A. Zanella-Calzada[1], Carlos E. Galván-Tejada[2(✉)],
Nubia M. Chávez-Lamas[3], Karen E. Villagrana-Bañuelos[2],
Jorge I. Galván-Tejada[2], and Hamurabi Gamboa-Rosales[2]

[1] LORIA, Université de Lorraine, Campus Scientifique BP 239, 54506 Nancy, France
laura.zanella-calzada@univ-lorraine.fr
[2] Unidad Académica de Ingeniería Eléctrica, Universidad Autónoma de Zacatecas,
Jardín Juárez 147, Centro, 98000 Zacatecas, Zac, Mexico
{ericgalvan,kvillagrana,gatejo,hamurabigr}@uaz.edu.mx
[3] Clínica Comunitaria de Tacoaleche, Unidad Académica de Odontología,
Universidad Autónoma de Zacatecas, Jardín Juárez 147, Centro, 98000 Zacatecas,
Zac, Mexico
nubiachavez@uaz.edu.mx

Abstract. This work proposes the analysis of a set of features related to breastfeeding and dental caries. The data was taken from NHANES 2013–2014, for the development of the model, the random forest algorithm is implemented, was evaluated through a statistical analysis based on the out-of-bag error (OOB), the receiver operating characteristic (ROC) curve and the area under the curve (AUC). Results; AUC = 0.669 and OOB = 36% were observed, which shows that the multivariate model developed is statistically significant and achieves an adequate generalization for the classification of the subjects. Conclusions; A model based on information related to breastfeeding is able to classify subjects with presence of dental caries in a generalized way, obtaining preliminary results for the development of a support tool for the diagnosis of this condition based on a new approach.

Keywords: Breastfeeding · Dental caries · NHANES · Classification · Random forest · Multivariate model

1 Introduction

According to Setiawati [19] and Guerrero [8], tooth decay can develop immediately as soon as the tooth erupts into the oral cavity. In quality of life studies it has been reported that dental caries is a condition that can damage the overall development of the child, because in advanced stages causes infectious processes, aesthetic problems, phonetic and hinders chewing [10,16]. In Mexico, the prevalence of dental caries in children outweighs any other health condition. According to estimates, six out of ten children suffer from dental caries at the age of six.

© Springer Nature Switzerland AG 2021
E. Roman-Rangel et al. (Eds.): MCPR 2021, LNCS 12725, pp. 325–334, 2021.
https://doi.org/10.1007/978-3-030-77004-4_31

Dental caries is considered a diet-induced infectious disease [17]. The "United Nations Children's Fund" recommends breast milk as the only food the infant needs during the first 6 months of life. In this regard, Ramírez et al. [14] consider breastfeeding as a protective factor in the development of early tooth decay.

In recent years, paediatric dentistry consultations have seen an upsurge in cases of severe early childhood caries, Severe-Early Childhood Caries (S-ECC), which are not related to the misuse of a bottle or pacifier but occur in children fed with prolonged, nocturnal and on-demand breastfeeding. The presence of childhood dental caries is an important issue that should be thoroughly investigated as it affects the well-being, quality of life and health of the child. It is disconcerting to observe rampant caries in young children [1]. Pain and infection caused by tooth decay can be extremely bothersome and can impact children quality of life and oral function [18]. Cavities in young children are often managed with repeated antibiotic prescriptions and tooth extractions under local or general anaesthesia [12]. In industrialized countries dental caries are responsible for one of the most frequent causes of hospitalization of children [7]. This disease represents one of the most preventable causes of hospitalization [11]. Children with Early Childhood Caries (ECC) are much more likely to have new tooth decay in both the primary and permanent dentition [6]. The hypothesis that could explain ECC cases is that certain breastfeeding styles, specifically prolonged breastfeeding beyond the first tooth eruption, offered on demand, nocturnal, and colostum, would increase the risk of tooth decay. In the case of daytime feedings the causal mechanism would be the repeated contact of a carbohydrate (breast milk) with the child's teeth, without subsequent hygiene or remineralisation time between feedings, and in the case of night-time feedings the prolonged contact of this carbohydrate (the residual breast milk that accumulates in the child's teeth when the child falls asleep to the breast), in conditions of reduced saliva and absence of oral hygiene, producing a maintained acid attack that would cause cavities.

Considering then that the etiology of caries is multifactorial, there are three essential factors to which time is added: host, microorganisms and diet. Environmental factors include the presence or absence of health services and oral health programmes, socioeconomic level, stress, ethnicity, culture, biodental engineering factors (biomechanical, biochemical and bioelectric) as well as sociodemographic, behavioural, physical-environmental and biological risk factors. However, many epidemiological studies correlate sugar consumption with caries prevalence and show a clear association between frequency of consumption, ingestion between meals and the development of dental caries. On the other hand, several characteristics of foods can influence their cariogenic potential, such as sucrose concentration, consistency, oral clarification, combination of foods, sequence and frequency of ingestion and pH of foods.

Taking into consideration the previous information, the main contribution of this work is the analysis of a set of features related to breastfeeding (infant who was breast fed, age whet stopped breastfeeding and first fed with other than breast milk), obtained from NHANES 2013–2014 survey, in order to develop a computer assisted diagnosis (CAD) multivariate model, with a random forest approach, that allows the automatic classification of subjects with presence of dental caries.

2   Materials and Methods

The methodology proposed in this work begins with the acquisition of data from the NHANES 2013–2014 database, then a data pre-processing stage is included, which consists of two main steps, the treatment of outliers and a balance of data. Continuing with the data classification, where a random forest (RF) approach is applied and finally a validation based on a statistical analysis was performed.

2.1   Data Description

NHANES is a program of studies that present a combination of interviews and physical examinations developed to assess the health and nutritional status of adults and children in the United States (US) [5]. Includes demographic, socioeconomic, dietary and health-related questions. In addition, an examination component presents medical, dental, and physiological measurements, as well as laboratory tests. In 2013–2014, 14,332 persons were selected for NHANES from 30 different survey locations. Of those selected, 10,175 completed the interview and 9,813 were examined.

The features extracted for the development of this work from the NHANES 2013–2014 survey, related to breast-feeding information and described in Table 1. These features are used as input data.

In addition, a feature related to the oral health status based on the presence or absence of dental caries is used as outcome feature, where '0' represents the absence of caries and '1' represents the presence.

From the total population, 1,082 subjects are selected since they were the ones who presented their complete record, without missing data, from which 894 belong to the absence of dental caries category and 188 belong to the presence of caries category.

Table 1. Features obtained from NHANES 2013–2014 contained by information related to breast-feeding.

Feature	Description
DRABF	Indicates whether the sample person was an infant who breast fed on either the two recall days
DRBD030	Indicates the age at which the sample person completely stopped breastfeeding or being fed breast milk
DBD055	Indicates the age at which the sample person was first fed anything other than breast milk or formula

2.2 Data Preprocessing

For the data preprocessing, two steps are performed, treatment of outliers and random data balance. The treatment of outliers consists on using the Cook's distance to identify the outliers. Cook's distance is commonly used to identify the influential outliers in a set of predictor variables in regression analysis. The calculation of this distance is a combination of each observation's leverage and residual values, becoming higher when the leverage and residuals are higher. When an observation, i^{th}, is identified, the Cook's distance is recalculated by removing it from the model, summarizing the change of all the values in the regression model when the ith observation is removed. This distance can be calculated with Eq. 1,

$$D_i = \frac{\sum_{j=1}^{n}(\hat{y}_j - \hat{y}_{j(i)})^2}{pMSE} \tag{1}$$

where $\hat{y}_j$ is the jth fitted response value, $\hat{y}_{ji}$ is the j_{th} fitted response value where the fit does not include the observation i, MSE is the mean squared error and p is the number of coefficients of the regression model.

The observations can be categorized as outliers if the value of the Cook's distance is more than three times the mean, any observations over $4/n$ (n being the number of observations) and a potential outlier's percentile of over 50 calculated through the F-distribution [13].

Once the outliers have been identified, those values are replaced by the extreme values of the quantiles 0.05 and 0.95, depending on the location of the outlier.

Taking into account the large difference between the amount of data that has an outcome of '1' and those that have an outcome of '0', a random balance is made, in order to have the same amount of data for each outcome. Therefore, 188 data were randomly selected with outcome of '0' from the 894 total data.

2.3 Classification

For the classification of the data, a RF approach is implemented, in order to develop a general model that allows to automatically identify the oral health status of the subjects based on the information contained in the input features.

RF is a learning method developed by Breiman et al. [4] that constructs a set of decision trees and outputs classes of the individual trees. Once the model is constructed, the prediction of the class is decided by majority vote, where the predicted class for a new observation is the most picked class among individual classifier. To measure the performance of the model developed by RF, the out-of-bag (OOB) error is measured, since, throughout the algorithm, each tree is built under a bootstrap training set, selected from the discovery cohort with replacement. Bootstrap aggregating (bagging) is used as a way to improve unstable classifiers. In bagging, a classifier is built under a different bootstrap sample of the training sets. The samples are randomly selected with replacement from the original training set, being of the same size. The bootstrap training set is contained by around two-thirds of the total data, from which a set of different training sets are created. A decision tree is fitted for each training set, obtaining together a random forest. The remaining one-third of the data, known as OOB samples, is used to estimate a generalization error (called an OOB error).

One of the problems that classifiers can present is not achieving adequate generalization through learning, properly classifying training data but not new observations, known as overfitting. However, by generating multiple training sets, fitting multiple trees and building a forest out of these tree classifiers, the risk of overfitting is decreased.

Two main scores are used in RF. The average decrease in the accuracy reflects an important measure to assess the prediction strength of each predictor. The OOB samples are used to calculate the error rate of the trees that are grown. Then, the values of a given predictor are randomly permuted, calculating the error rate again. A decrease in the accuracy caused by this permutation is averaged over all trees. The decrease importance in the Gini score provides the value of the improvement in the split-criterion at each split in each tree [20], which sums the total impurity measure decreased cause by partitioning upon a predictor among an entire tree, computing the average of this measure across all trees in a forest.

In the decrease importance of the permutation, if a predictor has a significant effect on the response, the algorithm could be losing prediction accuracy if the values of that predictor are randomized in the data set. Then, a strategy to alter the predictors values is by permutations. This procedure computes the prediction accuracy on the test set through the original test set. The values are then permuted for one predictor, j, across all observations, running this permuted data among the forest and computing the new accuracy. If the input, j, is important, the algorithm would be losing prediction accuracy by permuting the values of j in the test set. This process is repeated for all predictors and subsequently averaged across all trees, comparing this result with the averaged prediction accuracy. The variable is considered more important if the decrease in the accuracy is larger [2].

Therefore, some of the advantages of RF are that the OOB error provides an unbiased estimate of the classification error, while the bagging method decreases the chance of overfitting. In addition, RF can process non-parametric data, is robust to noise and accounts for weak classifiers [15].

For this work, the "randomForest" package for R is implemented, where the model is trained as follows, data is randomly split into training (2/3) and test (1/3) set. The model is trained on the training set, with 2,000 trees and one variable to try at each split. The OOB error is measured on the test set.

2.4 Validation

For the validation of the classification model obtained, the ROC curve and the AUC value are measured. The ROC curve is a common measure used to evaluate the classifiers performance. This curve is based on two measures, specificity and

sensitivity. Specificity represents the negative part or the false-negative proportion and it can be calculated with Eq. 2, where the samples without a condition
correctly classified are measured. TN are the true negatives and FP are the
false positives.

$$specificity = \frac{TN}{FP + TN} \tag{2}$$

Sensitivity represents the positive part or the true-positive proportion and
it can be calculated with Eq. 3, where the samples with a condition correctly
classified are measured. TP are the true positives and FN are the false negatives
[9].

$$sensitivity = \frac{TP}{FN + TP} \tag{3}$$

The specificity is represented on the x-axis of the ROC curve, while the
specificity is represented on the y-axis.

The AUC is measured trough the sensitivity and specificity and it has a range
from zero to one, with 0.5 as a 50-50 guess and one as an accuracy of 100 %.
An accurate predictor has a large AUC (closer to one and above 0.5), meaning
that the predictor performs well in both measures, specificity and sentivity. To
calculate the AUC, Eq. 4 is used, where $f(x)$ represents the function of the curve,
a represents the value where the curve begins and b represents the value where
the curve ends, on the x-axis [3].

$$AUC = \int_a^b f(x)dx \tag{4}$$

3   Results and Discussion

This section presents the results obtained and a their brief description.

From the preprocessing stage, Fig. 1 shows a graph of the samples vs their
correspondent Cook's distance. The main purpose of this graph is to identify the
outliers contained in the data set, from which is possible to observe that the data
with the positions 36, 505, 637, 965 and 1034, present higher Cook's distances
standing out from the other data, being considered as outliers. Therefore, these
outliers are imputed by replacing them with the values found at the extremes of
the quantiles 0.05 and 0.95, Therefore, these outliers are imputed by replacing
them with the values found at the ends of the quantiles 0.05 and 0.95, according
to where they are located.

The main objective of treating outliers is to avoid problems of data bias,
since, including a value that is particularly different from most data can cause
the results to be affected by providing values that do not correspond to the
average of them.

In Fig. 2 is presented a graph containing the boxplots corresponding to the
input features, where the small circumferences protruding from the limits of the

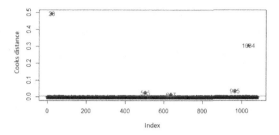

Fig. 1. Identification of outliers based on the Cook's distance. X-axis represents the samples while y-axis represents the Cook's distance.

box represent values that exceed the extreme quantiles; however, they are not imputed because they are not identified as outliers by Cook's distance. This is due to the fact that the outliers identified had much higher or lower values, which could affect the results of calculating with them and, the values that stand out from the quantiles in this graph are not significantly higher or lower compared to the outliers that were previously presented.

It is important to take into account that the treatment of outliers is strategic because, in a real phenomenon there will always be outliers present, so eliminating them could also be biasing the results to an application when only the values respect the limits of their distribution. Therefore, keeping some values that can be considered outliers but do not represent a risk of biasing the results, are helpful to represent the behavior of a natural phenomenon.

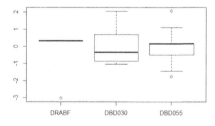

Fig. 2. Boxplot of the data contained in each feature after the treatment of outliers.

After the treatment of outliers, the random data balance is applied, where from the 1,082 total data, 188 corresponding to subjects with presence of dental caries (outcome = 1) and 894 corresponding to subjects with absence (outcome = 0), 188 subjects with absence of dental caries are randomly selected, obtaining a new data set contained by 376 subjects.

From the total data, a training set and a test set are randomly selected for the classification stage, where the RF technique is implemented. The training set is contained by 250 data and it is used by the algorithm to learn, while the test set is contained by 126 data, being used to auto-validate the training.

A confusion matrix of the results obtained from the training of RF, where the x-axis represents the outcome obtained, the y-axis represents the actual outcome. There are obtained 38 true negatives, 122 true positives, 5 false negatives, and 85 false positives, calculating a classification error of 0.691 for the samples with absence of dental caries and 0.039 for the samples with presence of caries. An OOB error value of 36 % is obtained. Therefore, it is evident that the results are being affected by the classification of the healthy subjects or those who do not present dental caries, being confused with subjects that do present the condition.

Then, in the validation stage, a statistical analysis, measuring the ROC curve of the model obtained through the subjection of the data to RF, and its correspondent AUC value, is performed.

In Fig. 3 is presented The ROC curve of the model developed by RF, the which obtained an AUC of 0.669. The specificity of the model corresponds to 0.354 and the sensitivity corresponds to 0.984, where it is shown again that the classification of subjects with caries absence are those that are generating an increase in error, since the value of specificity is significantly low, while the sensitivity value presents an almost perfect classification.

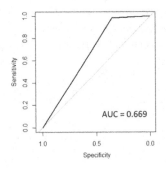

Fig. 3. ROC curve obtained from the classification of the data based on RF.

Finally, the series of ROC curves obtained from the univariate models developed through the relationship between each input feature and the outcome feature. The ROC curve represents the model of the feature DRABF, obtaining an AUC of 0.598; the curve represents the model of the feature DBD030, obtaining an AUC of 0.666 and the curve represents the model of the feature DBD055, obtaining and AUC of 0.630. As it is shown, the feature that the provides the least contribution in the classification of subjects is DRABF, which is related to the breast-feed of the subject of the recall days. The other two features, DBD030 and DBD055, related to the age at which the subject stopped breastfeeding and the age at which the subject was first fed by anything but breastfeeding, respectively, present a better performance in the classification of subjects, being DBD030 the one that represents the contribution.

Based on this, it is possible to notice that the classification behavior improves when the feature information includes data of the age of the subjects. This may occur because the age at which a person stops breastfeeding influences the likelihood of a person developing tooth decay, since breast milk provides, in addition to calcium and other minerals, different means of defense for the body that allow counteracting the attack of the bacteria on the denture, which makes it less vulnerable to the development of this condition. In this way, breastfeeding long enough, at the right age, allows to strengthen the immune system, helping in the oral health of people, avoiding acquiring dental caries.

4   Conclusions

Based on the results obtained, it can be observed that the features used for the development of a multivariate model allow the identification of subjects with the presence of dental caries with statistically significant precision. In this classification, the information of the features related to the age of the subjects in which they stopped their breastfeeding represents an important contribution, since, based on the ROC curves, they are those that present a better classification result, which is also statistically significant.

On the other hand, it is important to note that the classification achieves a significantly better result for subjects with presence of caries than for healthy subjects, based on the specificity value obtained, so that may be occurring due to a confusion when classifying these subjects based on their information. It is necessary to highlight that one of the limitations of this work is the limited amount of data that is available, which could be affecting the result of the classification of healthy subjects. To counteract this problem, it may be important to increase the number of samples in order to better describe healthy subjects and thus achieve a generalized modeling that allows them to be automatically classified with better accuracy.

Finally, it can be concluded that in this work it is obtained through the RF algorithm, a generalized multivariate model based on breastfeeding information, mainly in the age at which it was stopped, allowing the classification of subjects with presence of dental caries from healthy subjects. Nevertheless, it is important to mention that this model represents a preliminary work and is not intended to be used in clinical practice as a computer-assisted diagnostic tool for the support of specialists in the diagnosis of dental caries.

References

1. Bahuguna, R., Younis Khan, S., Jain, A.: Influence of feeding practices on dental caries. a case-control study. Eur. J. Paediatr. Dent. **14**(1), 55–58 (2013)
2. Beaulac, C., Rosenthal, J.S.: Predicting university students' academic success and major using random forests. Res. High. Educ. **60**(7), 1–17 (2019)
3. Bowers, A.J., Zhou, X.: Receiver operating characteristic (ROC) area under the curve (AUC): a diagnostic measure for evaluating the accuracy of predictors of education outcomes. J. Educ. Students Placed Risk (JESPAR) **24**(1), 20–46 (2019)
4. Breiman, L.: Random forests. Mach. Learn. **45**(1), 5–32 (2001)

5. CDC, NCHS: National health and nutrition examination survey data. https://wwwn.cdc.gov/nchs/nhanes/ContinuousNhanes/Default.aspx?BeginYear=2013. Accessed 09 Sept 2019

6. EzEldeen, M., Van Gorp, G., Van Dessel, J., Vandermeulen, D., Jacobs, R.: 3-dimensional analysis of regenerative endodontic treatment outcome. J. Endodontics **41**(3), 317–324 (2015)

7. Gionet, L., Roshanafshar, S.: Health at a glance. Select Health Indicators of First Nations People Living Off Reserve, Métis and Inuit (2013)

8. Juárez-López, M.L.A., Hernández-Guerrero, J.C., Jiménez-Farfán, D., Ledesma-Montes, C.: Prevalencia de fluorosis dental y caries en escolares de la ciudad de méxico. Gaceta Médica de México **139**(3), 221–226 (2003)

9. Kannan, R., Vasanthi, V.: Machine learning algorithms with ROC curve for predicting and diagnosing the heart disease. Soft Computing and Medical Bioinformatics. SAST, pp. 63–72. Springer, Singapore (2019). https://doi.org/10.1007/978-981-13-0059-2_8

10. Lauritano, D., et al.: Prevalence of oral lesions and correlation with intestinal symptoms of inflammatory bowel disease: a systematic review. Diagnostics **9**(3), 77 (2019)

11. Madan, N., Rathnam, A., Bajaj, N.: Palmistry: a tool for dental caries prediction!. Indian J. Dental Res. **22**(2), 213 (2011)

12. North, S., Davidson, L.E., Blinkhorn, A.S., Mackie, I.C.: The effects of a long wait for children's dental general anaesthesia. Int. J. Paediatric Dentistry **17**(2), 105–109 (2007)

13. Prabakaran, K.M., Saravanan, P., Manonmani, S., Anandhi, V.: Comparative study on multivariate outlier detection methods in sesame (sesamum indicum l.). Electronic J. Plant Breeding **10**(2), 809–815 (2019)

14. Ramírez, M.A.M., Hernández, A.G., Muñoz, E.E.H., Hernández, H.I., Flores, R.R.: Lactancia materna y caries de la infancia temprana. Rev Odontoped Latino Am ALOP **6**, 1–15 (2016)

15. Reece, N., Wingard, G., Mandakh, B., Reading, R.P.: Using random forest to classify vegetation communities in the southern area of ikh nart nature reserve in Mongolia. Mongolian J. Biol. Sci. **17**(1), 31–39 (2019)

16. Setiawati, F., Sutadi, H., Rahardjo, A.: Relationship between breastfeeding status and early childhood caries prevalence in 6–24 months old children in Jakarta. J. Int. Dental Med. Res. **10**(2), 308 (2017)

17. Sharna, N., Ramakrishnan, M., Samuel, V., Ravikumar, D., Cheenglembi, K., Anil, S.: Association between early childhood caries and quality of life: early childhood oral health impact scale and pufa index. Dentistry J. **7**(4), 95 (2019)

18. Sheiham, A., James, W.: Diet and dental caries: the pivotal role of free sugars reemphasized. J. Dental Res. **94**(10), 1341–1347 (2015)

19. Sugito, F.S., Djoharnas, H., Darwita, R.R.: Breastfeeding and early childhood caries (ECC) severity of children under three years old in DKI Jakarta. Makara J. Health Res. 86–91 (2010)

20. Toth, R., et al.: Random forest-based modelling to detect biomarkers for prostate cancer progression. bioRxiv p. 602334 (2019)

Lung-Nodule Segmentation
Using a Convolutional Neural Network
with the U-Net Architecture

Vicente Hernández-Solis, Arturo Téllez-Velázquez, Antonio Orantes-Molina,
and Raúl Cruz-Barbosa[✉]

Applied Artificial Intelligence Laboratory, Computer Science Institute,
Universidad Tecnológica de la Mixteca, 69000 Huajuapan de León, Oaxaca, Mexico
hesv880702ps@ndikandi.utm.mx, {atellezv,tonito,rcruz}@mixteco.utm.mx

Abstract. Lung cancer is one of the types of cancer that claims the most lives globally. For screening purposes, computed tomography scans are the most reliable source for nodule detection, as it reveals the structure of the chest, through a three dimensional representation, in which lung lesions can be fully observed. For early cancer detection, it is necessary to use computed radiography and tomography of the thorax, as well as searches for potentially malignant nodules by specialists. In this paper, lung nodule segmentation was performed using the LIDC IDRI public database, which includes images of computed tomographies, by means of a modified U-Net convolutional neural network. The experimental results have shown that our proposal achieves a Dice similarity coefficient of 88.1% and accuracy of 99.78%, which improves nodule segmentation performance in comparison with other architectures used in the literature.

Keywords: Lung cancer · Image segmentation · Convolutional neural network · U-Net · Computed tomography

1 Introduction

When it comes to lung cancer, an early clinical diagnosis allow specialists to rule out the presence of malignant nodules and can lead to the correct choice of an appropriate treatment to combat this cancer [7].

Among all the existing forms of cancer, lung cancer is the type that causes the most deaths annually [26]. To detect it, an experienced radiologist searches for lung nodules visually by using advanced medical tests such as computed radiography and tomography. This procedure is often a highly complex task, however, even for specialists. The test consists of making use of a series of digital images that are taken transversely in the form of equidistant cross sections (usually 3 mm apart from one another), from which it is possible to get a three-dimensional representation of the patient's lungs [28].

© Springer Nature Switzerland AG 2021
E. Roman-Rangel et al. (Eds.): MCPR 2021, LNCS 12725, pp. 335–344, 2021.
https://doi.org/10.1007/978-3-030-77004-4_32

With the development of deep learning, many convolutional-neural-network methods (CNN) have yielded surprising results in carrying out computed radiography and tomography image-segmentation tasks [17]. For example, some research papers have dealt with image segmentation using fuzzy logic, active contour algorithms, and clustering; but the effectiveness of these techniques has been largely outdone by machine learning and CNN [15,18,21].

This research paper tackles the subject of lung-nodule segmentation, making use of the LIDC-IDRI public database of tomographies and the U-Net CNN model in order to segment potentially malignant nodules in patients at risk of suffering lung cancer.

This article is organized as follows. Section 2 deals with papers that have tackled the subject of lung-nodule segmentation. Section 3 introduces our implementation of CNN, after which our experiment design will be laid out. Section 4, follows, in which the experiment's results are given; and finally, in Sect. 5, our conclusions are offered, and future work is laid out.

2   Related Work

The analysis of computed tomographies for the detection of nodules begins with the segmentation process. This stage is of vital importance, because an incorrect segmentation would result in false clinical diagnoses, which would directly affect patients. Some papers [1] estimate that test data may miss from 5% to 17% of lung nodules due to a segmentation algorithm's shortcomings. Next, we present some segmentation methods from the literature, which are used to segment pulmonary nodules.

One of the most common ways to perform image segmentation is through the region-based approach, such as the one presented in [20], which uses the fast-marching method to separate the image into regions with similar features. In order to segment lung nodules, multiple seed points are required to produce a set of regions on input image. Finally, they are merged by combining regions that grow applying k-means algorithm.

In one case in particular, Nithila and Kumar [18] developed a nodule segmentation technique based on a Fuzzy C-mean algorithm and an active contour model. The reconstruction of the lung parenchyma was performed by a Gaussian filter and the segmentation was completed with a cluster algorithm.

Another paper has proposed a hybrid system which makes use of the following techniques [14]: morphological operation, dot-enhancement filter based on the Hessian matrix, fuzzy-connectedness segmentation, local-density maximum algorithm, geodesic-distance map, and regression tree classification. First, all the potential nodules are generated to classify them among three types: peripheral, those attached to the chest wall, or those on the mediastinum. Finally, by means of a tree structure, the nodules are detected and classified according to their location, size, and shape.

By contrast, [12] employs discriminative random fields (DRF) to segment 3D volumes of lung nodules in computed tomographies using only one seed point per nodule. First, various features are calculated, such as the estimated radius and approximate segmentation, making use of morphological filtering. Next, a supervised training of the DRF model is conducted to achieve a more accurate general segmentation.

Other less conventional methods as [23], have used the vanilla optical flow method to process the computed tomography slices. To do this, they created an image frame sequence with timeline-ordered CT slices and thereby achieve lung nodule segmentation by computing the detected changes between frames.

In the case of CNN-based segmentation, an interesting proposal has been published in [4], which makes use of a fully CNN (FCN). Nodule detection is then carried out through binary thresholding within the lung area; next, the approximate nodule segmentation is done through the level set method. Finally, nodule segmentation is obtained based on the coordinate system transformation.

Another CNN proposal [2] uses a dual-branch residual network (DB-ResNet), which simultaneously captures intensity features from multiple views and scales of different nodules in CT images and consequently performs image segmentation. Additionally, they propose a central intensity pooling layer (CIP), to extract the intensity features of the central voxel of the block, and subsequently with CNN obtain the convolutional features of the central voxel. Regarding lung-nodule detection, other papers as [11] have tackled the problem of voxel-to-voxel segmentation by means of a multi-view CNN, by which it is possible to determine if a voxel corresponds to a nodule.

3   Convolutional Neural Networks

The CNNs arose from the study of the human eye's visual cortex, and have been used for image recognition since 1980. CNNs are not limited to computer-vision tasks; rather, they are also used in other endeavors, such as voice recognition and natural language processing [8].

A CNN is a supervised learning model that has the ability to identify objects, since it can extract features from their inputs, especially from images. To do this, a CNN is comprised of several specialized hidden layers that have certain hierarchy. This hierarchy is represented by different levels of abstraction, by which the composition of simple or lower-level features allow for the learning about complex or higher-level features. This means that the first layers can detect geometric primitives, and as we go deeper through the layers, they become more and more specialized, so that deeper layers are able to recognize more complex shapes [3].

Figure 1 illustrates the main operations involved in a CNN's processing. For example, Fig. 1a shows the convolution layer, while Fig. 1c depicts the pooling operation.

3.1   U-Net Architecture

The U-Net architecture was initially designed to segment neural structures into sets of images obtained by electronic microscope. However, this architecture can also be used to classify and segment biomedical images [19].

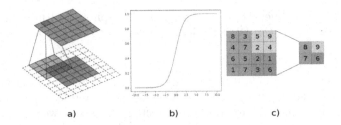

Fig. 1. Basic CNN operations: a) Convolution operation: cross product between a kernel and the image [6]. b) Activation function: it provides non-linearity to the network. c) Pooling operation: it reduces image size while preserving its main features [22]

The U-Net architecture (see Fig. 2), consists of two stages: contraction and expansion. The first stage is a standard CNN, which consists of the repeated application of convolutions with 3×3 filters without padding, which reduces the image's dimensions. Following this, a rectified linear unit layer (ReLU) and a 2×2 max-pooling layer with a stride of 2 is used to reduce the image's dimensions by half, while with each reduction the filter number is doubled, which is to say, one obtains double the feature maps. This stage is mainly used for automated feature extraction from the input images, which allows to improve the segmentation task.

In each step of the expansion stage, a transposed convolution of the feature map and a concatenation with the corresponding feature map cropped from its contraction counterpart are performed. Two convolutions with 3×3 filters and a ReLU layer are then added. Cropping the feature map is necessary, given that in each convolution the image's dimensions are reduced. A convolution with a $1 \times 1 \times n$ filter is used on the last layer to map each 64-component feature vector to the desired total number of classes n [19]. This stage combines both the features obtained from the first stage and the output of the transposed convolution layer to obtain accurate segmentations, although there is a loss of information due to cropping operation which adjusts the dimensions of the output.

The U-Net network is also called a fully convolutional network, since it only uses convolutional layers to perform image segmentation [13]. In other words, it has no fully connected layers, which reduces the number of weights to be estimated [9]. Additionally, this architecture does not require a large number of labeled images for training and it can obtain very accurate segmentations. These characteristics are particularly useful when working with biomedical images since a usual setting is that there are few labeled examples [19].

3.2   U-Net for Nodule Segmentation

In this work, a modified U-Net architecture was proposed to train the network with the LIDC-IDRI public database, as it is shown in Fig. 3. Unlike the original architecture, the input and output images preserve the same size, that is, a resolution of 128×128 pixels is used. This is because both the convolution and the transposed-convolution are carried out with zero padding, which avoids

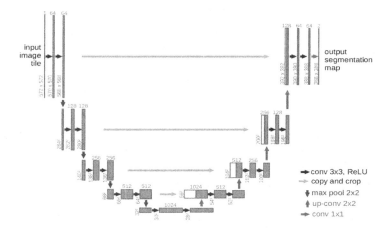

Fig. 2. U-Net deep neural network architecture [19]

that image dimensions have to be reduced in each convolution operation. As a consequence, the concatenation in the second stage (transposed-convolution) is performed without cropping. The number of initial filters is 32 and each time it is doubled (64, 128, and so on), while the image dimensions are reduced by half due to max-pooling layer. In the network's final layer, the segmentation is performed for two classes; in other words, it decides if a pixel belongs to a nodule or not. With our modified U-Net network, there is no information loss in the second stage. Also, the concatenation of the first-stage features and the transposed convolution layer output is direct, thus covering the entire input image.

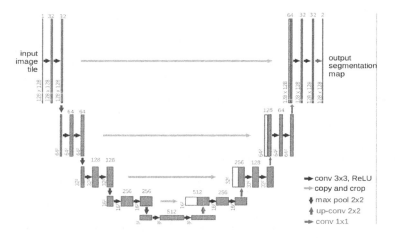

Fig. 3. Modified U-Net deep neural network architecture

Having both the segmentation performed by specialists and that performed by the CNN, the used evaluation criterion is the Dice Similarity Coefficient (DSC), which is given by the following equation [10]:

$$DSC = \frac{2\,|X \cap Y|}{|X| + |Y|} \tag{1}$$

where X is the segmented area by specialists and Y is the segmented area by U-Net. In other words, the DSC is used to measure the overlap between the two regions, which in this case are the nodule-segmentation results. When the DSC equals 1, it is because the segmented regions overlap completely, whereas if the DSC equals 0, there is no overlap between the segmented regions.

4   Results and Discussion

In this section, both the image set and the hardware and software used during implementation are described. Following is an analysis of our results, as well as a comparison with existing results in the literature.

The used image set was obtained from the public database LIDC-IDRI [5]. This database consists of 244,617 images from 1308 studies carried out on 1010 patients. The nodules were identified by as many as four specialists. The selected nodule images were those that were indicated by the four specialists, while the nodules identified by three or fewer specialists were ruled out. In total, there were 900 identified nodules with a diameter of greater than 3 mm.

Additionally, there is information for each study on the patient and on the nodules' properties, such as difficulty of detection, internal structure, calcification, sphericity, margin, degree of lobulation, extension of spiculation, texture, and an evaluation of the probability of malignancy.

To carry out the CNN training, the set of available nodules was divided into training (68%), validation (12%), and test (20%) subsets. The first two subsets were used to obtain the network's best hyperparameters, which turn out to be a learning rate of 0.0005, an initial filter number equal to 32, a batch size of 32, and a filter size of 3. Subsequently, using these hyperparameters, the network is retrained with different sizes of the training subset, in order to measure and compare the performance of the network using the corresponding test subset.

The experiments were conducted on a computer with an Intel(R) Xeon(R) CPU E5-2630 processor, which has 32 processing threads and runs the Ubuntu operating system with 16 GB of RAM memory. In terms of software, the Python programming language was used, along with the TensorFlow library.

Having conducted the corresponding experiments, the results analysis and discussion follow. As we have mentioned, different test-set sizes were used with the goal of making comparisons with other methods. For example, a size of 493 nodules was considered in [25]; also a size of 393 nodules was used in [24]; as well a size of 128 nodules was proposed in [16]. For the purposes of comparing the results with those reported in [16], sizes of 246 and 196 nodules were considered, that is, half of the aforementioned sizes. Table 1 shows the results obtained for each proposed test-set size, where classification accuracy and DSC coefficient are used as measures of convolutional network performance. Here it can be observed that as the test set decreases the classification accuracy and the DSC coefficient increases. This is expected behavior since the convolutional network learns to discriminate better with more information as the training set increases.

Table 1. Comparison of the performance of the U-Net architecture with different test-set sizes

Test size [Nod]	Accuracy [%]	DSC [%]
493	99.72	84.27
393	99.75	85.62
246	99.76	87.46
196	99.78	88.10

Table 2 presents the performance results of our U-Net proposal compared with other methods [16, 18, 24, 25, 27], which also deal with this problem of segmentation using the same database. Observe that the main performance measure for the comparison was DSC, although the test size and the classification accuracy are also included as complementary information. Note that in row 7, column 4 of Table 2, our U-Net proposal reached an average DSC of 88.10% in the test set, which indicates a high degree of similarity between the segmentations obtained by our proposal and those proposed by specialists.

Table 2. Comparison between our proposal (last line) and some other proposal on the state of the art, using the LIDC-IDRI database. The symbol '–' indicates that there is no available information about the accuracy measure or test size in the corresponding articles

Method	Test size [Nod]	Accuracy [%]	DSC [%]
PN-SAMP [27]	–	97.58	74.05
MV-CNN [24]	393	–	77.67
CF-CNN [25]	493	–	82.15
DLGC [16]	128	–	83.00
Fuzzy C-mean [18]	–	98.95	84.00
U-Net	196	99.78	88.10

Comparing the results in Tables 1 and 2, it is observed that the U-Net results are better, in terms of DSC, for all the test set sizes (493, 393, 128) used. That is, the DSC obtained with the U-Net is higher than the publications listed in Table 2, including the article using a small test set (128) compared to the smallest

U-Net set (196). To shed further light on the virtues of our proposal, which allow to improve the original U-Net architecture and related literature results (Table 2), some of the best visual results of the nodule segmentation on the test set are shown below in Fig. 4. For greater clarity, the images are shown in pairs (vertical orientation); the first image is the segmentation performed by the specialists (in green), and the second is the segmentation obtained by the CNN (in red). These segmentation results individually reach over 97% DSC due to the nodules' smooth shape, which is most often circular or oval. It is worth highlighting that the nodule's size also exercises a strong influence, given that the majority of these nodules have a diameter of greater than 4 mm, which aids in their identification.

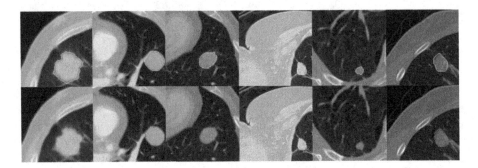

Fig. 4. Regularly shaped nodules segmented by experts in green (above) and nodules segmented by our U-Net proposal in red (below) (Color figure online)

Due to the great variety in lung nodules' shape and size, not all of them can be segmented correctly. For example, Fig. 5 shows some nodules, individually obtaining a DSC of less than 70%, that turned out to be difficult to segment under our proposal, since they did not have a smooth or regular shape. At times, nodules are spiculated or have a diameter close to 3 mm. These factors make their identification highly difficult.

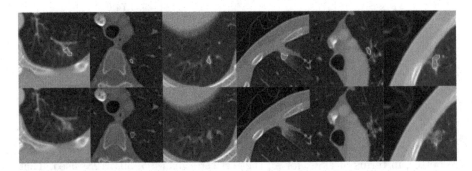

Fig. 5. Irregularly shaped (spiculated) nodules segmented by experts in green (above) and nodules segmented by our U-Net proposal in red (below) (Color figure online)

5   Conclusions

The impact of a modified U-Net deep architecture on the performance of lung-nodule segmentation was presented in this work. The experimental results have shown that the proposed U-Net modification obtains the highest DSC performance (88.10%) for the analyzed dataset, which outperforms other proposals on the state of the art. In spite of the fact that it has problems with performing nodule segmentation on irregular or spiculated shapes, the results are highly competitive.

As future work, several hybrid approaches could be explored with the aim to improve the DSC coefficient and consequently making efficiently progress on lung-nodule detection. For example, a hybrid approach composed of a U-Net-CNN and an adaptive morphological filter could be proposed. Additionally, this proposal should be scaled to distributed computing procedures, thus improving training times and, as a consequence, timely decision-making as well.

References

1. Armato, S.G., Sensakovic, W.F.: Automated lung segmentation for thoracic CT. Acad. Radiol. **11**(9), 1011–1021 (2004)
2. Cao, H., et al.: Dual-branch residual network for lung nodule segmentation. Appl. Soft Comput. **86** (2020)
3. Chollet, F.: Deep learning with Python, 1st. edn. Manning Publications Co. (2018)
4. Chunran, Y., Yuanvuan, W., Yi, G.: Automatic detection and segmentation of lung nodules on CT images. In: 11th International Congress on Image and Signal Processing. BioMedical Engineering and Informatics, pp. 1–6. Beijing, China (2018)
5. CIA: Lung image database consortium and image database resource initiative. https://wiki.cancerimagingarchive.net/display/Public/LIDC-IDRI. Accessed Nov 2019
6. Dumoulin, V., Visin, F.: A guide to convolution arithmetic for deep learning. ArXiv abs/1603.07285 (2016)
7. Fourcade, A., Khonsari, R.H.: Deep learning in medical image analysis: a third eye for doctors. J. Stomatol. Oral Maxillofacial Surg. **120**, 279–288 (2019)
8. Géron, A.: Hands-On Machine Learning with Scikit-Learn & Tensorflow, 1st edn. O'Reilly Media Inc. (2017)
9. Gulli, A., Kapoor, A., Pal, S.: Deep Learning with TensorFlow 2 and Keras, 2nd edn. Packt Publishing (2019)
10. Havaei, M., et al.: Brain tumor segmentation with deep neural networks. Med. Image Anal. **35**, 18–31 (2017)
11. Litjens, G., et al.: A survey on deep learning in medical image analysis. Med. Image Anal. **42**, 60–88 (2017)
12. Liu, B., Raj, A.: Discriminative random field segmentation of lung nodules in CT studies. Comput. Math. Methods Med. **2013**, 1–9 (2013)
13. Long, J., Shelhamer, E., Darrell, T.: Fully convolutional networks for semantic segmentation. arXiv preprint arXiv:1411.4038v2 (2015)
14. Lu, L., Tan, Y., Schwartz, L.H., Zhao, B.: Hybrid detection of lung nodules on CT scan images. Med. Phys. **42**(9), 5042–5054 (2015)

15. Manikandan, T., Bharathi, N.: Lung cancer diagnosis from CT images using fuzzy inference system. In: Das, V.V., Thankachan, N. (eds.) CIIT 2011. CCIS, vol. 250, pp. 642–647. Springer, Heidelberg (2011). https://doi.org/10.1007/978-3-642-25734-6_110

16. Mukherjee, S., Huang, X., Bhagalia, R.R.: Lung nodule segmentation using deep learned prior based graph cut. In: 14th IEEE International Symposium on Biomedical Imaging, pp. 1205–1208. Melbourne, VIC, Australia (2017)

17. Ni, J., Wu, J., Tong, J., Chen, Z., Zhao, J.: GC-Net: global context network for medical image segmentation. Comput. Methods Programs Biomed. **190**, 1–10 (2020)

18. Nithila, E.E., Kumar, S.S.: Segmentation of lung nodule in CT data using active contour model and Fuzzy C-mean clustering. Alex. Eng. J. **55**(3), 2583–2588 (2016)

19. Ronneberger, O., Fischer, P., Brox, T.: U-Net: convolutional networks for biomedical image segmentation. In: 18th Medical Image Computing and Computer-Assisted Intervention, pp. 234–241. Munich, Germany (2015)

20. Savic, M., Ma, Y., Ramponi, G., Du, W., Peng, Y.: Lung nodule segmentation with a region-based fast marching method. Sensors **21** (2021)

21. Sivakumar, S., Chandrasekar, C.: Lung nodule segmentation through unsupervised clustering models. ICMOC **38**(2012), 3064–3073 (2012)

22. Srinivas, M.: Max pooling in convolutional neural network and its features. https://analyticsindiamag.com/max-pooling-in-convolutional-neural-network-and-its-features/. Accessed Oct 2020

23. Suji, R.J., Bhadouria, S.S., Dhar, J., Godfrey, W.W.: Optical flow methods for lung nodule segmentation on LIDC-IDRI images. J. Digit. Imaging **33**, 1306–1324 (2020)

24. Wang, S., et al.: A multi-view deep convolutional neural networks for lung nodule segmentation. In: 39th Annual International Conference of the IEEE Engineering in Medicine and Biology Society, pp. 1752–1755. Jeju, Korea (South) (2017)

25. Wang, S., et al.: Central focused convolutional neural networks: developing a data-driven model for lung nodule segmentation. Med. Image Anal. **40**, 172–183 (2017)

26. WHO: Latest global cancer data. https://www.who.int/cancer/PRGlobocanFinal.pdf. Accessed Oct 2019

27. Wu, B., Zhou, Z., Wang, J., Wang, Y.: Joint learning for pulmonary nodule segmentation, attributes and malignancy prediction. In: 15th IEEE International Symposium on Biomedical Imaging, pp. 1109–1113. Washington, D.C., USA (2018)

28. Wu, J., Qian, T.: A survey of pulmonary nodule detection, segmentation and classification in computed tomography with deep learning techniques. J. Med. Artif. Intell. **2**(8), 1–12 (2019)

Multi-target Attachment for Surgical Instrument Tracking

Eberto Benjumea$^{(\boxtimes)}$, Juan S. Sierra , Jhacson Meza ,
and Andres G. Marrugo

Facultad de ingeniería, Universidad Tecnológica de Bolívar, Cartagena, Colombia
ebenjumea@utb.edu.co

Abstract. The pose estimation of a surgical instrument is a common problem in the new needs of medical science. Many instrument tracking methods use markers with a known geometry that allows for solving the instrument pose as detected by a camera. However, marker occlusion happens, and it hinders correct pose estimation. In this work, we propose an adaptable multi-target attachment with ArUco markers to solve occlusion problems on tracking a medical instrument like an ultrasound probe or a scalpel. Our multi-target system allows for precise and redundant real-time pose estimation implemented in OpenCV. Encouraging results show that the multi-target device may prove useful in the clinical setting.

Keywords: Multi-target ArUco marker · Pose estimation · Optical instrument tracking

1 Introduction

Camera pose estimation and object tracking are common problems in computer vision. These tasks require a high accuracy localization of the marker's features for applications such as virtual or augmented reality [2,9], robot navigation [5, 19], and even medical applications [13]. Marker-based methods have reached high popularity in recent years due to their easy usage, reliability, robustness, and high-speed detection. However, there is no general-purpose method that works efficiently for most applications.

Nowadays, it is challenging to choose from the many available solutions in terms of performance, speed, and overall accuracy [14]. Several authors have proposed different fiducial markers [7,9,10,16]. These markers have been used in augmented reality applications [1], to design wireless surgical knife attachment for medical usage [11,20], and automatic drone navigation system [17]. Nevertheless, there is still room for improvement in many of these applications.

For tracking surgical instruments, we need a clear line of sight between the marker and the camera. Due to instrument movement, marker occlusion occurs. This problem limits the physicians' freedom of movement in navigation systems

© Springer Nature Switzerland AG 2021
E. Roman-Rangel et al. (Eds.): MCPR 2021, LNCS 12725, pp. 345–354, 2021.
https://doi.org/10.1007/978-3-030-77004-4_33

where a needle, surgical knife, or ultrasound probe must be tracked, e.g., in 3D freehand ultrasound. Occlusion is a typical limitation when optical devices are adopted, but they are often more accurate compared to electromagnetic systems [4,12,18]. This problem has been assessed in several works [7,16] with partial success.

This work proposes a multi-target system for object tracking in clinical procedures under occlusion conditions. Its main novelties are the operation under occlusion and low cost, thanks to 3D printing and the use of a single camera, contrary to other proposed systems that use stereo vision [3]. Finally, this proposal is easily adaptable to any flat-faced structure as long as it contains nine markers: one source marker, four markers on the upper faces, and four markers on the lower faces. This feature allows improving the system's performance according to the type of surgical procedure: 3D reconstruction by ultrasound imaging, tool tracking, medical teaching tools, among others.

This paper is structured as follows. In Sect. 2, we explain the multi-target physical attachment with ArUco markers. Section 3 details how the pose is estimated with the multi-target system. Next, in Sect. 4, we show the proposed method's results and analysis. Finally, in Sect. 5, we draw several conclusions.

2   Multi-target Device

2.1   Physical Device

As a means to obtain a reliable detection regardless of the instrument pose or even with partial occlusions, we developed the multi-target physical attachment shown in Fig. 1. The multi-target attachment is a 3D printed solid piece designed in the computer-aided design software SolidEdge. It has a flat horizontal top face and eight diagonal faces oriented in multiples of 45 degrees. There is a unique marker on each face, as shown in Fig. 1. The bottom face is parallel to the top face and has a hole for attachment to a surgical or medical instrument.

Fig. 1. Multi-target attachment.

The existence of the nine markers increases the tracking system's robustness in case of occlusion of one or more markers. This advantage comes from the fact that each marker allows establishing the medical instrument's pose to a frame of reference (origin). We established the frame of reference on the top of the model. These coordinate transformations between markers will be explained in detail in Sect. 3.

2.2 ArUco Markers

ArUco is an open-source library for detecting squared fiducial markers in images [7,15]. Its use allows estimating the camera pose with respect to the markers for a calibrated camera. This library is written in C++ and requires OpenCV for its implementation [7,15]. There are some other libraries, like ArUco, used for the same function. Some of these libraries and their problems are mentioned below [6,7,15]: ARToolKit is prone to error and not very robust to illumination changes. ARToolKit+ is a new proprietary version of ARToolKit with a more robust error detection than ARToolKit. Also, ARTag is another proposal to prove ARToolKit, but it is a discontinued project. BinARyID does not consider the possibility of error detection and correction, and AprilTags detects and corrects errors, but its method is not adequate for a large number of markers.

ArUco library adapts to heterogeneous illumination, is highly accurate and fast at detecting markers, and is robust enough to do error detection and correction of the binary codes. These characteristics turned ArUco into the most popular system for marker detection [7,15]. Despite that, ArUco has problems when the lighting is poor or when the image undergoes extreme motion blur [8]. Deep ChArUco is a deep convolutional neural network system trained to overcome these situations for ChArUco marker detection and pose estimation [8].

The pose estimation using the ArUco library needs a previously acquired image. It starts with an image resize in order to reduce processing time [15]. Later, image segmentation is performed with a global threshold method. A contour extraction is applied, and these contours are filtered by their shape (polygonal). With a set of resized versions of the original image, an image pyramid is created [15]. Immediately, the marker code is extracted from the image using the image pyramid, and the precise corner localization of the marker corners is estimated [15]. Finally, its pose is estimated with respect to the camera by iteratively minimizing the reprojection error of the corners [7].

The multi-target attachment has on its top faces the markers with codes: ID0, ID1, ID2, ID3, and ID4 (See Fig. 2(a)). On its bottom faces are located the ID5, ID6, ID7, and ID8 markers (See Fig. 2(b)). These last four are respectively below the ID1, ID2, ID3, and ID4 markers. This geometrical configuration allows a marker to always be visible in front of the camera in spite of the translations or rotations of the medical device. The length of the markers is 19 mm.

3 Stages of the Pose Estimation of Multi-target Attachment Using ArUco Markers

There are five stages for the pose estimation of the attachment, as Fig. 3 shows. The stages of image acquisition, marker detection, and individual marker pose

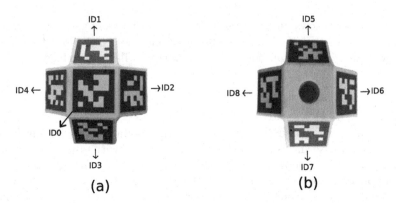

(a)   **(b)**

Fig. 2. Codes of the markers on the multi-target attachment. (a) Markers on the top faces, (b) Markers on the bottom diagonal faces

estimation are carried out using Python and the Open Source Computer Vision Library (OpenCV) libraries. Our novelties in the software implementation are the marker filtering and instrument pose estimation stages.

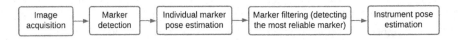

Fig. 3. Stages of the pose estimation of attachment using ArUco markers.

3.1 Image Acquisition, Marker Detection and Individual Marker Pose Estimation

First, we record a video of the surgical instrument. The proposed method was tested offline, and a real-time implementation is currently being developed. All the frames of the video are read. Each frame is processed for the detection of ArUco markers. The system can detect one or several markers in a frame. In this stage, we obtain the ID number and the corners of the markers in individual marker pose estimation. This data is taken for the individual pose estimation of the markers. For each detected marker, the pose is given in a rotation vector and a translation vector. These vectors are transformed in the extrinsic matrix of the marker.

3.2 Marker Filtering and Multi-target Pose Estimation

Prior camera calibration is required to obtain the intrinsic matrix of the camera. Since we established the frame of reference (origin) on the top of the model, it is necessary to calculate the relative position matrices between the origin marker and the other markers one by one (Fig. 4 shows some of these transformations). Therefore, we must estimate the pose of the origin marker and the pose of the other markers and formulate the following equation

$$
{}^{C}_{O}H = {}^{C}_{M}H \times {}^{M}_{O}H, \tag{1}
$$

where ${}^{C}_{M}H$ is the pose matrix of any target, ${}^{C}_{O}H$ is the pose matrix of the ID0 target, and ${}^{M}_{O}H$ is the relative position matrix of any target with respect to ID0 marker. From this equation, using matrix algebra, we obtain

$$
{}^{M}_{O}H = [{}^{C}_{M}H]^{-1} \times {}^{C}_{O}H, \tag{2}
$$

which allows us to calculate the relative position matrix of any marker.

Fig. 4. Matrices of relative positions.

Nevertheless, the estimation of relative position matrices based on a single image causes errors in the instrument's pose estimation. This problem is shown in the experiments and results section. Accordingly, it is necessary to estimate these matrices with many representative images of each pair of targets' possible poses. For this, we take the poses of each pair of markers, ID0 and IDX (IDX is the marker which we want to know its relative position matrix), in each image. These values are stored into two matrices which we stack the poses of ID0 and IDX on all processed images. Therefore, Eq. (2) turns into the following,

$$
\begin{bmatrix} {}^{C}_{O}H_1 \\ {}^{C}_{O}H_2 \\ {}^{C}_{O}H_3 \\ \cdot \\ \cdot \\ \cdot \\ {}^{C}_{O}H_n \end{bmatrix} = \begin{bmatrix} {}^{C}_{M}H_1 \\ {}^{C}_{M}H_2 \\ {}^{C}_{M}H_3 \\ \cdot \\ \cdot \\ \cdot \\ {}^{C}_{M}H_n \end{bmatrix} \times {}^{M}_{O}H, \tag{3}
$$

where n is the number of processed images, and the problem is solved by least-squares. The relative position matrices of the markers on the bottom faces are indirectly estimated through the top face's relative position matrices. The previously explained process is applied to these matrices, but instead of ID0 as a reference frame, we use the corresponding top face to each bottom marker. Equation (3) describes this estimation. Later, the matrix with respect to ID0 is calculated by Eq. (4).

$$\underset{0}{\text{Botton marker}} H = \underset{0}{\text{Top marker}} H \times \underset{Top\ marker}{\text{Botton marker}} H. \tag{4}$$

The camera center coordinates (CC) project in the coordinates system of the target ID0 through each detected marker's coordinates system. The resulting coordinates are averaged, and the marker with the closest coordinates is selected to estimate the surgical device's pose. We multiply this matrix with its corresponding relative position matrix to the origin marker (top marker with ID0), as shown in Eq. (1). The result is the pose of the surgical instrument. Finally, to visualize the result on the image, we use the following equation for the complete perspective projection, given by

$$\begin{bmatrix} x_1 \\ x_2 \\ x_3 \end{bmatrix} = K \times_O^C H \times^O P, \tag{5}$$

where K is the intrinsic camera matrix and $^O P$ are the axes points of the target in homogeneous coordinates. Then, the origin coordinates x_{im} and y_{im} on the image are given by $x_{im} = x_1/x_3$ and $y_{im} = x_2/x_3$.

4   Experiments and Results

We use a monocular system composed of a camera with a resolution of 640×480 pixels, the multi-target attachment, and a personal computer. As explained above, the software was implemented using Python and OpenCV. The camera calibration parameters are the following intrinsic values (K) and distortion coefficients $(dist)$

$$K = \begin{bmatrix} 491.0607 & 0 & 319.8941 \\ 0 & 492.8343 & 238.0494 \\ 0 & 0 & 1 \end{bmatrix},$$

$$dist = [0.0534, \ -0.2042, \ -0.00136, \ 0.0009, \ 0.1593].$$

The experiments were carried out with a distance of approximately 50 cm between the camera and the multi-target attachment. And the surgical instrument moved, like an ultrasound probe, in a volume of 4000 cm^3 composed of 20 cm $\times$ 20 cm $\times$ 10 cm. The video duration 40 s with a rate of 20 frames/seconds.

To test the accuracy of the proposed device and system, we carried out a graphical experiment. This consisted of drawing the target ID0: under the given pose estimation directly by the ArUco library and under the proposed method. The estimation of the relative position matrices with one and several images was analyzed in this test. Figure 5(a) shows two axes. The axes on the top face of the attachment were drawn with the given pose matrix by ArUco library. The axes which are floating were drawn with the proposed method but with the relative positions matrix based on only a single image. Figure 5b show us the same situation but with the relative positions matrix based on a group of twenty images. We can see that the two axes are almost superimposed. The multi-target attachment and its system obtained good results in the graphic experiment. Likewise, this test demonstrated the need to estimate the relative positions matrices with several images.

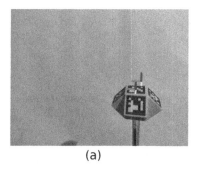 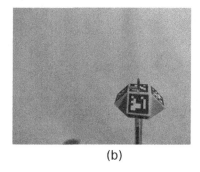

(a)   (b)

Fig. 5. Result of the graphic experiment to pose estimation of the surgical instrument. *a)* With relative position matrix based in a single image. *b)* With relative position matrix based in several images.

To present the system operation, we show the OpenCV-obtained poses for one of the multiple acquired images. The image showed in Fig. 6a was processed, and the ID0, ID1, and ID4 markers were detected, and their poses were calculated, obtaining the following data (See Fig. 6(b))

$$ID0\ marker\ pose = \begin{bmatrix} -0.9689 & -0.1715 & 0.1785 & -0.0144 \\ -0.2355 & 0.4176 & -0.8776 & 0.0122 \\ 0.0759 & -0.8923 & -0.4450 & 0.1383 \end{bmatrix},$$

$$ID1\ marker\ pose = \begin{bmatrix} -0.9737 & -0.2177 & -0.067 & -0.0185 \\ -0.1464 & 0.8235 & -0.5480 & 0.0271 \\ 0.1745 & -0.5238 & -0.8338 & 0.1161 \end{bmatrix},$$

$$ID4\ marker\ pose = \begin{bmatrix} -0.5916 & -0.1598 & 0.7903 & 0.0054 \\ -0.7611 & 0.4339 & -0.4820 & 0.0254 \\ -0.2659 & -0.8867 & -0.3783 & 0.1459 \end{bmatrix}.$$

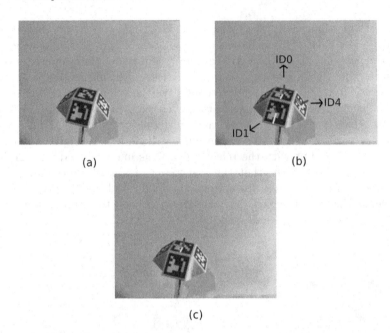

(a)   (b)

(c)

Fig. 6. Result of pose estimation of the surgical instrument. *a)* Input image. *b)* Axes plotted with the pose of each marker. *c)* Axes plotted with the pose of frame of reference.

Based on the target selection metric, the algorithm chooses the ID1 marker to estimate the pose of the frame of reference. Therefore, with the relative position matrix of the marker (See Eq. (6)), it uses Eq. (1) to obtain the optimal pose (See Eq. (7)). In Fig. 6c, we show the origin of the image coordinates.

$$
ID1\ relative\ position\ matrix = \begin{bmatrix} 0.9912 & -0.04989 & -0.12295 & 0.002 \\ -0.0229 & 0.8487 & -0.5285 & -0.0248 \\ 0.1306 & 0.5266 & 0.8400 & -0.0106 \\ 0 & 0 & 0 & 1 \end{bmatrix}, \quad (6)
$$

$$
Pose\ of\ the\ surgical\ instrument = \begin{bmatrix} 0.9912 & -0.04989 & -0.12295 & 0.002 \\ -0.0229 & 0.8487 & -0.5285 & -0.0248 \\ 0.1306 & 0.5266 & 0.8400 & -0.0106 \\ 0 & 0 & 0 & 1 \end{bmatrix}.
$$
$$(7)$$

In the future, an application of this multi-target attachment would be a robust and low-cost 3D free-hand ultrasound [13]. In the case showed in [13], we can change the three circular markers by our proposal and locate the camera any position with line of sight. Also, we would use an industrial robot to obtain a quantitative validation of the proposed method and errors of pose estimation [14].

We described a performance problem for pose estimation under poor lighting and fast motion of the experiments' attachment. We will focus our efforts to solve this situation, possibly using Deep ChArUco [8].

5 Conclusion

We implemented an offline system for pose estimation of a surgical instrument using ArUco markers. The developed system estimates the pose in the world coordinates even when some markers are occluded due to the device's movement. However, the existence of nine markers in the attachment guarantees the detection of at least one marker, and ultimately, the instrument pose. Future work involves exploiting the redundancy for improving pose estimation in challenging medical environments.

Acknowledgement. E. Benjumea thanks MinCiencias and Sistema General de Regalías (Programa de Becas de Excelencia) for a PhD scholarship. J. Sierra and J. Meza thank Universidad Tecnológica de Bolívar (UTB) for a post-graduate scholarship. J. Meza acknowledges support from MinCiencias, and MinSalud for a "Joven Talento" scholarship.

References

1. Avola, D., Cinque, L., Foresti, G.L., Mercuri, C., Pannone, D.: A practical framework for the development of augmented reality applications by using aruco markers. In: International Conference on Pattern Recognition Applications and Methods, vol. 2, pp. 645–654. SCITEPRESS (2016)
2. Azuma, R.T.: A survey of augmented reality. Presence: TeleoperatorsVirtual Environ. **6**(4), 355–385 (1997)
3. Bootsma, G.J., Siewerdsen, J.H., Daly, M.J., Jaffray, D.A.: Initial investigation of an automatic registration algorithm for surgical navigation. In: 2008 30th Annual International Conference of the IEEE Engineering in Medicine and Biology Society, pp. 3638–3642 (2008). https://doi.org/10.1109/IEMBS.2008.4649996
4. Colley, E., Carroll, J., Thomas, S., Varcoe, R.L., Simmons, A., Barber, T.: A methodology for non-invasive 3-D surveillance of arteriovenous fistulae using free-hand ultrasound. IEEE Trans. Biomed. Eng. **65**(8), 1885–1891 (2017)
5. DeSouza, G.N., Kak, A.C.: Vision for mobile robot navigation: a survey. IEEE Trans. Pattern Anal. Mach. Intell. **24**(2), 237–267 (2002)
6. Garrido-Jurado, S., Muñoz Salinas, R., Madrid-Cuevas, F., Medina-Carnicer, R.: Generation of fiducial marker dictionaries using mixed integer linear programming. Pattern Recogn. **51**(C), 481–491 2016). https://doi.org/10.1016/j.patcog.2015.09.023
7. Garrido-Jurado, S., Muñoz-Salinas, R., Madrid-Cuevas, F.J., Marín-Jiménez, M.J.: Automatic generation and detection of highly reliable fiducial markers under occlusion. Pattern Recogn. **47**(6), 2280–2292 (2014)
8. Hu, D., DeTone, D., Malisiewicz, T.: Deep charuco: dark charuco marker pose estimation. In: Proceedings of the IEEE/CVF Conference on Computer Vision and Pattern Recognition (CVPR), June 2019

9. Kato, H., Billinghurst, M.: Marker tracking and HMD calibration for a video-based augmented reality conferencing system. In: Proceedings 2nd IEEE and ACM International Workshop on Augmented Reality (IWAR 1999), pp. 85–94. IEEE (1999)

10. Knyaz, V.A.: The development of new coded targets for automated point identification and non-contact 3D surface measurements. IAPRS **5**, 80–85 (1998)

11. Koeda, M., Yano, D., Shintaku, N., Onishi, K., Noborio, H.: Development of wireless surgical knife attachment with proximity indicators using aruco marker. In: Kurosu, M. (ed.) HCI 2018. LNCS, vol. 10902, pp. 14–26. Springer, Cham (2018). https://doi.org/10.1007/978-3-319-91244-8_2

12. Mercier, L., Langø, T., Lindseth, F., Collins, D.L.: A review of calibration techniques for freehand 3-D ultrasound systems. Ultrasound Med. Biol. **31**(4), 449–471 (2005)

13. Meza, J., Simarra, P., Contreras-Ojeda, S., Romero, L.A., Contreras Ortiz, S.H., Arámbula Cosío, F., Marrugo, A.G.: A low-cost multi-modal medical imaging system with fringe projection profilometry and 3D freehand ultrasound. Proc. SPIE **11330**, 1133004 (2020)

14. Romero, C., Naufal, C., Meza, J., Marrugo, A.G.: A validation strategy for a target-based vision tracking system with an industrial robot. J. Phys.: Conf. Ser. **1547**, 012018 (2020). https://doi.org/10.1088/1742-6596/1547/1/012018

15. Romero-Ramirez, F., Muñoz-Salinas, R., Medina-Carnicer, R.: Speeded up detection of squared fiducial markers. Image Vision Comput. 76 (2018). https://doi.org/10.1016/j.imavis.2018.05.004

16. Romero-Ramirez, F.J., Muñoz-Salinas, R., Medina-Carnicer, R.: Fractal markers: a new approach for long-range marker pose estimation under occlusion. IEEE Access **7**, 169908–169919 (2019)

17. Sani, M.F., Karimian, G.: Automatic navigation and landing of an indoor AR. Drone quadrotor using arUco marker and inertial sensors. In: 2017 International Conference on Computer and Drone Applications (IConDA), pp. 102–107. IEEE (2017)

18. Treece, G.M., Gee, A.H., Prager, R.W., Cash, C.J., Berman, L.H.: High-definition freehand 3-D ultrasound. Ultrasound Med. Biol. **29**(4), 529–546 (2003)

19. Wang, J., Olson, E.: Apriltag 2: efficient and robust fiducial detection. In: 2016 IEEE/RSJ International Conference on Intelligent Robots and Systems (IROS), pp. 4193–4198. IEEE (2016)

20. Yano, D., Koeda, M., Onishi, K., Noborio, H.: Development of a surgical knife attachment with proximity indicators. In: Marcus, A., Wang, W. (eds.) DUXU 2017. LNCS, vol. 10289, pp. 608–618. Springer, Cham (2017). https://doi.org/10.1007/978-3-319-58637-3_48

W–net: A Convolutional Neural Network for Retinal Vessel Segmentation

Alan Reyes-Figueroa$^{(\boxtimes)}$ and Mariano Rivera

Centro de Investigación en Matemáticas AC, 36023 Guanajuato, GTO, México
{agreyes,mrivera}@cimat.mx

Abstract. In this paper we propose a method for retinal vessel segmentation based on a multi-stage deep convolutional neural network with short connections. The proposed method is a two-stage application of an improved U–net architecture. In the first stage, a probability score for the vascular structure presence is computed from a set of random patches taken from the image dataset. In the second stage, this probability is refined to obtain a final threshold image of the vessel structure.

The main contributions of this paper are the following: (1) We propose a modification for the distribution of weights in the U–net, called here the V–net model, which is more convenient for reconstruction tasks. (2) We propose a multi-stage version of our model, called here the W–net, and we conduct extensive experimental evidence in which the W–net produces high-quality results for retinal vessel segmentation. (3) We also propose a fast operating version of the W–net, and evaluate potential improvements when modify our proposal.

We evaluate the performance of our methods in various public available datasets, and compare our proposal versus other recently developed methods. The experimental results demonstrate the capabilities and potential of our proposal.

Keywords: Vessel segmentation · Neural networks · Medical imaging

1 Introduction

Blood vessel segmentation plays an important role in different clinical fields [1–5], both for diagnosis and for treatment planning and subsequent evaluation. The importance of vessel analysis is supported by the constant introduction into clinical practice of new medical technologies to improve the visualisation of the arterial structures [6,7] (Fig. 1).

Retinal vessels identification and localisation aim to separate the different retinal vasculature structure tissues, from the fundus image background and other retinal anatomical structures. Recently, retinal vessels segmentation studies have attracted attention, since valuable information contained in vessel structure is helpful for the detection and diagnosis of a variety of retinal pathologies. In recent years, artificial intelligent algorithms and deep learning approaches

© Springer Nature Switzerland AG 2021
E. Roman-Rangel et al. (Eds.): MCPR 2021, LNCS 12725, pp. 355–368, 2021.
https://doi.org/10.1007/978-3-030-77004-4_34

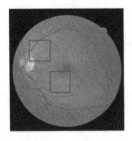

Fig. 1. Left: color fundus image of retina. Right: Manual segmentation of vessel structures. (DRIVE dataset). (Color figure online)

have obtained better results than other previous methodologies in vessel segmentation. The majority of these techniques are based of feature extraction at different scale-levels.

1.1 Related Work

There exist a vast literature on automatic retinal vessel segmentation. Detailed surveys and reviews on methods about 2D vessel segmentation can be found in [8–10]. Recently, the incorporation of deep learning convolutional-based methodologies can be found in [11–13]. In the recent years, one of the most popular architectures are the U–net [14] and the Densely Connected ConvNet (DCCNN) [15]. The U–net architecture has been used widely in biomedical imaging, since is one of the most successful and accurate architectures for segmentation. For example, [16–19] and other authors use the U–net for retinal vessel segmentation from color fundus images problem with success.

The purpose of this paper is to propose a new deep learning scheme for retinal vessels segmentation. The organisation of this paper is as follows: Sect. 2 describes the V–net and W–net architectures. The methodology and implementation details are described in Sect. 3. The material and experimental results are presented in Sect. 4.

2 The V–net and W–net Models

2.1 The V–net Model

In the literature, classification (image segmentation) and regression (image filtering) are usually approached differently, and may require different features. In this work we propose a U–net modification designed to achieve image filtering instead of image segmentation. Despite the computational cost that it implies, our network applies a larger number of filters on the input tensor (original image) in order to capture local details and achieve a precise reconstruction. Also, as opposed to the standard U–net, we reduce the number of filters as the layers are deeper on the encoder. Thus, the deepest layer in the encoder stage (bottom layer on Fig. 2) produces a tensor with the smallest dimension (spatial size and number of channels). These characteristics distinguish our architecture and provide our DNN with an advantage for the regression task. We call our improved model "V–net" since it uses tensors with few channels on deeper layers.

Recently, we have reported in Refs. [20–22] that V–net filter distribution outperforms the classic U–net filter distribution. In this work, we present the details of our proposed V–net. So, our approach can be seen as a contribution, that produces better results for the task of vessel segmentation and can be used in other image processing task. Other important feature of the V–net is the inclusion of Dropout layers [23] in the encoder part, in order to produce better and stable results.

The V–net encoder is composed by a sequence of K encoding blocks (Down–Blocks), followed by the decoder, which consist of a sequence of K decoding blocks (Up–Blocks), and a Tail (composed by two last convolutional layers), see Fig. 2 The kth Down–Block, $k = 1, 2, \ldots, K$, starts by applying two convolutional layers with n_k channels of size 3×3. This number n_k determines the amount of output channels at each stage. A complete description of each encoding and decoding block architectures is presented in Tables 1 and 2. In the following, x_k denotes the output tensor of the kth Down–Block, $k = 1, 2, \ldots, K$, as well as the second input of the $(k + 1)$th Up–Block, $k = 1, 2, \ldots, K - 1$. Similarly, y_k denotes the first input tensor of the kth Up–Block, $k = K, \ldots, 2, 1$, as well as the output for the $(k + 1)$th Up–Block, $k = K - 1, \ldots, 1, 0$.

The complete architecture of our V–net implementation is summarised in Table 3. In our implementation, we set $K = 5$ (so we have five spatial-size levels). The number of channels n_k, $k = 1, 2, \ldots, K$, is determined by the number of channels n_{k-1} in the previous Down–Block following the rule $n_k = \frac{1}{2} n_{k-1}$. The same occurs with the number of channels for each Up–Block. In our model, the respective number of channels is set as $n_k = 256, 128, 64, 32, 16$, for $k = $

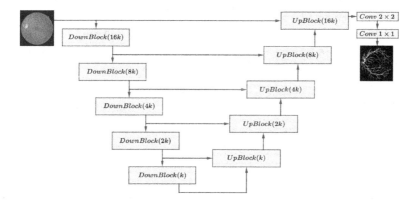

Fig. 2. The V–net architecture. The number of filters per block is inversely distributed: while U–net is designed for image segmentation (classification), the V–net (shown above) is for image reconstruction (regression).

Table 1. V–net Down–Block(a, b, f, p) architecture. Parameters: $(None, a, b)$ = shape of input tensor, f = number of filters, p = Dropout rate.

Layer	Output shape	# Params
Conv2D	(None, a, b, f)	$3 \times 3 \times f$
Conv2D	(None, a, b, f)	$3 \times 3 \times f$
Dropout	(None, a, b, f)	0
MaxPooling2D	(None, $\lfloor \frac{a}{2} \rfloor$, $\lfloor \frac{b}{2} \rfloor$, f)	0

Table 2. V–net Up–Block(a, b, f) architecture. Parameters: $(None, a, b)$ = shape of input tensor, f = number of filters.

Layer	Output shape	# Params
UpSampling2D	(None, $2a$, $2b$, f)	0
Conv2D	(None, $2a$, $2b$, $2f$)	$2 \times 2 \times f$
Concatenate	(None, $2a$, $2b$, $4f$)	0
Conv2D	(None, $2a$, $2b$, $2f$)	$3 \times 3 \times 2f$
Conv2D	(None, $2a$, $2b$, $2f$)	$3 \times 3 \times 2f$

Table 3. V–net architecture.

Block/Layer	Output shape	# Params	Inputs
01. Input Layer	(None, 32, 32, 1)	0	
02. DownBlock(32,32,256,0)	(None, 16, 16, 256)	592,640	01
03. DownBlock(16,16,128,0.25)	(None, 8, 8, 128)	442,624	02
04. DownBlock(8,8,64,0.25)	(None, 4, 4, 64)	110,720	03
05. DownBlock(4,4,32,0.25)	(None, 2, 2, 32)	27,712	04
06. UpBlock(2,2,32)	(None, 4, 4, 32)	592,640	05, 04
07. UpBlock(4,4,64)	(None, 8, 8, 64)	592,640	06, 03
08. UpBlock(8,8,128)	(None, 16, 16, 128)	592,640	07, 02
09. UpBlock(16,16,256)	(None, 32, 32, 256)	592,640	08, 01
10. Tail Conv2D	(None, 32, 32, 2)	578	09
11. Tail Conv2D	(None, 32, 32, 1)	3	10
Total params		3,721,669	
Trainable params		3,721,669	
Non-trainable params		0	

$1, 2, \ldots, 5$. Although more general configurations for the number of channels can be implemented, we have chosen as global parameter the number $F = n_K = 16$ of channels in the last Down–Block (bottom level), and the other n_k's are determined by F as is indicated in Table 3.

2.2   W–net

The W–net model is a two-stage application of the V–net. In the first stage, the purpose of the V–net is to detect the vascular structures and produce a score image which indicates the probability of presence of vessel structure at each pixel. This V–net is trained to compute this probability from a set of random patches taken from the training images in the dataset. In the second stage, again a V–net is applied. This V–net is trained in order to intensify this probability and produce final thresholded image which serves a characteristic function for the vessel structure. If necessary, the V–net stage could be applied n times in sequence, in order to achieve finer probability maps. The W–net architecture is illustrated in Fig. 3 for the case of $n = 2$ consecutive applications of the V–net stage.

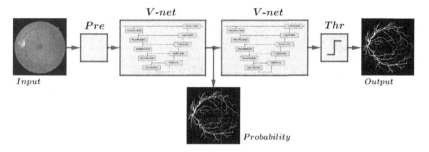

Fig. 3. W–net architecture: After a pre-processing stage, two V–net are applied in sequence. Finally a post-processing and thresholding algorithm is computed to produce a final segmentation.

3   Methodology and Implementation Details

The W–net implementation comprises four steps: 1) a pre-processing stage, 2) application of the first V–net and reconstruction of a probability map, 3) Application of a second V–net, and 4) thresholding and post-processing tasks. In the following we describe with detail the methodology and algorithms in each stage.

3.1   Pre-processing

All images are transformed to PNG format, in order to unify data treatment. Following [16], before training, the 40 images of the DRIVE datasets are pre-processed with the following transformations: gray-scale conversion, normalisation, contrast-limited adaptive histogram equalisation (CLAHE), and gamma adjustment.

Normalisation $Y/\max Y$ is then applied to force the images to be in the $[0, 1]$ range. Subsequently, we apply a contrast-limited adaptative equalisation

(CLAHE) using a bound of 0.01 normalised clipping limit, and a kernel size of 17×17 pixels, in order to highlight vessel structures. Finally, a gamma correction process is applied using $\gamma = 0.5$. In the case of the STARE dataset, the same procedure is applied, with the only exception of the gamma correction.

We have found experimentally that better results are obtained when the segmentation process is applied to the gray-scale images, rather than the original RGB images. When the process was tested on RGB images, the obtained results were not as good as possible. Similarly, in the case of DRIVE set, better results were attained when the gamma correction is applied. In the case of the STARE set, since the background of fundus images are not completely black (probably the camera was calibrated in a different manner), applying gamma correction only reduces the obtained metrics. We have not compared results by using different values of clipping limit and kernel size in CLAHE step, nor other gamma values in the gamma correction step. After this, both sets are split in training and test dataset.

3.2 First V–net

The V–net is designed to reconstruct small FP patches of 64×64 pixels. Thus, to reconstruct an entire FP, we generated a set of patches using a sliding window scheme, with a stride (pixels shifts step) of $s_x = s_y = 4$ pixels in both horizontal and vertical directions in the n images of size 565×584 images. All patches are fed to the V–net to compute their segmentation. Each pixel in the entire reconstructed probability map was computed as the average of the values in the same pixel position obtained from overlapped normalised patches. We preferred the mean because it is more efficiently computed than the median, and we did not appreciate a significant differences if the median is used instead.

Again, the pixel shifts s_x and s_y are user-defined parameters. We have also tested pixel shifts equal to 2 and 1, but the improvement in the reconstruction is not significant, and the selection of lesser values of s_x and s_y only increases the computational cost and time (nearly $\times 4$ times for the 2 stride, and $\times 16$ times in the case of the 1 stride). Higher values of s_x, s_y reduce the computational cost but can produce bad non-smooth reconstructions by introducing an undesired checker effect. Therefore, our choice of $s_x = s_y = 4$ responds to a trade-off between good reconstructions and computational cost.

For a 2-dimensional input image, let κ_d be the number of patches computed over the dimensions $d = 1, 2$ (rows and columns). Then $\kappa_d = q_d + \varepsilon_d$, where $q_d = \left\lfloor \frac{H_d - h_d}{s_d} \right\rfloor + 1$, H_d is the image size, h_d the patch size, s_d the stride step and

$$\varepsilon_d = \begin{cases} 1, & H_d - (q_d - 1)s_d - h_d > 0 \\ 0, & \text{otherwise.} \end{cases} \tag{1}$$

In the case of the DRIVE dataset, we set $H_1 = 565$, $H_2 = 584$, $h_d = 64$, $s_d = 4$ for $d = 1, 2$. Then, the number of patches required to reconstruct a single image is $\kappa_1 \times \kappa_2 = 127 \times 131 = 16,637$. On 20 training images, we have a total of $332,740$ patches. This quantity is substantially larger than the number of patches used as training set, with 25,000 patches. The expected number of patches per training image was 1250 (25,000/20).

In the case of the STARE dataset, we set $H_1 = 700$, $H_2 = 605$, $h_d = 64$, $s_d = 4$ for $d = 1, 2$. Then, the number of patches required to reconstruct a single image is $\kappa_1 \times \kappa_2 = 160 \times 137 = 21,920$. On 20 training images, we have a total of 438,400 patches.

In [16], the author suggest a training with a set of 190,000 patches of size 48×48. We have shown that good quality results can be obtained by using much more less training patches. The size difference was only to satisfy the requiring multiple of 32 size in the V–net model.

Although the patches overlap and may contain same part of the original image, no further data augmentation was performed. The first 90% of the patches was used for training, while the last 10% was used for validation. The first V–net was trained using ADAM [24] as optimisation algorithm, with 50 epochs and batch size of 32. We use a learning rate of $\alpha = 0.001$, with a decay rate of 0.001. Binary cross-entropy was used as loss function, while binary accuracy was computed as an alternate metric.

We tested other patches size $e.g.$ 32×32, 96×96 and 128×128. With patch size of 32×32, the training process if faster, but the output quality was not as good as the proposed size. In the other cases, the training process slows down and it requires much more iterations to attain low entropy and high accuracy. As the size of patches increase, the training becomes less efficient.

3.3 Second V–net

From the previous probability estimation, we repeat the same process described in previous section, to train the second V–net. An amount of 25,000 patches of size 64×64 are taken again uniformly distributed over all probability images. In order to reduce possible overfitting, we use a different random seed from the used in the first V–net stage. No further data augmentation is performed. The first 90% of the patches was used for training, while the last 10% was used for validation. The second V–net is trained with the same parameters as first V–net.

The purpose of this second V–net is to improve the probability estimation obtained in the first stage, rather than perform vessel segmentation (see Fig. 4). This improvement is done by intensifying the probability score at the most weak vessel ramifications, while the scores is maintained at principal vessel branches. Basically, this second stage improves the score passing an intensification filter where it is needed, giving the probability score a much more threshold-like or bump-function form. This second V–net is essential to attain better results. At the end, a second probability averaged estimation is computed by the same patch by patch algorithm used to compute first stage.

3.4 Thresholding Process

After second probability is computed we perform a threshold on the probability scores, by using a local Otsu's method [25]. Local Otsu's is performed using a

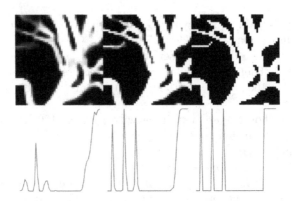

Fig. 4. Detail of the W–net process on a retina image. First V–net probability estimation (left), second V–net refinement result (center). The final threshold output image (right). Traversal cuts are shown in the second row.

disk structuring element of radius $r = 51$ pixels. Other global and local threshold methods were tested, but Otsu's algorithm produced the best results. As a result, with lower or higher radius some of the weak vessel ramifications can be lost, since the local the method only sees vessel/background quantity distributions and no other topological or morphological information. We suggest to use a radius in the range of 30 to 70 pixels. No other structuring element were tested.

3.5   The Fast V–net Implementation

Finally, a modification of our V–net implementation is proposed. This variant preserves the same architecture of the V–net described in Fig. 2 and Table 3, just modifies the shape of the input tensor. Now the reconstruction or inference process is done by passing the entire input image into the network, instead of covering patches. As a result, we obtain similar quality of reconstructions, but now the computational time needed to process a single image reduces to a fraction of the time consumed by the original V–net. The reduction is about 100 times faster that the original V–net implementation. It is identical to the architecture in Table 3, only that all output shapes are re-scaled according to the input shape. We call this variant the "Fast V–net". A fast version of the W–net, the "Fast W–net", is constructed in a similar way by applying two Fast V–net in sequence.

4   Experiments and Material

4.1   Material

A number of publicly available databases with associated GS has been published in the last few years: ARIA, CHASE, HRF, IMAGERET, MESSIDOR, REVIEW, ROC, VICAVR and VAMPIRE. Unfortunately, in the literature almost all previous results and testing evaluations are related to one of DRIVE [26,27] or STARE [28,29] datasets. We limit our evaluation of the proposed techniques to those two sets in order to compare to previous work.

Both image datasets present optical differences. For example, the FOV angle are distinct, the FOV mask sizes and shapes differ, and some contrast dissimilarities outside the field of view region. Due to these differences, we use the same W–net architecture for both experiments, but each dataset is trained with a different model. Also, different pre-processing techniques must be applied to each dataset. Using a general model trained with both datasets, can also be done but its performance metrics reduce significantly.

4.2   Results

A total of 10 different training runs for the W–net with different random patches were executed. Time performance depends on the number of train images, image size, patch size, patch stride, number of epochs and the number of parameters in each V–net. One of the most time-demanding steps is the probability prediction. For example, for the DRIVE dataset with 40 images, with 25,000 training patches of 64×64, and 50 epochs at each V–net, the total training time is about 70 min, using a Nvidia GeForce GTX TITAN GPU. The inference time is about 15 s per image. All implementations are done in Python 3.6 using Tensorflow Keras, preprocess and postprocess use Scikit-image library.

We have used the sensitivity, specificity and accuracy as comparison metrics. Table 4 summarises the experimental results. We indicate the mean value of the metric obtained for all 10 experiments. In parenthesis, we indicate a confidence interval corresponding to a significant level of $\alpha = 98\%$. The values of min, max are also shown.

Table 4. Metric performance on the DRIVE and STARE datasets (all 10 experiments).

DRIVE	F1-score	Sensitivity	Specificity	Accuracy	ROC auc
Min	0.8282	0.8287	0.9535	0.9386	0.8917
Max	0.8476	0.8501	0.9573	0.9436	0.9037
Mean	0.8360 ($\pm$ .004)	0.8400 ($\pm$ .005)	0.9553 ($\pm$ .0007)	0.9405 ($\pm$ .001)	0.8976 ($\pm$ .002)
STARE	F1-score	Sensitivity	Specificity	Accuracy	ROC auc.
Min	0.8382	0.8323	0.9508	0.9315	0.8737
Max	0.8496	0.8564	0.9553	0.9392	0.8915
Mean	0.8423 ($\pm$ .007)	0.8435 ($\pm$ .016)	0.9531 ($\pm$ .017)	0.9342 ($\pm$ .007)	0.8824 ($\pm$ .011)

From the methods discussed in some of the review in Sect. 1.1, we have chosen a subset of them for comparison purposes. Results are summarised in Table 5. Some of the segmentation results are shown in Figs. 5 and 6. Figure 5 corresponds to the results obtained in the case of the DRIVE dataset, for the first experiment (experiment 1 of 10). Similarly, Fig. 6 corresponds to the obtained results in the first experiment for the STARE dataset.

Table 5. Comparison of averaged performance metrics with other methodologies.

Dataset	Method	Year	F1-score	Sensitivity	Specificity	Accuracy
DRIVE	Roychowdhury [11]	2015	–	0.7250	**0.9830**	0.9520
	Liskowski [12]	2016	–	0.7763	0.9768	0.9495
	Qiaoliang Li [13]	2016	–	0.7569	0.9816	0.9527
	U-Net [17]	2018	0.8142	0.7537	0.9820	0.9531
	Residual U-Net [17]	2018	0.8149	0.7726	0.9820	0.9553
	Recurrent U-Net [17]	2018	0.8155	0.7751	0.9816	0.9556
	R2U-Net [17]	2018	0.8171	0.7792	0.9813	0.9556
	LadderNet [18]	2019	0.8202	0.7856	0.9810	**0.9561**
	Yan et al. [19]	2019	–	0.7631	0.7820	0.9538
	Proposed (ROI)	**2019**	**0.8360**	**0.8400**	0.9553	0.9405
	Proposed (all)	**2019**	**0.8360**	**0.8400**	0.9622	0.9515
STARE	Roychowdhury	2015	–	0.7720	0.9730	0.9510
	Liskowski	2016	–	0.7867	0.9754	0.9566
	Qiaoliang Li	2016	–	0.7726	0.9844	0.9628
	U-Net	2018	0.8373	0.8270	0.9842	0.9690
	Residual U-Net	2018	0.8388	0.8203	0.9856	0.9700
	Recurrent U-Net	2018	0.8396	0.8108	**0.9871**	0.9706
	R2U-Net	2018	**0.8475**	0.8298	0.9862	**0.9712**
	Yan et al.	2019	–	0.7735	0.9857	0.9638
	Proposed (all)	**2019**	0.8423	**0.8435**	0.9531	0.9342

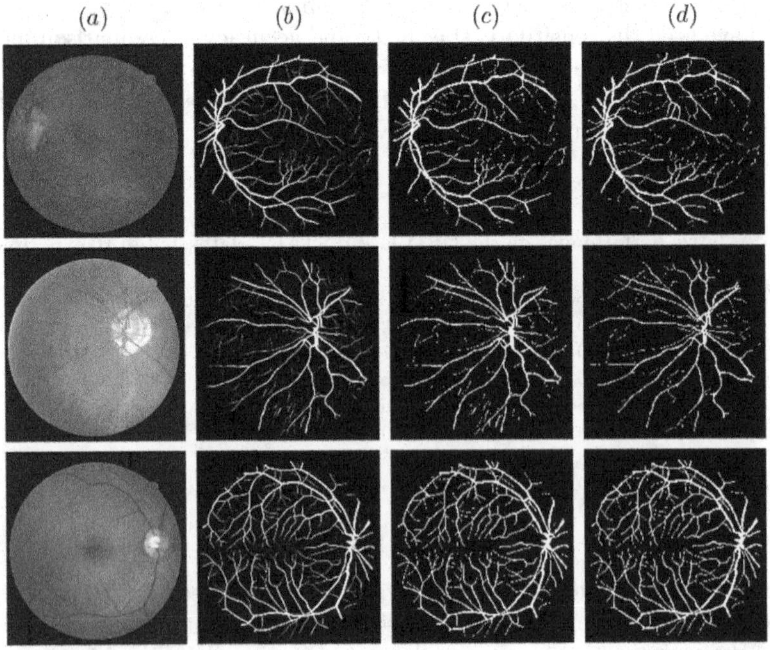

(a)   (b)   (c)   (d)

Fig. 5. Results for the DRIVE dataset: (a) input image. (b) initial probability estimation by the first V-net, (c) second probability estimation and refinement, (d) final binary segmentation.

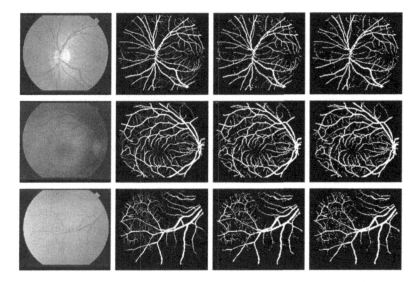

Fig. 6. Results for the STARE dataset: (a) input image. (b) initial probability estimation by the first V–net, (c) second probability estimation and refinement, (d) final binary segmentation.

5   Discussion and Conclusion

U–net, V–net and W–net models base their image segmentation by processing image patches with local information. This is an advantage in terms of computational efficiency, since the processing is done locally, and it subsequently can be transferred to a global information method as the proposed Fast W–net scheme. Also, other relevant advantage is that locally, all retinal vessel structures have the same local behaviour, following a geometrical tubular structure, only varying in size, radius, orientation and other geometrical parameters, that can be modelled in a general form. From this, our patch by patch prediction methodology in the W–net model could be interpreted as a local approach to describe this vascular structure pattern. It adapts the convolutional filtering process to the particular local details. On the other hand, the Fast W–net model produces almost the same quality in the segmentations with much lower computational time.

We also observed that W–net and Fast W–net models have limitations for filtering-out and produce a good segmentation of the vessel structure at points or regions with very low frequencies and radii; typically at places where the tubular structure is thin and presents lower radius. The majority of the differences between the predicted output segmentation and the ground-truth maps are located at the boundary of the vascular region, or at points near the end of vessel ramifications. Further refinements or variations of our basic model could correct this particularity. But even the manually produced ground-truth segmentations present this same limitation.

Even the limitations described above, the obtained results in Table 4 indicate that our method produces high quality results. All performance scores are above 0.8, which indicates the good performance of our proposal. In literature, one particularity of previous reported retinal vessel segmentation methods is that the sensitivity metric has been an unsolved issue. Usually, almost all reported methods have a sensitivity score in the range $[0.76, 0.785]$. In this case, our methodology produces sensitivity metrics above 0.83 in both evaluated datasets, and out-performs all other compared alternatives both in sensitivity and F1-score. Since sensitivity measures the proportion of positives that are correctly identified, our methodology has lower rate of false negatives (vascular structure pixels that are segmented as background). Moreover, from results in Table 5, we can conclude that our algorithm is competitive with other state-of-the-art segmentation methodologies, even out-performing them in various metrics. In the case of DRIVE dataset we include two versions of the evaluation metrics. ROI refers to the case in which only the masked pixels are evaluated, no background pixels are included. In the (all) version all pixels are evaluated. In general, the (all) version performs better since almost all background is correctly classified. Unfortunately, a lot of the previous methods in Table 5 do not explicit which pixels are taken into account in the metrics, we suggest to use the ROI version to get a better idea of the performance of our model. In the case of STARE dataset all pixels are evaluated.

Our method also produces visually high-quality segmentation maps. In Figs. 5 and 6, we observe part of this results. Even the first probability estimation map produced by the first V–net is a high-quality image. The authors suggest this probability map sometimes generates better visual results than the final binary segmentation. In this sense, it is possible that the use of those probability maps present better results than the usually used to compare binary classification methods. One possible line of research in this direction is the development of metrics (quantitative or visual) to compare these probability maps.

Finally, the V–net model has been applied successfully in a wide set of image processing tasks and context. For example, [20] discuss the case of the V–net and Fast V–net in the context of fringe pattern filtering and normalisation, while [21] compares this methodology to state-of-the-art methods. In [22] the authors constructs a multi-stage scheme, based on the V–net, called ModuleNet, and applies it the to the stereo depth estimation problem. Other applications of the V–net include the single image super-resolution problem, fusion, design of robust filtering, image inpainting, among others.

5.1   Conclusions

In this paper we effectively implement a new deep learning approach for retinal vessel segmentation. Our method is based on a multi-stage application of the V–net model. Our results show that this methodology is competitive with other state-of-the-art methods.

We observed that the W–net model can compute retinal vessel segmentation with lower error than other recent deep learning approaches, In our opinion, the reason is that the V–net filter distribution across the layers is designed to retain more details, as opposed to U–net which is designed to segment images. Also, the use of the multi-stage scheme is useful to refine the final output segmentation.

Acknowledgements. Both author want to thank Consejo Nacional de Ciencia y Tecnología (CONACYT), Mexico, for their financial support (ARF doctoral scholarship grant, MR grant A1-S-43858). Author 2 wants to thank NVIDIA Corporation for their support via the Nvidia Academic Program. Both authors want to thanks the Instituto Potosino de Investigación en Ciencia y Tecnología (IPICYT), Mexico, for their friendly and valuable hospitality during the development of this project.

References

1. Carmeliet, P., Jain, R.K.: Angiogenesis in cancer and other diseases. Nature **407**(6801), 249–257 (2000)
2. Campochiaro, P.A.: Molecular pathogenesis of retinal and choroidal vascular diseases. Prog. Retin. Eye Res. **49**, 67–81 (2015)
3. De Momi, E., et al.: Multi-trajectories automatic planner for Stereo Electro Encephalo Graphy (SEEG). Int. J. Comput. Assist. Radio. Surg. **9**(6), 1087–1097 (2014). https://doi.org/10.1007/s11548-014-1004-1
4. Essert, C., et al.: Statistical study of parameters for deep brain stimulation automatic preoperative planning of electrodes trajectories. Int. J. Comput. Assist. Radiol. Surg. **10**(12), 1973–1983 (2015). https://doi.org/10.1007/s11548-015-1263-5
5. Faria, C., et al.: Validation of a stereo camera system to quantify brain deformation due to breathing and pulsatility. Med. Physiol. **41**(11), 113502 (2014)
6. Piazza, C., Del Bon, F., Peretti, G., Nicolai, P.: Narrow band imaging in endoscopic evaluation of the larynx. Curr. Opin. Otolaryngol. Head Neck Surg. **20**(6), 472–476 (2012)
7. Cardinale, F., et al.: Cerebral angiography for multimodal surgical planning in epilepsy surgery: description of a new three-dimensional technique and literature review. World Neurosurg. **84**, 358–367 (2015)
8. Moccia, S., De Momi, E., El Hadji, S., Mattos, L.S.: Blood vessel segmentation algorithms: review of methods, datasets and evaluation metrics. Comput. Methods Programs Biomed. **158**, 71–91 (2018)
9. Fraz, M.M., et al.: Blood vessel segmentation methodologies in retinal images: a survey. Comput. Methods Programs Biomed. **108**(1), 407–433 (2012)
10. Srinidhi, C.L., Aparna, P., Rajan, J.: Recent advancements in retinal vessel segmentation. J. Med. Syst. **41**(4), 70 (2017)
11. Roychowdhury, S., Koozekanani, D., Parhi, K.: Blood vessel segmentation of fundus images by major vessel extraction and subimage classification. IEEE J. Biomed. Health Inform. **19**(3), 1118–1128 (2015)
12. Liskowski, P., Krawiec, K.: Segmenting retinal blood vessels with deep neural networks. Trans. Med. Imaging **35**(11), 2369–2380 (2016)
13. Li, Q., Feng, B., Xie, L., Liang, P., Zhang, H., Wang, T.: A cross-modality learning approach for vessel segmentation in retinal images. Trans. Med. Imaging **35**(1), 109–118 (2016)

14. Ronneberger, O., Fischer, P., Brox, T.: U-Net: convolutional networks for biomedical image segmentation. In: Navab, N., Hornegger, J., Wells, W.M., Frangi, A.F. (eds.) MICCAI 2015. LNCS, vol. 9351, pp. 234–241. Springer, Cham (2015). https://doi.org/10.1007/978-3-319-24574-4_28

15. Huang, G., Liu, Z., van der Maaten, L., Weinberger, K.: Densely Connected Convolutional Networks. arXiv preprint arXiv:1608.06993 (2018)

16. Orobix. Retina blood vessel segmentation with a convolution neural network (U-net) (2018). https://github.com/orobix/retina-unet

17. Zahangir, M., et al. Recurrent Residual Convolutional Neural Network based on U-Net (R2U-Net) for Medical Image Segmentation (2018). arXiv preprint arXiv:1802.06955

18. Zhuang, J.: LadderNet: Multi-Path Networks based on the U-net for Medical Image Segmentation (2019). arXiv preprint arXiv:1810.07810v4

19. Yan et al.: A Three-stage Deep Learning Model for Accurate Retinal Vessel Segmentation (2018). http://home.cse.ust.hk/~zyanad/pdf/jbhi2018.pdf

20. Reyes-Figueroa, A., Flores, V.H., Rivera, M.: Deep neural network for fringe pattern filtering and normalisation. Appl. Opt. **60**(7), 2022–2036 (2021)

21. Flores, V.H., Reyes-Figueroa, A., Carrillo-Delgado, C., Rivera, M.: Two-step phase shifting algorithms: where are we? Opt. Laser Technol. **126**, 1–13 (2020)

22. Renteria-Vidales, O.I., Cuevas-Tello, J.C., Reyes-Figueroa, A., Rivera, M.: ModuleNet: a convolutional neural network for stereo vision. In: Figueroa Mora, K.M., Anzurez Marín, J., Cerda, J., Carrasco-Ochoa, J.A., Martínez-Trinidad, J.F., Olvera-López, J.A. (eds.) MCPR 2020. LNCS, vol. 12088, pp. 219–228. Springer, Cham (2020). https://doi.org/10.1007/978-3-030-49076-8_21

23. Srivastava, N., Hinton, G., Krizhevsky, A., Sutskever, I., Salakhutdinov, R.: Dropout: a simple way to prevent neural networks from overfitting. J. Mach. Learn. Res. **15**, 1929–1958 (2014)

24. Kingma, D.P., Ba, J.: Adam: a method for stochastic optimization. In: 3rd International Conference for Learning Representations, ICLR 2015 (2014)

25. Otsu, N.: A threshold selection method from gray level histograms. IEEE Trans. Syst. Manuf. Cybern. **9**, 62–66 (1979)

26. Staal, J.J., Abramoff, M.D., Niemeijer, M., Viergever, M.A., van Ginneken, B.: Ridge based vessel segmentation in color images of the retina. IEEE Trans. Med. Imaging **23**, 501–509 (2004)

27. Niemeijer, M., Staal, J.J., van Ginneken, B., Loog, M., Abramoff, M.D.: Comparative study of retinal vessel segmentation methods on a new publicly available database. In: Fitzpatrick, J.M., Sonka, M. (eds.) SPIE Medical Imaging, SPIE, vol. 5370, pp. 648–656 (2004)

28. Hoover, A., Kouznetsova, V., Goldbaum, M.: Locating blood vessels in retinal images by piecewise threshold probing of a matched filter response. IEEE Trans. Med. Imaging **19**(3), 203–210 (2000)

29. Hoover, A., Goldbaum, M.: Locating the optic nerve in a retinal image using the fuzzy convergence of the blood vessels. IEEE Trans. Med. Imaging **22**(8), 951–958 (2003)

Novel Features for Glaucoma Detection in Fundus Images

Juan A. González Urquijo[1,2]($\boxtimes$) (ID), Jessica D. Sánchez Fonseca[1,2] (ID),
Juan M. López López[1] (ID), and Sandra Cancino Suárez[1] (ID)

[1] Escuela Colombiana de Ingeniería Julio Garavito, Ak. 45 No. 205 - 59,
Autopista Norte, Bogota, D.C, Colombia
`juan.gonzalez-u@mail.escuelaing.edu.co`
[2] Universidad del Rosario, Ak. 24 No. 63C-69, Barrios Unidos,
Bogota, D.C, Colombia
`https://www.escuelaing.edu.co/es/`

Abstract. Glaucoma is one of the leading causes of irreversible blindness worldwide, and a correct and early diagnosis can impact on the disease treatment. The development of automated solutions for glaucoma detection, using digital image processing techniques and machine learning classifier models may enhance the conventional diagnosis methods. In this work, a new approach for feature extraction, based on projection vectors, was proposed as input to a Multilayer Perceptron (MLP) classifier for accomplishing automated glaucoma detection. Experimental results show that the proposed method provides good classification performance compared to state-of-the-art techniques: 91.6% of sensitivity, 94.5% of specificity, and 93.5% of accuracy. The proposed vectors may be useful in other artificial vision tasks.

Keywords: Automatic detection · Digital image processing · Fundus image · Glaucoma · Machine learning · Optic disc

1 Introduction

Glaucoma is one of the leading causes of irreversible blindness in the world. This disease represents a great public health problem [11]. It is estimated that every year, 12% of the world population presents glaucoma and the number of people with glaucoma will be 111.8 million by 2040 [17,21]. Glaucoma consists on the degeneration of retinal ganglion cells, producing structural changes in the optic nerve head, also known as optic disc (OD), and in the nerve fibers [14]. These changes block the drainage system, causing an increase in the pressure inside the eye [22]. There is no cure for glaucoma, but one strategy to control the disease is a correct and timely diagnosis, taking into account that 50% of the population in the developed countries and 90% of the cases in third world countries that present glaucoma do not have a diagnostic [4,8].

Conventional techniques for glaucoma detection are the tonometry, for measuring the pressure inside the eye; the ophthalmoscopy, allows the visualization

© Springer Nature Switzerland AG 2021
E. Roman-Rangel et al. (Eds.): MCPR 2021, LNCS 12725, pp. 369–378, 2021.
https://doi.org/10.1007/978-3-030-77004-4_35

of the fundus of the eye and other structures; the perimetry, that measures the visual field function; the gonioscopy, used for evaluation of the anterior chamber angle, and the pachymetry, that measures the thickness of the cornea [9]. These tests are time-consuming, expensive and the reproducibility of the results is difficult. Besides, the results depend on the expertise of the ophthalmologist and accurate measurement needs a high level of skill in the glaucoma diagnosis. For these reasons, it is necessary to develop technologies that can improve the timely detection of glaucoma, using digital image processing and machine learning techniques to assess the structural changes of the optic nerve head [19].

Some of the automatic methods use digital image processing to analyze the fundus image and machine learning classifiers with high accuracy in glaucoma diagnosis [10]. Fundus images are useful for glaucoma detection, showing structures like fovea, macula, optic disc, and disc cup, which can provide relevant information of the health state of the patient. Some methods use the cup-to-disc ratio, defined as the ratio of the optic cup and the optic disc diameter. The presence of glaucoma is determined if this measurement is greater than 0.65. However, this feature needs the use of complex image processing techniques [18]. Many studies use machine learning models for glaucoma detection, such as artificial neural networks (ANN), support vector machine (SVM), random forest (RAN), transfer learning, K-nearest neighbor, or convolutional neural networks (CNN) [15]. Though a majority of these methods have been demonstrated a good response in glaucoma diagnosis, the development needs computationally expensive preprocessing and training stages. In this work, a multilayer perceptron (MLP) model is proposed for glaucoma detection with a novel technique for feature extraction, which provides relevant information of the intensity distribution in the region of interest.

2   Method

2.1   Dataset Description

In this work, two datasets were used. Dataset A contains 1255 fundus images that belong to the "Machine learn for glaucoma" dataset from Harvard University [7]. Each image size is 240×240 pixels, in addition, this dataset has 788 normal images and 467 glaucoma images. The dataset B was collected from an online web source named "Glaucoma Detection" from Kaggle [23]. In dataset B, there are 650 fundus images, 168 glaucoma images, and 482 normal images, each one with a size of 2072×2048 pixels.

2.2   Preprocessing

Contrast Enhancement: The OD has some unique features that can be useful for glaucoma detection (Fig. 1a), especially pixel intensity. An initial stage for contrast enhancement was applied to the images, after converting them from rgb to grayscale, to overcome uneven distribution of intensities across datasets (Fig. 1b), through a histogram equalization.

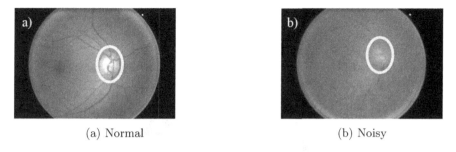

(a) Normal   (b) Noisy

Fig. 1. Comparison between normal and noisy fundus images

Optic Disc Detection: With the results of the contrast enhancement, and noticing that the region of interest (ROI) is located in the OD, an algorithm for detecting this region was developed. The final result of this method gives a squared area of 650×650 pixels that contain the desired region to be analyzed. These dimensions were selected based on the resolution of the fundus image. As images from dataset A just contain OD region, preprocessing for this dataset involves only contrast enhancement. On the other hand, dataset B contains full fundus images, so preprocessing includes contrast enhancement and optic disc detection. Also, because images from the two datasets have different resolutions, their machine learning models are independent.

Vectors V1 & V2: This vectors are one of the main components of this research, they are used for detecting the OD and they will be also used as the main feature of the data obtained from this preprocessing procedure. In a bidimensional matrix X of M rows and N columns where m represents a row and n a column, Vector 1 ($V1$) and Vector 2 ($V2$) are defined as shown in Eqs. 1 and 2. In this case X is the image acquired from contrast enhancement. V1 represent the sum of horizontal pixels and V2 the sum of vertical pixels.

$$\overrightarrow{V1} = \sum_{i=1}^{N} X_{m,i} \quad with \quad m = [1,2,3,...,M] \tag{1}$$

$$\overrightarrow{V2} = \sum_{j=1}^{M} X_{j,n} \quad with \quad n = [1,2,3,...,N] \tag{2}$$

Gaussian Function: As it can be seen in Fig. 2, some images have a high intensity in the borders from a vertical or horizontal point of view, so when Eq. 1 or 2 is applied, some high-intensity values will be found referring to this region, as a consequence, it can be confused with the OD. This artifact can be visible on both axis, so $V1$ and $V2$ are multiplied by two different Gaussian function (Eq. 3) as shown in Eq. 4 and 5, this gives the $V1G$ and $V2G$ vectors.

$$G(x; \sigma, c) = e^{\frac{-(x-c)^2}{2\sigma^2}} \quad with \quad x = 1,2,3... \tag{3}$$

$$\overrightarrow{V1G} = \overrightarrow{V1} \cdot G(x; \sigma, c) \quad with \quad x = [1, 2, 3, ..., M] \quad and \quad \sigma, c = M/2 \quad (4)$$

$$\overrightarrow{V2G} = \overrightarrow{V2} \cdot G(x; \sigma, c) \quad with \quad x = [1, 2, 3, ..., N] \quad and \quad \sigma, c = N/2 \quad (5)$$

As in fundus images the OD is usually located in a central position of the image, σ and c are set as in Eqs. 4 and 5.

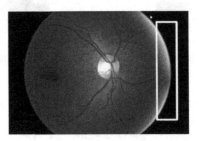

Fig. 2. Artifact in sample image of dataset B.

Optic Disc Location: The maximum value of V1G and V2G refers to the approximate location of the center of the OD, with this central location, the squared area mentioned of 650×650 pixels is around the detected center of the OD (see Fig. 3a and b). It is manually estimated that this method properly detects 97.98% of the OD location in Dataset B images.

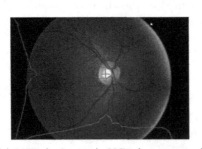

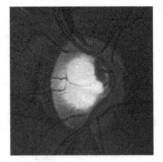

(a) VG1 (red curve), VG2 (green curve)   (b) OD extraction in an image

Fig. 3. Results of OD detection (Color figure online)

V1 and V2 vectors are obtained over the image with contrast enhancement. In order to obtain the image features, there is no need for Gaussian multiplication, as in the OD detection step. In addition, V1 and V2 are useful for reducing data dimensionality, so that they can have intrinsic information of the whole image, preserving valuable geometrical information, as well as the distribution of intensities. It has been shown in previous glaucoma studies, that the cup-to-disc ratio is one of the key features useful for diagnosis, so a couple of synthetic images following these criteria were created to evaluate the effect over V1 and V2. Figure 4a shows that V1 and V2 vectors can show the geometrical characteristics of images, indicating the relationship between the gray disc and the white one. This same procedure was applied, for discs with different size and positions (Fig. 4b and c). In Fig. 4b, the proportion between discs is different, this reduces the amplitude of V1 and V2, as well as the distribution. Finally, in Fig. 4c it can be seen a change in the symmetry, positioning the white disc slightly to the left, generating a change only in V2 but not in V1, then, it can be concluded, that the information in V2 is not the same as in V1. As a consequence, both vectors contain valuable information of the image. The final V1 and V2 over an image can be seen in Fig. 5.

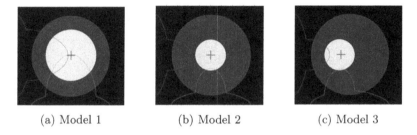

(a) Model 1   (b) Model 2   (c) Model 3

Fig. 4. Geometrical and intensity approximations of visual disc and cup (Color figure online)

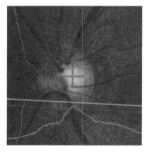

Fig. 5. Example of V1 (red) and V2 (green) over ROI. (Color figure online)

Model Training: The machine learning method selected is a MLP. The system input is the concatenation of V1 and V2 into only one vector, placing first V1 and then V2. The system arquitecture is the following: A MLP with 3 hidden layers and 50 neurons per layer, a train/test proportion of 80/20 (holdout validation), and a learning rate of 1e−9. This procedure was made for dataset A and dataset B separately, so the input layer for A has 480 units, and for B has 1300 units.

3   Results

With the main parameters defined, five different models were trained, as this process includes a random component, results were not the same always. As it can be seen in Fig. 6a, the sensitivity for dataset B is much better than dataset A, and for the total accuracy, the trained model with dataset B images has a better result, with a difference of 6.04%. To get better performance of the model, a centering around zero was made to the concatenation of V1 and V2 (input of the model); this was computed following the Eq. 6. The procedure ideally gets the data close to a 0 average and a variance of 1, by subtracting in each value of concatenated vector the average and dividing it by the standard deviation.

$$\overrightarrow{V_Z} = \frac{\overrightarrow{V_{1,2}} - \overline{V_{1,2}}}{SD(V_{1,2})} \tag{6}$$

After this method is applied, it can be seen in Fig. 6b the metrics improvement, except for the case of specificity of dataset A, with a small decrease in percentage (1.64%). As an additional test, the initial architecture is reduced to 15 neurons in each hidden layer, as the initial number of neurons seems to be more than necessary, even though there is not an exact criteria in the selection of MLP architecture. As Fig. 7 shows, there is a slight decrease in the general performance of the model, indicating that the 35 neurons per layer used in the initial model may increase the metrics between 1–2%.

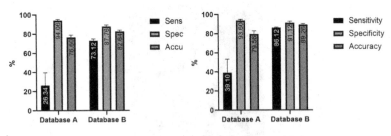

(a)   Training   architecture   five (b) Training architecture five times
times.   with scaled data.

Fig. 6. Performance of models for datasets A and B: averages and standar derivations,

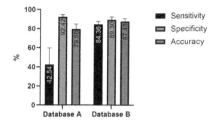

Fig. 7. Training five times with 3 hidden layers and 15 neurons per layer

4 Discussion

The ROC curves (Fig. 8) shows that the model presents a high level of sensitivity and specificity, which means it has a good ability to recognize the glaucoma and healthy instances. This is relevant for future disease recognition. On the other hand, the best validation performance results shows that the model training needs only 42 epochs for achieving the best results. In this work, the highest classification accuracy was 93.5%, the sensitivity was 91.6%, and the specificity was 94.5%.

Table 1. Studies reporting detection of glaucoma using fundus images

Authors	Features	Classifier	Sensitivity	Specificity	Accuracy	Images
Maheshwari, et al. [12]	Empirical wavelet tansform to obtain features	LS-SVM	78.99%	83.14%	81.32%	505
Singh, et al. [20]	Entropy and fractal dimensions	SVM	96.97%	93.33%	95.24%	63
Maheshwari, et al. [13]	Wavelet features	SVM	93.62%	95.88%	94.79%	488
Noronha, et al. [16]	HOS cumulants	NB	100%	92%	92.6%	272
Cristopher, et al. [6]	Disc center	TL-DL	88%	95%	91%	14882 (Optic nerve hypoplasia)
Al-Bander, et al. [3]	Extracted with CNN	SVM	85%	89.8%	88.2%	455
Abbas, Q. [1]	Extracted with CNN	DL	84.5%	98.01%	99%	1200 (retinography)
Bock, et al. [5]	GRI	SVM	69%	83%	76%	575
Acharya, et al. [2]	Gabor features	SVM	89.75%	96.2%	93.1%	510
Salam, et al. [18]	Local binary partitions and color moments	SVM	87%	90%	88%	100
This model	Intensity features	MLP	91.6%	94.5%	93.5%	680

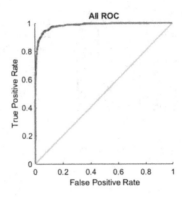

Fig. 8. ROC curves for train, test, validation and general groups

Glaucoma is detected in fundus images and the proposed method is not expensive, not in the preprocessing nor in the model training process. The vectors provide relevant information of the intensity distribution of the pixels, regarding to the studied disease. Considering that the images were cropped to the optic disc, the method is useful to identify structural differences caused by glaucoma, based on the vectors.

The performance metrics obtained were similar to those found in the literature (see Table 1). In contrast, the feature extraction stage is simple in comparison to wavelet transform, HOC, CNN, or deep learning techniques used by other authors [1–3,5,6,12,13,16,18,20]. On the other hand, the methods that extract features like pixel regularity, color moments, or use features extracted from the cup-to-disc ratio, used datasets with less than 100 images or data which does not present only the glaucoma disease. This can affect the accuracy of the results. In this work, to prevent overfitting, 467 in dataset A and 168 in dataset B glaucoma images were used.

The principal finding of this research is a novel feature, based in vectors, that allows the OD detection, as well as the classification of fundus images between glaucoma and healthy controls. As V1 and V2 have not been used before, this technique can be applied to the classification of other diseases visible from the fundus image. Finally, it is the simplicity of the method is valuable, and was based on a physiological point of view (cup-to-disc ratio).

5   Conclusion

Glaucoma causes structural changes in the optic nerve head and it can be observed in fundus images. The automatic detection models are useful to develop diagnosis tools for glaucoma. In this work, an accuracy of 93.5%, sensitivity of 91.6% and specificity of 94.5% is reported using 650 fundus images in a MLP that classify the glaucoma disease. The method for feature extraction proposed here shows a high performance in the results of the model, in comparison with other techniques. The vectors used as features are extracted from the cup-to-disc ratio providing information of structural changes caused by glaucoma disease. This features, in the future, may be useful for another eye diseases that affect the structure of the optic nerve, and may be detected using fundus images.

References

1. Abbas, Q.: Glaucoma-deep: detection of glaucoma eye disease on retinal fundus images using deep learning. Int. J. Adv. Comput. Sci. Appl. **8**(6), 41–5 (2017)
2. Acharya, U.R., et al.: Decision support system for the glaucoma using Gabor transformation. Biomed. Signal Process. Control **15**, 18–26 (2015)
3. Al-Bander, B., Al-Nuaimy, W., Al-Taee, M.A., Zheng, Y.: Automated glaucoma diagnosis using deep learning approach. In: 2017 14th International Multi-Conference on Systems, Signals & Devices (SSD), pp. 207–210. IEEE (2017)
4. Bettin, P., Di Matteo, F.: Glaucoma: present challenges and future trends. Ophthalmic Res. **50**(4), 197–208 (2013)
5. Bock, R., Meier, J., Nyúl, L.G., Hornegger, J., Michelson, G.: Glaucoma risk index: automated glaucoma detection from color fundus images. Med. Image Anal. **14**(3), 471–481 (2010)
6. Christopher, M., et al.: Performance of deep learning architectures and transfer learning for detecting glaucomatous optic neuropathy in fundus photographs. Sci. Rep. **8**(1), 1–13 (2018)
7. Dataverse, H.: Machine learn for glaucoma (2018)
8. Gupta, P., Zhao, D., Guallar, E., Ko, F., Boland, M.V., Friedman, D.S.: Prevalence of glaucoma in the United States: the 2005–2008 national health and nutrition examination survey. Invest. Ophthalmol. Vis. Sci. **57**(6), 2905–2913 (2016)
9. K, B.: Glaucoma diagnosis (2020)
10. Khalil, T., Khalid, S., Syed, A.M.: Review of machine learning techniques for glaucoma detection and prediction. In: 2014 Science and Information Conference, pp. 438–442. IEEE (2014)
11. Kingman, S.: Glaucoma is second leading cause of blindness globally. Bull. World Health Organ. **82**, 887–888 (2004)
12. Maheshwari, S., Pachori, R.B., Acharya, U.R.: Automated diagnosis of glaucoma using empirical wavelet transform and correntropy features extracted from fundus images. IEEE J. Biomed. Health Inform. **21**(3), 803–813 (2016)
13. Maheshwari, S., Pachori, R.B., Kanhangad, V., Bhandary, S.V., Acharya, U.R.: Iterative variational mode decomposition based automated detection of glaucoma using fundus images. Comput. Biol. Med. **88**, 142–149 (2017)
14. Mookiah, M.R.K., Acharya, U.R., Lim, C.M., Petznick, A., Suri, J.S.: Data mining technique for automated diagnosis of glaucoma using higher order spectra and wavelet energy features. Knowl.-Based Syst. **33**, 73–82 (2012)
15. Murtagh, P., Greene, G., O'Brien, C.: Current applications of machine learning in the screening and diagnosis of glaucoma: a systematic review and meta-analysis. Int. J. Ophthalmol. **13**(1), 149 (2020)
16. Noronha, K.P., Acharya, U.R., Nayak, K.P., Martis, R.J., Bhandary, S.V.: Automated classification of glaucoma stages using higher order cumulant features. Biomed. Signal Process. Control **10**, 174–183 (2014)
17. Quigley, H.A., Broman, A.T.: The number of people with glaucoma worldwide in 2010 and 2020. Br. J. Ophthalmol. **90**(3), 262–267 (2006)

18. Salam, A.A., Khalil, T., Akram, M.U., Jameel, A., Basit, I.: Automated detection of glaucoma using structural and non structural features. Springerplus **5**(1), 1–21 (2016). https://doi.org/10.1186/s40064-016-3175-4

19. Sarhan, A., Rokne, J., Alhajj, R.: Glaucoma detection using image processing techniques: a literature review. Comput. Med. Imaging Graph. **78**, 101657 (2019)

20. Singh, A., Dutta, M.K., ParthaSarathi, M., Uher, V., Burget, R.: Image processing based automatic diagnosis of glaucoma using wavelet features of segmented optic disc from fundus image. Comput. Methods Programs Biomed. **124**, 108–120 (2016)

21. Tham, Y.C., Li, X., Wong, T.Y., Quigley, H.A., Aung, T., Cheng, C.Y.: Global prevalence of glaucoma and projections of glaucoma burden through 2040: a systematic review and meta-analysis. Ophthalmology **121**(11), 2081–2090 (2014)

22. Yadav, K.S., Rajpurohit, R., Sharma, S.: Glaucoma: current treatment and impact of advanced drug delivery systems. Life Sci. **221**, 362–376 (2019)

23. Zhang, E.: Glaucoma dataset, Kaggle (2020)

Author Index

Printed in the United States
by Baker & Taylor Publisher Services